ITALY

MINING LAWS AND REGULATIONS HANDBOOK

VOLUME 1

STRATEGIC INFORMATION AND REGULATIONS

International Business Publications, USA
Washington DC, USA- Italy

ITALY

MINING LAWS AND REGULATIONS HANDBOOK
VOLUME 1 STRATEGIC INFORMATION AND REGULATIONS

UPDATED ANNUALLY

We express our sincere appreciation to all government agencies and international organizations which provided information and other materials for this handbook

Cover Design: **International Business Publications, USA**

2016 Edition Updated Reprint International Business Publications, USA
ISBN 1-4330-7762-0

For customer service and information, please contact:
in the USA: **International Business Publications, USA**
P.O.Box 15343, Washington, DC 20033
Phone: (202) 546-2103, Fax: (202) 546-3275.
E-mail: rusric@erols.com

Printed in the USA

ITALY

MINING LAWS AND REGULATIONS HANDBOOK

VOLUME 1
STRATEGIC INFORMATION AND REGULATIONS

TABLE OF CONTENTS

STRATEGIC AND BUSINESS PROFILES

STRATEGIC PROFILE

Capital and largest city	Rome 41°54′N 12°29′E41.900°N 12.483°E
Official languages	Italian[a]
Demonym	Italian
Government	Unitary parliamentary constitutional republic
- Acting President	Pietro Grasso
- Prime Minister	Matteo Renzi
Legislature	Parliament
- Upper house	Senate of the Republic
- Lower house	Chamber of Deputies
Formation	
- Unification	17 March 1861
- Republic	2 June 1946
- Founded the EEC (now the European Union)	1 January 1958
Area	
- Total	301,338 km^2 (72nd) 116,347 sq mi
- Water (%)	2.4
Population	
- 2013 estimate	60,782,668 (23rd)
- 2011 census	59,433,744 (23rd)
- Density	201.7/km^2 (63rd) 522.4/sq mi
GDP (PPP)	2014 estimate
- Total	$2.066 trillion (12th)
- Per capita	$34,455 (31st)
GDP (nominal)	2014 estimate
- Total	$2.13 trillion (8th)
- Per capita	$35,512 (27th)
Gini (2011)	31.9 medium
HDI	0.872 very high · 26th
Currency	Euro (€)[b] (EUR)
Time zone	CET (UTC+1)
- Summer (DST)	CEST (UTC+2)
Drives on the	right
Calling code	39[c]
ISO 3166 code	IT
Internet TLD	.it[d]

[a] French is co-official in the Aosta Valley; Slovene is co-official in the province of Trieste and the province of Gorizia; German and Ladin are co-official in South Tyrol.

[b.] Before 2002, the Italian Lira. The euro is accepted in Campione d'Italia, but the official currency there is the Swiss Franc.
[c.] To call Campione d'Italia, it is necessary to use the Swiss code +41.
[d.] The .eu domain is also used, as it is shared with other European Union member states.

Italy officially the **Italian Republic** (Italian: *Repubblica italiana*), is a unitary parliamentary republic in Southern Europe. Italy covers an area of 301,338 km^2 (116,347 sq mi) and has a largely temperate climate; due to its shape, it is often referred to in Italy as *lo Stivale* (the Boot). With 61 million inhabitants, it is the 5th most populous country in Europe. Italy is a very highly developed country and has the third largest economy in the Eurozone and the eighth-largest in the world.

Since ancient times, Etruscan, Magna Graecia and other cultures have flourished in the territory of present-day Italy, being eventually absorbed by Rome, that has for centuries remained the leading political and religious centre of Western civilisation, capital of the Roman Empire and Christianity. During the Dark Ages, the Italian Peninsula faced calamitous invasions by barbarian tribes, but beginning around the 11th century, numerous Italian city-states rose to great prosperity through shipping, commerce and banking (indeed, modern capitalism has its roots in Medieval Italy).

Especially during The Renaissance, Italian culture thrived, producing scholars, artists, and polymaths such as Leonardo da Vinci, Galileo, Michelangelo and Machiavelli. Italian explorers such as Polo, Columbus, Vespucci, and Verrazzano discovered new routes to the Far East and the New World, helping to usher in the European Age of Discovery. Nevertheless, Italy would remain fragmented into many warring states for the rest of the Middle Ages, subsequently falling prey to larger European powers such as France, Spain, and later Austria. Italy would thus enter a long period of decline that lasted until the mid 19th century.

After various unsuccessful attempts, the second and the third wars of Italian Independence resulted in the unification of most of present-day Italy between 1859-66. From the late 19th century to the early 20th century, the new Kingdom of Italy rapidly industrialised and acquired a colonial empire becoming a Great Power. However, Southern and rural Italy remained largely excluded from industrialisation, fuelling a large and influential diaspora. Despite victory in World War I, Italy entered a period of economic crisis and social turmoil, which favoured the establishment of a Fascist dictatorship in 1922. The subsequent participation in World War II at the side the Axis ended in military defeat, economic destruction and civil war. In the years that followed, Italy abolished the monarchy, reinstated democracy, and enjoyed a prolonged economic boom, thus becoming one of the most developed nations and the 5th largest economy in the world by 1990.

Italy plays a prominent role in global military, cultural and diplomatic affairs and thus is considered a major regional power. Italy is a founding and leading member of the European Union (on 1 July 2014, Italy replaced Greece as holder of the rotating EU Council Presidency.) Italy is a member of numerous international institutions, including the UN, NATO, the OECD, the OSCE, the DAC, the WTO, the G4, G6, G7, G8, G10, G20, the Union for the Mediterranean, the Latin Union, the Council of Europe, the Central European Initiative, the ASEM and the Uniting for Consensus.

Italy plays a prominent role in European and global military, cultural and diplomatic affairs. The country's European political, social and economic influence make it a major regional power. The country has a high public education level and is a highly globalised nation

Location/Size: Southern Europe/301,230 sq km (186,763 sq mi, slightly larger than Arizona)
Major Cities: Rome (capital), Milan, Naples, Turin, Palermo, Genoa
Languages: Italian, German (parts of Trentino-Alto Adige region are predominantly German speaking), French (small French-speaking minority in Valle d'Aosta region), Slovene (Slovene-speaking minority in the Trieste-Gorizia area)
Ethnic groups: Italian (includes small clusters of German-, French-, and Slovene-Italians in the north and Albanian-Italians and Greek-Italians in the south)
Religion: predominately Roman Catholic with mature Protestant and Jewish communities and a growing Muslim immigrant community
Population : 57.6 million
Defense: Army, 165,600; Navy, 40,000; Air Force, 63,600; Paramilitary forces, 255,700; Conscripts, 134,100

Background: Italy became a nation-state belatedly - in 1861 when the city-states of the peninsula and Sicily were united under King Victor EMMANUEL. The Fascist dictatorship of Benito MUSSOLINI that took over after World War I led to a disastrous alliance with Nazi Germany and Italian defeat in World War II. Revival followed. Italy was a charter member of NATO and the European Economic Community (EEC) and joined the growing political and economic unification of Western Europe, including the introduction of the euro in 2004. Persistent problems include illegal immigration, the ravages of organized crime, corruption, high unemployment, and the low incomes and technical standards of southern Italy compared with the more prosperous north.

GEOGRAPHY

Location: Southern Europe, a peninsula extending into the central Mediterranean Sea, northeast of Tunisia
Geographic coordinates: 42 50 N, 12 50 E
Map references: Europe

Area:
total: 301,230 sq km
land: 294,020 sq km
water: 7,210 sq km
note: includes Sardinia and Sicily

Area - comparative: slightly larger than Arizona

Land boundaries:
total: 1,932.2 km
border countries: Austria 430 km, France 488 km, Holy See (Vatican City) 3.2 km, San Marino 39 km, Slovenia 232 km, Switzerland 740 km

Coastline: 7,600 km

Maritime claims:
continental shelf: 200-m depth or to the depth of exploitation
territorial sea: 12 nm

Climate: predominantly Mediterranean; Alpine in far north; hot, dry in south
Terrain: mostly rugged and mountainous; some plains, coastal lowlands

Base 802446 (A04844) 3-96

Elevation extremes:
lowest point: Mediterranean Sea 0 m
highest point: Mont Blanc (Monte Bianco) 4,807 m

Natural resources: mercury, potash, marble, sulfur, dwindling natural gas and crude oil reserves, fish, coal, arable land
Land use:
arable land: 31% *permanent crops:* 10% *permanent pastures:* 15% *forests and woodland:* 23% *other:* 21%
Irrigated land: 27,100 sq km

Natural hazards: regional risks include landslides, mudflows, avalanches, earthquakes, volcanic eruptions, flooding; land subsidence in Venice

Environment - current issues: air pollution from industrial emissions such as sulfur dioxide; coastal and inland rivers polluted from industrial and agricultural effluents; acid rain damaging lakes; inadequate industrial waste treatment and disposal facilities

Environment - international agreements:
party to: Air Pollution, Air Pollution-Nitrogen Oxides, Air Pollution-Sulphur 85, Air Pollution-Sulphur 94, Air Pollution-Volatile Organic Compounds, Antarctic-Environmental Protocol, Antarctic Treaty, Biodiversity, Climate Change, Desertification, Endangered Species, Environmental Modification, Hazardous Wastes, Law of the Sea, Marine Dumping, Nuclear Test Ban, Ozone Layer Protection, Ship Pollution, Tropical Timber 83, Tropical Timber 94, Wetlands, Whaling
signed, but not ratified: Air Pollution-Persistent Organic Pollutants, Climate Change-Kyoto Protocol

Geography - note: strategic location dominating central Mediterranean as well as southern sea and air approaches to Western Europe

PEOPLE

Population: 56,735,130
Age structure:
0-14 years: 14% (male 4,161,841; female 3,925,413)
15-64 years: 68% (male 19,205,293; female 19,285,848)
65 years and over: 18% (male 4,169,098; female 5,987,637)
Population growth rate: -0.08%

Birth rate: 9.27 births/1,000 population
Death rate: 10.28 deaths/1,000 population
Net migration rate: 0.17 migrant(s)/1,000 population

Sex ratio:
at birth: 1.06 male(s)/female
under 15 years: 1.06 male(s)/female
15-64 years: 1 male(s)/female
65 years and over: 0.7 male(s)/female
total population: 0.94 male(s)/female

Infant mortality rate: 6.3 deaths/1,000 live births

Life expectancy at birth:
total population: 78.51 years
male: 75.4 years
female: 81.82 years

Total fertility rate: 1.22 children born/woman

Nationality:
noun: Italian(s)
adjective: Italian

Ethnic groups: Italian (includes small clusters of German-, French-, and Slovene-Italians in the north and Albanian-Italians and Greek-Italians in the south)

Religions: Roman Catholic 98%, other 2%

Languages: Italian, German (parts of Trentino-Alto Adige region are predominantly German speaking), French (small French-speaking minority in Valle d'Aosta region), Slovene (Slovene-speaking minority in the Trieste-Gorizia area)

Literacy:
definition: age 15 and over can read and write
total population: 97%
male: 98%
female: 96% (1990 est.)

GOVERNMENT

Country name:

conventional long form: Italian Republic
conventional short form: Italy
local long form: Repubblica Italiana
local short form: Italia
former: Kingdom of Italy

Government type:

republic

Capital:

name: Rome
geographic coordinates: 41 54 N, 12 29 E
time difference: UTC+1 (6 hours ahead of Washington, DC, during Standard Time)
daylight saving time: +1hr, begins last Sunday in March; ends last Sunday in October

Administrative divisions:

15 regions (regioni, singular - regione) and 5 autonomous regions (regioni autonome, singular - regione autonoma)
regions: Abruzzo, Basilicata, Calabria, Campania, Emilia-Romagna, Lazio (Latium), Liguria, Lombardia, Marche, Molise, Piemonte (Piedmont), Puglia (Apulia), Toscana (Tuscany), Umbria, Veneto (Venetia)

autonomous regions: Friuli-Venezia Giulia; Sardegna (Sardinia); Sicilia (Sicily); Trentino-Alto Adige (Trentino-South Tyrol) or Trentino-Suedtirol (German); Valle d'Aosta (Aosta Valley) or Vallee d'Aoste (French)

Independence:

17 March 1861 (Kingdom of Italy proclaimed; Italy was not finally unified until 1870)

National holiday:

Republic Day, 2 June (1946)

Constitution:

previous 1848 (originally for Kingdom of Sardinia and adopted by Kingdom of Italy in 1861); latest enacted 22 December 1947, adopted 27 December 1947, entered into force 1 January 1948; amended many times, last in 2012 (2013)

Legal system:

civil law system; judicial review of legislation under certain conditions in Constitutional Court

International law organization participation:

has not submitted an ICJ jurisdiction declaration; accepts ICCt jurisdiction

Suffrage:

18 years of age; universal except in senatorial elections, where minimum age is 25

Executive branch:

chief of state: President Giorgio NAPOLITANO (since 15 May 2006)
head of government: Prime Minister Matteo RENZI (since 22 February 2014); note - the prime minister is referred to as the President of the Council of Ministers
cabinet: Council of Ministers proposed by the prime minister and nominated by the President of the Republic
elections: president elected by an electoral college consisting of both houses of parliament and 58 regional representatives for a seven-year term (no term limits); election last held on 18-20 April 2013 (next scheduled for 2020); prime minister appointed by the president and confirmed by parliament; national parliamentary elections were last held on 24-25 February 2013
election results: Giorgio NAPOLITANO elected president on the sixth round of voting; electoral college vote - 738 out of a possible 1,007 (504 votes required); Enrico LETTA sworn in as prime minister on 28 April 2013 following formal talks between the center-left Democratic Party (PD), the center-right People of Freedom party (PdL), the centrist Civic Choice, and President NAPOLITANO that also led to the creation of a broad coalition government; the talks coming after the February 2013 legislative election produced a stalemate that impeded government formation; the PdL split into the Forza Italia and the New Center Right (NCD) in November 2013 and only the NCD remained in the governing

coalition

Legislative branch:

bicameral Parliament or Parlamento consists of the Senate or Senato della Repubblica (321 seats; members elected by proportional vote with the winning coalition in each region receiving 55% of seats from that region; members to serve five-year terms; and up to 5 senators for life appointed by the president of the Republic) and the Chamber of Deputies or Camera dei Deputati (630 seats; members elected by popular vote with the winning national coalition receiving 54% of chamber seats; members to serve five-year terms); note - it has not been clarified if each president has the power to designate up to five senators or if five is the number of senators for life who might sit in the Senate
elections: Senate - last held on 24-25 February 2013 (next to be held in 2018); Chamber of Deputies - last held on 24-25 February 2013 (next to be held in 2018)
election results: Senate - percent of vote by party - NA; seats by party - center-left coalition [Pier Luigi BERSANI] 123 (PD 111, SEL 7, SVP 2, other 3), center-right coalition [Silvio BERLUSCONI] 117 (PdL 98, LN 18, other 1), M5S 54, centrist coalition [Mario MONTI] 19, other 2; Chamber of Deputies - percent of vote by party - NA; seats by party - center-left coalition [Pier Luigi BERSANI] 345 (PD 297, SEL 37, CD 6 SVP 5), center-right coalition [Silvio BERLUSCONI] 125 (PdL 98, LN 18, FdI 9), M5S 109, centrist coalition [Mario MONTI] 47, other 4; note - President NAPOLITANO dissolved Parliament on 22 December 2012

Judicial branch:

highest court(s): Supreme Court of Cassation or Corte Suprema di Cassazione (organized into penal, civil, administrative, and military divisions, each with a president and several judges); Constitutional Court or Corte Costituzionale (consists of 15 judges)
judge selection and term of office: Supreme Court judges appointed by the Superior Council of the Judiciary, headed by the president, to serve NA terms; Constitutional Court judges - 5 appointed by the president, 5 elected by parliament, 5 elected by select higher courts; judges serve up to 9 years)
subordinate courts: various lower civil and criminal courts (primary and secondary tribunals, courts, and courts of appeal)

Political parties and leaders:

Center-right parties::
Forza Italia [Silvio BERLUSCONI]
The New Center-Right or NCD [Angelino ALFANO]
Northern League or LN [Roberto MARONI]
Brothers of Italy or FdI [Giorgia MELONI, Ignazio LA RUSSA, and Guido CROSETTO]
The Right or LD [Francesco STORACE]
other minor parties
Center-left parties::
Democratic Party or PD [Matteo RENZI]
Left Ecology Freedom or SEL [Nichi VENDOLA]
Italian Socialist Party or PSI [Riccardo NENCINI]
Democratic Centre or CD [Bruno TABACCI and Massimo DONADI]
South Tyrolean People's Party or SVP [Arno KOMPATSCHER]
Centrist parties::
Civic Choice or SC [Alberto BOMBASSEI]

Union of the Center or UdC [Pier Ferdinando CASINI]
Future and Freedom for Italy or FLI [vacant]
other coalitions and parties::
Five Star Movment or M5S [Beppe GRILLO]
Civil Revolution or RC [Antonio INGROIA]
Act to Stop the Decline or FiD [Michele BOLDRIN]

Political pressure groups and leaders:

manufacturers and merchants associations - Confcommercio; Confindustria
organized farm groups - Confcoltivatori; Confagricoltura; Roman Catholic Church
three major trade union confederations - Confederazione Generale Italiana del Lavoro or CGIL [Susanna CAMUSSO] which is left wing; Confederazione Italiana dei Sindacati Lavoratori or CISL [Raffaele BONANNI], which is Roman Catholic centrist; Unione Italiana del Lavoro or UIL [Luigi ANGELETTI] which is lay centrist

International organization participation:

ADB (nonregional member), AfDB (nonregional member), Australia Group, BIS, BSEC (observer), CBSS (observer), CD, CDB, CE, CEI, CERN, EAPC, EBRD, ECB, EIB, EITI (implementing country), EMU, ESA, EU, FAO, FATF, G-20, G-7, G-8, G-10, IADB, IAEA, IBRD, ICAO, ICC (national committees), ICRM, IDA, IEA, IFAD, IFC, IFRCS, IGAD (partners), IHO, ILO, IMF, IMO, IMSO, Interpol, IOC, IOM, IPU, ISO, ITSO, ITU, ITUC (NGOs), LAIA (observer), MIGA, MINURSO, MINUSMA, NATO, NEA, NSG, OAS (observer), OECD, OPCW, OSCE, Pacific Alliance (observer), Paris Club, PCA, PIF (partner), Schengen Convention, SELEC (observer), SICA (observer), UN, UNAMID, UNCTAD, UNESCO, UNHCR, UNIDO, UNIFIL, Union Latina, UNMISS, UNMOGIP, UNRWA, UNTSO, UNWTO, UPU, WCO, WHO, WIPO, WMO, WTO, ZC

Diplomatic representation in the US:

chief of mission: Ambassador Claudio BISOGNIERO (since 13 January 2012)
chancery: 3000 Whitehaven Street NW, Washington, DC 20008
telephone: (202) 612-4400
FAX: (202) 518-2154
consulate(s) general: Boston, Chicago, Houston, Miami, New York, Los Angeles, Philadelphia, San Francisco
consulate(s): Detroit, Newark (NJ), San Francisco

Diplomatic representation from the US:

chief of mission: Ambassador John R. PHILLIPS (since 16 August 2013); note - also accredited to San Marino
embassy: Via Vittorio Veneto 121, 00187-Rome
mailing address: PSC 59, Box 100, APO AE 09624
telephone: [39] (06) 46741
FAX: [39] (06) 4674-2244
consulate(s) general: Florence, Milan, Naples

Flag description:

three equal vertical bands of green (hoist side), white, and red; design inspired by the French flag brought to Italy by Napoleon in 1797; colors are those of Milan (red and white) combined with the green uniform color of the Milanese civic guard
note: similar to the flag of Mexico, which is longer, uses darker shades of red and green, and has its coat of arms centered on the white band; Ireland, which is longer and is green (hoist side), white, and orange; also similar to the flag of the Cote d'Ivoire, which has the colors reversed - orange (hoist side), white, and green

National symbol(s):

white, five-pointed star (Stella d'Italia)

National anthem:

name: "Il Canto degli Italiani" (The Song of the Italians)

ECONOMY

Italy has a diversified industrial economy, which is divided into a developed industrial north, dominated by private companies, and a less-developed, highly subsidized, agricultural south, where unemployment is higher. The Italian economy is driven in large part by the manufacture of high-quality consumer goods produced by small and medium-sized enterprises, many of them family-owned. Italy also has a sizable underground economy, which by some estimates accounts for as much as 17% of GDP. These activities are most common within the agriculture, construction, and service sectors.

Italy is the third-largest economy in the euro-zone, but its exceptionally high public debt and structural impediments to growth have rendered it vulnerable to scrutiny by financial markets. Public debt has increased steadily since 2007, topping 133% of GDP in 2013, but investor concerns about Italy and the broader euro-zone crisis eased in 2013, bringing down Italy's borrowing costs on sovereign government debt from euro-era records. The government still faces pressure from investors and European partners to sustain its efforts to address Italy's long-standing structural impediments to growth, such as labor market inefficiencies and widespread tax evasion. In 2013 economic growth and labor market conditions deteriorated, with growth at -1.8% and unemployment rising to 12.4%, with youth unemployment around 40%. Italy's GDP is now 8% below its 2007 pre-crisis level.

GDP (purchasing power parity):

$1.805 trillion
country comparison to the world: 12
$1.838 trillion (2012 est.)
$1.883 trillion (2011 est.)
note: data are in 2013 US dollars

GDP (official exchange rate):

$2.068 trillion

GDP - real growth rate:

-1.8%

country comparison to the world: 211
-2.4% (2012 est.)
0.4% (2011 est.)

GDP - per capita (PPP):

$29,600
country comparison to the world: 51
$29,800 (2012 est.)
$30,100 (2011 est.)
note: data are in 2013 US dollars

Gross national saving:

17.4% of GDP
country comparison to the world: 94
16.9% of GDP (2012 est.)
16.4% of GDP (2011 est.)

GDP - composition, by end use:

household consumption: 60%
government consumption: 20.6%
investment in fixed capital: 17.6%
investment in inventories: -0.3%
exports of goods and services: 30.1%
imports of goods and services: -27.9%

GDP - composition, by sector of origin:

agriculture: 2%
industry: 24.4%
services: 73.5%

Agriculture - products:

fruits, vegetables, grapes, potatoes, sugar beets, soybeans, grain, olives; beef, dairy products; fish

Industries:

tourism, machinery, iron and steel, chemicals, food processing, textiles, motor vehicles, clothing, footwear, ceramics

Industrial production growth rate:

-2.7%
country comparison to the world: 183

Labor force:

25.74 million
country comparison to the world: 26

Labor force - by occupation:

agriculture: 3.9%
industry: 28.3%
services: 67.8% (2011)

Unemployment rate:

12.4%
country comparison to the world: 125
10.7% (2012 est.)

Population below poverty line:

29.9%

Household income or consumption by percentage share:

lowest 10%: 2.3%
highest 10%: 26.8% (2000)

Distribution of family income - Gini index:

31.9
country comparison to the world: 109
27.3

Budget:

revenues: $984 billion
expenditures: $1.052 trillion

Taxes and other revenues:

47.6% of GDP
country comparison to the world: 18

Budget surplus (+) or deficit (-):

-3.3% of GDP
country comparison to the world: 130

Public debt:

133% of GDP
country comparison to the world: 4
126.9% of GDP (2012 est.)
note: Italy reports its data on public debt according to guidelines set out in the Maastricht Treaty; general government gross debt is defined in the Maastricht Treaty as consolidated general government gross debt at nominal value, outstanding at the end of the year, in the following categories of government liabilities (as defined in ESA95): currency and deposits (AF.2), securities other than shares excluding financial derivatives (AF.3, excluding AF.34), and loans (AF.4); the general government sector comprises the central government, state government, local government and social security funds

Fiscal year:

calendar year

Inflation rate (consumer prices):

1.2%
country comparison to the world: 31
3%

Central bank discount rate:

0.25%
country comparison to the world: 131
0.75% (31 December 2012)
note: this is the European Central Bank's rate on the marginal lending facility, which offers overnight credit to banks in the euro area

Commercial bank prime lending rate:

5.2%
country comparison to the world: 150
5.22% (31 December 2012 est.)

Stock of narrow money:

$1.138 trillion
country comparison to the world: 6
$1.162 trillion (31 December 2012 est.)
note: see entry for the European Union for money supply in the euro area; the European Central Bank (ECB) controls monetary policy for the 17 members of the Economic and Monetary Union (EMU); individual members of the EMU do not control the quantity of money circulating within their own borders

Stock of broad money:

$2.15 trillion
country comparison to the world: 8
$2.134 trillion (31 December 2012 est.)

Stock of domestic credit:

$3.407 trillion
country comparison to the world: 8
$3.438 trillion (31 December 2012 est.)

Market value of publicly traded shares:

$480.5 billion
country comparison to the world: 21
$431.5 billion (31 December 2011)
$318.1 billion (31 December 2010 est.)

Current account balance:

-$2.4 billion
country comparison to the world: 150
-$14.88 billion (2012 est.)

Exports:

$474 billion
country comparison to the world: 11
$478.9 billion (2012 est.)

Exports - commodities:

engineering products, textiles and clothing, production machinery, motor vehicles, transport equipment, chemicals; food, beverages and tobacco; minerals, nonferrous metals

Exports - partners:

Germany 12.63%, France 11.11%, United States 6.84%, Switzerland 5.72%, United Kingdom 4.72%, Spain 4.48%

Imports:

$435.8 billion
country comparison to the world: 13
$453.5 billion (2012 est.)

Imports - commodities:

engineering products, chemicals, transport equipment, energy products, minerals and nonferrous metals, textiles and clothing; food, beverages, and tobacco

Imports - partners:

Germany 14.73%, France 8.4%, China 8.4%, Russia 6.35%, Netherlands 5.85%, Spain 4.54%, Belgium 4.09%

Reserves of foreign exchange and gold:

$181.7 billion
country comparison to the world: 16
$173.3 billion (31 December 2011 est.)

Debt - external:

$2.604 trillion
country comparison to the world: 8
$2.516 trillion (31 December 2012 est.)

Stock of direct foreign investment - at home:

$466.3 billion
country comparison to the world: 18
$457.8 billion (31 December 2012 est.)

Stock of direct foreign investment - abroad:

$683.6 billion
country comparison to the world: 13
$653.3 billion (31 December 2012 est.)

Exchange rates:

euros (EUR) per US dollar -
0.7634
0.7752 (2012 est.)
0.755 (2010 est.)
0.7198 (2009 est.)
0.6827 (2008 est.)

ENERGY

Electricity - production:

299.3 billion kWh
country comparison to the world: 13

Electricity - consumption:

307.2 billion kWh
country comparison to the world: 13

Electricity - exports:

2.304 billion kWh
country comparison to the world: 42

Electricity - imports:

45.41 billion kWh
country comparison to the world: 3

Electricity - installed generating capacity:

124.2 million kW
country comparison to the world: 10

Electricity - from fossil fuels:

65% of total installed capacity
country comparison to the world: 120

Electricity - from nuclear fuels:

0% of total installed capacity
country comparison to the world: 111

Electricity - from hydroelectric plants:

18% of total installed capacity
country comparison to the world: 95

Electricity - from other renewable sources:

15.8% of total installed capacity
country comparison to the world: 13

Crude oil - production:

112,000 bbl/day
country comparison to the world: 48

Crude oil - exports:

6,300 bbl/day
country comparison to the world: 63

Crude oil - imports:

1.591 million bbl/day
country comparison to the world: 7

Crude oil - proved reserves:

521.3 million bbl (1 January 2013 est.)
country comparison to the world: 50

Refined petroleum products - production:

6,600 bbl/day
country comparison to the world: 107

Refined petroleum products - consumption:

1.454 million bbl/day
country comparison to the world: 15

Refined petroleum products - exports:

628,000 bbl/day
country comparison to the world: 12

Refined petroleum products - imports:

393,300 bbl/day
country comparison to the world: 15

Natural gas - production:

7.8 billion cu m
country comparison to the world: 47

Natural gas - consumption:

68.7 billion cu m
country comparison to the world: 10

Natural gas - exports:

324 million cu m
country comparison to the world: 48

Natural gas - imports:

67.8 billion cu m
country comparison to the world: 5

Natural gas - proved reserves:

62.35 billion cu m
country comparison to the world: 62

Carbon dioxide emissions from consumption of energy:

400.9 million Mt

COMMUNICATIONS

Telephones - main lines in use:

21.656 million
country comparison to the world: 13

Telephones - mobile cellular:

97.225 million
country comparison to the world: 14

Telephone system:

general assessment: modern, well-developed, fast; fully automated telephone, telex, and data services
domestic: high-capacity cable and microwave radio relay trunks
international: country code - 39; a series of submarine cables provide links to Asia, Middle East, Europe, North Africa, and US; satellite earth stations - 3 Intelsat (with a total of 5 antennas - 3 for Atlantic Ocean and 2 for Indian Ocean), 1 Inmarsat (Atlantic Ocean region), and NA Eutelsat

Broadcast media:

two Italian media giants dominate - the publicly owned Radiotelevisione Italiana (RAI) with 3 national terrestrial stations and privately owned Mediaset with 3 national terrestrial stations; a large number of private stations and Sky Italia - a satellite TV network; RAI operates 3 AM/FM nationwide radio stations; some 1,300 commercial radio stations

Internet country code:

.it

Internet hosts:

25.662 million
country comparison to the world: 4

Internet users:

29.235 million
country comparison to the world: 13

TRANSPORTATION

Airports:

129
country comparison to the world: 45

Airports - with paved runways:

total: 98
over 3,047 m: 9
2,438 to 3,047 m: 31
1,524 to 2,437 m: 18
914 to 1,523 m: 29
under 914 m: 11

Airports - with unpaved runways:

total: 31
1,524 to 2,437 m: 1
914 to 1,523 m: 10
under 914 m:
20

Heliports:

5

Pipelines:

gas 20,223 km; oil 1,393 km; refined products 1,574 km

Railways:

total: 20,255 km
country comparison to the world: 13
standard gauge: 18,611 km 1.435-m gauge (12,662 km electrified)
narrow gauge: 123 km 1.000-m gauge (123 km electrified); 1,290 km 0.950-m gauge (151 km electrified); 231 km 0.850-m gauge

Roadways:

total: 487,700 km
country comparison to the world: 14
paved: 487,700 km (includes 6,700 km of expressways) (2007)

Waterways:

2,400 km (used for commercial traffic; of limited overall value compared to road and rail)
country comparison to the world: 37

Merchant marine:

total: 681
country comparison to the world: 17
by type: bulk carrier 105, cargo 42, carrier 1, chemical tanker 164, container 21, liquefied gas 28, passenger 25, passenger/cargo 154, petroleum tanker 59, refrigerated cargo 4, roll

on/roll off 39, specialized tanker 9, vehicle carrier 30
foreign-owned: 90 (Denmark 4, France 2, Greece 7, Luxembourg 14, Netherlands 2, Nigeria 1, Norway 6, Singapore 1, Sweden 1, Switzerland 13, Taiwan 10, Turkey 4, UK 2, US 23)
registered in other countries: 201 (Bahamas 1, Belize 3, Cayman Islands 7, Cyprus 6, Georgia 2, Gibraltar 4, Greece 5, Liberia 47, Malta 45, Marshall Islands 1, Morocco 1, Netherlands 6, Panama 25, Portugal 12, Russia 14, Saint Vincent and the Grenadines 4, Singapore 5, Slovakia 2, Spain 1, Sweden 5, Turkey 1, UK 3, unknown 1)

Ports and terminals:

major seaport(s): Augusta, Cagliari, Genoa, Livorno, Taranto, Trieste, Venice
oil terminals: Melilli (Santa Panagia) oil terminal, Sarroch oil terminal
container port(s) (TEUs): Genoa (1,847,648), Gioia Tauro (2,264,798), La Spezia (1,307,274)

MILITARY

Military branches:

Italian Armed Forces: Army (Esercito Italiano, EI), Navy (Marina Militare Italiana, MMI), Italian Air Force (Aeronautica Militare Italiana, AMI), Carabinieri Corps (Arma dei Carabinieri, CC) (2011)

Military service age and obligation:

18-25 years of age for voluntary military service; women may serve in any military branch; Italian citizenship required; 12-month service obligation

Manpower available for military service:

males age 16-49: 13,865,688
females age 16-49: 14,003,755

Manpower fit for military service:

males age 16-49: 11,247,446
females age 16-49: 11,348,695

Manpower reaching militarily significant age annually:

male: 288,188
female: 281,671

Military expenditures:

1.69% of GDP
country comparison to the world: 53
1.72% of GDP (2011)
1.69% of GDP (2010)

TRANSNATIONAL ISSUES

Disputes - international:

Italy's long coastline and developed economy entices tens of thousands of illegal immigrants from southeastern Europe and northern Africa

Refugees and internally displaced persons:

refugees (country of origin): 12,682 (Eritrea); 10,817 (Somalia); 6,695 (Afghanistan) (2013)
stateless persons: 470

Illicit drugs:

important gateway for and consumer of Latin American cocaine and Southwest Asian heroin entering the European market; money laundering by organized crime and from smuggling

IMPORTANT INFORMATION FOR UNDERSTANDING ITALY

PROFILE

OFFICIAL NAME: Italian Republic

Geography
Area: 301,225 sq. km. (116,303 sq. mi.); about the size of Georgia and Florida combined.
Cities: *Capital*--Rome (pop. 2.8 million). *Other cities*--Milan, Naples, Turin.
Terrain: Mostly rugged and mountainous.
Climate: Generally mild Mediterranean; cold northern winters.

People
Nationality: *Noun and adjective*--Italian(s).
Population: 57.8 million.
Annual growth rate: 0.28%.
Ethnic groups: Primarily Italian, but there are small groups of German-, French-, Slovene-, and Albanian-Italians.
Religion: Roman Catholic (majority).
Language: Italian (official).
Education: *Years compulsory*--18. *Literacy*--98%.
Health: *Infant mortality rate*--5.76/1,000 live births. *Life expectancy*--76.08 years for men; 83.0 years for women.
Work force (23.8 million): *Services*--57.6%; *industry and commerce*--28.9%; *agriculture*--4.2%; *unemployed*--9.2%.

Government
Type: Republic since June 2, 1946.
Constitution: January 1, 1948.
Branches: *Executive*--president (chief of state), Council of Ministers (cabinet), headed by the president of the council (prime minister). *Legislative*--bicameral parliament: 630-member Chamber of Deputies, 315-member Senate (plus a varying number of "life" Senators). *Judicial*--independent constitutional court and lower magistracy.
Subdivisions: 94 provinces, 20 regions.
Political parties: Forza Italia, Democratic Party of the Left, National Alliance, Northern League, United Christian Democrats, Democrats, Italian People's Party, Christian Democratic Center, Socialist, Communist Renewal, Social Democratic, Republican, Liberal, Greens, Italian Renewal.
Suffrage: Vote for House; universal over 18; vote for Senate; universal over 18.

PEOPLE AND HISTORY

Italy is largely homogeneous linguistically and religiously but is diverse culturally, economically, and politically. Italy has the fifth-highest population density in Europe--about 200 persons per square kilometer (490 per sq. mi.). Minority groups are small, the largest being the German-speaking people of Bolzano Province and the Slovenes around Trieste. There are also small communities of Albanian, Greek, Ladino, and French origin. Immigration has increased in recent years, however, while the Italian population is declining overall due to low birth rates. Although Roman Catholicism is the majority religion--85% of native-born citizens are nominally Catholic--all religious faiths are provided equal freedom before the law by the constitution.

Greeks settled in the southern tip of the Italian Peninsula in the eighth and seventh centuries B.C.; Etruscans, Romans, and others inhabited the central and northern mainland. The peninsula subsequently was unified under the Roman Republic. The neighboring islands came under Roman control by the third century B.C.; by the first century A.D., the Roman Empire effectively dominated the Mediterranean world. After the collapse of the Roman Empire in the West in the fifth century A.D., the peninsula and islands were subjected to a series of invasions, and political unity was lost. Italy became an oft-changing succession of small states, principalities, and kingdoms, which fought among themselves and were subject to ambitions of foreign powers. Popes of Rome ruled central Italy; rivalries between the popes and the Holy Roman Emperors, who claimed Italy as their domain, often made the peninsula a battleground.

The commercial prosperity of northern and central Italian cities, beginning in the 11th century, combined with the influence of the Renaissance, mitigated somewhat the effects of these medieval political rivalries. Although Italy declined after the 16th century, the Renaissance had strengthened the idea of a single Italian nationality. By the early 19th century, a nationalist movement developed and led to the reunification of Italy--except for Rome--in the 1860s. In 1861, Victor Emmanuel II of the House of Savoy was proclaimed King of Italy. Rome was incorporated in 1870. From 1870 until 1922, Italy was a constitutional monarchy with a parliament elected under limited suffrage.

20th-Century History

During World War I, Italy renounced its standing alliance with Germany and Austria-Hungary and, in 1915, entered the war on the side of the Allies. Under the postwar settlement, Italy received some former Austrian territory along the northeast frontier. In 1922, Benito Mussolini came to power and, over the next few years, eliminated political parties, curtailed personal liberties, and installed a fascist dictatorship termed the Corporate State. The king, with little or no effective power, remained titular head of state.

Italy allied with Germany and declared war on the United Kingdom and France in 1940. In 1941, Italy--with the other Axis powers, Germany and Japan--declared war on the United States and the Soviet Union. Following the Allied invasion of Sicily in 1943, the King dismissed Mussolini and appointed Marshal Pietro Badoglio as Premier. The Badoglio government declared war on Germany, which quickly occupied most of the country and freed Mussolini, who led a brief-lived regime in the north. An anti-fascist popular resistance movement grew during the last two years of the war, harassing German forces before they were driven out in April 1945. A 1946 plebiscite ended the monarchy, and a constituent assembly was elected to draw up plans for the republic.

Under the 1947 peace treaty, minor adjustments were made in Italy's frontier with France, the eastern border area was transferred to Yugoslavia, and the area around the city of Trieste was designated a free territory. In 1954, the free territory, which had remained under the administration of U.S.-U.K. forces (Zone A, including the city of Trieste) and Yugoslav forces (Zone B), was divided between Italy and Yugoslavia, principally along the zonal boundary. This arrangement was made permanent by the Italian-Yugoslav Treaty of Osimo, ratified in 1977 (currently being discussed by Italy, Slovenia, and Croatia). Under the 1947 peace treaty, Italy relinquished its overseas territories and certain Mediterranean islands.

The Roman Catholic Church's status in Italy has been determined, since its temporal powers ended in 1870, by a series of accords with the Italian Government. Under the Lateran Pacts of 1929, which were confirmed by the present constitution, Vatican City is recognized by Italy as an independent, sovereign entity. While preserving that recognition, in 1984, Italy and the Vatican updated several provisions of the 1929 accords. Included was the end of Roman Catholicism as Italy's formal state religion.

Italy's Cultural Contributions
Europe's Renaissance period began in Italy during the 14th and 15th centuries. Literary achievements--such as the poetry of Petrarch, Tasso, and Ariosto and the prose of Boccaccio, Machiavelli, and Castiglione--exerted a tremendous and lasting influence on the subsequent development of Western civilization, as did the painting, sculpture, and architecture contributed by giants such as da Vinci, Raphael, Botticelli, Fra Angelico, and Michelangelo.

The musical influence of Italian composers Monteverdi, Palestrina, and Vivaldi proved epochal; in the 19th century, Italian romantic opera flourished under composers Gioacchino Rossini, Giuseppe Verdi, and Giacomo Puccini. Contemporary Italian artists, writers, filmmakers, architects, composers, and designers contribute significantly to Western culture.

GOVERNMENT

Italy has been a democratic republic since June 2, 1946, when the monarchy was abolished by popular referendum. The constitution was promulgated on January 1, 1948.

The Italian state is centralized. The prefect of each of the provinces is appointed by and answerable to the central government. In addition to the provinces, the constitution provides for 20 regions with limited governing powers. Five regions--Sardinia, Sicily, Trentino-Alto Adige, Valle d'Aosta, and Friuli-Venezia Giulia--function with special autonomy statutes. The other 15 regions were established in 1970 and vote for regional "councils." The establishment of regional governments throughout Italy has brought some decentralization to the national governmental machinery, and recent governments have devolved further powers to the regions. Many regional governments, particularly in the north of Italy, are seeking additional powers.

The 1948 constitution established a bicameral parliament (Chamber of Deputies and Senate), a separate judiciary, and an executive branch composed of a Council of Ministers (cabinet), headed by the president of the council (prime minister). The president of the republic is elected for seven years by the parliament sitting jointly with a small number of regional delegates. The president nominates the prime minister, who chooses the other ministers. The Council of Ministers--in practice composed mostly of members of parliament--must retain the confidence of both houses.

The houses of parliament are popularly and directly elected by a proportional representation system. Under 2005 legislation, the Chamber of Deputies has 630 members (12 of which are elected by Italians abroad). In addition to 315 elected members (six of which are elected by Italians abroad), the Senate includes former presidents and several other persons appointed for life according to special constitutional provisions. Both houses are elected for a maximum of five years, but either may be dissolved before the expiration of its normal term. Legislative bills may originate in either house and must be passed by a majority in both.

The Italian judicial system is based on Roman law modified by the Napoleonic code and subsequent statutes. There is only partial judicial review of legislation in the American sense. A constitutional court, which passes on the constitutionality of laws, is a post-World War II innovation. Its powers, volume, and frequency of decisions are not as extensive as those of the U.S. Supreme Court.

Principal Government Officials

Ministry	Minister	Party

President of the Council (Prime Minister)	Matteo Renzi	PD
State Secretary to the Prime Minister	Graziano Delrio	PD
Ministers with portfolio		
Minister of the Interior	Angelino Alfano	NCD
Minister of Foreign Affairs	Paolo Gentiloni	PD
Minister of Defense	Roberta Pinotti	PD
Minister of Justice	Andrea Orlando	PD
Minister of Economy and Finance	Pier Carlo Padoan	Independent
Minister of Economic Development	Federica Guidi	Independent
Minister of Infrastructures and Transports	Maurizio Lupi	NCD
Minister of Agriculture, Food and Forestry Policies	Maurizio Martina	PD
Minister of Education, Universities and Research	Stefania Giannini	SC
Minister of Labour and Social Policy (it)	Giuliano Poletti	Independent
Minister of the Environment, Protection of Land and Sea	Gian Luca Galletti	UdC
Minister of Heritage and Cultural Activities and Tourism	Dario Franceschini	PD
Minister of Health	Beatrice Lorenzin	NCD
Ministers without portfolio		
Minister for Constitutional Reforms and Parliamentary Relations	Maria Elena Boschi	PD
Minister for Regional Affairs	Maria Carmela Lanzetta	PD
Minister for Simplification of Public Administration	Marianna Madia	PD

Italy maintains an embassy in the United States at 3000 Whitehaven Street, NW, Washington, DC 20008 (tel. 202-612-4400).

POLITICAL CONDITIONS

Until recently, there had been frequent government turnovers since 1945. The dominance of the Christian Democratic (DC) party during much of the postwar period lent continuity and comparative stability to Italy's political situation.

From 1992 to 1997, Italy faced significant challenges as voters--disenchanted with past political paralysis, massive government debt, extensive corruption, and organized crime's considerable influence--demanded political, economic, and ethical reforms. In 1993 referendums, voters approved substantial changes, including moving from a proportional to a largely majoritarian electoral system and the abolishment of some ministries. However in 2005, parliament passed a new electoral law based on full proportional assignment of seats.

Major political parties, beset by scandal and loss of voter confidence, underwent far-reaching changes. New political forces and new alignments of power emerged in March 1994 national elections. The election saw a major turnover in the new parliament, with 452 out of 630 deputies and 213 out of 315 senators elected for the first time. The 1994 elections also swept media magnate Silvio Berlusconi--and his Freedom Pole coalition--into office as Prime Minister. Berlusconi, however, was forced to step down in January 1995 when one member of his coalition withdrew support. The Berlusconi government was succeeded by a technical government headed by Prime Minister Lamberto Dini, which fell in early 1996. New elections in 1996 brought a center-left coalition to government for the first time after World War II.

A series of center-left coalitions dominated Italy's political landscape between 1996 and 2001. In April 1996, national elections led to the victory of a center-left coalition (the Olive Tree) under the leadership of Romano Prodi. Prodi's government became the second-longest to stay in power before he narrowly lost a vote of confidence (by three votes) in October 1998. A new government was formed by Democratic Party of the Left leader and former-communist Massimo D'Alema. In April 2000, following a poor showing by his coalition in regional elections, D'Alema resigned. The succeeding center-left government, including most of the same parties, was headed by Giuliano Amato, who previously served as Prime Minister in 1992-93.

National elections, held on May 13, 2001, returned Berlusconi to power at the head of the five-party center-right Freedom House coalition, comprising the prime minister's own party, Forza Italia, the National Alliance, the Northern League, the Christian Democratic Center, and the United Christian Democrats. In April 2005, a poor showing in regional elections and dissatisfaction with the focus of the government's program among center-right coalition members forced Prime Minister Berlusconi to resign and form a new government. The 60th government since the liberation of Italy was formed on April 23, 2005, with a new program emphasizing economic concerns. The previous Berlusconi government was the longest serving in Italy's post-war history.

In national elections held April 9-10, 2006, Romano Prodi's center-left Union coalition won a narrow victory over Berlusconi's Freedom House coalition. The Union coalition includes the Democratic Party of the Left, the Daisy Party, Communist Refoundation, the Greens, the Social Democrats, and six other parties.

In May 2006, the parliament selected Giorgio Napolitano of the Democratic Party of the Left as the Republic's President. President Napolitano formerly served as a lifetime senator, Minister of the Interior, and a Member of the European Parliament. President Napolitano's term ends in May 2013. The Senate, lower house, and regional representatives will vote to elect his successor.

Political Parties
Italy's dramatic self-renewal transformed the political landscape between 1992 and 1997. Scandal investigations touched thousands of politicians, administrators, and businessmen; the shift from a proportional to majoritarian voting system--with the requirement to obtain a minimum of 4% of the national vote to obtain representation--also altered the political landscape.

Party changes were sweeping. The Christian Democratic party dissolved; the Italian People's Party and the Christian Democratic Center emerged. Other major parties, such as the Socialists, saw support plummet. A new populist, and free-market orientated movement, Forza Italia, gained wide support among moderate voters. The National Alliance broke from the neofascist Italian

Social Movement. A trend toward two large coalitions--one on the center-left and the other on the center-right--emerged from the April 1995 regional elections. For the 1996 national elections, the center-left parties created the Olive Tree coalition while the center right united again under the Freedom Pole. The May 2001 elections ushered into power a refashioned center-right coalition dominated by Berlusconi's party, Forza Italia. The April 2006 elections returned the center-left to power under the Union coalition, a successor to the Olive Tree. Freedom House now sits in the opposition. This emerging bipolarity represents a major break from the fragmented, multi-party political landscape of the postwar era, although it appears to have reached a plateau, since efforts via referendums to further curtail the influence of small parties were defeated in 1999 and 2000.

The largest parties in the Chamber of Deputies are Olive Tree (31.3%), now a party within the broader Union coalition comprised of the Democrats of the Left, the Daisy Party, and the European Republican Movement; Forza Italia (23.7%); the National Alliance (12.3%); the Union of Christian and Center Democrats (6.8%); and the Communist Refoundation Party (5.8%). Similar rankings generally apply in the Senate, in which the Olive Tree and Forza Italia are the dominant parties.

ECONOMY

Currency	Euro (EUR), except in Campione d'Italia (CHF)
Fiscal year	calendar year
Trade organisations	EU, WTO (via EU membership), OECD
	Statistics
GDP	$2.129 trillion (estimate by IMF)(nominal) 8th $2.065 trillion (estimate by IMF) (PPP; 12th)
GDP rank	8th (nominal) / 12th (PPP)
GDP growth	▼-0.1% Q3 2014
GDP per capita	▲$35,512 nominal (2014)$34,455 PPP
GDP by sector	agriculture: 1.8%; industry: 25%; services: 73% (2010 est.)
Inflation (CPI)	0,6 CPI, (april . 2014 ISTAT estimate)
Population below poverty line	8% 4,814,000 people below absolute line of poverty (about €520/month)(
Gini coefficient	36
Labour force	▲22.4 million (est.)
Labour force by occupation	services (68%), industry (28%), agriculture (4%)
Unemployment	12.3% (ISTAT estimate)
Average gross salary	▲€2,378/$3,270,
Average net salary	▲€1,898/$2,610, Average net income monthly €1472/$2003 (2014)
Main industries	tourism, communications, machinery, steel, chemicals, pharmaceuticals, food processing, textiles, motor vehicles, home appliances, clothing, fashion
Ease-of-doing-business rank	73rd
	External
Exports	▲$483 billion (2013 est.) (+3.2%)
Export goods	engineering products, textiles and clothing, production machinery, motor vehicles, transport equipment, chemicals; food, beverages and tobacco; minerals, and nonferrous metals
Main export partners	Germany 13%, France 11%, United States 6.6%,

	Switzerland 6%, United Kingdom 5%, Spain 4.8%,
Imports	▲$470 billion
Import goods	engineering products, chemicals, transport equipment, energy products, minerals and nonferrous metals, textiles and clothing; food, beverages, and tobacco
Main import partners	Germany 15.7%, France 9%, China 7%, Netherlands 6%, Spain 4.8%, Belgium 4%,
FDI stock	▲$369.5 billion
Gross external debt	▲$2.493 trillion
Public finances	
Public debt	▲134,6 % of GDP
Revenues	$956.6 billion
Expenses	$1.014 trillion
Economic aid	donor: $2.48 billion, 0.15% of GDP
Credit rating	Standard & Poor's: BBB- (Domestic) BBB- (Foreign) AAA (T&C Assessment) Outlook: Stable Moody's: BAA2 Outlook: Stable Fitch: BBB+ Outlook: Stable
Foreign reserves	▲US$152.689 billion

Italy has a diversified industrial economy with high gross domestic product (GDP) per capita and developed infrastructure. According to the International Monetary Fund (see List of countries by past and future GDP (nominal)) Italy in 2014 is the 8th-largest economy in the world, the 4th-largest in Europe and in the EU and the 3rd-largest in the Eurozone in terms of nominal GDP, and the 12th-largest economy in the world and 5th-largest in Europe in terms of purchasing power parity (PPP) GDP.

Italy is a member of the G7 and the G8 industrialized nations, the European Union and the OECD.

The Italian economy has changed dramatically since the end of World War II. From an agriculturally based economy, it has developed into an industrial state ranked as the world's sixth-largest market economy. Italy belongs to the Group of Eight (G-8) industrialized nations; it is a member of the European Union and the Organization for Economic Cooperation and Development (OECD).

Italy has few natural resources. With much land unsuited for farming, Italy is a net food importer. There are no substantial deposits of iron, coal, or oil. Proven natural gas reserves, mainly in the Po Valley and offshore Adriatic, constitute the country's most important mineral resource. Most raw materials needed for manufacturing and more than 80% of the country's energy sources are imported. Italy's economic strength is in the processing and the manufacturing of goods, primarily in small and medium-sized family-owned firms. Its major industries are precision machinery, motor vehicles, chemicals, pharmaceuticals, electric goods, and fashion and clothing.

Italy is in the midst of a slow economic recovery from the aftermath of September 11, 2001, and the global economy's tailspin. While Italy's economic growth averaged only 0.66% for the last five years, 2006 GDP growth should reach 1.5%, largely due to growth in the Euro zone area.

Italy continues to grapple with excessive budget deficits and high public debt--4.3% and 108% of GDP expected in 2006, respectively. Italy joined the European Monetary Union in 1998 by signing the Stability and Growth Pact, and as a condition of this Euro Zone membership, Italy must keep its budget deficit beneath a 3% ceiling. In June 2006, the European Commission warned Italy it must bring the deficit down to that level by 2007. Italy must either cut its spending dramatically and/or raise new revenue; most such measures will require real political will and buy-in from the Italian public. The rise in public debt has also caused some credit rating agencies to lower Italy's sovereign debt rating.

Italy's closest trade ties are with the other countries of the European Union, with whom it conducts about 54.4% of its total trade (2002 data). Italy's largest EU trade partners, in order of market share, are Germany (15.5%), France (11.6%), and the United Kingdom (5.9%). Italy continues to grapple with the effects of globalization, where certain countries (notably China) have eroded the Italian lower-end industrial product sector.

The Italian economy is also affected by a large underground economy--worth some 27% of Italy's GDP. This production is not subject, of course, to taxation and thus remains a source of lost revenue to the local and central government.

U.S.-ITALY ECONOMIC RELATIONS

The United States and Italy cooperate closely on major economic issues, including within the G-8. With a large population and a high per capita income, Italy was the United States' eleventh-largest trading partner in 2005, with total bilateral trade of $42.5 billion comprised of exports to Italy totaling $11.5 billion and imports from Italy worth $31.0 billion. The U.S. ran a $19.5 billion deficit with Italy in 2005, up from $17.4 billion in 2004. Part of this imbalance has been due to a strong dollar. Significant changes are occurring in the composition of this trade. Value-added products such as office machinery and aircraft are becoming important U.S. exports to Italy. U.S. foreign direct investment in Italy at the end of 2004 exceeded $33.3 billion.

Labor

Unemployment is a regional issue in Italy--low in the north, high in the south. The overall national rate is at its lowest level since 1992. Chronic problems of inadequate infrastructure, corruption, and organized crime act as disincentives to investment and job creation in the south. A significant underground economy absorbs substantial numbers of people, but they work for low wages and without standard social benefits and protections. Women and youth have significantly higher rates of unemployment than do men.

Unions claim to represent 40% of the work force. Most Italian unions are grouped in four major confederations: the General Italian Confederation of Labor (CGIL), the Italian Confederation of Workers' Unions (CISL), the Italian Union of Labor (UIL), and the General Union of Labor (UGL), which together claim 35% of the work force. These confederations formerly were associated with important political parties or currents, but they have evolved info fully autonomous, professional bodies. The CGIL, CISL, and UIL are affiliated with the International Confederation of Free Trade Unions (ICFTU) and customarily coordinate their positions before confronting management or lobbying the government. The confederations have had an important consultative role on national social and economic issues. Among their major agreements are a 4-year wage moderation agreement signed in 1993, a reform of the pension system in 1995, and an employment pact, introducing steps for labor market flexibility in economically depressed areas, in 1996. In April 2002, unions held a general strike to protest against labor reforms proposed by Prime Minister Berlusconi.

Agriculture
Italy's agriculture is typical of the division between the agricultures of the northern and southern countries of the European Union. The northern part of Italy produces primarily grains, sugarbeets, soybeans, meat, and dairy products, while the south specializes in producing fruits, vegetables, olive oil, wine, and durum wheat. Even though much of its mountainous terrain is unsuitable for farming, Italy has a large work force (1.4 million) employed in farming. Most farms are small, with the average farm only seven hectares.

FOREIGN RELATIONS

Italy was a founding member of the European Community--now the European Union (EU). Italy was admitted to the United Nations in 1955 and is a member and strong supporter of the North Atlantic Treaty Organization (NATO), the Organization for Economic Cooperation and Development (OECD), the General Agreement on Tariffs and Trade/World Trade Organization (GATT/WTO), the Organization for Security and Cooperation in Europe (OSCE), and the Council of Europe. It chaired the CSCE (the forerunner of the OSCE) in 1994, the EU in 1996, and the G-8 in 2001 and served as EU president from July to December 2003.

Italy firmly supports the United Nations and its international security activities. Italy actively participated in and deployed troops in support of UN peacekeeping missions in Somalia, Mozambique, and East Timor and provides critical support for NATO and UN operations in Bosnia, Kosovo, and Albania. Italy deployed 1,000 Alpini troops to Afghanistan in support of Operation Enduring Freedom (OEF) in February 2003. Italy also supports international efforts to reconstruct and stabilize Iraq through its military contingent of some 2,800 troops, as well as humanitarian workers and other officials. The troops remain in Iraq under UN mandate and at the request of the sovereign Iraqi Government.

The Italian Government seeks to obtain consensus with other European countries on various defense and security issues within the EU as well as NATO. European integration and the development of common defense and security policies will continue to be of primary interest to Italy.

U.S.-ITALY RELATIONS

The United States enjoys warm and friendly relations with Italy. Italy is a leading partner in the war against terrorism. The two are NATO allies and cooperate in the United Nations, in various regional organizations, and bilaterally for peace, prosperity, and security. Italy has worked closely with the United States and others on such issues as NATO and UN operations as well as with assistance to Russia and the New Independent States; the Middle East peace process; multilateral talks; Somalia and Mozambique peacekeeping; and combating drug trafficking, trafficking in women and children, and terrorism.

Under longstanding bilateral agreements flowing from NATO membership, Italy hosts important U.S. military forces at Vicenza and Livorno (army); Aviano (air force); and Sigonella, Gaeta, and Naples--home port for the U.S. Navy Sixth Fleet. The United States has about 16,000 military personnel stationed in Italy. Italy hosts the NATO War College in Rome.

Italy remains a strong and active transatlantic partner which, along with the United States, has sought to foster democratic ideals and international cooperation in areas of strife and civil conflict. Toward this end, the Italian Government has cooperated with the United States in the formulation of defense, security, and peacekeeping policies.

Principal U.S. Officials
Ambassador-- John Phillips

Ambassador John Phillips was nominated by President Barack Obama on June 14, 2013 to serve as the U.S. Ambassador to the Italian Republic and the Republic of San Marino. He was confirmed by the United States Senate on August 1, 2013, and sworn in on August 16, 2013

Deputy Chief of Mission--Anna Borg
Economic Affairs--Kathleen Reddy
Political Affairs--David Pearce
Consular Affairs--Barbara Cummings
Public Affairs--John P. Dwyer
Commercial Affairs--vacant
Regional Security Affairs--Nancy Rolph-O'Donnell
Agricultural Section--Geoffrey Wiggin
Defense Attache--Col. Rolf Yngve

Consular Posts
Consul General, Florence--Nora Dempsey
Consul General, Milan--Deborah Graze
Consul General, Naples--Suneta Halliburton

The U.S. Embassy in Italy is located at Via Veneto 119, Rome (tel. (39)(06) 46741.

TRAVEL AND BUSINESS INFORMATION

The U.S. Department of State's Consular Information Program provides Consular Information Sheets, Travel Warnings, and Public Announcements.

Consular Information Sheets exist for all countries and include information on entry requirements, currency regulations, health conditions, areas of instability, crime and security, political disturbances, and the addresses of the U.S. posts in the country. **Travel Warnings** are issued when the State Department recommends that Americans avoid travel to a certain country.

Public Announcements are issued as a means to disseminate information quickly about terrorist threats and other relatively short-term conditions overseas that pose significant risks to the security of American travelers. Free copies of this information are available by calling the Bureau of Consular Affairs at 202-647-5225 or via the fax-on-demand system: 202-647-3000. Consular Information Sheets and Travel Warnings also are available on the Consular Affairs Internet home page: http://travel.state.gov. Consular Affairs Tips for Travelers publication series, which contain information on obtaining passports and planning a safe trip abroad, are available on the Internet and hard copies can be purchased from the Superintendent of Documents, U.S. Government Printing Office, telephone: 202-512-1800; fax 202-512-2250.

Emergency information concerning Americans traveling abroad may be obtained from the Office of Overseas Citizens Services at (202) 647-5225. For after-hours emergencies, Sundays and holidays, call 202-647-4000.

The National Passport Information Center (NPIC) is the U.S. Department of State's single, centralized public contact center for U.S. passport information. Telephone: 1-877-4USA-PPT (1-877-487-2778). Customer service representatives and operators for TDD/TTY are available Monday-Friday, 8:00 a.m. to 8:00 p.m., Eastern Time, excluding federal holidays.

Travelers can check the latest health information with the U.S. Centers for Disease Control and Prevention in Atlanta, Georgia. A hotline at 877-FYI-TRIP (877-394-8747) and a web site at http://www.cdc.gov/travel/index.htm give the most recent health advisories, immunization recommendations or requirements, and advice on food and drinking water safety for regions and countries. A booklet entitled Health Information for International Travel (HHS publication number CDC-95-8280) is available from the U.S. Government Printing Office, Washington, DC 20402, tel. (202) 512-1800.

Information on travel conditions, visa requirements, currency and customs regulations, legal holidays, and other items of interest to travelers also may be obtained before your departure from a country's embassy and/or consulates in the U.S. (for this country, see "Principal Government Officials" listing in this publication).

U.S. citizens who are long-term visitors or traveling in dangerous areas are encouraged to register their travel via the State Department's travel registration web site at https://travelregistration.state.gov or at the Consular section of the U.S. embassy upon arrival in a country by filling out a short form and sending in a copy of their passports. This may help family members contact you in case of an emergency.

ITALIAN ADMINISTRATIVE STRUCTURE: REGIONS AND PROVINCES

ABRUZZO

Abruzzo holds a record: 30 per cent of its territory is protected by environmental legislation. No other region in Europe can boast as much. Not without good reason is it known as "the region of parks". Three national parks, a regional park and many protected sites and nature reserves. In a region like this, it seems natural that the regional capital is called L'Aquila ('The Eagle').

Dominated by an imposing sixteenth-century castle (which houses the National Museum of Abruzzo), L'Aquila has splendid civic and religious monuments from the medieval and renaissance eras. On the coast of Abruzzo (which vaunts popular bathing areas) one of the most popular locations is Pescara, birthplace of Gabriele D'Annunzio. The house where he was born is now a small and evocative museum.

At Chieti there is an important National Archaeological Museum, well-known for the modernity and effectiveness of its exhibitions (for which it has won prizes). The "show piece" of the museum is the Warrior of Capestrano, a funerary statue of the sixth century B.C., found in the province of L'Aquila in 1934.At Teramo the stupendous fifteenth-century Antepedium (inside the cathedral) made by the great goldsmith of Abruzzo, Nicola da Guardiagrele, should not be missed. But Abruzzo is surprisingly rich in architectural and artistic treasures, almost as much as it is full of natural treasures and folk traditions (such as the "festival of the serpents" in Cocullo, which brings thousands of people to this tiny village on the first Sunday of May).

APULIA

In Bari - Apulia's capital city - they say: "If Paris was by the sea, it would be like a small Bari". Presumption or arrogance? No, just pride (for which these people are famous, apart from their strong sense of humour). The pride of living in a city that successfully blends art and deep historic roots with a very modern spirit of business enterprise. Traditionally the "land's end" that bridged Italy with the worlds of Greece and the Middle East, Bari enjoyed its "golden age" during medieval times. The Cathedral and Church of St. Nicholas with their Romanesque forms, bear majestic witness to that period. Traces of the ancient trading and social contacts with the Greek world can be seen in the Archaeological Museum.

The blend of history and art that characterizes the monuments of Bari is reflected in many areas of Apulia, where you will often discover cathedrals built during the medieval era such as in Brindisi, Andria, Barletta, Trani, Ruvo di Puglia, Lucera, Troia, Manfredonia, Otranto, and Gallipoli. Belonging to another era yet equally precious and extraordinary is the flourishing of the baroque architecture in the town of Lecce. In Taranto, the Archaeological Museum has sections of the more remote past. And Alberobello, in the province of Bari, is the capital of the Trulli, singular domains dating back to pre-history no less. As to nature's wonders, Apulia offers an extraordinary intermingling of mountains, woods and uncontaminated sea, for which the promontory of the Gargano in the province of Foggia is so well renowned.

BASILICATA

A piece of prehistory in the modern world.. This is found at Matera, the second main city of Basilicata, and UNESCO, the UN organisation that deals with education, science and culture, has proclaimed it to be the "heritage of humanity". It is the "caves of Matera", one of the most peculiar, ancient and extraordinary human settlements in the world, which have drawn the attention of scholars and artists from all over the world (the Italian writer Carlo Levi spoke of them in his famous book "Christ stopped at Eboli").

In the "caves", the houses have been dug out of the tufa rock and the walls constructed with the excavated material. Inhabited until recently, the "caves" are now empty and have become the object of projects of cultural and touristic revaluation and restoration. A visit to the "caves of Matera" is a truly unique experience. But it is not the only reason to come to this small, secluded, and beautiful region boarded by two seas: the Tyrrhenian and the Ionian. In Basilicata there are Greek ruins (Metaponto), medieval churches and castles (Melfi, Lagopesole), beautiful beaches (Maratea), and unspoilt countryside (Basilicata shares the splendid park of Pollino with Calabria).

And Matera does not only have its "caves": the remarkable blend of Romanesque and Baroque styles in the Church of S. Francesco, for example, is also fascinating. Finally, why not plan a visit to Venosa, birthplace of the great and wise Latin poet Horace? Here, among other attractions, it is possible to admire the medieval Abbey of SS. Trinità and other interesting monuments. In the regional capital, Potenza, ancient and recent earthquakes have seriously damaged the historic centre. But the archaeological museum merits a visit.

CALABRIA

Eternal gratitude is due to the Riace Bronzes, the two stupendous Greek statues dredged from the sea and exhibited, from the early 1980s, in the Museo Nazionale della Magna Grecia in Reggio Calabria. Thanks to the irresistible attraction exercised by the two masterpieces (one of which is attributed to Fidia, the master Greek sculptor of the fifth century B. C.), hundreds of thousands of visitors arrived in Calabria. And in this way many of them finally discovered, as a joyous and marvellous surprise, a beautiful country, an unspoilt sea, a lush and sometimes wild countryside, with numerous architectural and artistic masterpieces of unexpected quality.

Extraordinary, fascinating Calabria, a land of a thousand surprises. Of exquisite beauty, for example, is the Codex Purpureus, a rare sixth-century Greek gospel conserved in the Museo Diocesano in Rossano, with silver lettering and illustrated with splendid elegant figures and religious scenes. A breathtaking surprise, for those who see it for the first time, is the picturesque and spectacular coast of Tropea, on the Tyrrhenian sea (Calabria is also boarded by the Ionian). But it bears repeating that in Calabria, the surprises never end.

CAMPANIA

The Neapolitan dialect is said to be the best known of the Italian language in the world. This comes as no surprise: music, as we know, is a universal language and it is easy to remember the accompanying lyrics. And Neapolitan songs are known throughout the world. Who has not heard or sung "O sole mio" at least once? And yet, the diffusion of the Neapolitan dialect hides another truth: Neapolitan is not a dialect, it is a true and proper language that expresses and transmits an autonomous culture, formed and consolidated over the centuries. Naples, in short, has a history apart.

And it is for this that it is so well-known, beloved and visited: because there is no other city like it in the world, with its inimitable characteristics. It fascinates and conquers whoever stays therefore even for a short time. And how could it be otherwise when confronted with the beauty of its sea, the fascination of its history, the good humour of its people, and the beauty of the innumerable architectural treasures of all eras and all styles that grace the city?

A fascination and ability to enchant, throughout the whole of Campania, the region of which Naples is the capital: in the splendid Neapolitan islands of Capri, Ischia, Procida, on the spectacular Amalfi coast, in the magnificent Reggia di Caserta, in the archaeological site of Paestum (in the province of Salerno) and so many other beautiful centres of Campania. The ancients called this land "felix" (happiness) with good reason.

EMILIA-ROMAGNA

The porticoes that shelter and shade your way through the streets of the historic centre of Bologna; the infinite, multicoloured sea of umbrellas on the sunny beaches of Romagna. The modern, dynamic and wealthy city, which at the same time is capable of preserving its "human face". The lengthy coastline, crowded with tourists drawn by the irresistible trinity sun-sea-fun. Is this Emilia-Romagna? Yes, it is all this. And much much more, starting from its extraordinary historic, artistic and cultural heritage.

One of the richest regions of Italy, Emilia-Romagna is a gigantic treasure house filled with architectural gems and artistic masterpieces, with ancient and famous universities, and modern centres of artistic and cultural learning. In Bologna, the home of the most ancient Italian university (eleventh century), the monuments of great artistic value are truly countless. Here we shall mention just the two ancient spectacular towers of the Asinelli and the Garisenda, both leaning, and Piazza Maggiore, with its great medieval buildings, and the gothic duomo of S. Petronio, where Charles V was crowned emperor in 1530.

Outside Bologna, you should not miss the Byzantine masterpieces of Ravenna, the medieval baptistery of Benedetto Antelami in Parma, the Tempio Malatestiano in Rimini, the Romanesque church of S.Mercuriale in Forlì, the ancient Palazzo comunale in Piacenza, the seventeenth-century Sanctuary of the Madonna della Ghiara in Reggio Emilia, the splendid Galleria Estense in

Modena, or the harmonious and well-preserved historic centre of Ferrara. And 'enjoy your meal!'. Why? Go into any restaurant of Emilia-Romagna and you will understand.

FRIULI-VENEZIA GIULIA

The last Doge of Venice, Ludovico Manin, retired to this area at the end of the eighteenth century when the Venetian Republic fell to the blows of Napoleon Bonaparte. These days, whoever visits Villa Manin in the province of Udine, detects a hint of twilight in the air, almost as if the memory of the old gentleman who came here to pass the autumn of his life was influencing the visitors and inducing a melancholic mood in them. But this is a pleasant sensation, that leads to a more intimate and intense kind of aesthetic enjoyment.

The same sensation recurs all over this beautiful and severe border region, where almost every town boasts a museum (those of Udine, Tolmezzo, Pordenone, Cividale del Friuli, Gorizia, and Aquileia are particularly important and interesting), and is able to surprise with the plurality of architectural styles (in the centre of Udine the Venetian Gothic of the Palazzo del Comune faces the beautiful twentieth-century Art Deco Caffé Contarena) and cultural attractions (at Udine again, there are galleries of historic and modern art).

Highly suggestive is the Basilica in Aquileia, now a small town but once an important city of the Roman Empire. Trieste, in Venezia Giulia, the most "middle-European" of Italian cities, rich in history and culture, with its important ancient and modern artistic heritage, has been loved and represented by great literary figures (James Joyce, Italo Svevo, Umberto Saba and many others). Grado in the province of Gorizia is the favourite of many tourists who regularly return for its sea and particularly healthy climate.

LATIUM

The regional capital of Latium is Rome. Everybody knows it: the pull of the Eternal City is great and irresistible, the capital of the Christian world, the seat of the Papacy, the incomparable home of architectural and artistic masterpieces of the ancient world. Is it possible to resist the fascination of Rome? It may be difficult, but why not try to spend a few days "exploring" Latium? In this way you would discover a region of fascinating nature and environment, with an extraordinary variety of landscape: wide beaches, great pinewoods, mountains like Terminillo (an excellent ski resort), gentle hills and expansive plains. A region rich in artistic monuments that bring to mind the long and extraordinary history of this region in the most immediate fashion.

At Tarquinia, Cerveteri and Tuscania, necropolises and museums bear evidence of ancient and mysterious Etruscan people (seventh to sixth centuries B.C.) who ruled central Italy before the rise of Rome. There are countless testimonies of the Roman and later historical eras outside Rome, in the other provinces of Latium and in the local centres: Rieti, Viterbo, Latina and Frosinone.

It is enough to think of the splendid and grandiose Villa Adriana in Tivoli (where the renaissance Villa d'Este can also be found), the seventeenth-century Palazzo Barberini in Palestrina, and the Cathedral in Anagni. The same grandiose style of the Roman religion seems to be projected and duplicated outside Rome: in the abbeys of Montecassino, Casamari, and Fossanova and in the monasteries of Subiaco, places dear to Saint Benedict of Norcia. Latium, therefore, is not just Rome. And Rome is also Latium.

LIGURIA

A spectacular land of mountains descending sharply to the sea. Mountains and cliffs that seem to rise directly out of the Tyrrhenian Sea, in the far northern reaches of the Mediterranean . This is the dominant landscape of Liguria, fascinating and breathtaking, which induces an intensity of emotions and sensations in the visitor that will never leave during a tour through this region, so full of historic memories and a dynamic and severe (the mythical Genoese thrift) participation in the modern world.

The regional capital is Genoa, one of the main ports of the Mediterranean, the birthplace of Christopher Columbus, the great navigator who discovered America. A powerful marine city since the Middle Ages, Genoa preserves the traces of its great history to a remarkable extent. Imposing buildings, sumptuous aristocratic houses and great churches testify to the splendour of the past and integrate perfectly with the fabric of the modern city. In the other provinces of Liguria (Imperia and the other two important port cities of the region, La Spezia and Savona) there are countless natural and artistic attractions.

The peninsula of Portofino and the Cinque Terre are exceptional examples of lush and intact Mediterranean landscape; just as Portovenere is a small, exemplary jewel of the Mediterranean coast and Sanremo (where the vastly hugely Festival of the Italian Song is held in the casino every year) is one of most typical and famous seaside towns in Italy. Among the many monuments of great historical-artistic worth, we will limit ourselves to the example of the splendid Benedictine abbey of S. Fruttuoso, in Camogli. The pleasure of discovering the others is yours.

LOMBARDY

The richest, most highly developed and most densely populated region of Italy. And it is precisely for this that it is one of most surprising and unexpected for the tourist who arrives there knowing little of its historic, architectural, artistic and natural heritage. Let us take Milan, the great city of industry and commerce. Here everything that is modern and advanced finds its home: from technological innovation to fashion, from advertising to design, from ways of life to political "experiments". Milan sets the trend. Yet, beneath its thick aspect of a dynamic and modern metropolis projected towards the future, Milan conceals extraordinary architectural and artistic treasures.

There is only the embarrassment of choice: the Duomo, the Castello Sforzesco, the La Scala theatre and the Brera picture gallery. And in the rest of Lombardy there are many splendid natural landscapes (the lakes, the Stelvio national park), and monuments and works of art of considerable value. At Monza, Varese, Como, Bergamo, Brescia, Lodi, Cremona, and Pavia, every era has made its cultural and artistic mark: in the urban structures, in the churches, in the civic buildings. >From the Romanesque to the Gothic, from the Renaissance to the Baroque, up to the most daring and innovative architectural and artistic solutions of the modern and contemporary eras: Lombardy boasts an impressive cultural and artistic heritage. And many people have yet to discover all this.

MARCHE

It is a matter of fact: Italy possesses the most remarkable artistic and cultural heritage in the world. And this is not all: its heritage is not just to be found in the great artistic cities, but is diffuse, "spread" throughout national territory as in no other country. The proof? Le Marche. A region in which a rich and varied countryside (the Adriatic sea, with its flat and sandy coast interrupted at intervals by rugged, rocky precipices; the harmonious agricultural landscape of its gentle hills; the deep and mysterious caves; the protected areas of natural beauty) is enriched with towns, villages, palaces, and religious buildings, all of them of important architectural and artistic value.

This is the case with the cathedral of Ancona, the regional capital and an important Adriatic port, or the cathedral of Pesaro. In Urbino, the Ducal Palace is a stupefying testimony of Renaissance grandeur. If you find yourself in Macerata during the summer it is an unpardonable not to book a seat at the majestic Sferisterio theatre for a play or musical performance. At Ascoli Piceno the blend of medieval and renaissance architecture (S. Francesco, Loggia dei Mercanti, Piazza del

Popolo, etc.) arrests the attention of even the most distracted visitor. But in almost all the centres of Le Marche, even the smallest, there are many genuine artistic treasures. It is difficult to single out one without doing the others an injustice. We will make an exception for Recanati, the birthplace of the most beloved Italian poet of all time: the tender, bitter, unhappy and sublime Giacomo Leopardi (1798-1837). It is difficult not to feel moved when visiting the building where the poet spent his childhood and adolescence. An emotion which is felt, in a rather different way, by the visitor to the Santa Casa at Loreto, the destination for continuous crowds of pilgrims.

MOLISE

We shall hazard a slogan for this small and delightful region of the southern Adriatic: "Pay a visit, before it becomes fashionable". Ah yes, because it is not difficult to predict the mass discovery of this land where everything still has the "flavour" of old times: from the splendid landscapes to the folk traditions, from the gastronomic attractions (fabulous cheeses, among the many other typical products) to the community life, from the hospitality of the inhabitants to the unspoilt sea, from the craftsmanship (the bells of Agnone are famous) to the quiet life in the villages of the interior.

It is a genuine pleasure to visit Molise. Starting from the regional capital, Campobasso, with its evocative tangle of historic streets and the fifteenth-century Monforte castle. At Termoli, the most important town of the province of Campobasso, the Mediterranean sunshine illuminates the ancient walls constructed by Emperor Frederick and the massive sixteenth-century castle that looms over the sea. And everywhere in Molise, nature seems to keep watch over history, preserving memories.

As in the esplanade at Sepino, whose archaeological zone testifies to the ancient Roman colony, and in the vicinity of Pietrabbondante, where another interesting archaeological site recalls the remote existence of the Sannites, an ancient Italic people which dared to challenge and fight the power of Rome. And again, in the province of Isernia (the second city of Molise, with a beautiful Cathedral and fourteenth-century fountain), where the ancient abbey of S. Vincenzo al Volturno rises, solitary and majestic. A visit to Molise really is worthwhile, then. Before it becomes fashionable.

PIEDMONT

Turin, the regional capital of Piedmont, is reputed to be a magical city. And it can only be by magic that a city, considered to be the capital of Italian heavy industry (FIAT, one of the biggest automobile producers in the world, is based here), is also one of the main tourist attractions of Italy. Of course, there are good reasons for this. In the cathedral of Turin is kept the Holy Shroud, the ancient linen winding-sheet in which, according to the tradition, the body of Christ was wrapped after his crucifixion. At Turin there is also the Egyptian Museum, which contains an extraordinary collection of art from Ancient Egypt, and the Sabauda Gallery, full of masterpieces by great European artists.

Finally, at Turin there are some great monumental testimonies to the important role played by Piedmont in modern Italian history, as the seat of the House of Savoy (the reigning dynasty of Italy until 1946) and the first capital of the Kingdom of Italy: the Royal Palace, Palazzo Madama, the Mole Antonelliana, and the Royal Villa at Stupinigi. Throughout the rest of Piedmont, in the cities and provinces of Novara, Vercelli, Cuneo, Alessandria, and Asti, there are numerous civic and religious edifices which bear witness to the past: fortresses, basilicae, convents. Too many to give even a few examples. The natural landscape is splendid and varied: mountains, valleys, hills (the Langhe are famous as the setting for many stories by Cesare Pavese and Beppe Fenoglio, famous writers from Piedmont), lakes (Maggiore, d'Orta, di Viverone), and the Valgrande National Park. The gastronomic and wine-producing culture is rich and prestigious (some of the great Italian wines are from Piedmont).

SARDINIA

David Herbert Lawrence, the famous English writer, loved Italy. He travelled through it far and wide, often on foot. Sardinia inspired him and he dedicated his fine book to it, "Sea and Sardinia", where he wrote: "Sardinia is left outside of time and history". Of course, nowhere is left outside of time and history. But Lawrence's affirmation has a certain "poetic" truth, which captures and sums up a sensation which unites everyone who goes to Sardinia: the sensation of finding oneself in a region where the stunning beauty of nature, the limpid waters of the sea, the reserved and genuine character of the people, the exquisiteness of the many typical dishes, the ancient traditions, and the various expressions of Sardinian culture, will never change.

In spite of the twists and turns of history, and in spite of the passing of time. The Phoenicians, Carthaginians, Romans, Arabs, Byzantines and Spanish all arrived in this splendid island: Sardinia assimilated and reinterpreted all these different influences, integrated them into its own culture, but did not allow its heart, its own profound way of feeling, to be touched or changed.

Just as the physical heart of Sardinia, the area of Gennargentu (now a splendid National Park), has always been inaccessible to foreigners. All this gives a unique and original flavour to a holiday in Sardinia. The visitor feels reassured, "guaranteed" by this sensation of unchangeability: as if here, even in the most modern and built-up areas of the island, everything continues to be more authentic, more genuine than elsewhere. It is so at Cagliari as it is at Nuoro, at Sassari as it is at Oristano, at Alghero as it is on the Emerald Coast: wherever the tourist chooses to enjoy the magnificent sea or visit museums, to study the mystery of the "nuraghi" or to try a delicious typical dish. Wherever you are, you will feel that you are doing the right thing, at the right time, in the right place.

SICILY

Do you want to learn about Greece? So come to Sicily. It is a paradox, for sure, but only to a certain extent. The Greek cities of Sicily (Agrigento, Selinunte, Segesta, Syracuse, to mention the most important) were among the most beautiful of the Hellenic world. Nowadays, to visit the Valley of Temples at Agrigento or to watch a summer performance in the great Greek Theatre of Syracuse is to plunge yourself into the remote Hellenic past. And this is also true in Sicily for many other historical eras and civilisations, from the Spanish to the French. With the sole exception of Arab rule, which has left scarce physical testimony. Sicily is a book of history and art history, a compendium of the greatest civilisations and cultures of all time. A sunny island whose landscape is rich in contrasts, with a splendid coastline and a refined, delicious and varied cuisine of traditional flavours and exquisite aromas: the quintessence of Mediterranean culture, yet also dense with intellectual complexity and refinement, so well represented by the literary masterpieces of Luigi Pirandello, Giuseppe Tomasi di Lampedusa, Leonardo Sciascia, Gesualdo Bufalino and today, Andrea Camilleri.Every style, every movement in art is richly represented in Sicily. In cities like Palermo, Catania, Caltanissetta, Enna, Syracuse, Ragusa, Trapani, Agrigento, and Messina. And in small towns, like Cefalù, clustered around its Norman cathedral, or Noto, with its extraordinary Baroque cathedral, or Taormina, with its splendid Greco-Roman theatre.

TUSCANY

Modern Italian was born in Tuscany, from the great literature of Dante, Petrarch and Boccaccio. Can there be a deeper bond, a greater and more noble debt owed by a nation to one of its regions, than that of the common language? But the whole of Europe is in debt to Tuscany for its extraordinary contribution to European culture. It was in Tuscany between the fourteenth and sixteenth centuries that the great era of humanism and the Renaissance was born and developed, movements which radically renewed the culture and art of the time, leaving a profound and indelible mark on the common civilisation of Europe.

Of that extraordinary period of history, Tuscany, starting from the regional capital Florence, bears the greatest witness. Great works of civic and religious architecture, sculpture and paintings of extraordinary artistic value, testify to the creative genius of great artists: Leonardo da Vinci, Michelangelo Buonarroti, and Filippo Brunelleschi.

But Tuscany is not just Florence. There is Siena too, with its Piazza del Campo, the theatre each summer for its famous Palio. In the province of Siena (also famous for its great wines, such as Chianti and Brunello) Montepulciano and Pienza stand out, extraordinary gems of renaissance art, and San Gimignano, with its famous towers and turreted houses. Then there is Pisa with its world-famous leaning tower; Carrara, with its Duomo clad in the precious marble that takes the name of the city; and also Lucca, Pistoia, Arezzo, Grosseto, Livorno, and Prato, that all boast churches and other monuments of great architectural and artistic value. The beauties of the Tuscan countryside are innumerable. Above all, its landscape: the typical, unique, gentle and warm Tuscan countryside.

TRENTINO-ALTO ADIGE

Apples, for example. Or the green of the valleys, the candour of the snow-capped mountains, or perhaps the placid lakes. Trentino-High Adige/Südtirol is a region that irresistably evokes images of genuineness, naturalness and quiet. [I took out a sentence at this point the meaning of which baffles me]. So whether your holiday will be spent on the banks of Lake Garda, in the Stelvio National Park, among the spectacular Dolomites Mountains, in one of the many verdant valleys, or skiing at Madonna di Campiglio or San Martino di Castrozza, you are sure to find exactly what you're looking for: splendid nature, excellent hospitality, excellent food and wine. For lovers of culture and history, this area has much in store: the provinces of Trento or Bolzen (both provinces with their own special autonomy) have their fair share of historic sites and monuments to admire. Trento's Romanesque/Gothic Cathedral dating from 1545 to 1563 hosted the most famous Council of Christianity. Also, the town of Rovereto vaunts two particular points of architectural interest, both dating back to the 15th century: the Castle and the Church of St. Mark.

On the hill of Miravalle, the great Bell of those fallen in war provides the suitable occasion for a civil pilgrimage. In Bolzen, a city where Italian and German cultures seamlessly blend together, between the many architectural sites we recommend beginning from a "lesser" work, yet one which have a great symbolic interest: the Porta del Vino (the “Wine Gate”) inside Bolzen's gothic Cathedral, artistically engraved with images of peasants at the work between the vines. A homage to wine, which here is produced with excellent results – just one more reason for this region's appeal. Not to be missed is the Domenican Church, with its 14th century fresco on the "Triumph of Death" in clear Giotto style. Finally, Merano is a pretty and highly popular tourist centre with ancient porticoes and a suggestive historic centre.

UMBRIA

Perhaps it is the evocative nature of the place, or a certain enchanted air (we might almost say “mystic”) that you breathe to some extent everywhere, but sooner or later whoever visits Umbria ends up thinking: Saint Francis, that great, gentle, tender and poetic Saint of happiness and meekness could only have been born here in Umbria. In this place of ever-green, enchanted and radiant nature. In these towns the concept of “historic centre” seems inadequate and reductive, so widespread is the monumental and artistic component in the towns of Umbria. Perugia, for example, the regional capital. Just to describe it is to lose oneself in the richness, complexity and magnificence of its architectural and artistic treasures: from the Etruscan walls to the splendid Palazzo Gallenga, seat of the prestigious university for foreigners, and many other buildings and historic monuments that lead out from the central Piazza IV Novembre, itself dotted with architectural and artistic jewels such as the Great Fountain and the magnificent Palazzo dei Priori.

The same is true for splendid Gubbio, rich with Franciscan memories and monuments from the medieval and renaissance eras. And then Todi, Spello, Spoleto, Orvieto, Città di Castello and many other small towns: all magnificently enriched by monuments, palaces and churches of high artistic merit. Even Terni, a modern industrial city, boasts jewels such as the churches of S. Salvatore and S. Francesco and, close by, the masterpiece of nature that is the Waterfall of Marmore. Finally Assisi, the town where Saint Francis was born (as was Saint Clare, founder of the Poor Clares), one of the best-known Christian destinations frequented by pilgrims. You have to see it for yourself.

MINERAL AND MINING SECTOR: IMPORTANT INFORMATION

ITALY

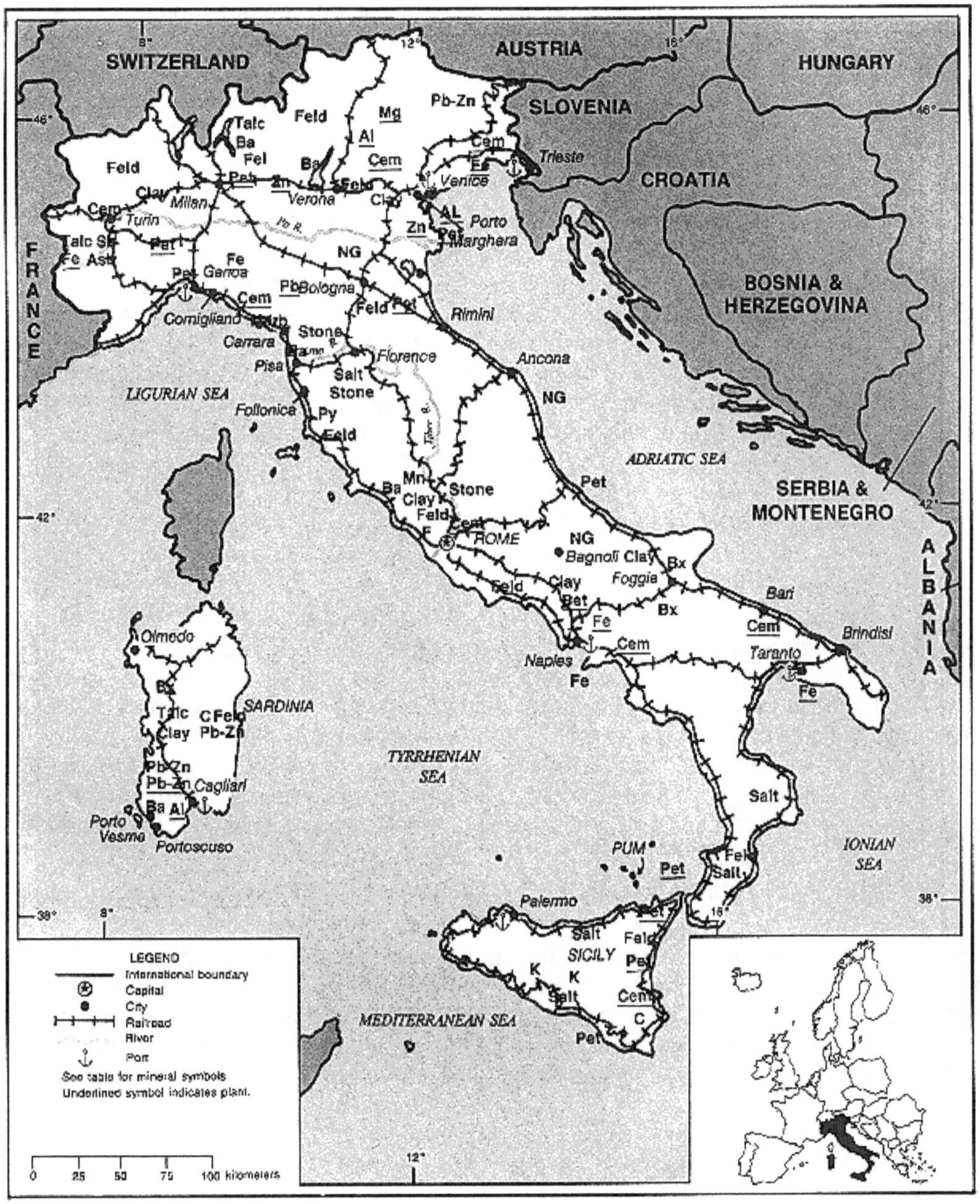

THE MINERAL INDUSTRY OF ITALY

By Alberto Alexander Perez

In 2009, Italy's gross domestic product (GDP) based on purchasing power parity amounted to an estimated $1.739 trillion, which was a decrease of 5.07% compared with that of 2008. In terms of its GDP based on purchasing power parity, the country ranked fourth in the European Union (EU) after Germany, the United Kingdom, and France. Italy's industrial sector accounted for about 25% of the GDP in 2009, which was a .7% decrease from that of the previous year. Industrial output as a whole decreased by 13.5% compared with output in 2008 owing to the effect of the world economic recession on its industries across the board. Italy's most important industrial facilities, in terms of value, are those for the production of aluminum, chemicals, and iron and steel; automotive assembly; machine tooling; and metal working.

These sectors continued to be heavily dependent on imported nonfuel and fuel mineral commodities. Italy is also well known for its industrial mineral resources. Its Carrara and Sienese marbles are appreciated for their natural qualities; the production of clays is extensive, and Italy was the 16th ranked manufacturer of cement in the world, measured by volume of production. Italy has gone through an economic development phase similar to those of France, Germany, and the United Kingdom, however, and has become mostly a services-based economy, which has led to specialization in its manufacturing and mineral industries. In 1970, industry's share of the GDP was 30% whereas that of services was 51.9%. In 2009, industry accounted for only 18.8% of the GDP and services accounted for 73.1% of the GDP. In 2009, Italy's national aggregate consumption fell slightly by .5%, reflecting the contraction in Italy's GDP (Cembureau, 2010, p. 4; Istituto Nazionale di Statistica, 2010, p. 21-25; U.S. Central Intelligence Agency, 2010).

Italy's construction and manufacturing industries suffered from the drop in world demand. As the world economy recovers, production in Italy will likely be reactivated. This is especially the case in the production of aluminum, cement, and steel, which are some of the sectors that have been most affected by the world economic downturn. As one of the largest EU members in terms of population and the size of its industrial sector, Italy is expected to continue to be a major consumer and producer of durable goods and to continue to rely on imported and recycled mineral materials. The country is likely to continue to rely on major imports of mineral fuels, despite increases in domestic production from new deposits coming onstream in the near term.

MINERALS IN THE NATIONAL ECONOMY

Italy's mineral industries produced such metals as copper, iron and steel, lead, and zinc, all of which were important materials for the country's manufacturing sector. The raw materials used to produce these and other metals were imported ores and concentrates or were obtained from secondary scrap recovery. Italy was a significant world producer of a variety of industrial minerals, which included cement, clays, feldspar, lime, marble, pumice, and sand and gravel (table 1).

Italy was highly dependent on imported mineral fuels, and Eni S.p.A. (Eni), which was 30% owned by the Italian Government, was the country's leading petroleum and natural gas company. Eni remained among the 20 leading energy companies in the world in 2008, which was the latest year for which data were available (Petroleum Intelligence Weekly, 2010).

GOVERNMENT POLICIES AND PROGRAMS

The Government plays a significant role in the economy through regulation of ownership of large financial and industrial companies; privatization and regulatory reform in accordance with EU directives, however, had reduced that role in recent years. Italy's basic mining legislation is mining law No. 1443 of July 29, 1927, which gives subsoil ownership of minerals to the state. The reimbursement of the state by mining concessionaires is regulated by law No. 752 of June 10, 1982. Quarrying operations are regulated by law No. 44 of September 1982.

All petroleum and gas upstream activities are supervised by the Ufficio Nazionale Minerario per gli Idrocarburi e la Geotermia [National Office for Mining, Hydrocarbons, and Geothermal Resources] (UNMIG), which operates within the Ministero dello Sviluppo Economico [Ministry of Economic Development]. After various organizational changes, the seven offices that compose the UNMIG now all operate within the Directorate General for Energy and Mineral Resources. Furthermore, by Presidential Decree in 2007, a committee was set up to carry out the UNMIG's duties. The Committee for Hydrocarbons and Mineral Resources (CIRM) groups together the functions of previous committees and performs technical advisory tasks related to mining, hydrocarbons, and royalties (Ministero dello Sviluppo Economico, 2010).

Environmental issues in Italy were focused on three main problem areas—air pollution from industrial emissions, such as sulfur dioxide; water pollution of coastal and inland rivers from industrial and agricultural effluents; and such natural hazards as avalanches, landslides, land subsidence in Venice, and volcanic eruptions (U.S. Central Intelligence Agency, 2010).

PRODUCTION

In 2009, the Italian mineral industry reflected the conditions of the global recession by posting severe decreases in the production of most mineral commodities. Pig iron production decreased by 45.1% to 5.69 million metric tons (Mt), alumina production decreased by 43.3%, ferromanganese production decreased by 35.3%, crude steel production decreased by 35.1% to 19.8 Mt, and silicomanganese decreased by 33%. Total aluminum production decreased by 31.5% compared with production in 2008. During the same period, copper production increased by 19.4%.

In the industrial minerals sector, bentonite production fell by 48%, granite production decreased by 31.8%, and estimated cement output decreased by about 15.5% compared with that of 2008. Nitrogen production, however, increased by 400%, and there were also increases in the production of ball clay (81%), salt (58%), common clay (41.4%), and silica sand (41.1%). Among mineral fuels, crude petroleum production decreased by 16.8% to 30,215,000 42-gallon barrels for 2009, and natural gas production decreased by 12.2% (table 1).

STRUCTURE OF THE MINERAL INDUSTRY

The Italian Government has ultimate control of all the mineral industry in Italy because mineral resources are by law the property of the Italian nation. However, private and mixed public and private entities were the principal owners of Italy's mineral industry. Full Government (public) ownership continued mainly in the mineral fuels sector and the Government has a 30% participation in Eni

MINERAL TRADE

Italy's demand for mineral raw materials was met by imports in 2009. The major commercial partners of Italy were, in order of the value of goods imported, Germany, France, China, and the Netherlands and Spain. Italy's principal partners were, in terms of the value of goods exported,

Germany, France, the United States, Spain, and the United Kingdom (Istituto Nazionale di Statistica, 2010, p. 25).

In 2009, exports from Italy to other countries in the EU included nonferrous metals[1] valued at $3.7 billion;[2] nonmetallic mineral manufactures, $5.78 billion; metalliferous ores and metal scraps, $458 million; and crude minerals, excluding coal, crude oil and precious stones, $266 million. Imports by Italy of goods originating from other countries in the EU included manufactured metals valued at $5.51 billion; nonferrous metals, $5.10 billion; and metalliferous ores and metal scrap, $1.73 billion. In contrast, Italy's most valuable mineral industry imports (not including mineral fuels) from a non-EU country were iron and steel, $5.28 billion, and nonferrous metals, $4.19 billion. The leading mineral exports to non-EU countries were iron and steel and manufactured metals, which were valued at $6.36 billion and $6.26 billion, respectively (Eurostat, 2010, p. 106-108, 114-116, 122-124,130-132).

The most significant component of Italy's mineral trade in 2009 was the net imports of mineral fuels; Italy imported 82.09 million metric tons (Mt) of crude petroleum in 2009, which was a decrease of 8% compared with the level of crude petroleum imports in 2008. Of this amount, Italy imported at least 34% from the Commonwealth of Independent States (CIS), principally from, in order of volume, Russia, Azerbaijan, and Kazakhstan. At least 26% of Italian crude petroleum came from Africa; Libya, which was the most important single country supplier of crude petroleum to Italy, provided 25% of Italy's crude petroleum imports; Iraq, 11%; Iran, 7%; Saudi Arabia, 5%; and Norway, 3%; the remaining 14% came from other sources.

Italy continued to be a net importer of petroleum products. In 2009, the country imported 11.27 Mt of petroleum products, which was a decrease of 2.64% compared with imports in the previous year, and it exported 21.4 Mt, which was a decrease of 19.2% compared with exports in the previous year (Eurostat 2010b, p. 2-5, 8).

METALS

Aluminum and Bauxite and Alumina.—In 2009, Italy's total output of alumina production decreased by 43.3 percent to 752,873 metric tons (t). United Company Rusal (RUSAL) suspended operations at its Eurallumina facility in Italy owing to the high cost of running the facilities and decreased production by 91% (United Company Rusal, 2010; table 1).

Primary and secondary aluminum production decreased by 31.6%. Secondary production decreased to 826,977 (t). Alcoa Inc. of the United States idled its smelting operations in Italy at Fusima and Portovesme after a ruling by the European Commission, which stated that a portion of the benefit received by Alcoa from the Italian Government based on an electricity tariff must be refunded because it did not comply with EU state aid rules. Alcoa appealed the decision (table 1; Alcoa Inc., 2010). These events had a major effect on Italian production, as the country's chief producers of alumina and primary aluminum were Rio Tinto-Alcoa Italia S.p.A. and Eurallumina S.p.A. (table 2).

Copper.—KME Group S.p.A. (a major European refiner and fabricator of copper headquartered in Florence) conducted its operations in Italy at Barga and at Scrivia under its subsidiary KME

[1]The classifications stated are from the United Nations Statistics Divisions' Standard International Trade Classification, Revision 4 (series M, no. 34, Rev. 4, March 2006).
[2]Where necessary, values have been converted from Eurozone euros (€) to U.S. dollars (US$) at an average exchange rate of €.719=US$1.00 for 2009.

Italy S.p.A. Secondary copper and copper semimanufactures were the main commodities produced at these locations (KME Group S.p.A., 2010, p. 4).

Simar S.p.A (Simar), which was a member of the Cordofin Group S.p.A., had a refinery at Porto Marghera, near Venice. It produced mainly copper-zinc-titanium alloys. Simar's main product was known commercially as Zintek, and Simar created a company with the same name to develop and promote this product, although it was produced in Simar's facilities in Porto Marghera (Simar S.p.A., 2010). For its copper production, Italy imported small amounts of copper concentrate and relied mainly on imports of copper metal and scrap recovery.

Iron and Steel.—In 2009, Italy's pig iron production decreased by about 45.1% from that of 2008 to 5.69 million tons (Mt), and the production of crude steel decreased by about 35.1% to 19.8 Mt compared with production in 2008, which was a contrast to Italy's highest ever production levels of 32 Mt achieved in 2007 (table 1).

Italy's apparent consumption of crude steel dropped to 19.5 Mt and ranked the country second in Europe (excluding the CIS) after Germany (World Steel Association, 2010, p. 88).

The international drop in steel demand owing to world economic conditions had a major effect on steel production in Italy. Tenaris S.A. ceased production at its plant for 13 weeks in August and the company expected a decrease in production of at least 60% for the second half of 2009 (Bloomberg L.P., 2009).

In December, the chairman of the steel industry organization Federacciai stated that Italy's forecasted production for 2010 would likely decrease by 40% compared with the output in 2009. As the second ranked producer of steel in Europe, Italy's production was sensitive to world and domestic demand (Reuters, 2009).

Lead and Zinc.—In 2008, Italy's mine output of lead remained static whereas that of zinc metal increased to an estimated 107,100 t. A minor amount of lead and zinc concentrate was produced in Sardinia. Domestic mine production of lead and zinc was not sufficient to meet demand, and the country imported most of its requirements for lead and zinc concentrates. Glencore International AG of Switzerland remained the country's principal processor (smelter and refinery) of lead and zinc (table 2).

INDUSTRIAL MINERALS

In 2009, Italy remained a leading European and global producer of such industrial minerals as feldspar (24.9% of world output), pumice (15.3%), bentonite (5.4%), gypsum (3.6%), lime (1.8%), and cement (1.5%) (Cordier, 2010; Crangle, 2010a, b; Miller, 2010; van Oss, 2010; Virta, 2010).

Cement.—Italian cement production decreased by 15.5% owing to a decrease in the construction sector, which was driven by a sharp reduction in activity in the residential construction sector. It is unlikely that the residential sector will recover in the short to medium term to lead a recovery in the cement market, which makes public investment the likely source of a revival in this sector. (Cembureau, 2010, p. 4, 10). Italcementi S.p.A. resumed production at its Borgo San Dalmazzo plant after it had been converted into a grinding plant (Cemweek, 2009).

MINERAL FUELS

Natural Gas and Petroleum.—In 2009, Italy's output of natural gas decreased by 12.2%, and crude petroleum production decreased by 16.8% to 30.2 million barrels compared with production levels in 2008 (table 1). The country was not well endowed with hydrocarbons and imported 82.09 Mt in 2009, which was a decrease of 8% from the previous year (table 1; Kröppl, 2010b).

Po Valley Energy Ltd. (Po Valley) took control of the Castello and the Sillaro gasfields and was expected to produce gas at the end of the year. The Castello field near Milan was calculated to have 6.3 billion cubic feet in reserves, and Po Valley expected it to have a reserve life of 10 to 12 years. Its initial production per day was expected to be 2.7 million cubic feet. Sillaro has a profile of 14 billion cubic feet and is situated near Bologna: initial offtake was expected to be 3.8 million cubic feet when the project comes online (Oilbarrel.com, 2010).

Algeria and Italy agreed to accelerate the construction of the Galsi gas pipeline between Algeria and Italy. The pipeline was set to export 282 billion cubic feet per year of gas to Italy; construction was set to start in 2010. Also, the Italian and Algerian ministers agreed to increase the TransMed pipeline capacity by 247 billion cubic feet per year (Magharebia, 2010).

ITALIAN MINING LEGISLATION

The **Italian mining legislation** is based on the Royal Decree of 29 July 1927 , No 1443 (inOfficial Gazette of the Kingdom of Italy , on 23 August 1927 No 194), updated and coordinated with Legislative Decree no. 4 August 1999 , No 213.

The marble quarries in the *municipal agricultural marble* of Carrara and Massa , were governed by a set of laws enacted between 1751 and 1852 by the Dukes of Massa and Carrara , and then by their successors, the Dukes of Modena . In part, this *system* , known as*the law Este* , named after the family d ' Este, who had succeeded to the dukedom Cibo-Malaspina, still has some residual application in Italian law.

The other area where the production of Italian extraction has had a secular nature - the Sicily - was able to maintain after the unification of certain rules peculiar law, even under pressure from the British government that it intended to defend its interests in the extraction of sulfurisland.

NATIONAL LEGISLATION

DR July 29, 1927, No 1443 (Sections 4 and following) - Rules of a legislative framework to govern the exploration and production of mines in the kingdom

DR December 18, 1927, No 2717 - Mandatory reporting of statistical data on the production of mines and quarries

RDL June 15, 1936, No 1347 - Provisions for the exploration and production of mines

DR January 25, 1937, No 218 - Covert RDL into law on June 15, 1936, No 1347

L. March 4th, 1958 No 198 - Delegation of powers to the executive power in policing in mines and quarries and for the reform of the Higher Council of the mines

April 9, 1959 Presidential Decree No 128 - Animal mining and quarrying

Presidential Decree of 14 January 1972, No 2 (Art. 1, Lett. A) - Transfer to the ordinary statute regions of the state administrative functions in areas of mineral and thermal waters, quarries and peat bogs and crafts and its staff

DPR July 24, 1977, No 616, Art. 61 and Article 82 - Implementation of the delegation referred to 'Article. A law July 22, 1975, No 382

Presidential Decree No 21 July 1982 727-Implementation of EEC Directive No 76/117 relating to electrical equipment intended to be used in "explosive atmosphere".

L. October 6, 1982, No 752 - Rules for the implementation of mining policy

L. June 15, 1984, No 246 - Additions and amendments to Presidential Decree 9 April 1959, No 128, containing rules for police in mines and quarries, as well as the Law of 6 October 1982, no 752, concerning the implementation of mining policy

L. July 8, 1986, No 349 (Art. 2, Lett. D) - Establishment of the Ministry for the Environment, Land and Sea and rules on environmental damage

Circular No 24 September 1988 30483 - Technical standards concerning the investigation of soils and rocks, stability of natural slopes and escarpments, the general criteria and requirements for the design, construction and testing of retaining the land and foundation work. Application Instructions

L. July 30, 1990, No 221 - New rules for the implementation of mining policy

DM 23 December 1991 - Ministry of the Environment, Land and Sea - Requirements for environmental projects to rehabilitate the areas subject to search or mining eligible for assistance and how to verify and control the projects themselves.

DPR 18 April 1994, No 382 - Discipline procedures for granting of exploration permits and production concessions of mineral deposits of national interest and local interest

Decree No 25 November 1996 624 - Implementation of Directive 92/91/EEC on the safety and health of workers in the extractive industries through drilling and Directive 92/104/EEC on the safety and health of workers in the extractive industries to the surface and underground

Circular No 19 May 1997 P1066 - Clarifications on the DL No 25 November 1996 624

Circular No 26 May 1997 600524 Clarification of the legislative decree 25 November 1996, No 624 by the Ministry of Industry and Trade and Crafts

DL March 30, 1999, No 96 - Statement for the replacement of the government allocation of administrative functions between regions and local authorities pursuant to Article 4, paragraph 5, of Law March 15, 1997, No 59, as amended (Article 9)

DL April 1, 2005 - Changes to the list of products approved for use in explosive mining.

HIGHLIGHTS

Distinction between the quarry and mining law, that is decided in a clear and unambiguous in the law itself, in Article 2, which lists resources which fields should be defined in either way.More precisely,

Mine

minerals used for the extraction of metals , metalloids and their compounds, although these minerals are used directly;

graphite , solid fuels , liquid and gaseous, asphaltic and bituminous;

phosphates , alkali metal salts and magnesium, alum, mica , feldspar , kaolin andbentonite , bleaching earth from, clay for porcelain and earthenware, lands with a degree of refractoriness above 1630 ° C ;

precious stones, garnet , corundum , bauxite , leucite , magnesite , fluorspar , mineralbarium and strontium , talc , asbestos , marl from concrete , stone lithographs;

radioactive substances , mineral waters and spas, vapors and gases ;

Cave

of peat ;

materials for building construction (except cement marl), road and hydraulic;

of earth colors, the diatomaceous earth, the quartz and sand silica , the millstones , thestone whetstones ;

other materials used industrially to the terms art. 1 and not included in the first category.

This distinction is very important because **the deposit subject to mining (except peat) falls in the act of public law and belongs to the state, instead of the reservoir that is the subject quarry is part of private law and is attributable to the owner the fund** .

The research can not be done without the required permit and the cultivation of a field (of course next to a mining research, which was successful for exploiting) can be performed only by those who possess the relevant license which is the priority owner of the research grant.

In regions with ordinary statute permits research and production concessions are required and approved by the Ministry of Economic Development (formerly Ministry of Industry), back in the regions with special status, these practices will be referred to the competent regional offices.

IMPORTANT LAWS AND REGULATIONS

FEDERAL MINING LAW

Norme of a legislative framework to govern the exploration and production of mines in the kingdom. Published in the Official Gazette. No. August 23, 1927, No 194.

TITLE I CLASSIFICATION OF CULTIVATION OF MINERALS

(Law of legitimacy)

1. The exploration and production of minerals and energy of the ground, used industrially, in any form or physical conduct, are governed by this Law (3).

(3) replaced by So. 1, L. November 7, 1941, No 1360.

(Law of legitimacy)

2. The work referred to in art. 1 is divided into two categories: mines and quarries.

The first category includes the exploration and production of substances and energies following:

a) used for the extraction of minerals, metals, metalloids and their compounds, although these minerals are used directly;

b) graphite, solid, liquid and gaseous (3 / a), asphaltic and bituminous;

c) phosphates, alkali metal salts and magnesium, alum, mica, feldspar, kaolin and bentonite, bleaching earth from, porcelain and earthenware clays, clays with a degree of refractoriness above 1630 degrees Celsius;

d) precious stones, garnet, corundum, bauxite, leucite, magnesite, fluorine, barium and strontium mineral, talc, asbestos, cement marl, lithographic stones;

e) radioactive substances, mineral and thermal waters, gases and vapors.

Belongs to the latter cultivation:

a) of peat;

b) building materials for construction, road and hydraulic;

c) of earth colors, the diatomaceous earth, quartz and silica sand, the millstones, whetstones of the stones;

d) other materials used industrially to the terms of Article. 1 and not included in the first category (3).

(3 / a) on the discipline of research and production of hydrocarbons, see, now, L. January 11, 1957, No 6, and the other measures reported under Hydrocarbons. But see the last paragraph of Art. 1 of the Act, added by Law March 8, 1958, No 231.

(3) replaced by So. 1, L. November 7, 1941, No 1360.

3. On membership and the category of substances not listed in the preceding article will be defined by Royal Decree (4), promoted by the Minister for corporations (5), the Board heard of the mines.

By Royal Decree (4), promoted by the Minister for corporations (5) in consultation with the Minister for Justice, after consulting the High Council of the mines and the State Council, the substances included in the second of the above categories may be included in the first.

In both cases, objects under the two preceding paragraphs, the following, as applicable, the transitional provisions contained in RD July 29, 1927, No 1443 (6).

(4) Now, the President of the Republic.

(5) Deleted by R.D. August 9, 1943, No 718. Responsible for mining is now the Ministry of Industry and Commerce, at which it was established, with L. January 4, 1951, No 2, the Directorate General of Mines.

(4) Now, the President of the Republic.

(5) Deleted by R.D. August 9, 1943, No 718. Responsible for mining is now the Ministry of Industry and Commerce, at which it was established, with L. January 4, 1951, No 2, the Directorate General of Mines.

(6) replaced by So. 1, L. November 7, 1941, No 1360. View Articles. 53 et seq. of this decree.

TITLE II MINES

Chapter I - Mineral Research.

(Law of legitimacy)

4. The search for minerals is allowed only to those who are in possession of a permit to be issued in the manner established by the following Article (7) (7 / a).

----

(7) replaced by So. 1, Presidential Decree June 28, 1955, No 620, reported to the No VI.

(7 / a) Article. 17, Presidential Decree April 18, 1994, No 382, reported to the No XXVII, repealed Art. 4 limited to the words "to be issued with the arrangements laid down below."

(Law of legitimacy)

5. [Permission is granted to those who so requests and has, at the discretion of the Administration, the necessary economic and technical capacity: the Minister of Industry and Trade, in the case of minerals in the national interest, by chief District of mining for minerals of local interest.

The chief engineer of the mining district is required to give notice to the Provincial Administration, the Chamber of Commerce, Industry and Agriculture and the municipalities concerned to the territory of the questions that are submitted for permission to search within its competence, these bodies may present their comments within thirty days from the date of the communication.

For areas of interest to the defense, the minister for industry and commerce, or the chief engineer of the mining district shall issue a research permit after hearing the military administration.

The decision by head of the Mining District, which grant or deny permission to search, is final.

Unless otherwise provided by the President of the Republic on the proposal of the Minister of Industry and Trade, the Board heard of the mines, are considered of national interest indicated in the minerals. 2, first-class, letter a), b), (except graphite) and e) (excluding mineral water springs) of this Decree and all other local interest (8).

The decree granting the exploration permit is registered with the fixed tax of 10 lira] (9) (9 / a).

----

(8) Just replaced the first three paragraphs of the original text of article. 2, Presidential Decree June 28, 1955, No 620, reported to the No VI.

(9) The registration fee has been abolished and replaced by government concession tax, fixed at L. 20,000 for permits by the Ministry of Trade and Industry, and L. 10,000 for the chief engineer of the jurisdiction permits the mining district, the DPR March 1, 1961, No 121, Table A, No 163, 1).

(9 / a) Repealed. 17, Presidential Decree April 18, 1994, No 382, reported to the No XXVII.

(Law of legitimacy)

6. The research permit can not agree to more than three years. May be extended prior finding to be made at the expense of the researcher, the works performed and results obtained.

----

7. The researcher must be proportionate to the State the right 160 pounds per year (10) for each hectare of land within the limits of the permit (10 / a).

----

(10) So high art. 1, L. December 21, 1961, No 1501. Previously, the original amount of L. 2 was raised to L. 20 art. 4, D.Lgs.C.P.S. January 7, 1947, No 24, and then quadrupled art. 1, L. January 21, 1949, No 8, measures listed under both State Property.

(10 / a) for the rent increase, see Art. 14, D.L. October 2, 1981, No 546, listed in item Stamp (Tax).

8. The research permit is not transferable without the prior permission of the Minister for the national economy (10 / b).

Any transfer is subject to the fee of 1,000 lire (11).

The sale has not been authorized in advance by the parties is nothing so much as in the administration.

(10 / b) now called the Ministry of Trade and Industry pursuant to the provisions of the RD August 9, 1943, No D. 718 and the Lieutenant. June 21, 1945, No 377.

(11) The registration fee has been abolished and replaced by government concession tax, fixed at L. 50,000, by Presidential Decree March 1, 1961, No 121, Table A, No 165.

9. The Minister for the national economy may make the loss of the allowed (12):

1) when any given principle in the work within the deadline and, in the absence of a specific term, within three months from the date on which the permit was issued;

2) when the work has remained suspended for over three months;

3) when not being complied with requirements or contravene the provisions of Articles. 8 and 12 of this Decree;

4) when the right is not paid in proportion indicated in Art. 7.

In any case, the researcher is entitled to any compensation or benefits to the State or to any subsequent researchers.

Against the decision pronouncing the forfeiture of an exploration permit shall be set aside. This is decided by the Ministry for the national economy (10 / b), after consulting the High Council of the mines.

Who speaks against the measure on the opposition shall not be any appeal or administratively or judicially (13).

----

(12) See, also, Art. 3, Presidential Decree June 28, 1955, No 620, reported to the No VI.

(10 / b) now called the Ministry of Trade and Industry pursuant to the provisions of the RD August 9, 1943, No D. 718 and the Lieutenant. June 21, 1945, No 377.

(13) See, also, Art. 113 of the Constitution to effect the constitutional provision and the provision mentioned in the previous note, the last two paragraphs of this Article shall be deemed repealed.

(Law of legitimacy)

10. The owners of the funds, including the scope to which the permission relates, can not oppose the research, subject to the prohibitions contained in the law of March 30, 1893 Mining Police, No 184 (14).

The researcher has the obligation to compensate damages caused by the research.

The owner of the land subject to the research has the power to require security.

When the parties do not siansi granted, the chief engineer of the mining district, after hearing, if necessary, the advice of an expert, will establish an office, provisionally, the amount of the deposit, which the researcher can run to execute the work .

Any further dispute between the owner of the land and the researcher will be decided by judicial authority.

----

(14) See, now, Articles. 62-66 and 104-113, Presidential Decree April 9, 1959, No 128, listed under Industrial accidents and hygiene (prevention).

(Law of legitimacy)

11. Within the limits of land included in a research permit or a concession may be given permission to other research, but for different substances, and provided that such works are not inconsistent with those of existing research or grant.

In case of disagreement between the parties concerned, the Minister for the national economy (14 / a) shall, after consulting the High Council of the mines.

(14 / a) Now, the Minister for Industry and Commerce, under RD August 9, 1943, No D. 718 and the Lieutenant. June 21, 1945, No 377.

12. It is prohibited to the researcher to perform the work of cultivation.

In no event may dispose of the minerals extracted without the consent of the Minister for the national economy (15).

The power to authorize the use that can be delegated to the engineer head of the mining district.

----

(15) Subject to government concession tax, now set in L. 20,000 by the Presidential Decree March 1, 1961, No 121, Table A, No 164. See, also, note 14 / a art. 11.

13. When the State intends to proceed directly to research, the area of exploration is determined by the Minister for the national economy (14 / a).

(14 / a) Now, the Minister for Industry and Commerce, under RD August 9, 1943, No D. 718 and the Lieutenant. June 21, 1945, No 377.

Chapter II - mining concessions.

(Law of legitimacy)

14. The mines can be cultivated only by those who have been granted.

May be the subject of granting the deposits of which the Administration has recognized the existence and cultivability (15 / a).

They can also be made more concessions in the same area, but for different mineral substances kept in mind what is required by Article 11.

(15 / a) Article. 17, Presidential Decree April 18, 1994, No 382, reported to the No XXVII, repealed Art. 14, paragraph 1, Article. 15, paragraphs 1 and 4, and art. 18, paragraph 1, only the words "after consultation with the Board of Governors of the mines."

15. The granting of a mine can be made to those who have, at the discretion of the Minister for the national economy (16) the technical and economic suitability to lead the company (15 / a).

They can make more concessions to the same person.

Where the grant is made to a company, as the leaders, the representatives of it should be appreciated by the Minister for the national economy (16).

For mines located in areas of interest to the defense, the Minister for the national economy (16) provides for the award after having heard of the Military Administration (15 / a).

----

(16) Now the chief engineer of the mining district, for the concessions within its competence: see Art. 4, Presidential Decree June 28, 1955, No 620, reported to the No VI. For Article. 5 of the decree, the jurisdiction to concessions for the production of deposits of mineral and thermal waters belong to the Prefect. See, also, note 14 / a art. 11.

(15 / a) Article. 17, Presidential Decree April 18, 1994, No 382, reported to the No XXVII, repealed Art. 14, paragraph 1, Article. 15, paragraphs 1 and 4, and art. 18, paragraph 1, only the words "after consultation with the Board of Governors of the mines."

(16) Now the chief engineer of the mining district, for the concessions within its competence: see Art. 4, Presidential Decree June 28, 1955, No 620, reported to the No VI. For Article. 5 of the decree, the jurisdiction to concessions for the production of deposits of mineral and thermal waters belong to the Prefect. See, also, note 14 / a art. 11.

(16) Now the chief engineer of the mining district, for the concessions within its competence: see Art. 4, Presidential Decree June 28, 1955, No 620, reported to the No VI. For Article. 5 of the decree, the jurisdiction to concessions for the production of deposits of mineral and thermal waters belong to the Prefect. See, also, note 14 / a art. 11.

(15 / a) Article. 17, Presidential Decree April 18, 1994, No 382, reported to the No XXVII, repealed Art. 14, paragraph 1, Article. 15, paragraphs 1 and 4, and art. 18, paragraph 1, only the words "after consultation with the Board of Governors of the mines."

16. The researcher is preferred to any other applicant, provided that the Minister for the national economy (16) recognizes that he has the technical and economic suitability.

The researcher, when you do not get the grant, has the right to obtain, out of the dealer, a premium in relation to the importance of the discovery and compensation on account of the works used.

The premium and the benefits are provisionally established in the act of granting. Any dispute concerning the jurisdiction of the court is.

----

(16) Now the chief engineer of the mining district, for the concessions within its competence: see Art. 4, Presidential Decree June 28, 1955, No 620, reported to the No VI. For Article. 5 of the decree, the jurisdiction to concessions for the production of deposits of mineral and thermal waters belong to the Prefect. See, also, note 14 / a art. 11.

17. The expenses necessary for the investigation of claims granted, shall be borne by the applicant.

----

18. The grant is made by the Minister for the national economy (16), after consultation with the Board of Governors of mines (15 / a).

The decree granting contains:

a) the indication of the dealer and his home to be established or elected in the province where the mine is found;

b) the duration of the concession;

c) the nature, circumstances, extent of the mine and its boundaries;

d) particulars of the right proportion to be paid by the dealer according to Article. 25;

e) the amount of the premium and the benefits which may be due to the researcher for art. 16;

f) all other obligations and the conditions which it intends to make the grant;

g) a statement of the State's participation in the profits of the company, to be determined after consultation with the Minister for Finance.

The decree will be joined the plan and the minutes of the concession boundary.

The decree, which will be recorded with the fixed tax of 10 lira (17), is published in the Official Gazette of the Kingdom (18) and transcribed to the office of mortgages.

----

(16) Now the chief engineer of the mining district, for the concessions within its competence: see Art. 4, Presidential Decree June 28, 1955, No 620, reported to the No VI. For Article. 5 of the decree, the jurisdiction to concessions for the production of deposits of mineral and thermal waters belong to the Prefect. See, also, note 14 / a art. 11.

(15 / a) Article. 17, Presidential Decree April 18, 1994, No 382, reported to the No XXVII, repealed Art. 14, paragraph 1, Article. 15, paragraphs 1 and 4, and art. 18, paragraph 1, only the words "after consultation with the Board of Governors of the mines."

(17) The registration fee has been abolished, and replaced by government concession tax, fixed at L. 40,000 by the Presidential Decree March 1, 1961, No 121, Table A, No 166, 1).

(18) Now, Official Gazette of the Italian Republic.

19. The owners of the funds can not resist the operations necessary for the demarcation of the grant, and affixing to the terms of the work of cultivation except the right to benefits payable in respect of any damage.

----

20. Where the grant has been made to the researcher, the licensee must, within three months from the date of communication of the decree granting, try the Ministry of National Economy (16), through the presentation of the receipt or certificate, the researcher to have paid the amount stated in the decree by way of premium or allowance, or to have made the deposit on the Deposits and Loans Fund.

Failure to comply with this requirement produces the forfeiture of the concession, to be pronounced by the Minister for the national economy (14 / a).

----

(16) Now the chief engineer of the mining district, for the concessions within its competence: see Art. 4, Presidential Decree June 28, 1955, No 620, reported to the No VI. For Article. 5 of this Decree, the competence to concessions for the production of deposits of mineral and thermal waters belong to the Prefect. See, also, note 14 / a art. 11.

(14 / a) Now, the Minister for Industry and Commerce, under RD August 9, 1943, No D. 718 and the Lieutenant. June 21, 1945, No 377.

CHAPTER III - EXERCISE OF THE CONCESSION.

21. The granting of the mine is temporary.

----

22. The mine and its appliances are subject to the provisions of law governing the property.

The registration of mortgages is subject to the Minister for the national economy (18 / a) (19).

(18 / a) See footnote to Article 16. 15.

(19) Subject to government concession tax, fixed at L. 5000 by Presidential Decree March 1, 1961, No 121, Table A, No 168.

(Law of legitimacy)

23. Appliances are of the mine buildings, stationary internal or external, wells, tunnels, and the machinery, equipment and tools for the cultivation of the mine, the works and installations for the enrichment of the mineral (20).

Are considered as furniture material extracts, stores, furniture.

----

(20) See, also, Articles. 817-819 of the Civil Code 1942.

24. The dealer may have the minerals that are associated with those that are the object of the concession.

----

25. The licensee is required to pay annually to the State the right proportion of ITL 400 (20 / a) for each hectare of land included within the limits of the concession (21).

(20 / a) So high art. 1, L. December 21, 1961, No 1501. See note 10 art. 7.

(21) To increase the fee, see Art. 14, D.L. October 2, 1981, No 546, listed in item Stamp (Tax).

26. The dates mining concession must be kept in operation except that, by the Minister for the national economy (21 / a), after consulting the High Council of the mines, is permitted to suspend the work or the progressive implementation of them (21 / b) .

The power to allow the suspension of the work belongs to the same authority which is vested with jurisdiction to issue the licenses for the cultivation of mineral deposits. That power belongs to the engineer in any case the head of the mining district in the case of suspension for periods not exceeding one year (22).

The dealer must cultivate the mine with the appropriate technical and economic importance of the field (23), and responds to the State of the regular maintenance of it, even during periods of suspension of work.

(21 / a) now known as Minister of Trade and Industry pursuant to the provisions of the RD August 9, 1943, No D. 718 and the Lieutenant. June 21, 1945, No 377.

(21 / b) Article. 17, Presidential Decree April 18, 1994, No 382, reported to the No XXVII, repealed Art. 26, paragraph 1, only the words "after consultation with the Board of Governors of the mines."

(22) Paragraph added by art. 6, Presidential Decree June 28, 1955, No 620, reported to the No VI.

(23) See, also, Art. 2, R.D.L. June 15, 1936, No 1347, reported to the No VI.

27. Any transfer, between the living act, the grant must be previously authorized by the Minister for the national economy (21 / a).

Every act which has not shown that the prior authorization, is void as against the Administration and between the parties.

Regardless of this void, the Minister for the national economy (21 / a) may order the forfeiture of the concession, observe the provisions of art. 41.

For mines located in areas of interest of national defense, the Minister for the national economy (21 / a) authorizes such transfers After hearing the Military Administration.

The decree authorizing the transfer is registered with the fixed tax of 10 lira (24).

(21 / a) now known as Minister of Trade and Industry pursuant to the provisions of the RD August 9, 1943, No D. 718 and the Lieutenant. June 21, 1945, No 377.

(21 / a) now known as Minister of Trade and Industry pursuant to the provisions of the RD August 9, 1943, No D. 718 and the Lieutenant. June 21, 1945, No 377.

(21 / a) now known as Minister of Trade and Industry pursuant to the provisions of the RD August 9, 1943, No D. 718 and the Lieutenant. June 21, 1945, No 377.

(24) The registration fee has been abolished, and replaced by government concession tax, now set in L. 50,000 by the Presidential Decree March 1, 1961, No 121, Table A, No 167.

28. The Minister for the national economy (21 / a) may require that the heir to the dealer is represented by a person of satisfaction of the Administration.

The heirs of the dealer must, within three months from the open succession, appointed by the majority indicated in Art. 678 of the Civil Code (25), one representative for all legal relations with the State and third parties.

After this deadline, the office said she will be appointed by the President of the Court, whose jurisdiction is found in the mine, the chief engineer at the request of the mining district, with no need to feel concerned.

(21 / a) now known as Minister of Trade and Industry pursuant to the provisions of the RD August 9, 1943, No D. 718 and the Lieutenant. June 21, 1945, No 377.

(25) See, now, the art. 1105, Civil Code 1942.

29. The concessionaires of mines must provide statistical data to the Public Administration (26) and any other information that is asked of them. They must also make available to all delegates to officials the means to inspect the work.

In case of refusal, the officials concerned may request the public authority with the necessary assistance (27).

----

(26) The obligation to report statistical data, see, also, the measures listed in paragraphs. II and III.

(27) See, also, Art. 5, Presidential Decree April 9, 1959, No 128, listed in item Industrial accidents and hygiene (prevention).

30. The expropriation of the dealer's right of mine can be brought only by mortgage lenders.

Both the expropriation proceedings as that graduation is conducted according to the rules of the Code of Civil Procedure. The precept of property should also be notified to the Minister for the national economy (21 / a).

The hammer price, which passeth after satisfying the creditors, it is for the dealer.

The contractor takes over all rights and obligations established in favor of the concessionaire in the act of loading and to grant and in this decree, provided that, at the discretion of the Minister for the national economy (21 / a) comply with the requirements established in 'Art. 15.

(21 / a) now known as Minister of Trade and Industry pursuant to the provisions of the RD August 9, 1943, No D. 718 and the Lieutenant. June 21, 1945, No 377.

(21 / a) now known as Minister of Trade and Industry pursuant to the provisions of the RD August 9, 1943, No D. 718 and the Lieutenant. June 21, 1945, No 377.

31. The licensee is required to compensate for any damage arising from the mine.

With regard to the provision of any security deposit you look at the rules laid down in Art. 10 (28).

----

(28) See, also, Articles. 62-65 and 104-113, Presidential Decree April 9, 1959, No 128, listed in item Industrial accidents and hygiene (prevention).

32. Within the perimeter of the concession, the works necessary for the storage, transport and processing of materials for the production and transmission of energy, and generally for the cultivation of the field and for the safety of the mine, will be considered a public utility all the effects of L. June 25, 1865, No 2359 (29).

In case of dispute about the need and modalities of the works mentioned above, decides the chief engineer of the mining district.

When the works specified in the first paragraph of this article should be executed outside the perimeter of the concession, the concessionaire may request a declaration of public utility for the purposes of the Act. This declaration is made by the Minister for the national economy (29 / a), after consulting the Board of Governors of mines (29 / b).

At the request of the licensee, the Minister for the national economy (29 / a), may order an expedited, resulting in temporary compensation and arranging for the deposit.

(29) On expropriation for the public interest.

(29 / a) now known as Minister of Trade and Industry pursuant to the provisions of the RD August 9, 1943, No D. 718 and the Lieutenant. June 21, 1945, No 377.

(29 / b) Article. 17, Presidential Decree April 18, 1994, No 382, reported to the No XXVII, repealed Art. 32, third paragraph, Article. 39 and paragraph 1 of article. 41, limited to the words "after consultation with the Board of Governors of the mines."

(29 / a) now known as Minister of Trade and Industry pursuant to the provisions of the RD August 9, 1943, No D. 718 and the Lieutenant. June 21, 1945, No 377.

Chapter IV - Termination of the concession.

33. The grant shall cease:

a) expiry of the period;

b) by resignation;

c) to decline.

----

a) Expiration of the term.

(Law of legitimacy)

34. The grant expired may be renewed if the licensee has complied with its obligations.

----

35. If the grant is not renewed, the licensee shall, at the end of the period, making delivery of the mine and its appurtenances to the Administration.

The licensee shall only be entitled to believe with the precautions laid down by chief purpose of the mining district, the items for the crop that can be separated without affecting the mine.

----

36. If at the expiry of the mine is granted to others, the dealer must take delivery from one to another with the intervention of the chief engineer of the mining district.

In case of disagreement between the parties, the engineer said provisionally determines the amount of the sum payable in respect of articles intended for cultivation, which can be separated without prejudice to the mine and that the new concessionaire intends to assume. The sum must be deposited to the Deposits and Loans Fund. Against such a settlement, the parties concerned may resort to the court.

----

37. The mortgages registered on the mine are resolved on things and on the amounts attributable to the dealer. The latter is bound to feel at least a month before, the registered mortgagees of the day in which we will proceed to the mine's operations for the delivery or administration of the new concessionaire.

----

b) Waiver.

38. The dealer who intends not to grant must make a statement to the Minister for the national economy (29 / a), without affixing any conditions.

From the day was made a declaration of surrender, the dealer is the guardian of the mine and is not required to do more work on mining, or to vary in any way the state.

The chief engineer of the mining district checks the status of the mine and prescribes safety and conservation measures that he believes necessary.

Failure to comply with its orders the execution of the office, at the expense of the dealer.

(29 / a) now known as Minister of Trade and Industry pursuant to the provisions of the RD August 9, 1943, No D. 718 and the Lieutenant. June 21, 1945, No 377.

39. Provides for the Minister to waive the national economy (29 / a), after consultation with the Board of Governors of mines (29 / b).

(29 / a) now known as Minister of Trade and Industry pursuant to the provisions of the RD August 9, 1943, No D. 718 and the Lieutenant. June 21, 1945, No 377.

(29 / b) Article. 17, Presidential Decree April 18, 1994, No 382, reported to the No XXVII, repealed Art. 32, third paragraph, Article. 39 and paragraph 1 of article. 41, limited to the words "after consultation with the Board of Governors of the mines."

c) Forfeiture.

40. The Minister for the national economy (29 / a) may make the revocation of the dealer, when:

1) fails to fulfill the obligations imposed by the act of granting;

2) has not complied with the provisions contained in articles. 25, 26 and 27 (30).

c) Forfeiture.

40. The Minister for the national economy (29 / a) may make the revocation of the dealer, when:

1) fails to fulfill the obligations imposed by the act of granting;

2) has not complied with the provisions contained in articles. 25, 26 and 27 (30).

(29 / a) now known as Minister of Trade and Industry pursuant to the provisions of the RD August 9, 1943, No D. 718 and the Lieutenant. June 21, 1945, No 377.

(30) See, also, Art. 2, R.D.L. June 15, 1936, No 1347, reported to the No IV.

41. The forfeiture of the award is announced, after it has notified the licensee of the reasons, by the Minister for the national economy (29 / a), after consulting the Board of Governors of mines (29 / b).

If the decree pronouncing the forfeiture, he may appeal to the Council of State, the courts, in cases provided for by art. 26 of the Consolidated laws of the State Council, approved by Royal Decree June 26, 1924, No 1054 (31).

(29 / a) now known as Minister of Trade and Industry pursuant to the provisions of the RD August 9, 1943, No D. 718 and the Lieutenant. June 21, 1945, No 377.

(29 / b) Article. 17, Presidential Decree April 18, 1994, No 382, reported to the No XXVII, repealed Art. 32, third paragraph, Article. 39 and paragraph 1 of article. 41, limited to the words "after consultation with the Board of Governors of the mines."

(31) provision applies also to actions for revocation of licenses for the art. 3, R.D.L. June 15, 1936, No 1347, reported to the No IV.

Provisions common to the waiver and forfeiture.

42. The decree of the resignation and what he says the forfeiture shall be published in the Official Journal of the office and recorded mortgages.

The date of the above decrees, the licensee is exempt from paying the right proportion and obligations imposed by the act of granting.

----

43. The mine which was subject to waiver or forfeiture may be granted again.

The new concessionaire has the right to use the works of installations and other appurtenances necessary for the cultivation of the mine. It may also consider the items for the crop that can be separated without affecting the mine, provided it corresponds to the price according to Article previous concessionaire. 36.

----

44. The Minister for the national economy (31 / a), after consulting the High Council of the mines, may make new grant of the mine that has been surrendered or revoked, even if it is included mortgages on it, by putting the burden of dealer prior acknowledgment of the obligation of members and determining the other creditors who see opportunities to give guarantees on behalf of third parties.

Within one year from the transcript of the decree of the resignation or a deprivation, mortgage lenders can enforce their rights, even if the agreed period has not expired, promoting the auction of the mining lease for which any non- provided the terms of the preceding paragraph. In this case, the auction price, satisfied mortgages or privileged, it is for.

The provision applies to the contractor in the last paragraph of Art. 30.

Course of this year, no further action is feasible on converting mining and the Minister for the national economy (31 / a) may proceed freely to the new concession.

Likewise, if you do not present any bidder for the auction, the mine remains free of any weight and may be subject to new license.

(31 / a) now known as Minister of Trade and Industry pursuant to the provisions of the RD August 9, 1943, No D. 718 and the Lieutenant. June 21, 1945, No 377.

(31 / a) now known as Minister of Trade and Industry pursuant to the provisions of the RD August 9, 1943, No D. 718 and the Lieutenant. June 21, 1945, No 377.

TITLE III CAVE

45. The quarries and peat bogs are left in the availability of the owner of the land (31 / b).

When the owner fails to undertake the cultivation of peat or quarry or it does not give sufficient development, the chief engineer of the mining district may prefixing a word for the beginning, the resumption or intensification of the work. After unsuccessfully the specified period, the chief engineer of the mining district may make the award (32) of the quarry and the bog in accordance with the provisions of Title II of this Order, as applicable. Where the grant has as its object the cultivation of the interesting bog land reclamation, it will be understood in advance the competent office of civil engineering.

Measures against the chief engineer of the District mining, quarrying granting or bog, hierarchical recourse is admitted to the Minister of Industry and Trade, who decides after hearing the High Council of the mines.

The owner is paid the value of the plant, the work of the extracted material usable and available at the quarry or peat bog.

The rights of third parties on the quarry or on the moor are resolved on the sums awarded to the owner in terms of the preceding paragraph.

Are applicable in every case to the quarries and peat bogs to the provisions of Articles. 29, 31 and 32 (33).

When the cultivation of quarries and peat bogs resulting danger of hydrogeological instability, such as to cause risk to the safety of persons and human settlements, the region, unless otherwise provided in the regional, may prescribe, by order of the President indicating a term interventions the securing of the charged conductor. In case of non-compliance with the requirements, the region may, by resolution of the Board reasoned, order the immediate revocation of the authorization and the acquisition of the quarry to the heritage of the region unavailable. If the quarry is part of the assets unavailable in the region, the Regional Government shall revoke the license (34).

(31 / b) During the 1940-45 war with RDLgs. June 1, 1946, No 593 (Official Gazette. July 23, 1946, No. 163), leases of quarries, concluded before June 10, 1940, and expire no later than December 31, 1949, were extended for a period equal to that of the suspension or reduction processing, due to the state of war, which had prevented the depreciation of the works of preparation and mechanical cultivation.

For peat, the R.D.L. May 18, 1942, No 617 (Official Gazette. June 17, 1942, No. 142), decided that they could be given in concession by the competent Ministry, when they were sufficiently grown, for a period not exceeding five years, to those who did application within one year after termination state of war.

(32) Subject to government concession tax, fixed at L. 20,000 by the Presidential Decree March 1, 1961, No 121, Table A, No 170.

(33) As amended by art. 7, Presidential Decree June 28, 1955, No 620, reported to the No VI.

(34) Paragraph added by art. 1, D.L. June 11, 1998, No 180, stated under public calamities, integrated in the text by its conversion law.

TITLE IV RELATIONS OF PROXIMITY AND MINING CONSORTIA

46. As a result of proximity or any other cause the work of a mine, quarry or cause any damage or bog produce a useful effect to another mine, quarry or peat, you rise to compensation or compensation between the parties concerned.

47. For the execution, maintenance and use of any work needed for the common good cultivation in mines, quarries and peat bogs, may be made compulsory or voluntary consortia.

The establishment of the consortium shall be required by the Minister for the national economy (31 / a), after consulting the High Council of the mines.

(31 / a) now known as Minister of Trade and Industry pursuant to the provisions of the RD August 9, 1943, No D. 718 and the Lieutenant. June 21, 1945, No 377.

48. Consortia mandatory and optional mines, quarries and peat bogs may be granted, by the Minister for the national economy (31 / a) with the power to levy privilege tax forms and club members.

All acts that are done in the direct interests of these associations are registered with the fee of 2000 pounds (35).

They are also subject to the right of lire in 2000 (35) all mortgage transactions made on behalf of the consortia mentioned above.

The increase in income from mines, quarries and peat bogs from the work carried out by consortia will be for twenty years from the date of completion of these works, exempt from land tax.

(31 / a) now known as Minister of Trade and Industry pursuant to the provisions of the RD August 9, 1943, No D. 718 and the Lieutenant. June 21, 1945, No 377.

(35) High to L. 500, from the original extent of L. 10, by art. 1 para. of L. February 15, 1949, No 33, and further, the amount indicated by art. 1 of L. July 21, 1961, No 707.

(35) High to L. 500, from the original extent of L. 10, by art. 1 para. of L. February 15, 1949, No 33, and further, the amount indicated by art. 1 of L. July 21, 1961, No 707.

49. If, within the time limits, the works are not performed, the Minister for the national economy (36) appoint a commissioner who, at the expense of the consortium, it assumes administration.

The Commissioner urges everyone concerned to deposit its share of spending, with, in case of default, the procedure established for the collection of direct taxes (37).

----

(36) now called, Minister of Trade and Industry pursuant to the provisions of the RD August 9, 1943, No D. 718 and the Lieutenant. June 21, 1945, No 377.

(37) See Articles. 173 et seq., Presidential Decree January 29, 1958, No 645, and the provisions of R.D. October 17, 1922, No 1401.

50. When the lack of units in the system of cultivation of adjacent or neighboring mines, belonging to different dealers jeopardize the existence of mines or safety of persons or the possibility of a more cost-effective cultivation, processing of these mines may be subject to a management only.

In this case, dealers are asked to agree to appoint the persons to be put before the administration of common interests.

If after the time limit prefix, does not fulfill any of the above, the Minister for the national economy (36) delegate one or more Commissioners to administer the common interests.

The Commissioner shall, in contradiction of the dealers, the assessment of individual interests, and, according to the results of the estimate, orders the apportionment of costs and products.

Appeals against the bases of apportionment are determined by the Court in whose jurisdiction the mines are found.

Such appeals have no suspensive effect.

----

(36) now called, Minister of Trade and Industry pursuant to the provisions of the RD August 9, 1943, No D. 718 and the Lieutenant. June 21, 1945, No 377.

TITLE V CRIMINAL PROVISIONS

51. Anyone engaged in research or production of minerals without the consent of the Minister for the national economy (36) is punished with administrative penalty of not less than one million lire (38), as well as the confiscation of the material excavated.

The same penalty is subject to the researcher who contravenes the provisions of art. 12.

----

(36) now called, Minister of Trade and Industry pursuant to the provisions of the RD August 9, 1943, No D. 718 and the Lieutenant. June 21, 1945, No 377.

(38) The sanction of the original fine was replaced with an administrative sanction art. 32, L. November 24, 1981, No 689, listed under judicial order, and as high art. 3, L. July 12, 1961, No 603, listed under Fines in Criminal Matters (Increase), as well as art. 114, first paragraph, the said L. November 24, 1981, No 689, related art. 113, first paragraph, the same law.

52. The dealer who neglects the regular maintenance of the mine shall be punished with administrative penalty of not less than one million lire (38), without prejudice of damages to the state.

Penalty is subject to the same dealer who contravenes the provisions of the first paragraph of art. 29.

----

(38) The sanction of the original fine was replaced with an administrative sanction art. 32, L. November 24, 1981, No 689, listed under judicial order, and as high art. 3, L. July 12, 1961, No 603, listed under Fines in Criminal Matters (Increase), as well as art. 114, first paragraph, the said L. November 24, 1981, No 689, related art. 113, first paragraph, the same law.

TITLE VI GENERAL AND TRANSITIONAL PROVISIONS

53. Concessions and the investiture of mines dates without time limit, according to rules in force up to now, are kept as perpetual concessions, when they are not incurred any grounds for revocation.

The temporary licenses remain in force until the deadline stated in the individual acts of concession, provided that they do not even committed any grounds for revocation.

----

54. In the territories in which, by virtue of the laws in force up to now, the availability of mining was left to the owner of the surface, the mines, at the discretion of the Minister for the national economy (36) resulting in normal cultivation to date publication of this decree, are given in perpetual concession to those who prove to be its rightful owner.

It also turned into granting the property, however acquired in other areas, mines in the normal cultivation of the date of publication of this decree.

----

(36) now called, Minister of Trade and Industry pursuant to the provisions of the RD August 9, 1943, No D. 718 and the Lieutenant. June 21, 1945, No 377.

55. The contracts for the mining operation at the date of publication of this decree shall be maintained for as long as they expected (39).

----

(39) See, also, the D.Lgs.C.P.S. March 2, 1947, No 216, extending the contracts of the operating mines of sulfur up to maximum period of 31 December 1956. For the exercise of mining concessions by the local authorities, cf. L. April 3, 1961, No 283.

56. In the territories indicated in Art. 54, the mines, of which the work has remained suspended or abandoned for any reason, are given in perpetual license to the owner that their commitments to reactivate within one year from the date of the decree of concession, or the major term which may be determined by the Minister for the national economy (36), the Board heard of the mines.

----

(36) now called, Minister of Trade and Industry pursuant to the provisions of the RD August 9, 1943, No D. 718 and the Lieutenant. June 21, 1945, No 377.

57. Confirmed or concessions granted under Articles. 53, 54 and 56 shall be subject to the rules of this Order, regardless of the arrangement in force at the time they were conferred and the mode and conditions of the consent.

----

58. Permits for mining research and investigations are kept for the time by which they were released, in compliance with the provisions of this Decree, when their owners have not incurred any of the cases of forfeiture provided for under the provisions hitherto in force.

----

59. In the territories indicated in Art. 54, anyone who has legitimately purchased the availability of mineral deposits, which has not yet undertaken the cultivation, has the opposite preference to other applicants to obtain a research permit, provided that, upon application within one year from the date of publication of this decree .

----

60. For the purposes of the preceding articles within one year after publication of this decree must be reported:

a) the concessions, whether perpetual or temporary;

b) the exercise or abandoned mines.

The complaint must be accompanied by evidence of formal qualifications or the availability of the mine property.

When a complaint is not made within that period, any law shall be deemed expired and the Minister for the national economy (40) can freely dispose of the soil in accordance with the standards contained in this decree.

----

(40) now called the Ministry of Trade and Industry pursuant to the provisions of the RD August 9, 1943, No D. 718 and the Lieutenant. June 21, 1945, No 377.

61. Where the right over a mine is very common to more people, they must appoint a majority indicated in Art. 678 of the Civil Code (41), one representative for all legal relations with the State and the third within six months from the publication of this decree.

After this period, the office will be appointed by the President of the Court requested the chief engineer of the mining district according to Article. 28.

----

(41) Now, Art. 1105, Civil Code 1942.

62. If the Administration recognizes that two or more mines, near or contiguous do not, taken individually, a suitable area of cultivation, can promote their work in common, pursuant to art. 50.

----

63. The cultivation of deposits of substances which, by virtue of Article. 2, become part of the class of mines, are given in perpetual license to the owner of the deposit and are subject to the provisions of this Title, as applicable.

(Law of legitimacy)

64. They repealed all provisions of laws and decrees in force up to now regarding the matters covered by this Decree.

Nothing has innovated:

a) the laws relating to mining Police (42);

b) the powers granted to the Minister for the national economy (40) for mineral exploration and production to be carried out on behalf of the State;

c) the legal system and the use of mines and mineral hot springs and the relevant State (43).

Within one year after publication of this decree, the towns of Massa Carrara and will issue a regulation (44), to be approved by the Minister for the national economy, to regulate their agricultural concessions marble.

----

(42) See Presidential Decree April 9, 1959, No 128, listed in item Industrial accidents and hygiene (prevention) which replaced the previously existing provisions.

(40) now called the Ministry of Trade and Industry pursuant to the provisions of the RD August 9, 1943, No D. 718 and the Lieutenant. June 21, 1945, No 377.

(43) See, also, the measures in the field of mineral and thermal waters reported under mineral waters.

(44) The municipality of Massa has not yet done so to adopt the regulation under this paragraph. On the marble quarries of Massa consider therefore still in force February 1, 1751 the Edict of Maria Theresa and the rescript of King Francis V of 19 November 1846.

The town of Carrara, with a Board resolution December 29, 1994, No 88 adopted this Regulation, approved by resolution of the Regional Council February 28, 1995, No 115 (B. U. R. Tuscany, April 5, 1995, No. 24 -

a). With regard to the marble quarries of Carrara, the edict of Maria Theresa and the Sovereign rescript mentioned above have therefore ceased to have effect.

Subsequently, the LR December 5, 1995, No 104 of the Tuscany region, supplemented by LR June 18, 1998, No 33, has dictated to these common principles to be followed by informants for the enactment of the regulation.

The town of Carrara, in compliance with such principles, with a Board resolution May 4, 1999, No 59 has modified the regulations previously adopted.

65. The Government of the King (45) is authorized to issue rules for the implementation of this Decree (46) which shall enter into force on the day of its publication in the Official Gazette of the Kingdom.

QUARRIES AND PEAT BOGS

Definition

The exploration and production of minerals and energy of the ground, industrially used in any form or physical condition are divided into two categories: mines and quarries.

Belong to the category of mines crops:

a) used for the extraction of minerals, metals, metalloids and their compounds, although these minerals are used directly;

b) graphite, solid, liquid and gaseous, asphaltic and bituminous;

c) phosphates, alkali metal salts and magnesium, alum, mica, feldspar, kaolin and bentonite, bleaching earth from, porcelain and earthenware clays, clays with a degree of refractoriness above 1630 degrees Celsius;

d) precious stones, garnet, corundum, bauxite, leucite, magnesite, fluorine, barium and strontium mineral, talc, asbestos, cement marl, lithographic stones;

e) radioactive substances, mineral and thermal waters, gases and vapors.

Belong to the category of quarries crops:

a) of peat;

b) building materials for construction, road and hydraulic;

c) of earth colors, the diatomaceous earth, quartz and silica sand, the millstones, whetstones of the stones;

d) other materials used industrially to the terms of Article. 1, not including

the first category.

The quarries are among the "public goods", so even if the enjoyment is left to the owners of the quarry land, the regional entity reserves the right to call back to the pits without compensation in the event of partial or total without use of the reservoir.

The general framework for the activities of quarries and peat is put off by the State (which did not produce a well-defined reference standards in this area) regional bodies. A situation of this kind has resulted in an overproduction of rules regarding the operation of quarries and peat bogs and a marked lack of homogeneity between all regional regulations.

Formalities for starting the

To start a company operating in quarries and peat bogs are necessary:

- Application for assignment of the number of VAT

- Application form to the Inland Revenue

- Application for registration in the Register of Companies with complaint login to the register of economic Administration (REA)

- Registration in the management of social security contributions and benefits at the INPS

- Subscribe to compulsory insurance against accidents at work at the Inail

- Compliance with national and regional guidelines in terms of public safety

National Building Regulations

- RD 29.7.1927, No 1443 (art. 4 et seq.) - Rules of a legislative framework to govern the exploration and production of mines in the kingdom

- RD 18 December 1927, No 2717 - Mandatory reporting of statistical data on the production of mines and quarries

- Royal Decree 15 June 1936, No 1347 - Provisions for the exploration and production of the mines into Law January 25, 1937, No 218

- April 9, 1959 Presidential Decree No 128 - Animal mining and quarrying

- Presidential Decree of 14 January 1972, No 2 (Art. 1, Lett. A) - Transfer to the ordinary statute regions of the state administrative functions in areas of mineral and thermal waters, quarries and peat bogs and crafts and its staff

- Presidential Decree of 24 July 1977, No 616, Art. 61 and Article 82 - Implementation of the delegation referred to 'Article. A law July 22, 1975, No 382

- L. 6. October 1982, no 752 - Rules for the implementation of mining policy

- L. June 15, 1984, No 246 - Additions and changes to the decree of the President of the Republic April 9, 1959, No 128, containing rules for police in mines and quarries, as well as the Law of 6 October 1982, no 752, concerning the implementation of mining policy

- L. July 8, 1986, No 349 (Art. 2, Lett. D) - Establishment of the Ministry of Environment and rules on environmental damage

- L. July 30, 1990, No 221 - New rules for the implementation of mining policy

- Presidential Decree of April 18, 1994, No 382 - Discipline procedures for granting of exploration permits and production concessions of mineral deposits of national interest and local interest.

- Legislative Decree no. March 30, 1999, No 96 - Statement by the Government for replacement of the distribution of administrative functions between regions and local authorities pursuant to Article 4, paragraph 5, of Law March 15, 1997, No 59, as amended (Article 9)

Normative References regional
- Abruzzo: LL.RR. July 26, 1983, No 54, October 23, 1987, No 67
- PROV. AUTON. BOLZANO: May 19, 2003 LP, No 7
- CALABRIA: LR 24 May 1980, No 14
- Campania: LL.RR. December 13, 1985, No 54, April 13, 1995, No 17
- Emilia Romagna: LR 18 July 1991, No 17
- LAZIO: LR 6. December 2006, no 17
- Liguria: LR 10. April 1979 No 12
- BRANDS: LR 1 December 1997, No 71
- MOLISE: LR 5 April 2005, No 11;
- Piedmont: LL.RR. November 22, 1978, No 69, LR 21 January 1985, No 4
- Apulia: LL.RR. April 10, 1985, No 15, May 22, 1985, No 37
- SARDINIA: LL.RR. May 7, 1957, No 15, June 7, 1989, No 30, June 11, 1990, No 16
- SICILY: LL.RR. October 1, 1956, No 54, December 27, 1978, No 71, December 9, 1980, No 127, 6 May 1981, No 96, March 26, 1982, No 22, June 14, 1983, No 64, December 6, 1984, No 105, May 27, 1987, No 28, May 15, 1991, No 24, March 1, 1995, No 19
- PROV. AUTON. TRENT: February 18, 1988, No 6, 16 December 1993 42; DPProv. June 5, 2003, No 10-131/Leg; DPProv. October 24, 2006, No 7
- Umbria: LR 19 July 1972, No 9
- Valle d'Aosta: LL.RR. February 23, 1981, No 15, July 11, 1996, No 15
- Venetia: LL.RR. September 7, 1982, No 44, August 16, 2002, No 26

Economic Activity Code ATECO
05.10.00 - Mining of hard coal and litantrace
05.20.00 - Mining of lignite
07.10.00 - Mining of iron ores

07.21.00 - Mining of uranium and thorium
07.29.00 - Mining of other non-ferrous metal ores
08.11.00 - Quarrying of ornamental and building stone, limestone, gypsum, chalk and slate
08.12.00 - Operation of gravel, sand mining of clays and kaolin
08.91.00 - Mining of the chemical and fertilizer production
08.92.00 - Extraction of peat
08.93.00 - Extraction of salt
08.99.01 - Extraction of natural asphalt and bitumen
08.99.09 - Extraction of pumice and other minerals nec

MINING POLICY IMPLEMENTATION RULES

New rules for the implementation of mining policy (1)

(1) European Commission decision of 22 July 1997 was the continuation of operations authorized under this Act after an adjustment of the EU definition of small and medium enterprises.

The Chamber of Deputies and the Senate have approved;
The President of the Republic:
Promulgates the following law:

ARTICLE 1. BROAD AND ACTIVITIES OF NATIONAL INTEREST

1. The Interministerial Committee for Economic Planning (CIPE), within three months from the date of entry into force of this Act, shall in the manner provided for in Article 2, second paragraph of the Law of 6 October 1982, no 752, to update the general guidelines of national policy in the mining sector on the basis of the results achieved with assistance arranged by the same law October 6, 1982, No 752, as amended and supplemented. The new mining policy should address, in particular, the objectives pursued, in view of the single European market, to raise the level of economy of the sector through the modernization, renovation or conversion of existing mining facilities in the country , to increase the technological level of industries, mining, by promoting research activities aimed at innovation of processes and products and metallurgical minerallurgici, and to foster a more extensive inclusion and a greater integration of the mining industry in the Italian international, in order to maintain and enhance the professionalism in the field.

2. Within the period referred to in paragraph 1, CIPE update the list of minerals which are of considerable interest for the country and indicates, based on the levels of mineralization observed throughout the country and the criteria for rationalization of the industry, mining activities, for the pre-eminent strategic value or social, must be maintained during production with assistance referred to in Article 7, although its cultivation would result in operating losses.

ARTICLE 2. FIVE-YEAR PROGRAMS, AND REPLACEMENT ACTIVITIES

1. In accordance with the new mining policy guidelines determined by the Committee pursuant to Article 1 and within three months after the relevant decision, the Minister of Industry, Trade and Industry, after consultation with the High Council of the mines and the Standing Conference relations between the state, regions and autonomous provinces of Trento and Bolzano referred to in Article 12 of Law 23 August 1988 400, in consultation with the Minister for Universities and Scientific and Technological Research and in agreement with the Ministers concerned, submit to the Interministerial Committee for Coordination of Industrial Policy (CIPI), (1) for approval, the

update on the steps of the five-year programs for basic research to operational research and the promotion of scientific and technological research in the mining sector.

2. In order to aid economic recovery and employment in areas affected by restructuring of the mining sector CIPI, the proposal of the Minister of Industry, Trade and Industry, in consultation, as far as his powers, with the participation of Ministers state and for routine work in the South, after hearing the regions concerned, fixed addresses coordination of the initiatives undertaken by government and public bodies, acting special program of promotion of new productive activities in which entrepreneurial initiatives are indicated by implement and issuing directives to the National Hydrocarbon (ENI) to a promotion action, advice and assistance to be carried out within these areas in favor of those who engage in alternative activities under Article 1 of Law February 3, 1989, No 41, as amended by Article 3 of this Act.

3. The CIPI, also distributes the authorization of expenditure referred to in Article 7 so that there at least 40 per cent of total supply is designed to work for the replacement activities referred to in Article 1 of Law February 3, 1989 No 41, as amended by Article 3 of this Act] (1).

(1) The CIPI has been deleted by art. 1, l. December 24, 1993, No 537. All his powers were distributed between the CIPE, the Ministry of Industry, Trade and Industry and the Ministry of Labour and Social Security based on the provisions of Art. 2, Presidential Decree April 20, 1994, No 373.

(2) The Ministry of State Shareholdings and that for routine work in the South were killed and their devolved powers to the Treasury, Budget and Economic Planning.

ARTICLE 3. CHANGES AND ADDITIONS TO THE CURRENT REQUIREMENTS FOR THE IMPLEMENTATION OF MINING POLICY

1. Art. 9, first paragraph, letter a) of the Act of 6 October 1982, no 752, amended and supplemented by. 3 of Law June 15, 1984, No 246, the word "Geomining 'is replaced by the following:" geogiacimentologici, mining, minerallurgici. "

2. Art. 10, third paragraph, the Law of 6 October 1982, no 752, the second sentence is replaced by the following: "The interests, the extent of 50 per cent of the official discount rate, starting from the date of production.."

3. Art. 11 of the Law of 6 October 1982, no 752, is added at the end, the following sentence: "The manner of recovery of outstanding payments are determined by the Minister of Industry, Trade and Industry, in consultation with the Secretary of the Treasury.."

4. Art. 13, second paragraph of the Law of 6 October 1982, no 752, replaced by. 3 of Law June 15, 1984, No 246, the words "under Article. 10 Law of May 2, 1976, No 183 'is replaced by the following: "under Article. 9, paragraph 4 of the Law of 1 March 1986, no 64. "

5. The Art. Law 15 of October 6, 1982, No 752, as last amended by Art. 5 of Decree-Law July 31, 1987, No 318, with amendments, into law October 3, 1987, No 399, is repealed.

6. Art. 17 of the Law of 6 October 1982, no 752, as last amended by Article. 6 of Decree-Law July 31, 1987, No 318, with amendments, into law October 3, 1987, No 399, paragraphs 1, 2 and 3 are replaced by the following:

«1. In order to promote and support the activities of foreign mining research, based on guidelines established by the Committee, may be granted ENI, IRI steel for minerals of interest, the institutions and mining companies to issue regional proven expertise in operations research, as well as mining companies holding concessions in production activities in the country in possession of the technical and economic requirements specified by the Committee, contributions of up to 70 percent of expenses incurred abroad for:

a) studies and surveys of character geophysical, geochemical, geological, geostatistical and mineral-minerallurgico;

b) operational research and feasibility studies;

c) infrastructure necessary for the performance of mining research;

d) acquisition of interests in mining research has already begun.

2. May be granted to the entities referred to in paragraph 1 interest loans up to 70 percent of the costs incurred to acquire mines abroad or shares of them, already in farming activities, to participate in consortia or companies managing mainly mining, or the realization of investment programs relating to the growing, preparation and exploitation of minerals. The soft loan with a maturity not exceeding fifteen years and a grace period of up to five years, must be repaid at an interest rate equal to 30 percent of the reference rate referred to in Article. 20 of the Decree of the President of the Republic November 9, 1976, No 902 and subsequent amendments thereto, at the date of issue of the decree was granted. By decree of the Minister of Industry, Trade and Industry have set the criteria and modalities of the withdrawal or repayment of the funding in cases of disposal of the object for which it was granted the loan.

3. The CIPI, with the participation of Minister of Foreign Affairs on the proposal of Minister of Industry, Trade and Industry, sets priorities in allocating grants and loans referred to in paragraphs 1 and 2, with particular reference to the needs supply of mineral raw materials needed for processing deficit, as well as the objectives of the maintenance and enhancement of the scientific, professional training, research and production operating in the mining sector in the country. Grants and loans are granted, after deliberation with the participation of the Committee to the Minister of Foreign Affairs, taking into account any benefits provided by international organizations, by decree of the Minister of Industry, Trade and Industry, after the Board of Governors mines. The decree also establishes the conditions for recovery of contributions referred to in paragraph 1 in the case of a positive outcome of the research.. "

7. Art. A law Feb. 3, 1989, No 41, paragraphs 1, 2 and 3 are replaced by the following:

«1. In mining areas affected by restructuring processes involving contraction of the labor or total or partial suspension of mining became uneconomic, resulting in displacement of labor, even if the suspension of the activity has occurred before the date of entry into force of this law, but in term of the mining concession, a mining concession holders or other persons as may be appropriate to engage in alternative activities in the municipalities which insists on mining, or in neighboring towns, with plans of hiring labor connected with the exodus, may be granted by resolution of the Interministerial Committee for Coordination of Industrial Policy (CIPI), proposed by the Minister of Industry, Trade and Industry, capital grants of up to 25 percent of global investment regarding the implementation of these activities and initiatives for re-employment up to 50 units, to be implemented in areas other than those defined as sensitive by the Community provisions in force.

2. The contributions referred to in paragraph 1 shall not be combined with the facilities provided by other state laws, regional laws and the autonomous provinces of Trento and Bolzano, except for the facilities provided by Community bodies and those related to agricultural activities.

3. The facilities referred to in paragraph 1 for areas located within the territories referred to in art. 1 of the Consolidated Law on interventions in the South, approved by Decree of the President of the Republic March 6, 1978, No 218, may be granted up to 50 percent of global investment, and up to the limit of 75 per cent in the case of overlapping facilities provided by other state laws and regional laws.. "

8. In the first paragraph of art. Law 41 of January 11, 1957, No 6, after the No 11) is added as follows:

"12) a senior executive of a senior executive and technical administration of the Directorate General of Mines."

(1) Change the bed. a) the first paragraph of art. 9, l. October 6, 1982, No 752.

(2) Change the third paragraph of art. 10, l. October 6, 1982, No 752.

(3) Amendment Article. 11, l. October 6, 1982, No 752.

(4) Change the second paragraph of Art. 13, l. October 6, 1982, No 752.

(5) Repeals the art. 15, l. October 6, 1982, No 752.

(6) Replace paragraphs 1, 2 and 3 of art. 17, l. October 6, 1982, No 752.

(7) Replace paragraphs 1, 2 and 3 of art. 1, l. February 3, 1989, No 41.

(8) No Adds 12) the first paragraph of art. 41, l. January 11, 1957, No 6. Subsequently, this paragraph was repealed by. 19, Presidential Decree April 18, 1994, No 484.

ARTICLE 4.CHANGES TO THE MANAGEMENT PROCEDURE OF THE FACILITIES

1. Changes in investment programs, admitted to the contributions referred to in Articles 12 and 17 of the Law of 6 October 1982, no 752, as last amended and supplemented by this Act, referred to in Article 1 of Law February 3, 1989, No 41, as amended by Article 3 of this Act and Article 9 of this law, which do not change the objectives and programs without increasing the total expenditure, are approved by the Minister of Industry, Trade and crafts.

2. The Minister of Industry, Trade and Industry, in the course of checks and controls on spending for the allocation of funds, at the request of the company and upon presentation of proper surety may liquidate up to 80 percent of payments made under Articles 9, 14 and 17 of the Law of 6 October 1982, no 752, as last amended and supplemented by this law, Article 1 of Law February 3, 1989, No 41, as amended by Article 3 of this Act and Articles 7 and 9 of this Act and prior recovery of advances already paid.

3. In order disbursement of the funds provided by the Law of 6 October 1982, no 752, as last amended and supplemented by this law, Article 1 of Law February 3, 1989, No 41, as amended by Article 3 of this Act, and Articles 7 and 9 of this Act, the costs can be documented in the manner provided in Article 18, fifth paragraph, of Law April 26, 1983, No 130.

4. The sums that grant recipients are required to return under the Law of 6 October 1982, no 752, as last amended and supplemented by this law and this law, which is normally the entry on the appropriate section of the state budget to be reallocated to the relevant chapters of the state budget of the Ministry of Industry, Trade and Industry for the implementation of mining policy. The reallocation of expenditure shall be introduced by decree of the Minister of the Treasury.

5. The Minister of Industry, Trade and Industry may, for the performance of specific tasks laid down in Articles 7 and 9 of this Law, also request the government of the State by name, including self-sorting, as well as public bodies, including economic, the command staff required by up to five units. Expenses related to such personnel are borne by the Administration of the State or of the membership.

6. To ensure the achievement of the objectives of this Act, the Minister of Industry, Trade and Industry, after notification of the proposed action to the Commission of European Communities issues the measures granting assistance under Article 14 the Law of 6 October 1982, no 752, as amended and supplemented, referred to in Article 1 of Law February 3, 1989, No 41, as amended by Article 3 of this Act and Article 7, paragraph 2 of this Law, within sixty days of the resolution of the Committee to (1).

(1) The CIPI has been deleted by art. 1, l. December 24, 1993, No 537. All his powers were distributed between the CIPE, the Ministry of Industry, Trade and Industry and the Ministry of Labour and Social Security based on the provisions of Art. 2, Presidential Decree April 20, 1994, No 373.

ARTICLE 5. BASIC SEARCH

1. For the continuation of research initiatives, described in Article 4 of the Law of 6 October 1982, no 752, as amended by Article 3 of Law June 15, 1984, No 246, has authorized the expenditure of 5 billion pounds for the year 1989, 5 billion lire for 1990 and 6 billion pounds for the year 1991

ARTICLE 6. RESEARCH AND DEVELOPMENT

1. For the continuation of research and development initiatives referred to in Article 9 of the Law of 6 October 1982, no 752, as amended by Article 3 of Law June 15, 1984, No 246, and Article 3 of this Act, have started and to start new initiatives on the basis of the results of basic research, has authorized the expenditure of 10 billion lire for 1991

ARTICLE 7. INTERVENTIONS TO SUPPORT MINING

1. For the actions referred to in Article 14 of the Law of 6 October 1982, no 752, as last amended by Article 5 of Decree-Law July 31, 1987, No 318, with amendments, into law October 3, 1987, No 399, for the award of the fees provided for in paragraph 2 of this Article as well as implementation of initiatives for the replacement of Article 1 of Law February 3, 1989, No 41, as amended by Article 3 of this Act, has authorized the expenditure of 43 billion lire for the year 1989, 43 billion lire for 1990 and 64 billion pounds for the year 1991. The breakdown of that available between the three types of intervention is made by resolution of the Committee to the proposal of the Minister of Industry, Trade and Industry, the Board heard of the mines.

2. Within the guidelines established by the Committee pursuant to Article 1, paragraph 1 of this Law mining units to dealers recognized the strategic value or social programs that present restructuring aimed at cost-recovery conditions of the management or conversion plans in alternative activities referred to in Article 1 of Law February 3, 1989, No 41, as amended by Article 3 of this Act, may be granted for the period during the production phase of the mine, capital grants to the fullest extent of the cost of labor, direct or through third-party services, support for the cultivation , preparation and exploitation of mineral, however, does not exceed the operating loss, excluding certain financial charges and taking into account depreciation of fixed assets related to the actual use for the production.

3. The restructuring plans are approved, the proposal of the Minister of Industry, Trade and Industry, after consultation with the region and the High Council of the mines, by resolution of the Committee to indicate that even the highest levels of production for each mine. The opinion of the region must be given within thirty days of the request, if no means expressed its support.

4. The grant is awarded annually, based on the income statement forecast, by decree of the Minister of Industry, Trade and Industry, in consultation with the Secretary of the Treasury. Financial assistance, based on the income statement period presented by the dealer for each mine is made by the Minister of Industry, Trade and Industry, following verification and control of expenditure by the Technical Commission referred to in Article 5, second paragraph, of Law June 15, 1984, No 246.

5. At their request the Minister of Industry, Trade and Industry may order the payment of advances to the extent not exceeding 40 percent of the assistance granted, upon presentation of proper surety in an amount equal to the plus 15 percent. Where in their assessment proves the contribution in whole or in part is not due on the amount of the advance shall be recovered in an interest rate equal to the official discount rate in force at the time of disbursement of the advance plus two points. The Minister for Industry, Commerce and Handicrafts, by decree to be issued in consultation with the Minister of the Treasury, sets out the procedures and modalities for the granting and payment of contributions and advances.

6. With effect from the date of entry into force of this Act and until December 31, 1991, employees of the mining units located in mining areas referred to in Article 1 of Law February 3, 1989, No 41, as amended by Article 3 of this Act, may be granted at the expense of the state budget, the benefit of early retirement conditions and in the manner provided for in Article 18 of Law April 23, 1981, No 155, as amended and supplemented.

7. The residues of Chapter 7903 of the state budget of the Ministry of Industry, Trade and Industry, not yet formally committed to the date of entry into force of this Act, shall be transferred, in an amount not more than 50 billion lire in residues account in Chapter 7902 of the same estimates and may be used for interventions and initiatives referred to in paragraph 1. The Minister of the Treasury is authorized to issue, by decree, the necessary changes in the account of arrears (1).

(1) The CIPI has been deleted by art. 1, l. December 24, 1993, No 537. All his powers were distributed between the CIPE, the Ministry of Industry, Trade and Industry and the Ministry of Labour and Social Security based on the provisions of Art. 2, Presidential Decree April 20, 1994, No 373.

ARTICLE 8. ACTIVITIES ABROAD

1. For the actions referred to in Article 17 of the Law of 6 October 1982, no 752, replaced by Article 6 of Decree-Law July 31, 1987, No 318, with amendments, into law October 3, 1987, No 399, and amended by this Act, is authorized the expenditure of 65 billion lire for the year 1991.

ARTICLE 9. STANDARDS FOR ENVIRONMENTAL PROTECTION

1. In order to ensure proper insertion of the mining environment, permit holders, research or mining lease must provide for the reorganization of the subject areas of environmental research or cultivation and they can be granted, in areas of the Centre-North, capital grants to a maximum of 15 percent of the total cost of development projects. Shall be granted up to a maximum of 20 percent of the total cost of contributions for the projects located in areas of the territories referred to in Article 1 of the Consolidated Law on interventions in the South, approved by Decree of the President on March 6 1978, No 218. Contributions can not be combined with benefits under other state laws, regional laws and the autonomous provinces of Trento and Bolzano, except for the facilities provided by Community bodies and those related to agricultural activities.

2. The subsidy is granted by the Minister of Industry, Trade and Industry, in consultation with the Minister, after considering the validity of the project by a technical committee composed of three representatives of the Ministry of Industry, of Trade and Industry - Directorate General of Mines, three representatives from the Ministry of the Environment and a representative of the Ministry of the Treasury.

3. The Minister for the Environment, by decree to be issued in consultation with the Minister of Industry, Trade and Industry, sets out the requirements of urban environmental projects eligible for assistance, as well as how to verify and control the execution of them.

4. For the implementation of the measures referred to in paragraph 1 shall be authorized the expenditure of 2 billion pounds for the year 1989 to 2 billion pounds for 1990 and 3 billion pounds for the year 1991.

5. Basins referred to in Article 1 of Law February 3, 1989, No 41, as amended by Article 3 of this Act, environmental restoration programs of abstracts estate, directly or indirectly related to mining activities, have already divested or affected by restructuring or conversion, to the satisfaction of needs for social, cultural and through projects of factories for the use and development of the territory and its resources, are allowed to work in facilities provided by the national laws. To promote the implementation of such programs, the Minister of Industry, Trade and Industry may make contributions to local stakeholders to design studies or feasibility plans, against the authorization of expenditure referred to in paragraph 4. The same program may be eligible under Article 1 of Law February 3, 1989, No 41, as amended by Article 3 of this Act, strictly limited to works aimed at creating new stable employment (1).

(1) See, also, Art. 17, l. August 7, 1997, No 266.

ARTICLE 10. TRAINING AND RETRAINING

1. Among the initiatives aimed at promoting the reuse of mining workers, until December 31, 1990 the holders of production concessions, and establishments and companies involved in the conversion plans basins referred to in Article 1 of Law February 3, 1989, n . 41, as amended by Article 3 of this Act, submit to the Ministry of Labour and Social Welfare projects for training and retraining programs prepared in accordance with the regulations of the European Social Fund.

2. The activities referred to in paragraph 1 may be financed, by decree of the Minister of Labour and Social Security, in consultation with the Minister of the Treasury, with a cost to the revolving fund referred to in Article 25 of the Law of 21 December 1978 No 845.

3. By decree of the Minister of Labour and Social Security, in consultation with the Secretary of the Treasury and the Minister for the coordination of Community policies, requirements are determined that the institutions and enterprises must observe in order to allow the use Community resources are aimed at the realization of social policy on the labor market.

ARTICLE 11. CHANGES TO THE ANIMAL MINING

1. The second paragraph of Art. 4 of the Decree of President of the Republic April 9, 1959, No 128, is replaced by the following:

"The chief engineer of the mining district and the chief engineer of the section of the National Mining for hydrocarbons and geothermal energy (which will be indicated in the text with the title of `` chief engineer") to ensure prevention of accidents occupational hygiene and environmental protection work in systems and processes subject to the animal of the mines, using the tasks of hygiene standards of local health units of doctors of Law December 23, 1978, No 833 and subsequent amendments and additions.. "

(1) Replace the second paragraph of Art. 4, Presidential Decree April 9, 1959, No 128.

ARTICLE 12. CO-OWNERSHIP RULES

1. The exploration permit and mining lease may be made payable to several parties, natural or legal persons Italian, the other Member States of the European Economic Community and third countries that practice conditions of reciprocity with regard to the Italian legal and natural persons, provided that:

a) demonstrate the necessary technical and economic capacity;

b) possess or undertake to provide technical and administrative structures in Italy appropriate to the activities provided.

2. The joint holders are jointly and severally liable for the obligations of the government relating to the exercise of mining and also meet jointly and severally even as against third parties. They must appoint a single representative for all dealings with the administration and third parties.

3. The only representative referred to in paragraph 2, in addition to the requirements of paragraph 1, must be in possession of special qualifications and technical expertise in the field.

4. The Minister of Industry, Trade and verify that the sole representative meets the requirements of paragraph 3.

5. Each of the joint holders of a mining lease is entitled to acquire direct ownership of a part of the products of mining to be determined by agreement between co-owners themselves, in the manner agreed between them. In the absence of express agreement, the portion owned by each joint owner is the value of their share.

6. The costs, expenses and charges resulting from mining, although supported by only representative referred to in paragraph 2 on the basis of a mandate without representation, impact directly on account of their share, the co-owners, unless their liability .

7. The loss of the requirements referred to in paragraph 1 by one or more co-owners for any reason or the withdrawal of one or more co-owners does not involve the forfeiture or revocation of the mining concession if the other co-owners shall bear the share or shares of individuals who have less, without prejudice to any rights of third parties.

8. The share of one or more joint holders may not be transferred without the consent of the Minister of Industry, Trade and Industry, after consultation with the other joint holders of a permit or license.

9. The consent decrees are subject to any transfer, the government license fee of five million pounds.

10. The sale has not been previously authorized by the parties that nothing is in the administration, subject to the authority of the Minister of Industry, Trade and Industry to forfeit the permit holder or grant.

ARTICLE 13 FINANCIAL COVERAGE

1. Burden resulting from the implementation of this law, amounting to 50 billion pounds for the year 1989, 50 billion lire for 1990 and 148 billion lire for the year 1991, provides:

a) As at 50 billion pounds for the year 1989 by reducing the appropriations entered in Chapter 9001 of the Ministry of the Treasury for the same year, using the specific provision "Mining Policy";

PROCEDURES FOR THE GRANTING OF EXPLORATION PERMITS AND PRODUCTION CONCESSIONS OF MINERAL DEPOSITS.

Presidential Decree April 18, 1994, No 382

Published in the Official Gazette. No. June 18, 1994, No 141.

THE PRESIDENT OF THE REPUBLIC

Given the art. 87, fifth paragraph, of the Constitution, Art Seen. 17, paragraph 2, of the law of 23 August 1988 400; Given the Law of 7 August 1990 241; Given the Law of 24 December 1993 537, and in particular art. 2, paragraphs 7, 8 and 9; Seen the Royal Decree of 29 July 1927, No 1443, the Order of the President of the Republic June 28, 1955, No 620; Given the preliminary resolution of the Council of Ministers, adopted at the meeting of 11

February 1994, Whereas the terms for issuing the opinion of the competent parliamentary committees

the Senate and House of Representatives pursuant to art. 2 of the Law of 24 December 1993 537, respectively, expired on 9 April 1994 and March 6, 1994, heard the opinion of the Council of

State expressed during the Assembly of March 24, 1994; Considering not having to comply with the opinion of the Council of State in relation to

on the formulation of Art. 5, paragraph 1, as the forecast contained in it is justified

functional activity as a requirement of the conference services;

Given the resolution of the Council of Ministers, adopted at its meeting on April 12, 1994; On the proposal of the Prime Minister and the Minister for the Civil Service, in consultation with the Minister of Industry, Trade and Industry;

Issues the following regulations:

TITLE I GENERAL

Chapter I - Scope and definitions

1. Subject to Regulation.

1. This regulation governs the procedures for the granting of exploration permits and production concessions of mineral deposits of national interest and local interest.

Definitions.

1. Under Article. 5, paragraph 5, of the Royal Decree of 29 July 1927, No 1443, as amended by Presidential Decree of 28 June 1955, No 620, are of national interest: the minerals used for the extraction of metals and metals and their compounds, although these minerals are used directly, the solid, liquid and gaseous fuels, asphalt and bituminous rocks, radioactive substances, vapors , the gas is of local interest, all other minerals.

2. For the purposes of this Regulation, "Minister" means the Ministry of Industry, Trade and Industry, for "Royal Decree", the Royal Decree of 29 July 1927, No 1443, with subsequent amendments and additions.

TITLE II RESEARCH PERMITS

Chapter I - Granting permission to search

3. Assumptions.

1. The exploration permit may be granted to those who have the necessary technical and financial capability.

4. Question.

1. The request for transfer of an exploration permit shall be submitted to the competent mining district, who shall transmit copies to the Ministry.

2. Be annexed to the question: the topographic map, the geo-mining report, the program works. The formalities are not required on reporting and certification mafia, under the law May 31, 1965, No 575, as amended by Act March 19, 1990, No 55.

3. The chief engineer of the mining district authority within fifteen days of receipt of the application, by publishing the same, together with all attachments referred to in paragraph 2, in the 'hall of the town, in order to allow adequate publicity of the project. The copy for posting in the 'Praetorium is sent within twenty days of the mining district of the report for publication and provided with any objection, subject to the application of Articles 7 and 8 of the Law of 7 August 1990 241.

5. Inquiry.

1. The chief engineer of the mining district authority in order to acquire the observations of the province, the chamber of commerce and the municipality or municipalities, territorially interested,

2. in art. 5, paragraph 2, of the Royal Decree, as replaced by art. 2 of Presidential Decree of 28 June 1955, No 620, within ten days of receipt of the request, a conference of index services, pursuant to art. 14 of the Law of 7 August 1990 241, to be held within sixty days after receipt of the application. The conference will examine the application for service provision for an exploration license, together with its annexes and any opposition.

2. In the conference services referred to in paragraph 1 of this article are also acquired, pursuant to paragraph 2 of art. 14 of the Law of 7 August 1990 241, acts of understanding, concerts, clearances and permissions that other government departments and institutions shall, in accordance with state and regional laws.

3. If the conference does not reach determinations of services agreed, and provided for the agreement or the act of consent, however, called the government intervened, we proceed in accordance with Art. 14, paragraph 2-bis of the Law of 7 August 1990 241, as introduced by art. 2, paragraph 13 of Law No 24 December 1993 537.

6. Granting of license to explore for mineral deposits of local interest.

1. For the mineral deposits of local interest, the chief engineer of the mining district authority within ten days from the acquisition of the determinations of conference services, issue the decree which grants or denies permission to search for mineral deposits of local interest.

7. Granting of license to explore for mineral deposits of national interest.

1. For the mineral deposits of national interest, the chief engineer of the mining district shall, within ten days from the acquisition of the determinations of conference services, sending a report to the Ministry.

2. The Ministry, within thirty days of receipt of the report, issue the decree which grants or denies permission to search for mineral deposits of national interest.

8. Terms of proceedings.

1. The procedure for granting of license to explore for mineral deposits of local interest shall be completed within a maximum period of one hundred and thirty days from the date of application.

2. The procedure for granting of license to explore for mineral deposits of national interest shall be completed within a maximum period of one hundred and sixty days from the date of application.

3. The Minister for Industry, within fifteen days after the entry into force of this Regulation provides for the adjustment of the Ministerial Decree of 26 March 1993, No 329, the implementation of Articles 2 and 4 of 7 August 1990, No 241, indicating the end of the two preceding paragraphs.

Chapter II - Proceedings relating to the granting of exploration permits

9. Extension, expansion or reduction of the voluntary, transfer, forfeiture, surrender.

1. The application for renewal of an exploration permit, or the application for extension of the voluntary reduction of the permit application for transfer of the permit, the engineer must be submitted to the competent head of the mining district. The chief engineer shall convene, in cases of particular relevance, conference services, of which art. 5 of this Regulation.

2. For the mineral deposits of local interest, the chief engineer shall by decree in order to extend the authorization, or extension of the voluntary reduction, transfer, within a maximum of eighty days from the date of application.

3. For the mineral deposits of national interest, the chief engineer shall, within sixty days of receipt of the request, sending a report to the Ministry. The Ministry decree in order to extend the authorization, or extension of the voluntary reduction, transfer, within a maximum of one hundred ten days from the date of application.

4. The decay of the holder of an exploration permit is issued, advance notice, in cases of particular importance, from the chief engineer of the mining district jurisdiction, the conference facilities, of which art. 5 of this Regulation. It shall, as a result of the dispute and the grounds for revocation prefissione a reasonable period of deductions for the owner, chief engineer with the decree of the mining district responsible for the mineral deposits of local interest, and by decree of the Minister for mineral deposits of national interest, respectively, within sixty and eighty days from office of the proceedings.

5. The chief engineer, for mineral deposits of local interest, or the Ministry, for mineral deposits of national interest, shall issue an order accepting the resignation, no later than forty and fifty days from the reasoned request of the permit holder.

TITLE III EXPLOITATION CONCESSIONS

Chapter I - Transfer of production concessions

10. Assumptions.

1. May be subject to the granting of mineral deposits such as the administration has recognized the existence and cultivability.

2. The granting of a field may be issued to those who have the technical and economic suitability to lead the company.

11. Question.

1. The request for transfer of mining lease must be submitted to the competent mining district, who shall transmit copies to the Ministry and is responsible for the investigation.

2. Be annexed to the question: the topographic map, the geo-mining report, the program works. The formalities are not required on reporting and certification mafia, under the law May 31, 1965, No 575, as amended by Act March 19, 1990, No 55.

3. The chief engineer of the mining district authority within fifteen days of receipt of the application, by publishing the same, together with all attachments referred to in paragraph 2 of this article, in the 'hall of the town and, by the person concerned, in sheet of legal announcements in the province, in order to allow adequate publicity of the project. The copy for posting in the 'Praetorium is sent within twenty days of the mining district of the report for publication and provided with any objection, subject to the application of Articles 7 and 8 of the Law of 7 August 1990 241.

12. Inquiry.

1. The chief engineer of the mining district authority in order to acquire the observations of the province, the chamber of commerce and the municipality or municipalities, regional authorities concerned, under Article. 5, paragraph 2, of the Royal Decree, as replaced by art. 2 of Presidential Decree of 28 June 1955, No 620, within ten days of receipt of the request, a conference of index services, pursuant to art. 14 of the Law of 7 August 1990 241, to be held within sixty days after receipt of the application. The conference will examine the application for service provision for an exploration license, together with its annexes and any opposition.

2. In the conference services referred to in paragraph 1 of this article are also acquired, pursuant to paragraph 2 of art. 14 of the Law of 7 August 1990 241, acts of understanding, concerts, clearances and permissions that other government departments and institutions shall, in accordance with state and regional laws.

3. If the conference does not reach determinations of services agreed, and provided for the agreement or the act of consent, however, called the government intervened, we proceed in accordance with Art. 14, paragraph 2-bis of the Law of 7 August 1990 241

13. Contribution of mining lease of mineral deposits of local interest.

1. For the mineral deposits of local interest, the chief engineer of the mining district authority within ten days from the acquisition of the determinations of conference services, issue the decree which grants or denies the mining lease of mineral deposits of local interest.

14. Contribution of mining lease of mineral deposits of national interest.

1. For the mineral deposits of national interest, the chief engineer of the mining district shall, within ten days from the acquisition of the determinations of conference services,

2. sending a report to the Ministry.

2. The Ministry, within thirty days of receipt of the report, issue the decree which grants or denies the mining lease of mineral deposits of national interest.

15. Terms of proceedings.

1. The process of granting of mining lease of mineral deposits of local interest shall be completed within a maximum period of one hundred and thirty days from the date of application.

2. The process of granting of mining lease of mineral deposits of national interest shall be completed within a maximum period of one hundred and sixty days from the date of application.

3. The Minister for Industry, within fifteen days after the entry into force of this Regulation provides for the adjustment of the Ministerial Decree of 26 March 1993, No 329, the implementation of Articles 2 and 4 of 7 August 1990, No 241, indicating the end of the two preceding paragraphs.

Chapter II - Proceedings relating to the granting of exploitation concessions

16. Renewal, or extension of the voluntary reduction, suspension of work, transfer, forfeiture, surrender.

1. The application for renewal of the concession, the question of the voluntary extension or reduction of the concession, the application for suspension of work, the demand for transfer of the license must be submitted to the engineer responsible head of the mining district. The chief engineer shall convene, in cases of particular relevance, conference services, of which art. 5 of this Regulation.

2. For the mineral deposits of local interest, the chief engineer issue decrees which grants or denies permission for an extension, or expansion of the voluntary reduction or suspension of work, transfer, within the period of up to seventy days from the date of application.

3. For the mineral deposits of national interest, the chief engineer shall, within sixty days of receipt of the request, sending a report to the Ministry. The Ministry, issue decrees which grants or denies permission for an extension, or expansion of the voluntary reduction or suspension of work, transfer, within a maximum period of ninety days from the date of application.

4. The forfeiture of the concession holder is announced, advance notice, in cases of particular importance, from the chief engineer of the mining district jurisdiction, the conference facilities, of which art. 5 of this Regulation. It shall, as a result of the dispute and the grounds for revocation prefissione a reasonable period of deductions for the owner, chief engineer with the decree of the mining district responsible for the mineral deposits of local interest, and by decree of the Ministry, for mineral deposits of national interest, respectively, within sixty and eighty days from office of the proceedings.

5. The chief engineer, for mineral deposits of local interest, or the Ministry, for mineral deposits of national interest, shall issue an order accepting the resignation, no later than forty and fifty days from the reasoned request of the permit holder.

17. Repeal of rules.

1. Under Article. 2, paragraph 8 of the Law of 24 December 1993 537, the date of entry into force of this Regulation shall be repealed: Articles 3 and 4 of Presidential Decree of 28 June 1955, No 620, art. 4, only the words "to be issued in the manner established by art. the following, "art. 5, art. 14, second paragraph, Article. 15, first and fourth paragraph of Article 18, first paragraph,

limited to the words "after consultation with the Board of Governors of the mines', Article. 26, first paragraph, limited to the words "after consultation with the Board of Governors of the mines', Article. 32, third paragraph, limited to the words "after consultation with the Board of Governors of the mines', Article. 39, limited to the words "after consultation with the Board of Governors of the mines', Article. 41, first paragraph, limited to the words "after consultation with the Board of Governors of the mines," the Royal Decree of July 29, 1927, No 1443.

18. Entry into force.

1. This Regulation shall enter into force one hundred and eighty days after its publication in the Official Gazette.

STRATEGIC INFORMATION FOR CONDUCTING BUSINESS IN ITALY

ENERGY SECTOR PROFILE

ENERGY OVERVIEW

Proven Oil Reserves: 622 million barrels
Oil Production : 172,000 barrels per day (bbl/d), of which 107,000 bbl/d is crude oil
Oil Consumption : 2.1 million bbl/d
Crude Oil Refining Capacity: 2.45 million bbl/d
Net Oil Imports : 1.89 million bbl/d
Natural Gas Reserves: 8.1 trillion cubic feet (Tcf)
Natural Gas Production : 680 billion cubic feet
Natural Gas Consumption : 2 Tcf
Net Natural Gas Imports : 1.4 Tcf
Recoverable Coal Reserves : 37 million short tons (Mmst)
Coal Production : 0.2 Mmst
Coal Consumption : 16.9 Mmst
Electric Generation Capacity : 61 million kilowatts
Electricity Generation : 235 billion kilowatthours
Electricity Consumption : 257 billion kilowatthours

ENVIRONMENTAL OVERVIEW

Total Energy Consumption : 8.0 quadrillion Btu* (2.1% of world total energy consumption)
Energy-Related Carbon Emissions : 120.0 million metric tons of carbon (2.0% of world carbon emissions)
Per Capita Energy Consumption : 139.0 million Btu (vs U.S. value of 350.7 million Btu)
Per Capita Carbon Emissions : 2.1 metric tons of carbon (vs U.S. value of 5.5 metric tons of carbon)
Energy Intensity : 6,700 Btu/ $1990 (vs U.S. value of 13,400 Btu/ $1990)**
Carbon Intensity : 0.10 metric tons of carbon/thousand $1990 (vs U.S. value of 0.21 metric tons/thousand $1990)**
Sectoral Share of Energy Consumption : Industrial (44.0%), Transportation (25.7%), Residential (23.3%), Commercial (6.6%)
Sectoral Share of Carbon Emissions : Industrial (41.3%), Transportation (30.0%), Residential (22.5%), Commercial (6.2%)
Fuel Share of Energy Consumption : Oil (54.0%), Natural Gas (28.2%), Coal (5.7%)
Fuel Share of Carbon Emissions : Oil (63.9%), Natural Gas (27.0%), Coal (9.1%)
Renewable Energy Consumption : 552 trillion Btu* (2% increase from 1996)
Number of People per Motor Vehicle : 1.7 (vs U.S. value of 1.3)
Status in Climate Change Negotiations: Annex I country under the United Nations Framework Convention on Climate Change (ratified April 15th, 1994). Under the negotiated Kyoto Protocol (signed on April 29th, 1998, but not yet ratified), Italy, as a member of the European Union, has agreed to reduce greenhouse gases 8% below 1990 levels by the 2008-2012 commitment period.
Major Environmental Issues: Air pollution from industrial emissions such as sulfur dioxide; coastal and inland rivers polluted from industrial and agricultural effluents; acid rain damaging lakes; inadequate industrial waste treatment and disposal facilities

Major International Environmental Agreements: A party to Conventions on Air Pollution, Air Pollution-Nitrogen Oxides, Air Pollution-Sulphur 85, Air Pollution-Sulphur 94, Air Pollution-Volatile Organic Compounds, Antarctic-Environmental Protocol, Antarctic Treaty, Biodiversity, Climate Change, Desertification, Endangered Species, Environmental Modification, Hazardous Wastes, Law of the Sea, Marine Dumping, Nuclear Test Ban, Ozone Layer Protection, Ship Pollution, Tropical Timber 83, Tropical Timber 94, Wetlands and Whaling . Has signed, but not ratified: Air Pollution-Persistent Organic Pollutants

* The total energy consumption statistic includes petroleum, dry natural gas, coal, net hydro, nuclear, geothermal, solar and wind electric power. The renewable energy consumption statistic is based on International Energy Agency (IEA) data and includes hydropower, solar, wind, tide, geothermal, solid biomass and animal products, biomass gas and liquids, industrial and municipal wastes. Sectoral shares of energy consumption and carbon emissions are also based on IEA data.
**GDP based on EIA International Energy Annual 1998

ENERGY INDUSTRY

Oil and Gas Company: Ente Nazionale Idrocarburi (ENI); Chief Subsidiaries: Agip (hydrocarbons exploration and production), Snam (gas supplies and hydrocarbon transportation), Enichem (petrochemicals)
Major Pipelines (gas): TransMed, Trans-Austria Gasleitung
Major Ports: Cagliari (Sardinia), Genoa, La Spezia, Livorno, Naples, Palermo, Trieste, Venice
National Electricity Company: Ente Nazionale per l'Energia Elettrica (ENEL, soon to be privatized)

GENERAL BACKGROUND

Italy has the world's fifth largest economy. It is one of the original members of the European Union (EU). Under the Prodi government (which fell in October 1998), Italy decided to join the European currency, the euro, at its initiation on January 1, 1999. It is also a member of the North Atlantic Treaty Organization (NATO, 1949), the Organization for Economic Cooperation and Development (OECD, 1961), and the General Agreement of Tariffs and Trade/World Trade Organization (GATT/WTO). It is one of the "Group of Seven" (G-7) industrialized countries.

Italy's 56th government since 1945 came to power in October 1998. The current government, headed by Prime Minister Massimo D'Alema, has continued many of the policies of the preceding government. There is considerable continuity in the energy sector, as Industry Minister Pierluigi Bersani and Bersani's undersecretary with special responsibility for energy, Umberto Carpi, were re-appointed.

EU membership has initiated important changes in Italy's energy sector, requiring privatization of Italy's dominant energy monopolies. Hence, Italy's energy sector has been undergoing considerable restructuring in recent years. ENI, the state-held oil and gas conglomerate, along with its main subsidiaries, Agip (hydrocarbons exploration and production) and Snam (gas supplies and distribution), and the state-owned electricity company, ENEL, had to be privatized. Both ENEL and ENI became joint stock companies in 1992. The Italian government sold off shares of ENI between 1995 and 1998, and now holds 35% of the company. Privatization of ENEL has stalled. According to EU directives, plans for privatization must proceed quickly in coming years.

With limited domestic energy sources, Italy is highly dependent on energy imports. As of 1998, Italy was estimated to be less than 20% self sufficient in terms of energy. Historically, the country has relied heavily on imported oil, much of it from North Africa. In recent years, oil consumption has declined (although Italy remains one of the largest oil consumers in Western Europe) in favor of natural gas. Natural gas is a much cleaner fossil fuel that helps Italy to meet domestic, European, and broader international requirements for a cleaner environment. As with oil, North Africa is a large exporter of natural gas to Italy. Algeria is the single largest supplier, and a new agreement with Libya makes the region an even more important supply source. There have been concerns that this reliance on North African sources has potentially negative implications for Italian security.

OIL

Italy is one of the largest oil consumers in Western Europe, but is in the process of decreasing its reliance on oil as a fuel source, most notably in favor of natural gas. Especially in the electricity sector, the use of oil has decreased substantially since 1998 (see graph). In order to promote this change in fuel mix, the Italian government has adjusted taxation for the next five years. By 2004, the tax on natural gas will rise by 2%-7% (and will *decrease* by 23% for natural gas vehicular use), while the tax on oil will rise between 33% and 61%.

Italy is currently about 95% reliant on imports to meet oil demand. The major suppliers are largely in North Africa (Egypt, Libya, and Algeria). In order to bolster energy security and reduce dependence on foreign sources, Italy is in the process of increasing domestic production. ENI and several foreign companies (including Mobil) are planning to develop production capacity in Italy that could double Italy's current crude production levels.

In the summer of 1999, the final major regulatory hurdle was cleared for the first phases of ENI's development of massive reserves at Val d'Agri, in the southern Appenine region, considered to be Europe's most promising onshore development area. Pipeline construction to connect the area to the Taranto refinery should be complete by 2004, clearing the way for fairly rapid expansion of Italian oil production to around 250,000 barrels a day (bbl/d) beginning in 2004, compared to 1998 output of 108,000 bbl/d.

With regional approval for a pipeline from the central processing center that incorporates Val d'Agri and nearby Monte Alpi, initial flows of 45,000 bbl/d are planned for 2004 and should rise to 120,000 bbl/d after 2003. UK independent Enterprise is still seeking approval for a 50,000-bbl/d development of the nearby Tempa Rossa field. Tempa Rossa oil may enhance flows through the Val d'Agri center and via a shared or separate pipeline to ENI's Taranto refinery and on to a planned export terminal.

In addition to increasing domestic production, Italy is seeking new sources abroad. In March 1999, ENI and France's Elf Aquitaine signed a $1-billion contract with the National Iranian Oil Company to upgrade the production capacity of an Iranian oil field in the Persian Gulf. The buy-back contract provides for costs borne by the two companies and the remuneration of capital to be paid back through a share of the oil produced. ENI (with a 45% share) and Elf will implement the upgrading plan. Extracted oil will be processed and transported for export.

REFINING

To ensure access to foreign oil, the Italian government has promoted Italy as an export refining center. There are large facilities along the Mediterranean coast and on Mediterranean islands, capable of processing a wide range of crude oils from North Africa and the Persian Gulf. As a result, Italy now has Europe's largest surplus of refining capacity. ENI operates six of the 16 major refineries in Italy. While underutilized, the Italian refineries remain attractive because of their ability to handle large tankers and process many different fuel types, and also because of their catalytic and hydro cracking abilities.

NATURAL GAS

Italy's reliance on natural gas imports has risen substantially since they began in the early 1970s, with then state-held Ente Nazionale Idrocarburi's (ENI) gas purchases from the Netherlands and Russia. Italy is currently the third largest gas market in Europe, behind Germany and the United Kingdom. Natural gas use has increased sharply in recent years, especially for power generation. Gas now represents about 30% of total energy consumed in Italy, and this share is expected to grow in the coming years. According to ENEL officials, 60% of electricity in Italy will be generated by natural gas and only 10% by oil by 2010; currently, oil accounts for about 60% of generation, and gas only 10%.

ENI, a massive oil and gas conglomerate, has monopoly control over the Italian gas market through its subsidiary, Snam. As in the electricity sector, an EU directive requires deregulation in the Italian gas sector. ENI has been a publicly traded, joint stock company since 1992. Shares were sold off in four separate offerings between 1995 and 1998, and the state now holds 35% of ENI. Snam has retained its monopoly in the gas market; it currently controls 90% of the market. According to the EU directive, 30% of the sector must be deregulated by June 2003, 38% by 2003, and 43% by 2008.

Edison Gas is the leading independent power producer (IPP) in Italy, and its role in and share of the gas industry are expected to increase as deregulation continues. Edison Gas signed a deal to have Algerian gas delivered to Italy through the TransMed pipeline beginning in 2003. Edison has not yet negotiated with Snam, the operator of the pipeline, for use of the TransMed to complete the deal. Edison Gas is also pushing for a marine pipeline to link Algeria and the Italian island of Sardinia and the French island of Corsica.

Diversification of supply is an important issue, as Italy relies heavily on Algeria and Russia. In 1997, Italian gas sources were estimated to be 30% domestic, 30% Algerian, 26% Russian, and 10% Dutch (the remaining 4% was in the form of liquefied natural gas, and was imported from Algeria). The major alternative suppliers that Italy is considering are Libya and Norway. The biggest project under consideration is the proposed construction of a pipeline to link Libya and Italy's southern island, Sicily. This "West Libya Gas Project" was finalized in July 1999 as a joint venture between Libya's state-held National Oil Company and ENI. A 600-kilometer (372-mile) pipeline will run under the Mediterranean and connect with the TransMed, delivering a total of 8 billion cubic meters per year (282 Bcf), starting in 2003/2004. Snam has also signed a 25-year contract to receive 6 billion cubic meters per year (212 Bcf) of Norwegian natural gas through existing pipelines, beginning in 2003.

Prior to the outbreak of hostilities in Yugoslavia in the spring of 1999, a conference was held in Italy to discuss the possible construction of pipelines to connect the Caspian region, Libya, and Russia. The connection of the pipelines would have made Italy a transit center for the producing regions. No further action has been taken on these plans. Problems in Yugoslavia also halted a deal between Snam and Romania's SNGN Romgaz. According to their agreement in the summer of 1998, gas would be piped from Romania to Italy via an extension of the Adria line that links Croatia to the European network. It is uncertain whether the project will continue.

ENI is also involved in projects outside Italy. In the late winter of 1999, the Russian natural gas monopoly Gazprom and ENI signed an agreement to cooperate on the Blue Stream project. The project will involve laying a 400-kilometer (250-mile) pipeline on the floor of the Black Sea to connect Russia and Turkey. Each company will hold a 50% share in the project, and the gas will be sold jointly by the two companies in Turkey. Snam is also planning to be involved in a joint venture with South Korea's Hyundai Engineering and Construction in a gas project in Qatar.

LIQUEFIED NATURAL GAS

Liquefied natural gas (LNG) accounts for less than 5% of total Italian gas consumption. Italy receives Algerian LNG at its La Spezia terminal, under a 25-year contract that runs until 2015. ENEL also signed a contract in 1992 under which Nigerian LNG will be delivered to ENEL for 22 years, beginning in 1999. In 1996, ENEL attempted to terminate the contract because environmental restrictions had blocked its planned construction of re-gasification terminals in Italy. The attempt was unsuccessful. The Nigerian gas will be delivered to a Gaz de France terminal, and an equal volume of Algerian and Russian gas will be delivered to Italy in a "roundabout" system.

COAL

Coal consumption in Italy is dominated by power generation, which is increasing, and coke production for steel, which is decreasing. Coal has played a small role in the Italian energy sector, and Italy produces almost no coal domestically. In 1997, only 6% of Italy's primary energy demand was met with coal. The power sector is expected to dramatically increase its coal consumption in coming years, as ENI works to decrease reliance on imported oil. Clean coal technology will figure prominently in this increased coal usage, as EU environmental stipulations, Kyoto targets, and Italian public opinion demand that Italy's energy sector become increasingly clean.

The increased coal usage will be supplied by a combination of increased domestic production and increased imports. Coal mines on the island of Sardinia, previously closed by ENI, are scheduled to be re-opened. Imports are also predicted to double in coming years. Main exporters to Italy are the United States, Australia, and South Africa.

ELECTRICITY

State-held ENEL owns 85% of Italy's generating capacity, and is the world's fifth largest power generator. It owns 100% of transmission and 93% of distribution in Italy. ENEL is also the country's only cross-border trader (Italy imports about 15% of its electricity, mostly from France and Switzerland). ENEL has had a monopoly in Italy's electricity sector since the industry was nationalized in the early 1960s. A 1996 EU electricity directive bans any generator from supplying more than 50% of its national market. EU member countries had a February 19, 1999 deadline for implementing the directive.

Italy met the EU deadline with a decree issued on that day that ends ENEL's monopoly. Before the end of 1999, 30% of Italy's electricity market will be opened to competition, and 40% by 2002. In November 1999, ENEL plans to form three new power generation companies out of its current holdings, in what most likely will be the largest initial public offering in the world for the year. The three companies will account for about 25% of ENEL's current generation (15,000 megawatts).

In addition to opening up the Italian electric power generation market, the February decree also will end ENEL's monopoly on imports and sales. Finally, it will allow independent power producers (IPPs) to sell directly to industrial consumers, whereas IPPs currently can sell only to ENEL.

As ENEL reduces its Italian holdings, it is becoming increasingly involved in joint ventures abroad. In August 1999, ENEL signed an agreement with the Greek firm Prometheus Gaz to establish ENELCO, which will develop, finance, and implement energy projects in Greece and other Southeastern European countries. This joint venture makes it unlikely that plans for the construction of a pipeline under the Adriatic Sea linking Greece and Italy will come to fruition.

Italy is heavily reliant on oil for its electricity generation. Largely for environmental reasons, Italy is shifting more toward natural gas for electricity generation. Coal is far more polluting than either gas or oil, and EU and Kyoto Protocol agreements, as well as strongly opposed public opinion, have prevented Italy from opening any new coal-fired plants.

Nuclear
Italy has four nuclear power plants, all owned by ENEL. None is in operation. In 1987, a public vote decided against the use of nuclear power. The plants have remained idle since that time, and no nuclear generation is expected in the foreseeable future.

BUSINESS AND INVESTMENT CLIMATE

INVESTMENT CLIMATE AND BASIC REGULATIONS

For the most part, foreign investors do not find major impediments to investing in Italy, although bureaucratic requirements can be burdensome. 100 percent foreign ownership of Italian firms is allowed. Some restrictions to foreign investment exist. The government has the authority to block mergers involving foreign firms for "reasons essential to the national economy" or if the home government of the foreign firm applies discriminatory measures against Italian firms. There are industry sectors which are either closely regulated or prohibited outright to foreign investors, such as aircraft manufacturing and the state monopolies (although liberalization of the railroad and tobacco products manufacturing monopolies is under consideration).

Outside these sectors, there are no screening or blocking procedures directed solely at foreign investment. Italian anti-trust law (which applies to domestic and foreign investors) gives the government the right to review mergers and acquisitions over certain financial thresholds. Italy provides national treatment to foreign investors except in a few instances. The exceptions include limits to access to government subsidies for the film industry, some additional capital requirements for banks from countries not in the European union (EU), and restrictions on non-EU airlines operating domestic routes.

Italy also maintains restrictions in shipping. Also, companies may bring in non-EU workers only after certifying that no unemployed Italian is available to carry out the expected duties. Industrial projects require a multitude of approvals and permits from the many-layered Italian bureaucracy. Foreign investments often receive close scrutiny.

These lengthy procedures can, in and of themselves, present extensive difficulties for the uninitiated foreign investor. Firms incorporated in European union (EU) countries may offer investment services in Italy without establishing a presence. U.S. and other firms which are not from countries that belong to the EU may operate based on authorization from CONSOB, the securities oversight body. CONSOB may deny such authorization to firms from countries which discriminate against Italian firms. The financial sector is seeing a good deal of foreign investment activity. In the banking sector, the formerly dominant role of the state is being reduced by privatizations and a wave of mergers and other alliances.

Authorization by the Bank of Italy, the country's central bank, is required to acquire more than five percent of a financial institution's capital (or to gain effective control of a financial institution, regardless of the amount of capital acquired). Non-bank companies (either Italian or foreign) may not acquire more than 15 percent of a bank's capital. Foreign companies are increasingly active in the Italian insurance market, opening branches or buying shares in Italian firms. Government authorization is required to offer life and property insurance and usually based on reciprocal treatment for Italian insurers. Foreign insurance firms must prove that they have been active in life and property insurance for not less than ten years and must appoint a general agent domiciled in Italy. There some limits regarding foreign private ownership in banks. For instance, according to the banking law a foreign institution willing to increase its stake in a bank above 5 percent needs the authorization by the bank of Italy.

Boi has not been reluctant to use this power. For example, it is widely assumed that the Boi blocked German insurer Allianz's bid to increase its stake in the Italian bank Credito Italiano from 5 to 10 percent and warned against the sale of 10 percent of Banca Nazionale del Lavoro to Credit Suisse First Boston. These actions are not always directed against foreign companies, however: the BOI also reportedly prevented Italian insurer Assicurazioni Generali from increasing its stake in Banca Commerciale Italiana.

The expansion of modern, large-scale distribution units, such as chain stores, department stores, and large supermarkets, is restricted by local practice and national legislation which subjects applications for retail units above a certain merchandising surface to a lengthy and cumbersome authorization process. The Italian privatization program begun in 1992 has resulted in the sale of all or part of several formerly state-owned enterprises to private investors. Foreign investors are not prevented from investing in firms to be privatized, except in the defense sector. Privatization sales techniques have included private placement, worker shareholdings and management buy-outs and public stock offerings. Often the government establishes a "hard-core" group of shareholders (who agree to keep their shares for a minimum period, say three years), or retains a "golden share" (modest government stake, but with controlling influence). Completed privatizations include the telecommunications company and several banks. Upcoming privatizatons include a significant share of gas and oil parastatal eni and the last bank controlled by the treasury ministry. The Italian tax system does not discriminate between foreign and domestic investors.

PRIVATE OWNERSHIP There is no limitation in either the Italian constitution or Italian civil law on the right to private ownership and establishment. In general, there is competitive equality between the private and public sectors. For years, Italian government bonds absorbed a large share of available domestic investment, but this share has declined as interest rates on those bonds have dropped in the runup to European economic and monetary union. As an alternative, Italian investors have turned to stocks and corporate bonds, significantly increasing the Milan stock exchange's capitalization as a result.

PROTECTION OF PROPERTY RIGHTS

The United States Government considers intellectual property rights protection in Italy to be inadequate. From 1989 through 1997, the U.S. Trade Representative placed Italy on the intellectual property rights "watch list" under the special 301 provision of the united states trade act of 1988, because of inadequate copyright protection for computer software, sound recordings and film videos. In 1998, a heightened level of concern resulted in Italy being placed on the special 301 "priority watch list" because of two additional problems: (1) a delay in passing effective anti-piracy legislation; and (2) the introduction of European content requirements (tv broadcast quotas) at the national level that are more strict than those required by the EU broadcast directive.

In recent years, the Italian government has substantially increased enforcement actions against video and software pirates. Piracy rates and piracy losses for U.S. copyright industries have dropped but remain unacceptably high. U.S. citizens generally receive national treatment in acquiring and maintaining patent and trademark protection in Italy. After filing a patent application in the united states, a U.S. citizen is entitled to a 12-month period within which to file a corresponding application in Italy and receive the benefit in Italy of his or her first u.s. filing date (rights of priority). Patents are granted for 15 years from the effective filing date of application. They are assignable and transferable. U.S. authors can obtain copyright protection in Italy for their work first copyrighted in the United States merely by placing on the work, their name, date of first publication, and the symbol .

ADEQUACY OF LAWS AND REGULATION GOVERNING COMMERCIAL TRANSACTIONS
Laws governing physical property are adequate and enforced.

FOREIGN TRADE ZONES/FREE PORTS

There are two free trade zones in Italy, located in Trieste and Venice, both in the Northeast of the country. Goods of foreign origin may be brought in without payment of taxes or duties, as long as the material is to be used in the production or assembly of a product that will be exported. The free-trade zone law also allows a company, of any nationality, to employ workers of the same nationality under that country's labor laws and social security. Benefits of a free-trade zone include: - customs duties deferred for 180 days from the time that the goods leave the free trade zone to enter another EU country; - the goods may undergo transformation free of any customs restraints; - absolute exemption from any duties on products coming from a third country.

PERFORMANCE REQUIREMENTS/INCENTIVES

Investors do not face performance requirements specifically directed at foreigners. However, in the telecommunications sector, many new entrants are subject to performance requirements and must post a performance bond to receive a license necessry to operate. The European Union has challenged some of Italy's performance criteria for telecoms licenses. The Italian government offers incentives designed to encourage private sector investment (by both italian and foreign firms) in depressed areas, particularly in the underdeveloped "Mezzogiorno" in the south of Italy. A regulation that provided tax breaks nationwide for companies which reinvested earnings has expired, but the concept remains under discussion. Foreign investors are able to participate in government research and development programs based on reciprocal treatment for Italian firms.

TRANSPARENCY OF THE REGULATORY SYSTEM

Italy is subject to single market directives mandated by the European Union, which are intended to harmonize many regulatory structures across EU countries. This includes the mutual recognition agreements negotiated between the EU and the U.S. The EU directives are intended to benefit EU member countries by creating a non-discriminatory, less restrictive trade regime. The directives are expected to yield significant benefits to non-EU trading partners (such as the U.S.) as well. Harmonization of standards relating to labeling, content, production, safety, etc., Should reduce development costs and contribute to economies of scale for companies which wish to operate in Italy. Several EU directives deal with the issue of transparency in public sector contracts and subcontracts.

The process of incorporating these directives into Italian law has focused new public attention on governmental and political party practices for public works, an area traditionally known for corrupt practices. Italy's parliament is currently completing legislation governing public works projects that is designed to increase transparency in that sector. Even if this sector sees improvement, though, difficult bureaucratic procedures will likely impede new investment in Italy for both Italian and foreign firms.

CORRUPTION

According to a study by the International Monetary Fund, the level of corruption in Italy is among the worst in Western Europe, but the situation is improving. The study cited the weight of bureaucracy, confusing regulations, the financing of political parties and the level of wages of civil servants as factors fostering corruption. Corruption is punishable under Italian law. Much discretion for punishment is left to the presiding judge. Most corruption in the recent past has involved government procurement or bribes to tax authorities to hide income. In surveys, businesses routinely identify corruption as a disincentive to investing, or even doing business, in certain relatively less-developed areas of Italy, particularly in the south. The principal government authority for combating financial corruption is the Guardia di Finanza, a law enforcement entity responsible for customs and financial crimes.

The national police and the Carabinieri (military police with civilian duties) also play roles. Paying bribes to foreign officials is not a criminal act under current Italian law. However, Italy, like the U.S., is a signatory to the 1997 OECD convention on combating bribery, and is taking steps to modify its domestic legislation to conform to the treaty. Consistent with an earlier recommendation by OECD, tax deductibility of bribes paid to foreign officials is not allowed. The Tangentopoli, or "bribesville" scandal of the early 1990s, resulted in the wholesale turnover of the existing political class, the dissolution of the major political parties, and sharp cutbacks in public works programs (which had been the source for kickbacks). A campaign by the judiciary has made significant inroads in uncovering major financial scandals. The presence of organized crime groups, particularly in the south, has contributed to corrupt activity.

LABOR

Unemployment continues to be a serious problem in Italy. The national unemployment rate in April 1998 was 12.5 percent, up from 12.4 percent in January 1997. The breakdown by geographic area shows that it is much higher in the south of the country (23.1) than in the north (6.6 percent) and center (10.0 percent) and is also much higher for women (17.0 percent) than for men (9.8 percent). The unemployment rate for young people (15-24) was 33.3 percent nationally, with southern youth unemployment at 55.9 percent. There is a skilled labor pool in the north, where industries and services are more developed.

Labor shortages exist in the fields of engineering, nursing, and computers, and there is also a scarcity of skilled manual workers. Marketing skills and high level human resources are also in relatively short supply. The south, where agriculture and the underground economy are more widespread, has an overabundance of unskilled labor and of well-educated young people who do not want to leave their regions to find a job. Immigrant workers are employed for seasonal harvesting. The labor market is rather rigid, but is getting more flexible. The Pact for Employment signed by the Government, labor and management in September 1996 recognized the need to introduce greater flexibility into Italy's labor market in the struggle to reduce unemployment. In the course of 1997 and 1998, legislation and regulation gave shape to some of these measures. The hiring of part-time employees was encouraged by reducing the level of social security contributions which employers have to pay for certain types of these workers.

The door was opened to temporary workers, and many temporary help agencies started operations in 1998. The scope for their activities is substantial although not perhaps as wide as it is in other countries which have had greater experience with this type of employment. A program decentralizing the public employment service was underway, and legislation allowing private employment agencies to function was enacted.

The need to keep a tight reign on public spending left little room for economic stimulus to promote job creation, and unions were disappointed with the Government's investment plans for the economically depressed south. Nevertheless, targeted investments in the area are likely as the Government turns its post-EMU attention to bringing down persistent high rates of unemployment. Existing legislation provides for compulsory hiring of a given number of disabled workers. There are positive inducements for employers who hire the long term unemployed in the form of lower rates for social security contributions.

Wages and salaries represent only a part of labor cost to management. There are also the costs of indirect pay, i.e., annual leave, holidays, bonuses, seniority allowances and severance pay. In addition, social security contributions can account for up to 45 percent of gross salary. Italian workers enjoy substantial legal protection from dismissal, often with complex and costly consequences. Labor relations in Italy are relatively good, although strikes remain common in a number of industries.

Eight million three hundred thousand hours were lost due to strikes in 1997, down from 13 million in 1996. A number of labor and union rights are enshrined in the Constitution, and these core rights and others are the subject of a considerable body of supplementary legislation. The Workers' Statute (Law 300 of May 1970) is a major legislative landmark, and it deals, in part, with the right of association, granting most workers the right to establish unions in workplaces with more than 15 employees (5 in agriculture). Most Italian unions are grouped in three major national confederations: the Italian General Confederation of Labor - CGIL; the Italian Confederation of Labor Unions -- CISL; the Italian Union of Labor -- UIL. All three organizations are now affiliates of the International Confederation of Free Trade Unions.

The three major labor confederations negotiate collective bargaining agreements at the national level with employers associations, and the agreements are for all intents and purposes binding on all employers in a sector or industry. Through the July 1993 tripartite agreement, the confederations accepted wage moderation and consult with the government on economic and social policy.

EFFICIENCY OF CAPITAL MARKETS AND PORTFOLIO INVESTMENT

Financial resources flow relatively freely in Italian financial markets and credit is allocated on market terms. Foreign participation in Italian markets is not restricted. Capitalization on the Italian stock market is small relative to that of other g-7 countries and suffers from thin trading in a number of its stocks. The market is technologically modern and efficiently administered, however. The Italian government bond market, among the worlds largest, is predominantly an electronic screen-based market, and is also administered efficiently.

The Italian banking system is highly fragmented and generally regarded as inefficient, with high operating costs and excessive dependence on interest rate spreads for income. The top five Italian banks account for roughly 40 percent of total bank assets, lower than equivalent shares in several other EU countries. State ownership of financial institutions, both direct and indirect, has declined sharply as a result of privatization.

The return on equity system-wide - at 0.39 percent in 1997 - is well below the European average. ABI, Italy's banking association, contends that the average tax rate of 53.2 percent, compared to

37 percent EU average, hurts Italian banks' profitability. There are percentage limits on cross-shareholding among banks and between banks and non-bank companies (banks cannot hold more than 10 percent of the shares of another bank; non-bank companies cannot hold more than 15 percent of a bank's shares). Complex cross-shareholding has been used to fight off takeover attempts in the financial sector. This has not been directed at takeovers by foreign companies; in fact, there are cases where foreign investors have been part of the core shareholder group defending against the takeover. Legislation permits corporations to set a maximum percentage of shares for any single investor.

CONVERSION AND TRANSFER POLICIES

In conformance with EU directives, Italy has no foreign exchange controls. There are no special exchange rates and currency transfers are freely permitted. There are no restrictions on repatriation of capital and earnings, or on payments to foreign creditors. Italians are free to undertake financial transactions abroad, including direct investments and purchases and sales of foreign securities, real estate and loans. Regulations formerly prohibiting residents from entering or leaving the country with bearer securities worth more than 20 million lire (about $12,500) have been lifted.

Residents may freely hold foreign exchange and Italian lire in any form in Italy and abroad. Banks and authorized intermediaries must submit data on their foreign exchange transactions exceeding 20 million lire to the foreign exchange office of the bank of Italy. The Italy Italy-U.S. tax treaty contains provisions to avoid the double taxation of income for firms with operations in both countries. Royalties from patents and like properties are exempt from tax withholding under the treaty. They are freely remittable, subject to documentation requirements. Italian and us tax authorities are negotiating an update to the treaty which should be concluded in 1998.

EXPROPRIATION AND COMPENSATION

The Italian constitution permits expropriation of private property for "public purposes". Compensation is guaranteed and must adequately compensate the legitimate proprietor for losses. Lenders are not covered by the same constitutional guarantee as proprietors. The constitution also authorizes the nationalization of enterprises, which provide essential public services or are indispensable to the national economy. There are three longstanding disputes in Italy involving u.s. citizens who assert that municipal governments unjustly expropriated their real property or inadequately compensated them.

DISPUTE SETTLEMENTS

U.s. investors in Italy have a choice in selecting a means of dispute resolution, which should be specifically set forth in the contract. Given the slowness of the Italian judicial system (normally 3 - 5 years for trial in a civil matter and two automatic appeals), investors are advised to choose arbitration, which can be Italian or international.

POLITICAL VIOLENCE

Political violence is considered a low threat to foreign investments in Italy. There have been recent demonstrations over unemployment, especially in the south, but they have been non-violent and carried no anti-foreign undertones.

BILATERAL INVESTMENT AGREEMENTS

Italy has bilateral investment agreements with the following countries: Albania Kazakistan Algeria Kuwait Argentina Malaysia Bangladesh Mongolia Bolivia Oman Bulgaria Peru Chile Philippines China Poland Cuba Romania Egypt Russia Ethiopia South Korea Hungary Sri Lanka Indonesia Tunisia Jamaica Vietnam The 1948 U.S.-Italy friendship, commerce and navigation treaty contains provisions that may protect U.S. investment in Italy. Generally, existing bilateral investment accords create favorable conditions and guarantees for capital investment. They include reciprocal guarantees of equal treatment vis- -vis domestic firms and most-favored-nation status vis- -vis third countries, assurances against expropriation without fair market compensation and indemnities against losses suffered during war or revolution.

Agreements also include statements allowing for the free transfer of returns, royalties and funds to maintain investments. They usually detail the procedures under which disputes would be arbitrated.

OPIC AND OTHER INVESTMENT INSURANCE PROGRAMS OPIC does not operate in Italy. Italy is a member of the multilateral investment guarantee agency (MIGA).

MAJOR FOREIGN INVESTORS

Italy has for several years been a net source of foreign investment. In 1997, Italian direct investment abroad exceeded foreign direct investment in Italy by $6.7 billion. Italian direct investment abroad totaled $10.2 billion (0.9 percent of Italian GDP), up from $6.2 billion in 1996 (0.5 percent of GDP). Direct investment inflows totaled $ 3.5 billion (0.3 percent of GDP), about the same as in 1996.

The services sector remained the largest recipient of inflows at $2.3 billion, down from $ 2.9 billion registered in 1996. Investment in banking and insurance led the list, although it declined somewhat compared to 1996. Investment inflows in industrial activity increased from $619 million in 1996 to $1.2 billion in 1997.

Key areas of foreign industrial investment in Italy include the mechanical, chemical, food and mineral/metal sectors.

The largest share of Italian investments abroad, roughly 60 percent of the total, was in services: $5.9 billion, up from $3.8 billion in 1996. Investment in the banking and insurance sectors overseas was $4.9 billion, more than double the level of 1996. Italian overseas investment in industry almost tripled from $1.3 billion in 1996 to $3.0 billion in 1997. Investment in the mechanical sector increased from $363 million in 1996, to $1.2 billion in 1997.

The Bank of Italy (BOI) estimates that the stock of total foreign direct investment in Italy at the end of 1997 was $81.2 billion (7.3 percent of GDP), of which U.S. investment amounted to $11.8 billion (14.6 percent of total). The stock of total Italian direct investment abroad was $125.1 billion (11.2 percent of GDP). Italian investment in the US was valued by the Bank of Italy at $10.0 billion (9.8 percent of total Italian direct investment overseas). According to BOI data, Switzerland has the largest stock of foreign direct investment in Italy (17.1 percent of the total), followed by the U.S.

Among EU countries, which as a whole account for 58.5 percent of foreign investment in Italy, France is the largest investor, followed by the U.K., Netherlands, Luxembourg and Germany. Although Japan is a net investor in Italy, both Italian investments in Japan and Japanese investment in Italy (mostly in the banking and insurance sectors) are modest: 1.9 and 1.0 percent of the respective totals. Except for Sweden, Germany and France, Italy's European union partners are net recipients of Italian investment.

Among non-EU countries, the largest recipients of Italian investment are Brazil and Argentina, and Italian investment in eastern and central Europe is rising. About two-thirds of U.S. investment in Italy is in industry and one-third is in services. The chemical sector has the largest share of U.S. industrial investment-- $2.6 billion. Investment in the other sectors, such as food, mechanical and transportation equipment sectors registered increases in value between 1996 and 1997.

The largest portion of service sector investment was in banking and insurance $4.9 billion. More than half of Italy's $12.3 billion direct investment in the u.s. was in the services sector, with the remainder in industry (40 percent) and energy (10 percent). The value of direct investment in banking and insurance activities was $2.0 billion.

The top category among industrial investments was mechanical, where the level of investment dropped from $1.6 billion in 1996 to $1.4 billion in 1997. Many well known major multinationals, both U.S. and foreign, have a presence in Italy. General Electric, AT&T, Boeing, ITT Sheraton, Pfizer, and McDonalds are just a few of the American companies with sizeable investments in Italy.

TRADE AND PROJECT FINANCING REGULATIONS

BANKING SYSTEM

There are numerous banking offices located throughout the country, with over 800 banks and 22,000 branches performing commercial services. Among the most important are the Istituto Bancario San Paolo di Torino, Banca di Roma, Cassa di Risparmio delle Provincie Lombarde (CARIPLO), Banca Commerciale Italiana, Credito Italiano, Banco di Napoli and Banca Nazionale del Lavoro. These banks are a principal source of credit information. Several U.S. banks perform banking services in Italy through branches, subsidiaries, or representatives. Many American banks can also provide their commercial customers with bank reports on an overseas buyer as well as provide assistance on letters of credit and foreign exchange.

U.S. banks with offices in Italy include Chase, Citibank, Morgan Guaranty Trust, Bank of New York, and Bank of America and numerous smaller, regional banks. Banks in Italy that have the authority to participate in foreign exchange usually have an U.S. correspondent. Foreign currency transfers and foreign exchange transactions must be channeled via authorized intermediaries (the Bank of Italy, the Italian Foreign Exchange Office, and authorized banks). The larger banks in Italy have branches in one or more U.S. cities. The Bank of Italy, Italy's central bank, is widely respected both nationally and internationally as a non-political overseer of the Italian economy responsible for controlling inflation and balance of payments pressures.

FOREIGN EXCHANGE CONTROLS

Italy has no restrictions on the amount of foreign exchange instruments, currency, or checks that may be brought into the country. Normally, lire 20 million may be taken out of the country, but any amount declared on entry may be reexported. Italian exchange regulations are issued by the Italian Exchange Office (Ufficio Italiano dei Cambi--UIC), Via Quattro Fontane 123, Rome 00184) under authority of the Ministry of Foreign Trade. Foreign exchange may be sold or acquired from the Bank of Italy or any of the banks authorized by the Bank of Italy. In practice, all commercial banks are authorized to conduct foreign exchange transactions. Dollar currency, travelers checks, and, in some cases, personal checks, may be exchanged at banks, exchange offices, and authorized tourist offices and hotels. Major credit cards are accepted with proper identification. It is best to first confirm what form of payment is accepted.

GENERAL FINANCING AVAILABILITY

Italy has a well-developed banking and credit system with numerous correspondent U.S. banks. Italian banks are subject to close government supervision. The Bank of Italy must authorize the establishment of a new bank. Until 1993, the Italian banking system was divided into two categories, differentiated by length of lending authorized. The Single Banking Law passed in 1993 abolished this division, effectively allowing all Italian banks to lend at any maturity. Due to this historical legacy, those institutions that focused on longer-term lending, including the Istituto Mobiliare Italiano (IMI) and Mediobanca, remain at the forefront for this type of finance. Short-term business and trade finance is available from a wide range of Italian and U.S. banks. U.S. firms desiring to finance major portions of their capital investment outside the United States may find capital available in the Eurodollar market. U.S. bank branches in Italy can assist in financing capital investment.

HOW TO FINANCE EXPORTS / METHODS OF PAYMENT

When providing the Italian buyer with a price quote, American firms most frequently provide a quote that includes packing costs, insurance, and freight. This is called the c.i.f. price. The average Italian business representative can then usually determine the charges for customs, taxes, and local transportation to arrive at the final landed cost to importer. The customary terms of sale in Italy are either cash or net. Sales made on cash terms call for payment before delivery, on delivery, or shortly after delivery -- usually within 10 days from the date of delivery. A 2 to 5 percent discount is made for payment of the full amount of the transaction at the end of the specified period from 1 to 4 months from the date of the invoice. The length of the period depends on the commodity involved, the credit standing of the buyer, and the motivation of the seller.

A period of up to 2 years is often allowed for payment of capital goods, store equipment, trucks, and similar heavy equipment. Italian firms indicate that some American suppliers are too rigid in their payment terms and have thus lost business to other suppliers because of their rigidity. Financing is considered as much a competitive factor as the product itself, the delivery date, or after-sales service. While some U.S. manufacturers request payment upon receipt of the goods, more successful sellers are offering terms allowing settlement of the account from 60 to 120 days following receipt of the order.

The use of irrevocable letters of credit for the Italian market has declined appreciably in recent years. Although such instruments are still required by American exporters, especially when the Italian customer's credit reputation is not well known, the growing reluctance of Italian firms to provide letters of credit has required American exporters to utilize other methods to assure payment or lose the sale to other suppliers in the competitive Italian market. The Italian businessperson is reluctant to pay a high fee for a letter of credit when other suppliers or means of payment are available.

American firms have put to greater use the export credit insurance and guarantee programs available through the Foreign Credit Insurance Association (FCIA). Just as the terms of any sales offer should be presented in a clear and detailed manner, shipments should conform to the contract and to any samples that may have been sent to the Italian importer. Special attention should be given to the prompt observance of agreed delivery schedules, as prompt delivery may be a decisive and possibly an overriding consideration of the importer in placing additional orders.

When shipping on letter of credit, all terms specified on the letter of credit must be strictly observed. If the terms are no followed, the letter of credit may not be honored by the bank.

TYPES OF AVAILABLE EXPORT FINANCING AND INSURANCE

As a member of the G-7, Italy as a market for U.S. exporters does not warrant any special USG credit assistance. The network of Italian banks with branches in the U.S. will offer limited export credit assistance. Similarly, large U.S. banks and/or local banks located in the exporter's state can offer factoring; exchange fluctuation hedging and limited exporter's credit services. The EXIM bank and FCIA consider Italy a low political risk country. Italy is classified as a "rich" country under the OECD rate classification. Small business exporters may obtain assistance under the SBA's Export Revolving Line of Credit (ELRC) loan program.

PROJECT FINANCING AVAILABLE

Several programs exist to help finance exports. The following export financing programs may be of interest to an U.S. exporter: - The Small Business Administration (SBA) provides financing for the establishment, operation, or expansion of a small business, including firms engaged in exporting. the SBA's Export Revolving Line of Credit Guarantee Program provides pre-export financing for sales and for foreign market development. SBA also has a program in cooperation with the Export-Import Bank of the United States (Eximbank) to participate in loans to small firms. -

The Export-Import Bank of the United States (Eximbank) is an independent U.S. Government agency that helps to finance the sale of U.S. goods and services to foreign buyers. Eximbank can provide loans directly to foreign buyers, provide U.S. suppliers and their banks with credit risk protection, or originate direct financing. Eximbank has regional offices located in New York, Chicago, Houston, Miami, and Los Angeles. - The Foreign Credit Insurance Association (FCIA) is a private sector association of insurance companies. The FCIA acts in conjunction with, and as an agent for, Eximbank to cover export sale repayment losses due to political or commercial causes. - The Overseas Private Investment Corporation (OPIC) assists U.S. private investment to promote the economic and social progress of developing countries. Programs include political risk insurance, special insurance coverage for natural resource projects, leasing, and contractor's risks. - The International Bank for Reconstruction and Development (IBRD), under the World Bank Group, promotes development of member countries mainly by extending conventional loans for specific high-priority projects.

EXPORT-IMPORT REGULATIONS

TRADE BARRIERS

BROADCAST DIRECTIVE AND MOTION PICTURE QUOTAS

Italy passed legislation in 1998 to significantly tighten European content requirements (TV quotas). The new law replaces Italy's previous requirement that a majority of television broadcast time for feature films be reserved for EU-origin films, and that half of the European quota be dedicated to Italian films. The new quota goes beyond the EU "Broadcast without Frontiers" Directive by applying quotas specifically to prime time broadcasting, and by excluding talk shows from the types of programming that may be counted towards fulfilling the quota. (The Directive excludes only news, sports, game shows, advertising, teletext and teleshopping. The Italian law excludes these categories as well, but additionally excludes talk shows.)

A separate but related issue concerns films shown in Italian theaters. The film sector law approved by parliament on February 23, 1994, eliminated obligatory screen quotas for Italian films (heretofore 25 days per quarter subject to closing of the theater, under a 1965 law), and in their place substituted discretionary rebates on Italy's box office tax for theaters that show Italian films. The rebates and eligibility thresholds (percentages of screenings required to qualify) vary according to the category of the film. The United States continues its efforts both to obtain elimination of discriminatory laws and regulations in the audiovisual sector and to limit their impact in the interim.

CIVIL AVIATION

Since 1990, the United States/Italy civil aviation relationship has undergone some liberalization, including the entry of new U.S. carriers in 1991, 1992, and, most recently, in 1996. Nevertheless, the market remains somewhat restrictive. U.S. carriers have expressed concern over a range of issues, a number of which relate to the lack of competition in the provision of certain ground handling services at international airports.

Discussions that may lead to a liberal "open skies" civil aviation agreement between the U.S. and Italy are scheduled to begin in the summer of 1998.

GOVERNMENT PROCUREMENT

In Italy, fragmented, often non-transparent government procurement practices and previous problems with corruption have created obstacles to U.S. firms' participation in Italian government procurement. Italy has, however, made some progress in making the laws and regulations governing government procurement more transparent, although Italy has not yet fully updated its government procurement code, nor has it completely implemented EU directives on government procurement. The pressure to reduce government expenditures while increasing efficiency is resulting in increased use of competitive procurement procedures and somewhat greater emphasis on best value rather than automatic reliance on traditional suppliers. This trend should benefit U.S. firms.

CUSTOMS VALUATION

Prior to signing a long-term contract or sending a shipment of considerable value, it may be prudent for a U.S. exporter to first obtain an official ruling on the customs classification, duty rate, and taxes. Such requests should be sent to: Ministry of Finance, Rome, Italy. The request should describe the product, the material it is made from, and other details needed by customs authorities to classify the product correctly. While customs will not provide a binding decision, the advance ruling usually will be accepted if the imported goods are found to correspond exactly to the full description provided when requesting the ruling.

IMPORT LICENSES

With exception of a small group of largely agricultural items, practically all goods originating in the United States and most other free-world countries can be imported without import licenses and free of quantitative restrictions. There are, however, monitoring measures applied to imports of certain sensitive products. The most important of these measures is the automatic import license for textiles. This license is granted to Italian importers when they provide the requisite forms.

Various apparel and textile products, and controlled items such as arms and munitions are the most frequently regulated items. Import licenses are generally rapidly granted for goods of U.S. origin and delays are usually from lack of proper documentation or information.

Licenses are not transferable. They may be used to cover several shipments within the total quantity authorized. In general, the goods involved are indicated on the license by the Harmonized System classification number and the corresponding wording of the tariff position.

EXPORT CONTROLS

For the purpose of national security, foreign policy, or the short supply of materials, the United States controls the export of goods and technology by two broad categories of export licenses -- general and validated.

The vast majority of U.S. exports are shipped abroad under general licenses that do not require formal application or approval. To determine which kind of export license is required, exporters should consult the U.S. Export Administration Regulations for complete details or obtain assistance from the local U.S. Department of Commerce district office.

As an overview, the first step in the export licensing process is to determine whether a product requires a general or validated license. Determine what is being exported, the destination of the product, its end-use, and the organization that will be using the product. Check the schedule of Country Groups listed in the U.S.

Export Administration Regulations to determine the destination category; check the Commodity Control List to determine if the product requires a validated license for shipment to that particular country; and determine if any special restrictions are in effect.

If the product is not on the control list, then it can be exported under a general license. The U.S. exporter simply completes the "U.S. Shippers Export Declaration", Form 7525-V, providing details of the shipment; includes a commercial invoice; and exports the goods. If the product is on the control list, a
validated license is needed.

An application must be made and an export license granted. As a general rule, an exporter will need a validated license (1) if the products are controlled or in short supply regardless of the country of destination; (2) for any commodity to a destination with foreign policy concerns; or (3) for unpublished technical data to certain destinations. Certain special licenses are also issued to cover large projects or repeated sales through a foreign distributor.

For assistance in determining what type of license is needed and to initiate the processing of an application, contact your local Department of Commerce district office or the Bureau of Export Administration, Office of Export Assistance, Room H-1099D, U.S. Department of Commerce, Washington, DC 20230, (202) 482-4811.

IMPORT/EXPORT DOCUMENTATION

Documents required for exporting include the usual shipper's commercial invoice and the bill of lading or air waybill, none of which require consular legalization. For textiles and apparel, it is good practice to provide a certificate of origin, available through most state chambers of commerce. For other products, however, if substantive proof of U.S. origin is provided through other accompanying documents as well as through characteristic trademarks, a certificate of origin is not normally necessary.

For additional information or assistance on export documentation, readers should consult publications such as the Exporter's Encyclopedia, published by Dun's Marketing Services or contact a local U.S. Department of Commerce International Trade Administration Export Assistance Office.

TEMPORARY IMPORTS

Material may temporarily be imported into Italy without payment of duties and tax if such material is to be used in the production or manufacture of a product that is to be exported. The importer gives security, usually in the form of a guarantee from a bank or insurance company, for the amount of the usual duties and taxes. Upon exportation of the finished product, the guarantee is released or the deposit returned.

Temporary entry of goods intended to be re-exported in the same condition is permissible free of import duties and taxes upon approval of an application by Italian Customs.

Samples without commercial value are admitted free of duty and taxes. Product literature should be marked "product Literature - no commercial value". Samples with commercial value are also admitted duty and tax free, provided that the following conditions are complied with:

(a) The samples are accompanied by a representative of the U.S. firm with a statement, notarized by an Italian Consulate, identifying the commercial traveler and attesting to the intention that the samples are being imported into Italy for the purpose of being shown or demonstrated and they are to be reexported in due course.

(b) A certificate of origin from a recognized chamber of commerce is submitted to identify the source of the goods.

(c) A deposit or bond, in the amount of the applicable customs duties and taxes, is made at the point of entry. This will be refunded when the goods are reexported.

(d) A list (in duplicate) with a full description of each sample, including weight and value, is submitted. It is helpful to have such a list in Italian.

U.S. traders should be aware of another and more simplified procedure in the form of a carnet for the temporary importation of samples without posting guarantees.

In practice, samples valued in excess of lira 1 million (or about 1,250 USD) are practically impossible to clear through Italian customs. In such cases, it is advisable to engage the services of a local freight forwarder.

GOODS IN TRANSIT

Goods may clear customs with an EU transit procedure that provides for the issuance of a single transit document under which the goods may be easily shipped across frontiers of the EU member states. These transit documents are completed for the importer by a freight forwarder in Italy. The EU transit document provides the basis for a single, comprehensive procedure covering the goods within the Community. Since single transit document is an EU form, the European importer, customs house broker, freight forwarder, or shipper must prepare the document at the point of entry.

INWARD AND OUTWARD PROCESSING

Inward processing is the temporary importation of raw material or products for additional manufacture or processing. Merchandise imported for additional processing and eventual reexport out of the EU is eligible for custom-free treatment.

The reexported goods may be partly or totally processed. The import duty and taxes are levied only on those goods that are not reexported and are finally sold in the EU.

To qualify for inward processing, an Italian (or EU) firm must satisfy customs that it is necessary to use imported goods instead of EU goods; state an intention to export products manufactured from the imported goods (or equivalent goods available in the EU); and assure that, upon reexportation, the conditions set forth in the authorization are satisfied, the exported products are accounted for, and the entered goods are identifiable and relate to specific importations.

In outward processing, a firm in Italy may export goods for further manufacture or processing from the EU customs area and then reimport the final product. Duties and taxes are levied only on the increased value added by the expatriate manufacturing or processing when the goods are returned to Italy and not to the total value of the product. Only firms located in Italy or another EU country are eligible to take advantage of this option, and they should first gain approval of the Customs authorities.

LABELING, MARKING REQUIREMENTS

There is no general requirement that imports be marked as to country of origin. Under Italian legislation, the origin of imported merchandise is established through documentation accompanying the shipments arriving in Italy and not through marking of products or their containers. Certain specified commodities, however, must be marked or labeled to show composition, and name and location of manufacturer, in accordance with various laws and regulations.

he following articles are subject to special marking or labeling regulations: lime, cement and similar binding agents; pianos, automatic pianos, harmonicas and similar instruments; clinical thermometers; ethical medicines; cosmetics. Hallmarking of gold and silver articles is required before they can be offered for sale. Only small tolerances are allowable for manufacturing errors. The hallmarking may be done by a hallmarking office after importation.

Imports of certain commodities such as packaged foods, distilled spirits, beer, wine, vinegar and foodstuffs) are subject to special regulations regarding the manner in which they must be labeled to show manufacturer, composition, content (in metric units), and country of origin. In view of the complexity of these regulations and changing requirements, information should be requested from the importer prior to shipment. When the services of an importer are not available, information can be obtained directly from the appropriate Italian Government authority listed at the end of this publication. or agricultural and food products, see "Trade Regulations and Standards for Agriculture" below.

PROHIBITED IMPORTS

There are a number of Italian regulations and European Community directives that prohibit certain foodstuffs, food colorings, drugs and narcotics, animal products, plants, seed grains, alcohol, cosmetics and toiletries, etc. It is therefore recommended American exporters contact the Italian importer prior to the shipment or use their freight forwarder to make the determination.

STANDARDS

As a member of the EU, Italy applies the product standards and certification approval process developed by the European Community. Italy is required by the Treaty of Rome to incorporate approved EU directives into its national laws. However, there is frequently a long lag in implementing these directives at the national level. In addition, in some sectors such as pollution control, the uniformity in application of standards may vary according to region, further complicating the certification process.

Italy has been slow in accepting test data from foreign sources, but is expected to adopt EU standards in this area. U.S.-EU negotiation of mutual recognition agreements should, over time, reduce problems in this area. In the Spring of 1997 the U.S. and EU concluded mutual recognition agreements in the following areas: network and electromagnetic compatibility (EMC) for telecommunications and information technology equipment and radio transmitters; EMC and electrical safety for electrical and electronic products; good manufacturing practices inspections for pharmaceutical products and certain medical devices; product assessment for medical devices; and safety of recreational craft.

As part of the unification program to establish common standards for all member countries, key product areas are being regulated by the Community. Mandatory requirements to protect the health and safety of consumers, as well as the environment are constantly being developed and implemented.

To indicate conformance to the mandatory EU requirements, a CE mark must be placed on all regulated products by the manufacturer or a representative before they can be sold on the EU market. The applicable product testing and certification requirements for individual product categories are specified in the various EU directives.

The CE mark relates only to the mandatory health, safety, and environmental requirements established by the EU; it does not indicate conformity to European product standards. Thus, national marks of conformity with product standards remain compatible with the CE mark and both may be applied to the product. It should be noted, however, that the CE mark does replace all national safety marks for the regulated products.

U.S. firms exporting to Italy are confronted with both national and EU product standards. Further, these regulations occasionally change to meet new technology and more stringent demands.

Exporters can stay fully informed of the latest EU technical standards activities by contacting the Standards Information Service of the National Institute of Standards and Technology (NIST) at (301) 975-4040. A part of the U.S. Department of Commerce, NIST offers industry an in-depth reference system on EU standards information gathered from the two European standards bodies tasked to write the EU norms --the European Committee for Standards (CEN) and the European Committee for Electrotechnical Standardization (CENELEC). NIST also can provide updated information from the EU which will elaborate on directives and provide assistance in identifying EU and member state standards and regulations.

Other valuable sources of information with regard to Italian standards include: the American National Standards Institute, 1430 Broadway, New York, NY 10018, (212) 354-3300; the Department of Commerce's National Technical Information Service, Springfield, VA 22161, (703) 557-4733; UNI, Ente Nazionale Italiano di Unificazione, Via Battistotti Sassi, 20133 Milan (Italian National Bureau of Standards) or through the American National Standards Institute, 1430 Broadway, New York, NY 10018, (212) 354-3300; as well as various trade associations that follow international activities for their membership.

Electrical power supplies are generally 220 volts, 50 cycles, single-phase and 380 volts, 50 cycles, three-phase. Electricity at 60 cycles is not available. American appliances, such as electric shavers or hair dryers, do not work and will be damaged if used without a transformer.

Service interruptions are rare and the frequency of the current is stable. The electrical plug is the standard plug B. This is a plug that has two round pins instead of the flat prongs. Some outlets may require different plugs in other parts of the country.

Italy uses the metric system of weights and measures, which is called the International System of Units (SI). The European Community has established standardized packaging units for numerous products which should be consulted by U.S. exporters. Labeling must be in metric units for all imported products to be sold in Italy. Products are allowed to be imported and then labeled in SI metric units prior to sale.

Dual labeling information is permitted, but the nonmetric information must not predominate. The U.S. exporter would be well advised to first check with the Italian importer to ensure that the package size and labeling complies with all requirements prior to shipment.

FREE TRADE ZONES / WAREHOUSES

There are two free trade zones in Italy located in Trieste and Venice. Goods of foreign origin may be brought in without payment of taxes or duties, as long as the material is to be used in the production or assembly of a product that will be exported.

Benefits of a free-trade zone include:

- customs duties deferred for 180 days from the time that the goods leave the free-trade zone to enter another EU country;
  - the goods may undergo any transformation free of any customs restraints;
  - absolute exemption from any duties on products coming from a third country.

The free-trade zone law also allows a company, of any nationality, to employ workers of the same nationality, under that country's labor laws and social security.

Italy also has numerous general warehouses that are located throughout Italy in all the port areas and cities. There are no limitations as to the type or origin of merchandise that can be stored in free trade zones or bonded or customs warehouses. The time limit for such storage is 5 years. Merchandise deteriorated while in storage can be destroyed without payment of duty.

The advantage of a free trade zone or bonded warehouse to American firms is having a European base of supply to assure customers prompt delivery and service. Being able to maintain inventory at low cost with a minimum of customs paperwork is also a distinct advantage.

SPECIAL IMPORT PROVISIONS

Italy participates in the International Convention to Facilitate the Importation of Commercial Samples and Advertising Materials. Samples of negligible value imported to promote sales are accorded duty-free and tax-free treatment. Prior authorization is not required. To determine whether the samples are of negligible value, their value is compared with a commercial shipment of the same product. Granting of duty-free status may require that the samples be rendered useless for future sale by marking, perforating, cutting, or other means.

Imported samples of commercial value may be granted a temporary entry and exemption from custom charges. However, a bond or cash deposit may be required as security that the goods will be removed from the country. This security is the duty and tax normally levied plus 10 percent. Samples may remain in the country for up to 1 year. They are not permitted to be sold, put to their normal use (except for demonstration purposes), or utilized in any manner for remuneration. Goods imported as samples may be imported only in quantities constituting a sample according to normal commercial usage.

CARNETS

As a result of various customs agreements, simplified procedures are available to U.S. business and professional people for the temporary importation of commercial samples and professional equipment. A carnet is a customs document that facilitates customs clearance for temporary imports of samples or equipment. With the carnet, goods may be imported without the payment of duty, tax, or additional security.

The carnet also usually saves time since formalities are all arranged before leaving the United States. A carnet is usually valid for 1 year from the date of issuance and is issued at moderate cost. A bond or cash deposit of 40 percent of the value of the goods covered by the carnet is also required. This will be forfeited in the event the products are not reexported and duties and taxes are not paid.

Carnets are sold in the United States by the U.S. Council for International Business at the following locations: 1212 Avenue of the Americas, New York, NY 10036, (212) 354-4480; 3345 Wilshire Boulevard, Los Angeles, CA 90010, (213) 386-0767; and 1930 Thoreau Drive, #101, Schaumburg, IL 60173.

MEMBERSHIP IN FREE TRADE ARRANGEMENTS

Italy has been a member of the European Union (EU) since its inception in 1958. The other EU members are Belgium, Denmark, France, Germany, Greece, Ireland, Luxembourg, the Netherlands, Portugal, Spain, the United Kingdom, Austria, Finland and Sweden. Other countries have applied for membership. The EU forms a customs union and a large unified market having free trade among the member states. It levies a common tariff on imported products coming from non-EU countries such as the United States, Japan, and Canada. The EU also has a common agricultural policy, joint transportation policy, and free movement of goods and capital within the member states. Other aspects of commercial activity are being harmonized.

The EU grants tariff preferences to more than 100 developing countries and about 40 overseas territories under the EU's Generalized System of Preferences (GSP). Imports of nearly all semimanufactured and manufactured goods originating in these countries and territories enter the Community duty free. Annual duty-free quotas are established for those products and a system of providing certificates of origin has been established to ensure that goods are not diverted through the GSP countries to take advantage of the lower tariff concessions.

Free trade agreements have been developed between the European Union and the European Economic Area (EEA), which includes Norway, Iceland, Liechtenstein, and Switzerland. Under the terms of these agreements, most industrial products and certain processed agricultural products are exempt from import duties if traded within this trading bloc. The result of the agreements reached between the EU members and the EEA members is an open trading area for most industrial products of 19 nations with an affluent population of 380 million.

While customs duty rates are the same for all 15 EU countries, the value-added tax (VAT) and excise tax on products and services usually differ from country to country. These taxes are levied in the country of final destination. See the "Value-Added Tax" section for the Italian rates.

TRADE REGULATIONS AND STANDARDS FOR AGRICULTURE

Since Italy is a member of the European Union (EU), virtually all of its agricultural sector is governed by the Common Agricultural Policy (CAP). Similarly, Italy employs the same tariffs, levies and other EU regulations as the other fourteen member states.

For example, Italy imposes variable levies (on grain products) and quotas (on meat, cheese, bananas) as required by the European Union. Italy also applies a value added tax on most food/agricultural items (ranging from 4 percent for semi processed commodities to 19 percent for "luxury" high value food items).

In general, if a U.S. food product is imported into one EU member state it can be transhipped to Italy, provided it has a label written in Italian, and provided the product does not present a public or animal/plant health risk. However, if the product is directly imported into Italy it must meet all Italian food safety and quality standards, as well as Italian labeling and packaging regulations. Many of these standards and regulations have been harmonized within the European Union. For example, the EU has adopted a number of regulations covering production standards, analytical characteristics, product specifications, allowable additives, and labeling. Specific EU regulations exist for cocoa and chocolate products, sugars, fruit juices, fruit jams and jellies, milk and casein products.

However, where EU standards do not exist, Italy can set its own national requirements and some of these have been known to hamper imports of game meat, processed meat products, frozen foods, alcoholic beverages, and snack foods/confectionary products. U.S. exporters of "health" foods, weight loss/diet foods, baby foods and vitamins should work closely with an Italian importer, since Italy's labeling laws regarding health claims can be particularly stringent.

Italian legislation sets forth orders, obligations and criminal sanctions for violations. Food law is divided into two basic categories: rules dealing with hygiene/sanitary issues and rules governing labeling and packaging. All laws apply equally to domestically produced and imported goods.

Italy is still working on specific sectors of the food law to bring the regulations up to date scientifically in the areas of hygiene/sanitation. In the case of food additives, coloring and modified starches, Italy's laws are considered to be close to current U.S. laws, albeit sometimes more restrictive.

BASIC LABELING REQUIREMENTS IN THE EU/ITALY:

Name of products (physical condition or specific treatment)
Name/address of manufacturer, packer, seller or importer in
EU Local language
Country of origin
Ingredients in descending order of weight
Metric weight and volume
Additives by category name
Special storage conditions
Minimum shelf life date
Special preparation instructions

U.S. exporters should be aware that any food or agricultural product transhipped through Italian territory must meet Italian requirements, even if the product is transported in a sealed and bonded container and is not expected to enter Italian commerce.

PRACTICAL INFORATION FOR CONDUCTING BUSINESS

DOING BUSINESS IN ITALY BASICS

MARKET OVERVIEW

Italy is the world's 7th largest economy with a GDP of $2.1 trillion. Italy's economy is expected to grow 1.1 percent in 2010 following two years of decline due to the global recession. Italy's population is 60 million.

Italy is the 18th largest market for U.S. exports, totaling $15.5 billion in 2008. The U.S. is Italy's 10th largest supplier. The top four supplier nations are Germany, France, China, and the Netherlands. U.S. imports from Italy totaled $35 billion.

U.S. cumulative direct investment in Italy was $28.7 billion in 2008, ranking Italy 11th in Europe. Approximately 41 percent of U.S. investment is in manufacturing. Italy maintains the highest proportion of manufacturing jobs among the G7 countries.

Industrial activity is concentrated in the north in a swath that runs from Turin in the west through Milan to Venice in the east. This is one of the most industrialized and prosperous areas in Europe and accounts for some 50 percent of national income. By contrast, Italy's southern region, or "Mezzogiorno" is less developed.

Italy is a founding member of the European Union (EU) and uses the Euro as its national currency.

MARKET CHALLENGES

Italy is a mature and sophisticated market. U.S. entrants face strong competition from local and other EU companies in all market segments.

Italy's regulatory environment is complex and at times lacks the transparency, clarity, efficiency and certainty found in other developed economies.

Products that involve health, safety, or environmental concerns are likely to be highly regulated. While EU-wide regulations often apply, Italian laws may go beyond the basic EU requirements.

The economy is dominated by small, family owned companies (90 percent of Italian firms are small or medium size).

MARKET OPPORTUNITIES

U.S. firms enjoy good opportunities in sectors where new regulations or programs (often imposed or initiated at the EU level), are creating demand; with new products/services where there is little or no domestic competition; and/or where the American product offers clear technological, design, or price advantages.

Best prospect sectors include information technology, security, healthcare, and environment. Italy offers attractive incentives for renewable energy generation and energy efficient construction ("green building").

Italy's changing demographics and lifestyle also create opportunities. Italy's birthrate is low and its population is aging. More women are entering and remaining in the workforce.

Italy hosts major trade shows that attract buyers from throughout Europe, the Mediterranean, and beyond. This includes events in information technology, health care, franchising, travel and tourism, safety and security, solar power, construction, pets, automotive, and marine recreation, among others. The Commercial Service offers on-site support for U.S. exporters at most of the major international shows, or by request.

The U.S. sold $1 billion worth of agricultural products to Italy in 2008, mainly as inputs to Italian food and related industries. Principal exports included durum wheat for pasta and confectionary, forest products for furniture and housing components, tree nuts for bakery products, tomato paste and seafood for the restaurant sector, and soybeans for the livestock sector. Consumer-ready products are in increasing demand but face constraints, e.g. resistance to GMO ingredients and cultural differences.

MARKET ENTRY STRATEGY

The cultivation and maintenance of personal relationships are a vital part of doing business in Italy. This is even truer for foreign businesses that lack an intimate understanding of Italy's business culture and regulatory environment. Finding the right Italian agent, distributor, or business partner is therefore essential to enter the Italian market.

The ideal candidate should already have a network of relationships that will open doors in the market. They should also have a solid understanding of local business practices and applicable regulations. For technical products, the potential partner should have the ability to provide Italian customers with after-sales service. Patience is essential as it may take two to three times longer than expected to establish a business.

The U.S. Commercial Service offers services to help U.S. firms identify an ideal partner, from customized Gold Key matchmaking to participation in U.S. Pavilions at leading trade exhibitions.

TRADE AND PROJECT FINANCING

METHODS OF PAYMENT

American firms most frequently provide the Italian buyer with a price quote that includes packing costs, insurance, and freight (CIF price). The average Italian business representative can then usually determine the charges for customs, taxes, and local transportation to arrive at the importer's final landed cost. The customary terms of sale in Italy are either cash or net. Sales made on cash terms call for payment before delivery, on delivery, or shortly after delivery -- usually within 10 days. A two to five percent discount is made for payment of the full amount of the transaction at the end of the specified period from one to four months from the date of the invoice. The length of the period depends on the commodity involved, the credit standing of the buyer, and the motivation of the seller. A period of up to two years is often allowed for payment of capital goods, store equipment, trucks, and similar heavy equipment.

Some U.S. suppliers have lost business because Italian firms believe their payment terms are too rigid. Exporters should regard financing as another competitive factor, on par with the product itself, the delivery date, or after-sales service. U.S. manufacturers will be more competitive by allowing accounts to be settled from 60 to 120 days following receipt of the order.

Although originally an Italian creation, the use of irrevocable letters of credit has declined appreciably in Italy in recent years. Because of the growing reluctance of Italian firms to pay high fees associated with letters of credit, American exporters should explore other mechanisms to ensure payment from Italian customers of uncertain credit worthiness, or risk losing the sale. Alternatives include export credit insurance and guarantee programs available through the Foreign Credit Insurance Association (FCIA).

Just as sales offer terms should be clear and detailed, shipment terms should conform to contract specifications and should be consistent with any samples that were sent to the Italian importer.

Agreed delivery schedules should be met, as prompt delivery may be a decisive consideration of the importer in placing additional orders. When shipping on letters of credit, all terms specified in the letter of credit must be strictly observed. If all the terms are not followed, the bank may not honor the letter of credit.

HOW DOES THE BANKING SYSTEM OPERATE

Italy has a well-developed banking and credit system with numerous correspondent U.S. banks. Italian banks are subject to close government supervision, and the Bank of Italy must authorize the establishment of any new bank.

U.S. firms seeking to finance major portions of their capital investment outside the United States may find capital available in the Eurodollar market. U.S. bank branches in Italy can assist in financing capital investment. There almost 800 banks and over 34,000 branches performing commercial and other services throughout Italy. Currently, the country's largest banks are: Unicredit Group (established in 2007 by merger of Unicredit and Capitalia), Intesa San Paolo (established in 2007 by merger of Banca Intesa and Sanpaolo IMI), Monte dei Paschi di Siena, Banco Popolare, and UBI Banca. These banks are a principal source of credit information. Unicredit Group is the largest bank in Italy by market value and the second largest in Europe. Intesa Sanpaolo is the second largest bank in Italy by market value and the sixth largest in Europe.

The banking sector has undergone significant consolidation since the mid-nineties, with about 60 percent of total Italian banking assets involved. Since his appointment as new Governor of the Central Bank on January 16, 2006, Mario Draghi has publicly called for fragmented Italian banks to further consolidate, set aside their regional rivalries to prepare for international competition or face foreign takeovers. From 1996 to 2006, through mergers and acquisitions involving 349 banks, the number of banks decreased from almost 1,000 to less than 800 at end-2008, resulting in 81 Italian banking groups. Currently banking groups continued to rationalize their structure in the wake of past mergers, and no further significant acquisitions or mergers occurred in 2009 as the industry digested the previous years' deals. This consolidation process, already the largest among European countries in terms of bank assets, is expected to continue over the next several years as the Italian banking sector becomes more competitive in the single European market.

Banks in Italy that have the authority to participate in foreign exchange usually have a U.S. correspondent. Foreign currency transfers and foreign exchange transactions must be channeled via authorized intermediaries (for example, the Bank of Italy or the Italian Foreign Exchange Office). Larger Italian banks usually have branches in one or more U.S. cities.

The Bank of Italy, Italy's central bank, follows euro notes issues, performs credit, financial and market supervision, and regulates bank mergers. The financial market oversight reform bill, passed at end-2005 and drafted in consultation with the European Central Bank (ECB), cuts the Central Bank Governor's term from life to six years, limits the Governor to two terms in office, and divides the Central Bank's banking competition oversight responsibilities with Italy's anti-trust authority. The bill also authorizes CONSOB, Italy's security markets and company accounting regulator, to raid firms suspected of securities violations and to impound evidence.

In early December 2006, the Italian Cabinet approved legislation modifying this same financial market oversight reform law passed at the end of 2005 to eliminate overlapping authority and increase transparency. The new decree law gives CONSOB increased authority in the insurance sector. The decree law also transfers banking anti-trust authority from the Bank of Italy to the national Antitrust Authority. Finally, the decree law revises the voting structure of Italy's thirty-six cooperative banks (banche popolari) to make it easier for financial sector consolidation to move ahead.

A prohibition on non-bank companies (either Italian or foreign) acquiring more than 15 percent of a bank's capital was abolished by the legislature in late 2008, with the aim of implementing a new European directive. Firms have used complex cross-shareholding arrangements to fight off takeover attempts in the financial sector. Still, the presence of foreign intermediaries in the Italian market increased in the last several years. At end of 2008, 82 subsidiaries of foreign groups accounted for 11.7 percent of system assets. A year earlier, 21 subsidies of foreign banks accounted for 9.3 percent of system assets. Throughout 2008-09, however, various foreign banks closed or significantly scaled back operations in Italy, with accompanying layoffs and lost business. Several U.S. banks perform services in Italy, through branches, subsidiaries, or representatives. Many American banks can also provide their commercial customers with services, such as bank reports on overseas buyers, assistance for letters of credit, and foreign exchange. U.S. banks with offices in Italy include Citigroup, JP Morgan Chase, and Bank of America, as well as numerous smaller, regional banks.

FOREIGN-EXCHANGE CONTROLS

Italy has no restrictions on the amount of foreign exchange instruments, currency, or checks that may be brought into the country. Normally, 10,000 euros may be taken out of the country, but any amount declared upon entry may be re-exported.

Italian exchange regulations are issued by the Italian Exchange Office, Ufficio Italiano dei Cambi (UIC), Via Quattro Fontane 123, Rome 00184, Italy. Foreign currency may be sold or acquired from the Bank of Italy or any of the banks authorized by the Bank of Italy. In effect, all commercial banks are authorized to conduct foreign exchange transactions.

Dollar currency, travelers checks, and, in some cases, personal checks, may be exchanged at banks, exchange offices, authorized tourist offices, and hotels. Major credit cards are accepted with proper identification, and ATMs are ubiquitous.

U.S. BANKS AND LOCAL CORRESPONDENT BANKS

(A large number of Italian banks have correspondence relationships with U.S. banks. Below is a listing of Italian banks with branch offices in the U.S.

Intesa Sanpaolo S.p.A.
(Merger between Sanpaolo IMI S.p.A. and Banca Intesa in January 2007)
Piazza San Carlo, 156
10121 Torino
Tel.: +39-011-555-1

WEB: WWW.INTESASANPAOLO.COM

CEO Americas Area
New York – Branch
One William Street
New York NY 10004
Tel: (212) 6073500
Fax: (212) 809 2124
Gianluca Corrias, Manager
E-mail: gianluca.corrias@intesasanpaolo.com

Los Angeles – Representative Office
444 South Flower Street
23rd Floor Suite 2360
Los Angeles, CA 90071
Tel.: (213) 489 3100
Fax: (213) 622 2514
E-mail: losangeles.repoffice@intesasanpaolo.com
Donald Brown, Director
E-mail: donald.brown@intesasanpaolo.com

International Network
Piazza della Scala, 6
20121 Milano
Tel.: +39-02-87943059
Fax.: +39-02-87942940
Carlo Persico, Manager
E-mail: carlo.persico@intesasanpaolo.com

Unicredit Group S.p.A.
(Established in May 2007 with merger of Unicredito Italiano S.p.A. and Capitalia S.p.A. Capitalia S.p.A. was established in 2002 with merger of Banca di Roma, Bibop-Carire and Banco di Sicilia)
Piazza Cordusio
20121 Milano
Tel.: +39-02-886-211
Web: www.unicreditgroup.eu
www.unicredit-capitalia.eu
New York – Branch
150 East 42nd Street
New York NY 10017
Tel.: (212) 672 6000
Fax.: (212) 546 9675
Email: newyorkbranch@unicreditgroup.eu

HVB Corporates & Markets – New York Branch
150 East 42nd Street
New York NY 10017
Tel.: (212) 672 6000
Fax.: (212) 672 5555

Pioneer Alternative Investments
535 5th Avenue
New York NY 10017
us.pioneerinvestments.com

Pioneer Funds Distributor Inc.
701 Brickell Avenue, Suite 3260
Miami FL 33131-2847
us.pioneerinvestments.com

Pioneer Investment Management Inc.
60 State Street
Boston MA 02109
us.pioneerinvestments.com

Banca Nazionale del Lavoro BNL S.p.A.
(Incorporated in BNP Paribas in 2006)
Via Vittorio Veneto 119
00187 Roma
Tel.: +39-06-470-21
Web: www.bnl.it

Miami – Representative Office
201 South Biscayne Blvd., Suite 1800 Miami, FL 33131 Tel.: (305) 539 2000 Fax: (305) 539 1421
Also available: list of BNP Paribas Group branches in the United States:
http://www.bnpparibas.com/en/locations/cartography.asp

Banca Monte dei Paschi di Siena S.p.A.
Piazza Salimbeni 3
53100 Siena
Tel.: +39-0577-294-111
Web: www.mps.it

New York – Branch
55 East 59th Street – 9thFloor
10022 New York, NY
Tel.: (212) 891 3600
Fax: (212) 891 3661/3
Renato Bassi, Direttore Titolare
E-mail: renato.bassi@banca.mps.it

PROJECT FINANCING

EU financial assistance programs provide a wide array of grants, loans, loan guarantees and co-financing for feasibility studies and infrastructure projects in a number of key sectors (e.g., environmental, transportation, energy, telecommunications, tourism, public health). From a commercial perspective, these initiatives create significant market opportunities for U.S. businesses, U.S.-based suppliers, and subcontractors.

The EU supports projects within its Member States, as well as EU-wide "economic integration" projects that cross both internal and external EU borders. In addition, the EU provides assistance to accession countries in Eastern and Southern Europe and Turkey, as well as some of the former Soviet republics.

The European Union provides project financing through grants from the European Commission and loans from the European Investment Bank. Grants from the Structural Funds are distributed through the Member States' national and regional authorities, and are only available for projects in the 27 EU Member States. All grants for projects in non-EU countries are managed through the EuropeAid Cooperation agency in conjunction with various European Commission departments, called "Directorates-General."

The CSEU Tenders Database

The U.S. Commercial Service at the U.S. Mission to the European Union offers a tool on its website to help U.S.-based companies identify European public procurement opportunities. The database features all current public procurement tenders issued by all national and regional public authorities in the 27 Member States of the European Union, plus four other European countries, and that are open to U.S.-based firms under the terms of the Government Procurement Agreement (GPA) implemented in 1995. The database is updated twice weekly and is easy to use with a range of search options, including approximately 20 industry sectors. The database also contains tenders for public procurement contracts relating to structural funds. Readers may access the database at http://www.buyusa.gov/europeanunion/eu_tenders.html.

EU Structural Funds

The EU Structural Funds, including the European Regional Development Fund, were created in 1975 to assist economically depressed regions of the European Union that required industrial restructuring. The EU earmarked EUR 308 billion for projects under the Structural Funds and the Cohesion Fund programs for the 2007-2013 period for the EU-27. In addition to funding economic development projects proposed by Member States or local authorities, EU Structural Funds also support specialized projects promoting EU socioeconomic objectives. Member States negotiate regional and "sectoral" programs with officials from the regional policy Directorate-General at the European Commission. For information on approved programs that will result in future project proposals, please visit: http://ec.europa.eu/regional_policy/atlas2007/fiche_index_en.htm.

For projects financed through the Structural Funds, Member State officials are the key decision-makers. They assess the needs of their country; investigate projects; evaluate bids; and award contracts. To become familiar with available financial support programs in the Member States, it is advisable for would-be contractors to meet with local officials to discuss local needs.

Tenders issued by Member States' public contracting authorities for projects supported by EU grants are subject to EU public procurement legislation if they meet the EU minimum contract value requirement for the eligible sector. Below this threshold, tender procedures are subject to national procurement legislation. There are no overt prohibitions against the participation of U.S. companies, either as developers or concessionaires of projects supported partially by the Structural Funds, or as bidders on subsequent public tenders related to such projects, but it is advisable to team up with a local partner. All Structural Fund projects are co-financed by national authorities and most may also qualify for a loan from the European Investment Bank. The private sector is also involved in project financing. For more information on these programs, please see the market research section on the website of the US Mission to the EU: http://www.buyusa.gov/europeanunion/mrr.html

The Cohesion Fund

The Cohesion Fund is another instrument of EU structural policy. Its EUR 61.5 billion (2007-2013) budget seeks to improve cohesion within the EU by funding transport infrastructure and environmental projects in Portugal, Spain, Greece and the twelve new (since 2004) EU Member States from Central and Eastern Europe. These projects are generally co-financed by national authorities, the European Investment Bank, and the private sector.

The Trans-European Networks

The European Union also provides financial support to the Trans-European Networks (TENs) to develop infrastructure, strengthen cohesion and increase employment across greater Europe. Launched at the Essen Counsel (Germany) in 1994, the TENs are a series of transport, telecommunications and energy projects that are continually being expanded and upgraded. The TENs are largely financed by private sector and non-EU sources. The EU does, however, provide grants from the Cohesion Fund, loans from the European Investment Bank (and loan guarantees from the European Investment Fund), and partial feasibility study grants for the TENs. There are no overt EU restrictions on the participation of U.S. firms in the TENs.

Other EU Grants for Member States

Another set of sector-specific grants offers assistance to EU Member States in the fields of science, technology, communications, energy, environmental protection, education, training and research. Tenders related to these grants are posted on the various websites of the directorates-generals of the European Commission. Conditions for participation are strict and participation is usually restricted to EU firms or tied to EU content. Information pertaining to each of these programs can be found on: http://ec.europa.eu/grants/index_en.htm

External Assistance Grants

The EuropeAid Cooperation Office is the European Commission agency in charge of managing the EU's external aid programs. This Agency is responsible for the management of the entire project cycle, from identification to evaluation, while the Directorates-General in charge of External Relations and Development, are responsible for the drafting of multi-annual programs. The EuropeAid website offers extensive information on the range of grant programs, the kind of projects that are eligible, as well as manuals to help interested parties understand the relevant contract law. However, participation to calls for tender for contracts financed by EuropeAid is reserved for enterprises located in the EU Member States and requires that the products used to respond to these projects are manufactured in the EU or in the aid recipient country. But consultants of US nationality employed by a European firm are allowed to form part of a bidding team. European subsidiaries of U.S. firms are eligible to participate in these calls for tender.

All tenders related to EU-funded programs outside the territory of the European Union (including the accession countries) are located on the EuropeAid Cooperation Office website: http://ec.europa.eu/europeaid/work/funding/index_en.htm

• IPA replaces the following programs: PHARE (Poland and Hungary Assistance for Restructuring of the Economy), ISPA (Instrument for Structural Pre-Accession financing transport and environment projects), SAPARD (projects in the agriculture sector), CARDS (aid to southern Balkans) and the Turkey Facility Fund. IPA focuses on priorities linked to the adoption of the *acquis communautaire* (the body of European Union law that must be adopted by accession candidate countries as a precondition to accession), i.e., building up the administrative and institutional capacities and financing investments designed to help them comply with European Commission law. IPA will also finance projects destined to countries that are potential candidate countries, especially in the Balkans. The budget of IPA for 2007-2013 is EUR 11.4 billion.

• ENPI: replaces the former TACIS and MEDA programs. The European Neighborhood Policy program covers the EU's neighbors to the east and along the southern and eastern shores of the Mediterranean i.e. Algeria, Armenia, Azerbaijan, Belarus, Egypt, Georgia, Israel, Jordan, Lebanon, Libya, Moldova, Morocco, the Palestinian Authority, Syria, Tunisia and Ukraine. ENPI budget is €11,9 billion for 2007-2013.

Loans from the European Investment Bank

Headquartered in Luxembourg, the European Investment Bank (EIB) is the financing arm of the European Union. Since its creation in 1958, the EIB has been a key player in building Europe. As the EIB's lending practices evolved over the years, it became highly competent in assessing, reviewing and monitoring projects. As a non-profit banking institution, the EIB offers cost-competitive, long-term lending in Europe. Best known for its project financial and economic analysis, the Bank makes loans to both private and public EU-based borrowers for projects in all sectors of the economy, such as telecommunications, transport, energy infrastructure and environment.

While the EIB mostly funds projects within the EU, it lends outside the EU as well (e.g., in Central, Eastern and Southeastern Europe; Latin America; and Pacific and Caribbean states). In 2007, the EIB approved loans for projects worth EUR 56.4 billion, of which around 16% was lent outside the EU. The EIB also plays a key role in supporting EU enlargement with loans used to finance improvements in infrastructure, research and industrial manufacturing to help those countries prepare for eventual EU membership.

Projects financed by the EIB must contribute to the socioeconomic objectives set out by the European Union, such as fostering the development of less favored regions; improving European transport and telecommunication infrastructure; protecting the environment; supporting the activities of SMEs; assisting urban renewal; and, generally promoting growth, competitiveness and employment in Europe. Last year, the EIB created a list of projects to be considered for approval and posted the list on its website. As such, the EIB website is a source of intelligence on upcoming tenders related to EIB-financed projects: http://www.eib.org/projects/pipeline/index.htm

The EIB presents attractive business opportunities to U.S. businesses. EIB lending rates are lower than most other commercial rates. Like all EIB customers, however, U.S. firms must apply the loan proceeds to a project that contributes to the European objectives cited above.

The EIB's i2i (Innovation 2010 Initiative) is designed to highlight projects that support innovative technology in the European Union, in particular by financing broadband and multimedia networks; the physical or virtual infrastructure providing local access to these networks; and research and development infrastructures, especially in the less developed regions of the European Union. i2i will also finance projects to computerize schools and universities and to provide information technology training in conjunction with public authorities.

The US Mission to the European Union in Brussels has developed a database to help US-based companies bid on EIB public procurement contracts in non-EU countries in particular. The EIB-financed contracts that are open to US-based companies are featured in this database. All the tenders in this database are extracted from the EU's Official Journal. The EIB database contains on average 50 to 100 tenders and is updated twice per week.

WEB RESOURCES

EU WEBSITES:

Future project proposals: http://ec.europa.eu/regional_policy/atlas2007/fiche_index_en.htm .
The EU regional policies, the EU Structural and Cohesion Funds:
http://ec.europa.eu/regional_policy/index_en.htm
The Trans-European Networks (TENs): http://ec.europa.eu/ten/transport/index_en.htm
EU Grants and Loans index: http://ec.europa.eu/grants/index_en.htm
EuropeAid Co-operation Office: http://ec.europa.eu/europeaid/index_en.htm
IPA: http://ec.europa.eu/enlargement/how-does-it-work/financial-assistance/index_en.htm
The European Investment Bank http://www.eib.org/
EIB-financed projects: http://www.eib.org/projects/index.htm?lang=-en .
The EIB's i2i (Innovation 2010 Initiative):
http://www.eib.org/Attachments/thematic/innovation_2010_initiative_en.pdf

U.S. WEBSITES:

CSEU Tender Database:
http://www.buyusa.gov/europeanunion/eu_tenders.html
Market research section on the website of the US Mission to the EU:
http://www.buyusa.gov/europeanunion/mrr.html
European Union Tenders Database: http://www.buyusa.gov/europeanunion/euopportunities.html
Export-Import Bank of the United States: http://www.exim.gov
Country Limitation Schedule: http://www.exim.gov/tools/country/country_limits.html
OPIC: http://www.opic.gov
Trade and Development Agency: http://www.tda.gov/
SBA's Office of International Trade: http://www.sba.gov/oit/
USDA Commodity Credit Corporation: http://www.fsa.usda.gov/ccc/default.htm
U.S. Agency for International Development: http://www.usaid.gov
European Bank for Reconstruction and Development: http://www.ebrd.com/

IMPORTANT CONTACTS FOR BUSINESS AND INVESTMENTS

ITALY – CONTACTS

U.S. Commercial Service Web Site: www.buyusa.it
Commercial Service Contacts in U.S. Embassy Rome
Thomas Moore, Minister Counselor for Commercial Affairs
U.S. Embassy
Via V. Veneto, 119/A, 00187 Rome, Italy
Tel.: +39-06-4674-2202
Fax: +39-06-4674-2315
Rome.Office.Box@mail.doc.gov

Robert Bannerman, Counselor for Commercial Affairs
U.S. Embassy
Via V. Veneto, 119/A, 00187 Rome, Italy
Tel.: +39-06-4674-2820
Fax: +39-06-4674-2113
Rome.Office.Box@mail.doc.gov

Commercial Service Contacts at U.S. Consulates in Italy
Rick de Lambert, Principal Commercial Officer
American Consulate Milan
Via Principe Amedeo 2/10
20121 Milan, Italy
Tel.: +39-02-626-8851
Fax: +39-02-659-6561
Email: Milan.Office.Box@mail.doc.gov

Albina Parente, Economic/Commercial Specialist (Dept. of State)
American Consulate Naples
Piazza della Repubblica
80122 Naples, Italy
Tel.: +39-081-583-8206
Fax: +39-081-761-1592
Email: ParenteA@state.gov

Anya Sarkisov, Commercial Specialist

American Consulate Florence
Lungarno A. Vespucci 38 - 50123 Florence, Italy
Tel: +39 055 292 266 (Direct Line)
Tel: +39 055 266 95 230 (Main Switchboard Extension)
Fax: +39 055 283780
Email: SarkisovA@mail.doc.gov
Embassy Web Site: http://italy.usembassy.it

Contacts for the Foreign Agricultural Service in U.S. Embassy Rome
http://italy.usembassy.gov/agtrade/default.asp
James R. Dever, Minister Counselor for Agricultural Affairs
American Embassy
Via Veneto 119A
00187 Rome, Italy
Tel.: +39-06-4674-2362
Fax: +39-06-4788-7008
Email: agrome@usda.gov

Robin H. Gray, Agricultural Attaché
American Embassy
Via Veneto 119A
00187 Roma, Italy
Tel.: +39-06-4674-2362
Fax: +39-06-4788-7008
Email: agrome@usda.gov
C
ontacts in the Economic Section in U.S. Embassy Rome
George White
Minister Counselor for Economic Affairs
American Embassy
Via Vittorio Veneto 119/A
00187 Rome, Italy
Tel.: +39-06-4674-2107
Fax: +39-06-4674-2398
Email: delaret@state.gov

William Meara, Economic Counselor
Tel: +39-06-4674-2107
Fax: +39-06-4674-2398
Email: mearawr@state.gov

AMERICAN CHAMBER OF COMMERCE IN ITALY

American Chamber of Commerce in Italy
Umberto Paolucci, President
Via Cantù 1
20123 Milano
Tel.: +39-02-869-0661
Fax: +39-02-805-7737
Email: amcham@amcham.it
Web: www.amcham.it

ITALIAN GOVERNMENT AGENCIES

Banca d'Italia (Bank of Italy)

Credit Institutions Supervision Service
Via Nazionale 91
00184 Roma
Tel.: +39-06-47921
Web: www.bancaditalia.it

CONSOB-Commissione Nazionale per le Società e la Borsa
(Securities Regulatory Agency)
Via G.B. Martini 3
00198 Roma
Tel.: +39-06-847-71
Fax: +39-06-841-7707
Email: consob@consob.it
Web: www.consob.it

The Italian Embassy
Commercial Section
3000 Whitehaven St. N.W.
Washington, DC 20008
Tel.: (202) 612-4400
Fax: (202) 518-2154
Web: www.ambwashingtondc.esteri.it

Ente Nazionale Italiano per il Turismo (ENIT)
Italian Government Tourist Board
630 Fifth Avenue, Suite 1565
New York, NY 10111
Tel.: (212) 245-5618
Fax: (212) 586-9249
Email: enitny@ italiantourism.com
Web: www.italiantourism.com

The Italian Trade Commission
(Assists in locating Italian suppliers and products.)
Offices are located in the following cities:
ITC Atlanta
2301, Peachtree Center - Harris Tower
233, Peachtree Street N.E.
P.O.Box 56689
Atlanta Georgia 30343
Tel.: (404) 525-0660
Fax: (404) 525 -5112
Email: atlanta@ice.it
Web: http://www.italtrade.com

ITC Chicago
401, North Michigan Avenue
Suite 3030
Chicago, Illinois 60611
Tel.: (312) 670-4360
Fax: (312) 670-5147
Email: chicago@ice.it
Web: www.italtrade.com

ITC Los Angeles
1801 Avenue of the Stars
Suite 700
Los Angeles, CA 90067
Tel.: (323) 879-0950
Fax: (310) 203-8335
Email: losangeles@losangeles.ice.it
Web: www.italtrade.com

ITC Miami
4000 Ponce de Leon
Suite 590
Coral Gables, FL 33146
Miami
Tel.: (305) 461-3896
Fax.: (305) 374-7945
Email: miami@ice.it
Web: www.italtrade.com

ITC New York
33 East 67th Street
New York, NY 10021-5949
Tel.: (212) 980-1500
Fax: (212) 758-1050
Email: newyork@ice.it
Web: www.italtrade.com

Istituto Nazionale per il Commercio Estero (ICE)
Italian Trade Commission
Viale Liszt 21
00144 Roma
Tel.: +39-06-5992-1
Fax: +39-06-5929-9743
Email: ice@ice.it
Web: www.ice.gov.it

ITALIAN TRADE ASSOCIATIONS

GENERAL/INDUSTRIAL:
ABI - Associazione Bancaria Italiana
(Italian Banking Association)
Piazza del Gesú 49 (Palazzo Altieri)
00186 Roma
Tel.: +39-06-67671
Fax: +39-06-6767-457
Email: abi@abi.it
Web: www.abi.it

AIAD – Associazione Industrie per l'Aerospazio, i Sistemi e la Difesa
(Italian Association of Aerospace and Defense Industries)
Via Nazionale 54
00184 Roma
Tel: +39-06-488-0247
Fax: +39-06-482-7476

Email: aiad@aiad.it
Web: www.aiad.it

AIDDA - Associazione Imprenditrici e Donne Dirigenti d'Azienda
(Italian Association of Women Entrepreneurs and Business Executives)
Via degli Scialoja 18
00196 Roma
Tel.: +39-06-3230-578
Fax: +39-06-3230-562
Email: aidda@aidda.org
Web: www.aidda.org

ANCE - Associazione Nazionale Costruttori Edili (Italian Association of Building Contractors)
Via Guattani, 16 - 00161 Roma –
Tel.: +39-06-845-671
Fax. +39-06-8456-7550
Email: info@ance.it
Web: www.ance.it
ANFIA - Associazione Nazionale fra Industrie Automobilistiche
(Italian Automotive Industry Association)
Corso Galileo Ferraris 61
10128 Torino
Tel.: +39-011-554-6511
Fax: +39-011-545-986
Email: anfia@anfia.it
Web: www.anfia.it

ANIA - Associazione Nazionale fra le Imprese Assicuratrici
(Italian Association of Insurance Companies)
Via della Frezza 70
00186 Roma
Tel.: +39-06-326-881
Fax: +39-06-322-7135
Email: info@ania.it
Web: www.ania.it

ANIE – Associazione Nazionale Imprese Elettroniche ed Elettriche
(Italian Association of Electrical and Electronic Industries)
Via Gattamelata 34
20149 Milano
Tel: +39-02-326-41
Fax: +39-02-326-4212
Email: info@anie.it
Web: www.anie.it

ASSINFORM – Associazione Nazionale Produttori Tecnologie e Servizi per l'Informazione e la Comunicazione
(Italian Association of Office Machine Industries)
Via G. Sacchi, 7
20121 Milano
Tel: +39-02-0063-28-1
Fax: +39-02-0063-28-24
Email: segreteria@assinform.it
Web: www.assinform.it

ASSOFRANCHISING – Associazione Italiana del Franchising
(Italian Franchising Association)
Via Melchiorre Gioia, 70
20125 Milano
Tel.: +39-02-2900-3779
Fax. +39-02-655-5919
Email: assofranchising@assofranchising.it Web: www.assofranchising.it

CONFAGRICOLTURA - Confederazione Generale dell'Agricoltura Italiana
(General Confederation of Italian Agriculture)
Corso Vittorio Emanuele II, 101
00186 Roma
Tel.: +39-06-685-21
Fax: +39-06-686-1726
Email: info@confagricoltura.it
Web: www.confagricoltura.it

CONFAPI - Confederazione Italiana della Piccola e Media Industria
(Italian Confederation of Small and Medium Industries)
Via della Colonna Antonina 52
00186 Roma
Tel.: +39-06-690-151
Fax: +39-06-679-1488
Email: mail@confapi.org
Web: www.confapi.org

CONFARTIGIANATO - Confederazione Generale Italiana dell'Artigianato
(Italian General Confederation of Craft)
Via San Giovanni in Laterano 152
00184 Roma
Tel.: +39-06-703-741
Fax: +39-06-7045-2188
Email: confartigianato@confartigianato.it
Web: www.confartigianato.it

CONFCOMMERCIO - Confederazione Generale Italiana del Commercio, del Turismo, dei Servizi e delle P.M.I.
(Italian General Confederation of Trade, Tourism, Services, and Small and Medium Enterprises)
Piazza G.G. Belli 2
00153 Roma
Tel.: +39-06-586-61
Fax: +39-06-580-9425
Email: confcommercio@confcommercio.it
Web: www.confcommercio.it

CONFETRA – Confederazione Generale del Traffico e dei Trasporti
(Italian General Confederation of Transport Enterprises)
Via Panama 62
00198 Roma
Tel: +39-06-855-9151
Fax: +39-06-841-5576
Email: confetra@confetra.com
Web: www.confetra.com

CONFINDUSTRIA - Confederazione Generale dell'Industria Italiana
(The Confederation of Italian Industry is a principal trade association in Italy acting as an umbrella organization covering numerous industry trade associations)
Giampaolo Galli, General Director
Viale dell'Astronomia 30
00144 Roma
Tel.: +39-06-59-031
Fax: +39-06-59-19615
Email: confindustria@confindustria.it
Web: www.confindustria.it

FARMAINDUSTRIA – Associazione Nazionale dell'Industria Farmaceutica
(Italian National Association of Pharmaceutical Industries)
Largo del Nazareno 3/8
00187 Roma
Tel: +39-06-675-801
Fax: +39-06-678-6494
Web: www.farmindustria.it

FEDERACCIAI – Federazione Imprese Siderurgiche Italiane
(Italian Federation of Steel Industries)
Viale Sarca 336
20126 Milano
Tel: +39-02-661-461
Fax: +39-02-661-46219
Email: direzione@federacciai.it
Web: www.federacciai.it

FEDERAZIONE GOMMA PLASTICA – Unione Nazionale Industrie Trasfomatori Materie Plastiche
(Italian Union of Plastic Industries)
Via San Vittore 36
20123 Milano
Tel: +39-02-439-281
Fax: +39-02-435-432
Email: info@federazionegommaplastica.it
Web: www.federazionegommaplastica.it/

FEDERCHIMICA – Federazione Nazionale dell'Industria Chimica
(Italian Federation of Chemical Industries)
Via Giovanni da Procida 11
20149 Milano
Tel: +39-02-345-651
Fax: +39-02-345-65310
Email: federchimica@federchimica.it
Web: www.federchimica.it

FEDERLEGNO – Federazione Italiana delle Industrie del Legno, del Sughero, del Mobile e dell'Arredamento
(Italian Federation of Wood Product Industries)
Foro Bonaparte 65
20121 Milano
Tel: +39-02-806041
Fax: +39-02-80604392

E-mail: fla@federlegno.it
Web: www.federlegnoarredo.it

UCINA - Unione Nazionale Cantieri e Industrie Nautiche ed Affini (Italian National Union of Shipyards, Nautical Industries and Related Sectors)
Piazzale J. F. Kennedy 1
16129 Genova
Tel.: +39-010-576-9811
Fax: +39-010-553-1104
Email: ucina@ucina.it
Web: www.ucina.net

UNIONCAMERE - Unione Italiana delle Camere di Commercio Industria Agricoltura e Artigianato (Italian Union of the Chambers of Commerce, Industry, Handicraft and Agriculture)
(Umbrella organization responsible for all chambers of commerce in Italy)
Piazza Sallustio 21
00187 Roma
Tel.: +39-06-470-41
Fax: +39-06-489-070-4240
Email: segreteria.generale@unioncamere.it
Web: www.unioncamere.it

AGRICULTURAL:
FEDECOMLEGNO (Wood Trade Federation)
Via Toscana 10
00187 Roma
Tel.: +39-06-4200-681
Fax: +39-06-4281-7391
Email: fedecomlegno@federlegno.it
Web: www.federlegnoarredo.it

FEDERAGROALIMENTARE
La Federazione Nazionale delle Cooperative Agricole ed Agroalimentari
Via Torino, 146
00184 Roma
Tel.: +39-06-4697-81
Fax: +39-06-4881-469
Email: fedagri@confcooperative.it
Web: www.fedagri.confcooperative.it

ITALIAN MARKET RESEARCH FIRMS:

ACNielsen Italia S.p.a.
Via Giuseppe di Vittorio 10
20094 Corsico (MI)
Tel.: +39-02-451-971
Fax: +39-02-458-66235
Web: www.acnielsen.it

C.R.A. (Customized Research & Analysis)
Via Montecuccoli 32
20147 Milano
Tel. +39-02-414-921
Fax. +39-02-412-71623

Email: info@cra-research.com
Web: www.cra-research.com

Databank S.p.A.
Corso Italia 8
20122 Milano
Tel.: +39-02-809-556
Fax: +39-02-7210-7333
Email: databank@cerved.com
Web: www.databank.it

Demoskopea S.p.a
Via Porlezza 16
20123 Milano
Tel.: +39-02-721-451
Fax.: +39-02-8909-6128
Email: info@demoskopea.it
Web: www.demoskopea.it

Inter@ctive Market Research
Via Scarlatti 150
80127 Napoli
Tel. +39-081-229-2473
Fax. +39-081-229-2463
Email: info@interactive-mr.com
Web: www.imrgroup.com

M&T Marketing & Trade S.r.l.
Corso di Porta Ticinese 60
20123 Milano
Tel. +39-02-894-02219
Fax. +39-02-581-01117
Email: segreteria@marketingtrade.it
Web: www.marketingtrade.it

Pragma S.r.l.
Via Nizza 152-154
00198 Roma
Tel: +39-06-844-881
Fax: +39-06-844-88298
Email: pragma@pragma-research.it
Web: www.pragma-research.it

ITALIAN COMMERCIAL BANKS:

Intesa Sanpaolo S.p.A.
(Merger between Sanpaolo IMI S.p.A. and Banca Intesa in January 2007)
Piazza San Carlo, 156
10121 Torino
Tel.: +39-011-555-1
www.intesasanpaolo.com

Unicredit Group S.p.A.
(Established in May 2007 with merger of Unicredito Italiano S.p.A. and Capitalia S.p.A.

Capitalia S.p.A. was established in 2002 with merger of Banca di Roma, Bibop-Carire and Banco di Sicilia)
Piazza Cordusio
20121 Milano
Tel.: +39-02-886-211
www.unicreditgroup.eu
www.unicredit-capitalia.eu

Banca Nazionale del Lavoro BNL S.p.A.
(Incorporated in BNP Paribas in 2006)
Via Vittorio Veneto 119
00187 Roma
Tel.: +39-06-470-21
www.bnl.it

Banca Monte dei Paschi di Siena S.p.A.
Piazza Salimbeni 3
53100 Siena
Tel.: +39-0577-294-111
www.mps.it

WASHINGTON-BASED U.S. GOVERNMENT CONTACTS FOR ITALY

U.S. Department of Commerce
Trade Information Center
Tel.: 1-800-USA-TRADE
http://www.export.gov/
E-mail inquiries: tic@ita.doc.gov (including requests for country duty and tax information)

U.S. Department of Commerce
Market Access & Compliance Office
Robert McLaughlin
Italy Desk Officer
Room H-3042
14th Street and Constitution Ave, NW
Washington, DC 20230
Tel.: (202) 482-3748
Fax: (202) 482-2897
Email: Robert_McLaughlin@ita.doc.gov
Web: www.mac.doc.gov

U.S. Department of Agriculture
Foreign Agricultural Service
1400 Independence Ave. S.W.
Washington, DC 20250
Trade assistance and promotion office:
Tel.: (202) 720-7420
Web: www.usda.gov

Overseas Private Investment Corporation
1100 New York Avenue, NW
Washington, DC 20527
Tel.: (202) 336-8400

Fax: (202) 408-9859
Email: info@opic.gov
Web: www.opic.gov

U.S. - BASED MULTIPLIERS RELEVANT FOR ITALY

National Italian American Foundation (NIAF)
(NIAF conducts cultural and educational events, sponsors exchange programs, works to enhance cultural, political, and economic relations between the United States and Italy and serves as an advocacy group)
1860 19th Street, NW
Washington, DC 20009
Tel.: (202) 387-0600
Fax: (202) 387-0800
Web: www.niaf.org

Delegation of the European Commission to the United States
2300 M Street, NW
3rd Floor
Washington, DC 20037
Tel.: (202) 862-9500
Fax: (202) 429-1766
Web: www.eurunion.org

AGRICULTURAL CONTACTS BY INDUSTRY

For the U.S.-based multipliers listed below when dialing from Italy, the country code **001** is to be dialed before dialing the listed phone number. Also, the European Based Multipliers whose listed offices are listed below must be reached by dialing **011** before the telephone numbers as needed.

Ag Export Councils
National Association of State Departments of Agriculture (NASDA)
Stephen Haterius, Executive Director
Dewit Ashby, Director, Trade Shows
1156 15th Street, N.W.
Suite 1020
Washington, DC 20005-1704
Tel.: (202) 296-9680
Fax: (202) 296-9686
Email: dewitt@nasda.org
Web: www.nasda.org

Forest and Fishery Products
American Hardwood Export Council
1111 19th Street, N.W., Suite 800
Washington, DC 20036
Michael Snow, Executive Director
Tel.: (202) 463-2720
Fax: (202) 463-2787
Email: michael_snow@afandpa.org
Web: www.ahec.org

Softwood Export Council
PO Box 80517 Portland, Oregon 97280 6980 SW Varns Street, Tigard
Oregon 97223

Craig Larsen, President
Tel.: (503) 620-5946
Fax: (503) 684-8928
Email: clarsen@softwood.org
Web: www.softwood.org

Grain and Feed
The Pet Food Institute
2025 M Street, N.W.
Suite 800
Washington, DC 20036
Carol Jewel, Administrator
Tel.: (202) 367-1120
Fax: (202) 367-2120
Email: info@petfoodinstitute.org
Web: www.petfoodinstitute.org

Horticultural and Tropical Products
California Ag Export Council
915 L Street, #C 409
Sacramento, CA 95814
Frederick W. Klose, Executive Director
Tel.: (916) 863-0311
Fax: (916) 863-0304
Fred Klose, Manager
Email: info@caec.net
Web: www.caec.net

Organic Trade Association
60 Wells Street
Greenfield, MA 01301
Christine Bushway, Executive Director
Tel.: (413) 774-7511
Fax: (413) 774-6432
Email: info@ota.com
Web: www.ota.com

EU – CONTACTS

United States Department of Commerce - Contacts at the U.S. Mission to the EU:
Minister Counselor for Commercial Affairs
Beryl Blecher 32.2.508.27.47 beryl.blecher@mail.doc.gov
Deputy Senior Commercial Officer
Val Huston 32.2.508.27.55 val.huston@mail.doc.gov
Standards Attaché
Louis Santamaria 32.2.508.26.74 louis.santamaria@mail.doc.gov
Market Access and Trade Compliance Attaché
Ashley Miller 32.2.508.27.69 ashley.miller@mail.doc.gov
Commercial Attaché

John Fay 32.2.508.28.40 john.fay@mail.doc.gov
NOAA Fisheries Representative
Stephane Vrignaud 32.2.508.28.42 stephane.vrignaud@mail.doc.gov
U.S. Commercial Service

U.S. Mission to the European Union
Rue Zinner 13
B-1000 Brussels, Belgium
Tel.: 32.2.508.27.46
Fax: 32.2.513.12.28
E-mail: brussels.ec.office.box@mail.doc.gov
Website: http://www.buyusa.gov/europeanunion

United States Department of Agriculture - Contacts at the U.S. Mission to the EU:
Office of Agricultural Affairs
U.S. Mission to the European Union
Rue Zinner 13
B-1000 Brussels, Belgium
Tel.: 32.2.508.27.60
Fax: 32.2.511.09.18
E-mail: AgUSEUBrussels@fas.usda.gov
Website: http://www.fas.usda.gov/posthome/useu/

The European Commission:
European Commission
Rue de la Loi 200 / Wetstraat 200
B-1049 Brussels, Belgium
Tel: 32.2.299.11.11 (switchboard)
Fax: 32.2.295.01.38 (also 295.01.39 and 295.01.40)
Websites: http://ec.europa.eu/index_en.htm (European Commission)
http://ec.europa.eu/comm/external_relations/us/intro/index.htm (EU-U.S. relations)

For general information about the European Union:
Delegation of the European Commission to the United States
2300 M Street, N.W.
Washington, D.C. 20037
Tel: (202) 862-9500
Fax: (202) 429-1766
Website: http://www.eurunion.org/

EFTA – European Free Trade Association
Rue Joseph II, 12-16
B – 1000 Brussels
Tel: 32.2.286.17.11
Fax: 32.2.286.17.50
Website: http://www.efta.int/

For Information on Customs-related Matters within the European Union:
Mr. Robert Verrue, Director General
Directorate General Taxation and Customs Union
Rue de la Loi 200
B-1049 Brussels
Tel: 32.2.295.43.76
Fax: 32.2.296.90.46
Website: http://ec.europa.eu/taxation_customs/customs/index_en.htm

National Centers for Standards and Certification Information (NCSCI)
National Institute of Standards & Technology
100 Bureau Dr.

Mail Stop 2100
Gaithersburg, Maryland 20899
Tel: (301) 975-2573
Website: http://ts.nist.gov/Standards/Global/about.cfm

CEN – European Committee for Standardization
Avenue Marnix 17
B – 1000 Brussels, Belgium
Tel: 32.2.550.08.11
Fax: 32.2.550.08.19
Website: http://www.cen.eu/

CENELEC – European Committee for Electrotechnical Standardization
Avenue Marnix 17
B – 1000 Brussels, Belgium
Tel: 32.2.519.68.71
Fax: 32.2.519.69.19
Website: http://www.cenelec.eu/

ETSI - European Telecommunications Standards Institute
Route des Lucioles 650
F – 06921 Sophia Antipolis Cedex, France
Tel: 33.4.92.94.42.00
Fax: 33.4.93.65.47.16
Website: http://www.etsi.org/
European Commission -Directorate - General Enterprise and Industry
Avenue d'Auderghem 45/Rue Belliard 100
B – 1049 Brussels, Belgium
Tel: 32.2.299.56.72
Fax: 32.2.299.16.75
Website: http://ec.europa.eu/enterprise/standards_policy/index_en.htm

NORMAPME – European Office of Crafts Trades and Small and Medium-Sized Enterprises for Standardization
Rue Jacques de Lalaing 4
B – 1040 Brussels, Belgium
Tel: 32.2.282.05.30
Fax: 32.2.282.05.35
Website: http://www.normapme.com/

ANEC - European Association for the Co-ordination of Consumer Representation in Standardization
Avenue de Tervueren 32, Box 27
B – 1040 Brussels, Belgium
Tel: 32.2.743.24.70
Fax: 32.2.706.54.30
Website: http://www.anec.org

ECOS – European Environmental Citizens Organization for Standardization
rue d'Edimbourg 26
B – 1050 Brussels, Belgium
Tel: 32.2.894 46 55
Fax: 32.2.894 46 10
Website: http://www.ecostandard.org/

EOTA – European Organization for Technical Approvals (for construction products)
Avenue des Arts 40
B – 1040 Brussels, Belgium
Tel: 32.2.502.69.00
Fax: 32.2.502.38.14
Website: http://www.eota.be/

PRIVATE SECTOR ASSOCIATIONS:

AmchamEU
53 Avenue des Arts
B-1000 Brussels, Belgium
Tel: 32.2.513.68.92
Fax: 32.2.513.79.28
Website: http://www.amchameu.eu/

Business Europe
The Confederation of European Business
Avenue de Cortenbergh 168
1000 Brussels
Tel: 32.2.237.65.11
Fax: 32.2.231.14.45
Website: www.businesseurope.eu

European-American Business Council – EU Office
Rue de l'Industrie 26
B-1040 Brussels, Belgium
Tel: 32.2.513.38.72
Website: http://www.eabc.org/

European-American Business Council – US Office
919 18th Street, NW #220
Washington, DC 20006
Tel: (202) 828-9104
Fax: (202) 828-9106
Website: http://www.eabc.org/

The European Institute
1001 Connecticut Avenue, N.W., Suite 220,
Washington DC, 20036-5531
Tel: (202) 895-1670
Website: http://www.europeaninstitute.org/

Centre for European Policy Studies (CEPS)
1 Place du Congres
B-1000 Brussels, Belgium
Tel: 32.2.229.39.11
Fax: 32.2.219.41.51
Website: http://www.ceps.eu/index.php

The European Policy Centre
Residence Palace
155 Rue de la Loi

1040 Brussels, Belgium
Tel: 32.2.231.03.40
Fax: 32.2.231.07.04
Website: http://www.epc.eu

European Round Table of Industrialists (ERT)
Place des Carabiniers 18a
B-1030 Brussels
Tel: 32 2 534 31 00
Fax: 32 2 534 73 48
Website: http://www.ert.be/

The Transatlantic Policy Network
Rue Froissart 115, 1st floor
B-1040 Brussels, Belgium
Tel: 32.2.230.61.49
Fax: 32.2.230.58.96
Website: http://www.tpnonline.org/

TransAtlantic Business Dialogue – TABD EU Office
Residence Palace
115 Rue de la Loi, 4th floor
B-1040 Brussels, Belgium
Tel: 32.2. 238.52.40
Fax: 32.2.238.52.42
Website: http://www.tabd.com/

TransAtlantic Business Dialogue – TABD US Office
TABD c/o CSIS
1800 K Street, NW, Suite 400
Washington, DC 20006
Tel: (202) 775 32 51
Fax: (202) 775 31 99
Website: http://www.tabd.com/

The Trans European Policy Studies Association (TEPSA)
11 Rue d'Egmont
B-1000 Brussels, Belgium
Tel: 32.2.511.34.70
Fax: 32.2.511.67.70
Website: http://www.tepsa.be/

KEY EU-RELATED WEBSITES:

For general information on the European Union
The EU's portal website
http://www.europa.eu

Resource for EU news, policy positions and actors
http://www.euractiv.com/

A to Z index of European Union websites
http://www.eurunion.org/infores/euindex.htm

For information on topics related to doing business in the European Union
EU's "One Stop Internet Shop for Business" (EU funds, technical standards, intellectual property law, and free access to public procurement tender notices via the Tenders Electronic Daily (TED) database).
http://ec.europa.eu/youreurope/business/index_en.htm

EU Member State Chambers of Commerce in the U.S.
http://www.eurunion.org/eu/index.php?option=com_content&task=view&id=2345&Itemid=9

EU market access database (information on tariffs and other trade information)
http://madb.europa.eu/

EURLEX – Access to EU law
http://eur-lex.europa.eu/en/index.htm

CORDIS – Community Research and Development Information Service (EU research and innovation website)
http://cordis.europa.eu/

European Commission Statistical Office (Eurostat)
http://epp.eurostat.ec.europa.eu/

EU Office of Official Publications
http://publications.europa.eu/

EU official website on the euro
http://ec.europa.eu/euro/index_en.html

European Central Bank, Frankfurt
http://www.ecb.int/

European Investment Bank, Luxembourg
http://www.eib.org/

Council of the European Union
http://www.consilium.europa.eu/

European Parliament
http://www.europarl.europa.eu/

European Court of Justice
http://curia.europa.eu/

EU Who is Who – The Official Directory of the European Union
http://europa.eu/whoiswho/public/

CONDUCTING BUSINESS IN ITALY[3]

STRUCTURE OF BUSINESS INVESTMENTS

1. SUMMARY OF TYPES OF BUSINESS ENTITIES UNDER ITALIAN LAW

A. 'Societa` in nome collettivo' (Unlimited Partnership)

This type of business entity is a partnership whose partners have unlimited liability for all the acts and transactions entered into by the partnership. All or any of the partners may be appointed as directors of the partnership. Italian law generally restricts the transfer of a partner's interest in the partnership.

B.'Societa` in accomandita semplice' (Limited Partnership)

This entity has a combination of limited and unlimited liability. There are two categories of partners: general partners who have unlimited liability, and special partners who are liable only to the extent of their capital contributions to the partnership. Only general partners may be appointed as directors of the partnership.

C. 'Societa` in accomandita per azioni' (Partnership Limited by Shares)

The structure and characteristics of this type of business entity are similar to a limited partnership, except that:

the capital contribution of the partners is represented by shares; and generally, the law relating to limited liability companies will apply.

D. 'Societa` a responsabilita` limitata' (Limited Liability Company)

This type of business entity (usually indicated as "S.r.l.") is equivalent to a private limited company in which the capital participation of the members is represented by quotas instead of shares. Shares are physically represented by certificates but quotas are only registered in the quotaholders book maintained by the company. The company's articles of association may restrict the transfer of quotas. The minimum capital requirement is Lire 20,000,000.

E. 'Societa` per azioni' (Public Corporation)

This type of company is the equivalent of a public limited company (usually indicated as "S.p.A."). There is a minimum capital requirement of Lire 200,000,000. The interests of shareholders in the share capital of an S.p.A. are represented by shares. An S.p.A. can issue different classes of shares with different rights attached to each class. For example, not all classes of shares issued to the shareholder give the right to vote at company meetings. Limitations apply under Italian law to the issuance of shares with limited voting rights. All shares must be issued for a minimum of par value and must be in nominative form. However saving shares (see next page), if fully paid-up, may be issued to the bearer. The following is a brief description of the various classes of shares issued by an S.p.A.

---

[3] *This materials, provided by the Italian Embassy in Washington, was prepared with the assistence of the Arthur Anderson Worldwide Organization.*

a.Ordinary Shares:
Ordinary shares confer on their holders all rights in the company, subject to any rights preserved to other classes of shares.

b.Preferred Shares:
The holder has a right of priority in the distribution of the company's net profits and net assets upon liquidation. Limited voting rights may be established in the company's articles of association.

c.Employee Shares:
Shares may be issued by an S.p.A. to distribute profits to employees. The articles of association of an S.p.A. may establish specific rules governing the form and the transferability of the shares and the rights of the shareholders.

d.Redeemed Shares:
Shares may be issued for redeemed ordinary shares. The issued shares usually do not give the holder the right to vote at shareholders' meetings. These shares confer a right to a dividend only after other shareholders have obtained a dividend equivalent to at least the legal interest rate. Upon liquidation, shareholders participate in the distribution of the assets remaining after other shareholders are reimbursed for the nominal value of their shares.

e.Saving Shares:
Shares may be issued only by S.p.A.'s listed on a stock exchange in the event of an increase in capital or in the event of the redemption of ordinary or other shares. These shares may be listed on a stock exchange. Saving shares do not give the holder the right to attend and vote at the ordinary shareholders' meetings. Furthermore, the law provides for special rules concerning the method of subscription and the distribution of a company's profits and assets upon liquidation.

Only S.p.A. and S.r.l. entities confer limited liability on all their members, subject to certain conditions. They are the most common business organizations used by investors to conduct business in Italy. A subsidiary of a non-Italian parent company may be set up as either an S.p.A. or an S.r.l. Below is further information on the incorporation, management, acquisition and mergers of S.p.A. and S.r.1. entities.

1.2 Incorporation of a joint stock company (S.p.A. or S.r.l.)

The S.p.A. is the legal entity preferred by large enterprises. Most of the regulations which apply to S.p.A.'s also apply to S.r.l.'s.

Government authorization is normally not required for the establishment of an S.p.A. except in specific cases. For example, the incorporation of a bank requires prior authorization by the Bank of Italy.

Incorporation occurs by a 'public deed' which is drafted by a notary public. The promoters can be either individuals or corporations. They may appear personally or by proxy to execute the deed of incorporation, approve the company's memorandum and articles of association and appoint the company director(s).

At incorporation there must be at least two shareholders. After incorporation, all shares may be held by a single shareholder. In the event of insolvency, a single shareholder will have unlimited liability for all acts and transactions undertaken by the company during his period of ownership. Through Legislative Decree 88, enacted March 3, 1993, the Government adopted EC Directive

89/667. The Directive provides for the recognition of limited liability companies (S.r.l.) with only one shareholder under the company law system of the E.U. Member States. Formerly, Italian limited liability companies (S.r.l.) could only be incorporated with at least two shareholders.

Prior to incorporation the minimum capital requirement (Lire 200,000,000 for an S.p.A. and Lire 20,000,000 for an S.r.l.) must be fully subscribed and at least 3/10ths of the subscribed capital must be deposited with an authorized commercial bank in Italy. This deposit will be repaid to the company after registration. The company becomes a creditor of the original subscribers for the unpaid balance of any capital subscribed. The request for payment of the balance is left to the discretion of the company's director(s).

The deed of incorporation may provide for capital contributions to be made in cash or for consideration other than cash. For noncash capital contributions, the subscribed shares must be fully paid-up and specific procedural rules followed.

Once executed, the deed of incorporation, along with the memorandum and articles of association, must be filed with the District Court where the legal seat of the company is located. The Court, after verifying compliance with legal procedural requirements, issues a decree ordering the registration of the company in the company register. The company must then also register with the local Chamber of Commerce.

The above discussion summarizes the main steps for incorporating an S.p.A. After incorporation, the company may begin to trade.

1.3 Structure and organization of an S.p.A.

1.3.1 Shareholders' meetings and shareholders' rights

a.Shareholders' meetings are called by the directors through a written notice specifying the date and time of the meeting and the agenda. The notice may indicate an alternate date in the event that a quorum is not reached on the date of the originally scheduled meeting. An S.p.A. must publish this notice in the Official Gazette of the Italian Republic at least 15 days before the meeting date. A valid shareholders' meeting may be held in the absence of these formalities if all the shareholders, all the directors and all the statutory auditors are in attendance. The meeting agenda must clearly specify the matters to be discussed to ensure that the shareholders receive adequate information.

b.The Italian Civil Code requires that ordinary meetings be held at least annually, within four months of the end of the Company's financial year. The articles of association may provide that, in certain circumstances, the four-month period may be extended to six months.

c.Ordinary meetings are required for:

approval of the company's balance sheet;

appointment of directors, statutory auditors and the chairman of the board of statutory auditors;

determination of the remuneration of directors and the statutory auditors, unless already provided for in the articles of association;

other matters regarding the management of the company which are reserved to the ordinary meeting by the articles of association or submitted to the meeting by the directors;

the liability of directors and auditors for loss and damage caused to the company.

d.Ordinary meetings must include shareholders representing at least one half of the company's share capital. Resolutions are passed by an absolute majority unless a higher majority is required in the articles of association. If a quorum is not reached, a second meeting may be held on another date. No quorum is required for the second scheduled ordinary meetings.

e.Extraordinary meetings are required for amendments to the memorandum and articles of association, the issuance of bonds, the liquidation of the company and the appointment and powers granted to the liquidators.

f.As a general rule, extraordinary meetings adopt resolutions by the votes of shareholders representing more than one half of the company's share capital. In the event of a second meeting, votes of shareholders representing more than one third of the company's share capital are sufficient. However, the law provides that in a second meeting, resolutions concerning amendments of the company's objectives, the re-organization of the company, its dissolution, the transfer abroad of the company's legal seat and the issuance of preferred shares, may only be adopted with the votes of shareholders representing more than one half of the company's share capital.

Corporations listed on a stock exchange may have a third meeting at which resolutions may be passed with the votes of shareholders representing more than one fifth of the company's share capital. The articles of association of a company may provide for a different quorum for the passing of resolutions.

g.Shareholders have the right to attend and vote at shareholders' meetings. Voting rights may also be exercised by proxy. The proxy must be in writing and granted for a specific meeting. An individual shareholder who has a specific conflict of interest with the company must abstain from voting. Failure of an affected shareholder to abstain would allow the adopted resolution to be challenged if it causes damage or loss to the company or if the quorum would not have been reached without the vote of that shareholder. Voting arrangements are often entered into by shareholders providing for voting agreements. A breach of such arrangements may give rise to a claim for damages. Shareholders who dissent or who do not attend the shareholders' meeting may challenge in court the validity of any resolution adopted on the grounds of a breach of law or of the company's articles of association.

h.Any shareholder who uncovers illegal or unauthorized acts by the management of the company may report them to the statutory auditors. If the shareholder filing the complaint represents at least 5% of the company's share capital, the statutory auditors must investigate without delay and address the shareholders' meeting. If the statutory auditors believe the allegation is well-founded and a shareholders' meeting is not already scheduled, the statutory auditors must call a meeting.

i.Shareholders representing 10% of the company's share capital can file complaints with a court against the directors and statutory auditors for breach of duties.

j.Shareholders have the right to examine the company books which contain information on the shares of the company, the names of the shareholders, transfers, charges, and minutes of the shareholders' meetings.

k.Draft company financial statements, as well as the draft reports of the directors and the statutory auditors, must be prepared according to regulations and deposited at the company's legal seat 15 days before the date of the shareholders' meeting to approve such documents. The shareholders' must be free to examine these documents.

1.3.2 Management of the company

a.An S.p.A. can be managed by a board of directors or by a sole director. If the company is managed by a board of directors, but the articles of association specify only a minimum and maximum number of board members, the exact number of members may be determined at a shareholders' meeting. Directors need not be Italian citizens or residents.

b.The articles of association of a company determine the powers of the sole director and the board of directors. The board may delegate, within legal limits and within the company's articles, some of its powers to an executive committee composed of board members, or to one or more managing directors. The day to day management of the company may be delegated by the board or by the sole director to general managers, managers, and other executives.

c.Directors have the power to represent the company and perform all acts delegated to them by the company. The power of representation granted to directors may be limited by the articles of association or by a resolution of a shareholders' meeting. However, these limitations cannot be used against third parties acting in good faith unless it is proven that they participated in a breach of duty by a director.

d.Meetings of the board are generally called by the chairman. Unless the articles require a special quorum, a quorum is achieved by the presence of a majority of directors. The law provides that resolutions are adopted by an absolute majority, but the articles of association may establish special majorities. Voting by proxy, absentee ballots and alternate directors is not permitted under Italian law.

e.Directors have a general fiduciary duty to the company. They cannot become partners with unlimited liability in competing companies for their own account, or for the accounts of third parties which may be in competition with the company's activities, without specific authorization at a shareholders' meeting. In the case of a breach of this duty, directors may be removed from office and may be liable for damages caused to the company.

f.A director who has a conflict of interest with the company with respect to a specific transaction must notify the other directors and the board of statutory auditors and must abstain from taking part in the decision concerning the transaction.

g.Directors may be liable to the company, the company's creditors, shareholders and third parties for breach of their duties. However, liability does not extend to a director who, without being negligent, has declared his dissent with any board decision in the minutes book of the directors meetings and has given written notice of his dissent to the chairman of the board of auditors.

h.Upon liquidation, an action for breach of duty may be brought against the directors by the liquidator.

1.3.3 Statutory Auditors

a.An S.p.A. must have a board of statutory auditors. The board is a committee of individuals (usually professionals) who are responsible for overseeing the management of the company. In an S.r.l. a board of statutory auditors is required if the share capital is Lire 200,000,000. If the capital is below Lire 200,000,000, statutory auditors may still be required when specific conditions concerning employees, assets and revenues are met.

b.The main functions of the board of statutory auditors are to supervise the management of the company, to ensure compliance with the law, to ensure compliance with the memorandum and articles of association and to verify company accounts. The board of statutory auditors does not audit the company. Company financial audits are performed by independent accounting firms.

c.The auditors board has the right to request information from directors with regard to the company's general business or specific transactions. The board may also, at any time, inspect the company's accounts. Statutory auditors are required to inspect the company's accounts quarterly and report on the company's financial statement at the shareholders' meeting.

2. REPRESENTATIVE OFFICE AND BRANCH

There are two types of business organizations used by foreign companies to conduct business in Italy. These are the representative office (Ufficio di Rappresentanza) and the branch (Sede Secondaria). Neither the representative office nor the branch are separate legal entities.

2.1 Representative office

The simplest business structure available to a foreign company is the 'representative office.' It is often used by foreign companies to research the market before deciding to establish a branch or a subsidiary. A representative office does not allow a foreign investor to handle commercial or financial transactions of any kind, nor can it act as an agent or distributor of a foreign company. Failure to comply with such rules may create a permanent establishment resulting in income generated by the activities or services rendered by the representative office deemed fully taxable income in Italy.

In summary, a representative office serves mainly as a marketing tool with no tax implications, as long as the structure is kept within the strict limitations referred to above. There are no legal registration formalities, no financial statement is required to be filed, and no corporate tax is payable.

To open a representative office the foreign investor must enroll with the local Chamber of Commerce.

The following documents are needed:

a.A certified copy of a resolution of the board of directors of the foreign company (along with a sworn Italian translation) authorizing the opening of the representative office in Italy and containing:

The name of the representative office;

Full address;

Name of the individual legally responsible for the office (Preposto); and

List of powers granted to the individual legally responsible for the office.

b.Certificate (with a sworn Italian translation) showing membership of the foreign parent company in an official foreign Companies' Register or Chamber of Commerce.

The day-to-day management of the office requires a bank account to be opened in the name of the representative office with signatory powers in the name of the appointed representative.

The representative office must comply with the following tax requirements:

The representative office must obtain from the Italian tax authorities its own tax code number (codice fiscale) which must appear on all documents relating to the office (no VAT number is required). A written application on the stationery of the foreign parent company must be filed with the tax office to obtain a tax code number.

The representative office must also obtain a taxpayer identification number (codice contribuente) to be used for any withholding tax paid by the representative office.

The individual legally responsible for the office will also have to apply for his own personal tax code number.

Written notice of the establishment of a representative office must be given to the following employment institutions:

the National Institute for Social Security (INPS);

the National Institute for Insurance against Labor Accidents (INAIL);

the Employment Office.

Social security tax contributions for employees are payable by the representative office; contributions are calculated on a variable percentage based on the salary paid.

For an exact calculation of the various social security tax payments, professional advice is recommended.

2.2 Branch

Foreign investors who do not want to incorporate an Italian subsidiary may conduct their business in Italy through a registered branch. The formation of a branch is often advisable when the foreign company is likely to incur losses during the initial year which can be offset against profits earned from other activities. It may also be advisable to form a branch when there is no double taxation treaty between Italy and the country of origin of the foreign investor. The financing of the branch may be carried out through a specific loan agreement with the parent company. There is no requirement for statutory auditors to be appointed.

The following documents are needed to establish a branch of a foreign company in Italy:

a.a certified copy of the deed of incorporation of the company;

b.a certified copy of the minutes of the board of director or shareholders' meeting approving the establishment of the Italian branch indicating:

the full address of the branch in Italy;

the personal details of the individual representing the branch;

c.a certified signature of the branch's representative;

d.a certificate showing membership of the foreign company in an official foreign Companies' Register or Chamber of Commerce.

The above documents must be certified by a notary public and legalized by means of the "Apostille" procedure provided by the Convention de la Hague dated October 5, 1961. An Italian translation is also required.

The following formalities must be complied with;

Documents (a) and (b), set out in Paragraph 3.2.2 above, must be deposited with an Italian notary public;

30 days from the above deposit, documents (a), (b) and (c) must be filed with the competent court for registration in the Companies' Register;

30 days from the deposit with the notary public, a VAT number must be requested;

30 days from the deposit of documents with the Court, the branch status must be requested with the local Chamber of Commerce together with a VAT number; and

30 days from the registration with the Court the name of the branch must be published in the bulletin kept by the local Chamber of Commerce (BURSAL).

These formalities are normally executed by the notary public.

Profits earned in Italy by the branch are subject to Italian corporate tax. The branch is considered a permanent establishment and must file its own corporate income tax return together with an annual financial statement of the parent company including profit and loss accounts. The branch's profits are taxable at an aggregate corporate tax rate of 52.2% (IRPEG at 36% and ILOR at 16.2%). The branch must keep proper books and file VAT returns.

The branch may be terminated at any time by ceasing to trade. It is then necessary to apply to the court for removal from the Companies' Register. A liquidator is appointed to fulfill all administrative and tax requirements. On conclusion of the liquidation, a final liquidation balance sheet is filed with the Court.

3. ACQUISITIONS

3.1 General

It is difficult to summarize the problems and applicable regulations regarding acquisitions, as each transaction will have its own circumstances. The following description is designed to provide a general summary of the rules concerning acquisitions under Italian law and to outline problems which may arise in the course of negotiations and the drafting of purchase agreements.

Acquisitions of companies listed on a stock exchange are subject to specific disclosure requirements and regulations.

3.2 Acquisition of a company through the purchase of shares or quotas

Generally, the transfer of shares does not require the execution of any specific agreements. The transfer may take place through a simple endorsement in favor of the purchaser on the share certificate(s). The endorsement must be certified by a notary public or by an authorized stockbroker and the transfer must then be registered in the shareholders' book kept by the company. Until this last step is accomplished, the transfer is not valid.

An S.r.l., whose share capital is represented by quotas, must transfer quotas through a public act or a certified private writing. The act of transfer must be deposited within 30 days by the notary public in the Companies' Register. The registration of the transfer of quotas in the quotaholders' book must take place within 30 days following the deposit, on request of the transferor or the transferee upon exhibition of the document evidencing both the transfer and the deposit.

If an investor intends to acquire the entire stock of a company or large percentage of its share capital it is recommended that a purchase agreement be executed.

The transfer procedures described in 4.2.1 and 4.2.2 give limited protection to purchasers. In order to expand the protection of the purchaser it is common, especially for acquisitions of the entire capital or large percentage of the share capital, to draft and execute a purchase agreement. This agreement sets out representations and warranties given by both parties. It is customary that purchase agreements contain clauses in which the seller gives representations and warranties with regard to important aspects of the company's organization and business. For example, the seller may give warranties with regard to tax matters such as filing of tax returns, payment of taxes and the existence of any tax liability, pending litigation, and compliance with safety regulations. The agreement may also discuss labor law requirements, social security contributions, trade marks and trade names, and other properties owned by the company. Agreements may provide for indemnities in the case of a breach of warranties and may provide that all or part of the purchase price shall be paid into an escrow account to be released on the occurrence of certain events.

It is also advisable that a due diligence investigation of the target company is carried out by experts working for the purchaser. A preliminary agreement may provide for a period of time during which the experts have free access to the company's premises to carry out the investigation.

The transfer of shares takes place in accordance with the formalities set out in paragraph 4.2.1. However, an entry detailing that the transfer has taken place pursuant to the purchase agreement may be endorsed on the certificate(s) as well as in the shareholders' company book. The purchase agreement must then be certified by a notary public.

3.3 Acquisition of a business as a going concern

The Italian Civil Code defines a going concern as "... the aggregate of property used by the entrepreneur for the conduct of the business." The transfer of a going concern must be effected through a public act or a certified private writing. The act of transfer must be deposited, within 30 days, by the notary public in the Companies' Register.

Generally a transfer of a going concern has two consequences:

The seller is prevented from starting any activity which may be in competition with the activity of the going concern transferred; and

the purchaser takes on all existing contractual liabilities of the going concern transferred.

Under the Italian Civil Code the seller is bound by a noncompetition restriction for a period of five years. This restriction is limited to activity actually carried out by the going concern at the time of the transfer. The parties may agree on wider limits provided that the seller is not prevented from performing his professional activities.

The duration of the noncompetition agreement cannot extend beyond five years. If the parties agree upon a longer duration, or they do not provide for any duration at all, the noncompetition rules will remain in force for the five year period. A violation of noncompetition restrictions by the seller gives the purchaser the right to claim for damages and to terminate the purchase agreement.

The purchaser automatically takes on all contracts of the business, with the exception of contracts of a personal nature. However, a third party may, within three months from the notice of the transfer, end the contract if it would not have signed the contract if it knew of the transfer or it would have signed the contract under different conditions. If the seller terminates a contract, the purchaser has the right to claim damages from the seller. Employment contracts, provided they are not terminated by the seller, are transferred to the purchaser. Employees retain their legal rights derived before the transfer. Collective labor agreements may, however, establish specific rules applicable in the event of the transfer of businesses.

Debts may be transferred without notifying the debtor. Payments made by debtors in good faith to the seller after the transfer are valid and the debtors are released from their debt obligations. However, the seller is not released from any debts unless the creditors have given prior consent. The purchaser is liable for the debts of the transferred business provided these debts are recorded in the transferred company's accounting books.

The transfer of a business is subject to the payment of a registration tax. The seller and the purchaser are jointly and severally liable for the payment for this tax. The parties may, however, agree to vary their respective liability for the tax. The rates of the registration tax vary in accordance with the type of business assets. The value of the business considered for the calculation of the registration tax is the value declared by the parties in the purchase agreement. This value must not differ from the open market value and is calculated by taking into account the assets of the business to be transferred, including goodwill, less all recorded liabilities.

If tax authorities believe that the value declared is lower than market value, they may issue a reassessment. The authorities have two years from the date of payment of the registration tax to do so. The tax authorities may carry out investigations and inspections to ascertain the true market value.

The law does not establish criteria to be considered in evaluating the business goodwill. In the case of a tax reassessment, the evaluation of goodwill is left to the discretion of the tax authorities who may follow different methods depending on the facts and circumstances.

4. MERGERS

The rules governing merger transactions, both under civil and tax law, have been amended to comply with E.U. Directives 78/855 and 82/891 and to prevent merger transactions carried out solely for tax reasons.

Under Italian law, the merger of two companies may be carried out either by the incorporation of a new company into which the two existing company are merged or by the merger of one of the two companies into the other company.

According to rules established by the Civil Code, as amended by Law 22 of January 16, 1991, the directors of the companies participating in the merger must prepare a merger proposal giving details of the merger and the companies involved. The merger proposal must be filed with the District Court and must be published in the Official Gazette of the Italian Republic at least 30 days before the date set for the extraordinary shareholders' meeting called to approve the merger.

The directors of the merging companies must prepare financial statements. These financial statements must be drafted in compliance with rules established under Italian law. The directors must also prepare a report on the merger, explaining the reason for the merger and giving details of the merger proposal. In particular the share exchange ratio must be described.

In addition to the above requirements, one or more experts appointed by the Court must prepare a report on the fairness of the share exchange ratio giving details of the calculation of the exchange ratios and evaluations.

The merger proposal, the directors report, the experts report, the financial statements prepared for the merger, the financial statement for the last three years, and the reports of the board of directors and the board of statutory auditors, must be deposited at the company offices 30 days prior to the extraordinary shareholders' meeting. These items must remain in the offices until the merger has been approved.

Resolutions adopted at the shareholders' meetings approving the merger proposal must be filed with the Court. After verifying compliance with the law, the Court will order registration in the Companies' Register. Subsequently, an excerpt of the resolutions must be published in the Official Gazette.

A merger can generally only take effect two months after the registration of the above resolutions. During this period the creditors of the companies may challenge the merger. However, the Court, notwithstanding the objections of the creditors, can authorize the merger to occur sooner provided the company gives an acceptable guarantee to the creditors.

A deed of merger must then be executed before a notary public and registered in the Companies' Register within 30 days from the date of execution.

The newly created merged company assumes all rights and liabilities of the company extinguished by the merger.

5. DIVISIONS

Legislative Decree 22 of January 16, 1991 implemented the Sixth E.U. Directive on corporate divisions.

A corporate division may occur through the transfer of all or part of a company's assets and liabilities to two or more new or existing companies in exchange for the issuance of the transferee company's shares or quotas to the transferor company's shareholders.

As required for mergers, directors of companies participating in a division transaction must draw up a formal "division plan," proper financial statements of the companies, and a detailed written report illustrating and justifying the legal and economic aspects of the division plan. Particular reference must be made to the distribution formula of shares or quotas and the net asset values distributed to companies and kept by the divided companies. The same rules provided for merger procedures also apply for corporate divisions.

6. ANTITRUST AND MONOPOLY CONTROL LAW

6.1 Coordination with European Union rules

When considering corporate mergers or acquisitions in Italy, European Union antitrust regulations and domestic regulations must be considered.

Law 287 ('the Law') of October 10, 1990, repeats most of the provisions set out in E.U. Regulations 4064/89, but also introduces new regulations to prevent control of banks and industrial enterprises. The new Italian antitrust law is generally regarded as subordinate to existing E.U. rules and its interpretation is to be considered subject to the principles contained in the E.U. antitrust legislation. This means that acts, even if restricted to the Italian market, will be governed by Italian law only when not already subject to E.U. legislation.

6.2 Definition of trusts and prohibited cases

The Law guarantees free competition in the Italian market and states that a trust occurs when:

two or more undertakings merge; or

where one or more persons, in a position of control of at least one or more undertakings, acquires directly or indirectly, through share acquisition or assets acquisition, the control of all or part of one or more undertakings; or

where two or more undertakings create a joint venture by setting up a new undertaking.

Control of an undertaking does not exist where a bank or financial institution, upon the incorporation or the increased authorized capital of an undertaking, acquires securities in order to re-sell them. This applies only if the bank or financial institution does not exercise voting rights in respect of those securities during the period it holds them.

The purpose of the present antitrust law is to protect and guarantee the rights of economic initiative. It primarily concentrates on abuse of dominant positions by undertakings which are not covered by Articles 65/66 of the European Coal and Steel Community Treaty or Articles 85/86 of the Treaty of Rome.

Italian antitrust legislation only applies if E.U. law does not apply. Accordingly, domestic law applies to undertakings not having a 'community dimension.' This means undertakings with a combined aggregate world wide turn-over of less than 5 billion ECU (Exchange Currency Unit) and an aggregate community wide turn-over not exceeding 250 million ECU or where each of the undertakings achieves more than 2/3 of its aggregate community wide turn-over within Italy.

6.3 Definition of 'control'

To establish whether a trust exists, it is necessary to define control. Article 7 of the Law states that an undertaking controls another when:

it owns the majority of shares or quotas; or

it can influence behavior through its shareholding or by any other contractual agreement; or

an undertaking is controlled through another undertaking which is under the control of the party in question.

Control is also defined with reference to rights under contracts or by any other means which, given the facts and laws, allow for the possibility of exercising decisive influence on an undertaking, in particular through:

ownership;

rights to use all or part of the assets of an undertaking;

rights or contracts which confer decisive influence on the composition, voting or decisions of the undertaking.

Control is also acquired by person(s), or undertaking(s) which hold rights or are entitled to rights under contracts or, while not holders of such rights, have the power to exercise these rights.

The only undertakings exempted from the application of the above provisions are state monopolies.

Italian legislation provisions must be coordinated with Article 37 of the Treaty of Rome which is designed to prevent commercial state monopolies from discriminating against nationals of other member states.

6.4 The Antitrust Authority

Control and investigation of compliance with the provisions of the Antitrust Law are performed by an 'Antitrust Authority' ('the Authority').

Investigations can be initiated by the Authority at the request of any interested person or ministry or by notification of the relevant undertakings.

Notification of the Authority is required when the aggregate turnovers involved in the operation (merger, acquisition, takeover bid etc.) exceed approximately Lire 560 billion, or when the turnover of the undertaking to be acquired exceeds approximately Lire 56 billion.

After notification or in the case of an intention to proceed with a takeover bid, the Authority can start proceedings to determine whether such an action infringes upon the Law. The final decision of the Authority must be issued within 45 days from the beginning of the proceedings. This period can be extended for 30 days when the undertaking involved does not supply all the requested information.

During the Authority's proceedings, the operation or takeover bid is suspended.

The investigation may end with the prohibition or the authorization of the operation or takeover bid.

Fines are provided for undertakings not complying with the Authority's decisions.

Special provisions exist for banks, insurance companies, broadcasting companies and publishers.

The Authority may also issue, with the permission of the government, exemptions for mergers otherwise prohibited by the Law. Exemptions are allowed for transactions deemed necessary to the national economy in order to achieve greater European economic integration, provided the merger does not lead to the restriction of competition.

6.5 Control over banks

The most innovative part of the Law deals with share participation in banks by industrial undertakings.

It has been Italian economic policy to avoid mergers between industrial enterprises and banks which could lead to control of the market and a substantial increase of major private groups dominating the economy. This policy has led to strict limitations on the purchase, holding and exploitation of shareholdings in banks.

The Law states that any shareholding exceeding 5% of the shares issued by a bank or any other controlling interest in a bank must be authorized by the Bank of Italy. Acquisitions of shareholdings not exceeding 5% but exceeding 1% must be reported to the Bank of Italy. Any variation of shareholdings exceeding 5% must also be authorized in cases where it involves at least 2% of the share capital of the bank.

There is a general ban on holdings owned by institutions exceeding 15% of the share capital of a bank.

In the case of a breach of the above provisions, directors may be held liable for both civil and criminal offenses with a maximum fine of Lire 20 million or imprisonment for a maximum period of 5 years.

Italian antitrust legislation may affect foreign investors evaluating the possibility of a merger or acquisition in Italy. However, it should be noted that the provisions are in accordance with the E.U. legislation and similar laws of the other E.U. member states.

7. OTHER FORMS OF FOREIGN INVESTMENT

7.1 Agency Agreements

Agency contracts are governed under Italian law by the following provisions:

the Civil Code (articles 1742 - 1753);

the Collective Economic Agreement of June 20, 1956 for the agents of industrial companies extended by the Presidential Decree of January 16, 1961 to cover foreign principals;

Law n. 316 dated May 3, 1985, whereby persons wishing to work as agents in Italy must be enrolled in a special Agents' Register after sitting for an examination held by the local Chamber of Commerce. Failure to enroll in the Agents Register results in the agency agreement being deemed void and administrative sanctions are applied to both the agent and the principal;

The Legislative Decree n. 303 of September 10, 1991, implementing the EEC Directive 653/86 of December 18, 1986, on commercial agents. The provisions of the Decree are effective from January 1, 1994, for those contracts already in force as of January 1, 1990. However the provisions referring to the severance indemnity are applicable from January 1, 1993.

7.2 Form of Agency Contract

In accordance with Italian law, there is no specific form of agency contract. In general, an agency agreement is presumed to be exclusive unless the agreement states otherwise.

7.3 Commissions

Italian law entitles the agent to earn commissions only on completed transactions. Partially completed transactions may be subject to apportioned payments. No commission is due in the case of the buyer's insolvency.

The agent is not entitled to a commission for a contract canceled by the principal. The agent may claim a reimbursement to cover expenses equal to 50% of the commission he would have earned had the contract been completed.

Law 303/1991 entitles the agent to a commission on transactions completed after the termination of the agency contract if the completion of the transaction is due primarily to the agent's participation.

7.4 Agent's Liability

In the case of the buyer's insolvency, Italian law allows the parties to an agency agreement to seek a indemnity against the agent. The indemnity cannot exceed 20% of the loss suffered by the principal for each year or half of the commissions accrued to the agent during that year.

In some businesses a higher indemnity is agreed to on the condition that a higher commission is payable.

7.5 Duration and withdrawal

Law 303/91 defines agency agreements as an agreement of indefinite duration where performance continues even after the date of the natural expiration of the agreement. Each party may terminate the contract by sending to the other party a notice of termination. Advance notice of at least 30 days is required for the first year of the contract, at least 60 days for the second year of the contract, and at least 90 days for the third and subsequent years of the contract.

Payment may be made in lieu of notice and is calculated on the basis of the expected commission earned if the agent had worked out his notice.

7.6 Severance indemnity

If an agency agreement of an indefinite duration is terminated through no fault of the agent's, a severance indemnity may be due to the agent in the following cases:

if the agent has procured new customers or has substantially developed the principal's business from which the principal continues to benefit;

the payment of such an indemnity is reasonable with regards to circumstances and to the loss of commission by the agent.

The amount of the indemnity cannot exceed the total commission paid during a year based on the average commission paid over the past five years.

Payment of the indemnity does not prevent the agent from claiming possible damages for any losses or damage suffered.

The indemnity is not payable if:

the principal terminates the agreement for breach of contract by the agent and the breach cannot be remedied; or

the agent terminates the agreement unless the termination is caused by the principal or due to the agent's ill health; or

pursuant to an agreement with the principal, the agent assigns to a third party the contract rights.

The agent automatically waives his right to an indemnity if he fails to notify the principal of his intention to claim an indemnity within one year from the date of the termination.

8. DISTRIBUTION AGREEMENTS

There are no specific provisions for distribution agreements regulated by the Civil Code ('contratto di somministrazione'). It is therefore advisable to regulate all aspects of the contractual relationship by drafting a distribution agreement.

However, it is worth noting that distribution contracts of indefinite duration require the parties to give reasonable notice of termination. Failure may result in a claim for damages. A severance indemnity is not generally provided for upon the termination of distribution contracts.

THE TAX SYSTEM

The Italian tax system is based on two types of taxes: direct taxes and indirect taxes.

A: DIRECT TAXES ('IMPOSTE DIRETTE')

IRPEF ('Imposta sul Reddito delle Persone Fisiche') - income tax on individuals;

IRPEG ('Imposta sul Reddito delle Persone Giuridiche') - income tax on corporations;

ILOR ('Imposta Locale sui Redditi') - local income tax

B: Indirect taxes ('imposte indirette')

IVA ('Imposta sul Valore Aggiunto') - Value Added Tax (VAT);

Registration tax;

Inheritance and gift tax;

INVIM ('Imposta sull'Incremento del Valore degli Immobili') - tax on the appreciation of real estate;

Stamp duty;

ICI ('Imposta Comunale sugli Immobili') - municipal tax on buildings;

Other minor taxes.

1. DIRECT TAXES

1.1 Personal Income Tax (IRPEF)

1.1.1 Basis of the tax

Personal income tax (IRPEF) is based upon income earned, whether in money or in kind, in the following categories:

Income from land and buildings;

Income from capital;

Income from employment;

Income from self-employment;

Business income;

Miscellaneous income.

1.1.2 Persons subject to the tax

All individuals, whether resident or non-resident, are subject to the IRPEF.

For income tax purposes, those persons who for most of the tax year are registered in the Office of Records of the Resident Population or who are resident or domiciled within Italy are considered as resident.

1.1.3 Taxable base

The tax is applied on the aggregate income. Aggregate income for residents includes all income earned. Aggregate income for non-residents includes solely that income earned within Italy.

Income from continuous employment abroad, when that is the sole purpose of the labor relationship, is excluded from the taxable base.

1.1.4 Taxation of non-residents

Non-residents are taxable in Italy on the following types of local source income:

Income from real estate located in Italy;

Income from capital when received from the State, residents or local branches of non-resident entities;

Income from employment for services rendered in Italy;

Income from self-employment services performed in Italy;

Business income derived from activities carried out in Italy through a permanent establishment;

Miscellaneous income derived from activities performed in Italy or related to assets located in Italy (quotas in partnerships and limited liability companies are always considered to be located in Italy, whereas shares of corporations are only considered to be located in Italy if the share certificates are physically located there);

Capital gains realized by individuals on the sale of going concerns ('aziende') located in Italy;

Income from Italian partnerships attributable to non-resident partners;

Pensions and royalties when received from Italian resident entities or local branches of non-resident entities;

Income from artistic and professional performances carried out in Italy.

1.1.5 Income from farmland, agriculture and buildings

Income from farmland is derived by every owner or possessor under title of ownership, a life estate (usufruct) or other real right to the land. The land must be suitable for agricultural production but must not be attached to urban dwellings, used for free public services or used for commercial activities.

Agricultural income is income derived by every owner of farmland who directly engages in agricultural operations on the land.

Income from buildings is income derived by every owner or possessor under a title of ownership, a life estate, or other real right to buildings or other construction of a permanent nature that is capable of producing income.

Income from land and buildings is calculated using a special method referred to as "cadastral value."

The cadastre is the tax office that keeps land and building registers. These registers record the characteristics of all land and buildings in Italy and the names of the owners.

The cadastral value is the value attributed to land and buildings by the cadastre office. This value is determined as follows:

For land, multiply the average ordinary income (fixed by the cadastre) for the surface area taking into consideration the kind of culture and the location of the land;

For buildings, multiply the surface area by a pre-determined amount (fixed by the cadastre), taking into consideration the location of the building and the quality of the building.

1.1.6 Income from capital

The following types of income are considered to be from capital:

Income derived from loans;

Interest and other income from deposits and current accounts;

Income from participation in corporations, associations and other entities, excluding partnerships;

Interest, premiums and other income derived from bonds and similar securities;

Interest payable for late payment;

Compensation for guarantees and similar obligations;

Perpetual annuities;

Other income derived from the use of capital.

Income from capital is taxed on a cash basis and deductions are allowed from gross income.

1.1.7 Income from Employment

Income from employment includes salaries, fees, wages, emoluments or other compensation paid in money or in kind from employment earned during the year. Pensions and severance indemnities are also considered employment income.

1.1.8 Income from self-employment

Self-employment income includes all income earned from the practice of the arts and professions. The following types of income are also considered to be self-employment income:

Income from the rendering of services offered on the basis of a continuous and coordinated collaboration, such as a director, a statutory auditor or a journalist;

Income from royalties or fees received by the author or inventor for the use of copyrights, patents, designs, processes, formulae, trademarks or similar rights, not received in the conduct of a business or by general or limited partnerships;

Income from participation in a joint venture ('associazione in partecipazione') in which the sole contribution consists of rendering personal services.

In addition, indemnities received for the termination of agency relationships and other continuous and coordinated forms of collaboration are treated as self-employment income.

1.1.9 Income from business activities

Profits from business and industry earned by the individual businessman are taxed on an accrual basis from financial statements in the tax period. Rules for determining taxable income are similar to those applicable for corporate income tax purposes.

1.1.10 Income from Miscellaneous Sources

Income from miscellaneous sources includes the income earned from activities not considered in the previous categories, such as capital gains arising from:

The sale of real estate not directly used by the purchaser or his relatives, or owned for less than five years;

The sale or exchange of interests in companies.

1.1.11 Allowable reductions from the gross IRPEF tax

The individual taxpayer is entitled to deduct from the gross IRPEF tax due an amount equal to 27% of selected expenses such as:

Mortgage interest paid;

Social security tax contributions and life insurance premiums;

Medical and surgical expenses.

These deductions must be documented.

The law provides conditions and limits on the deductibility of these expenses, particularly for non-resident individuals.

1.1.12 Personal tax allowances

A taxpayer is also entitled to personal tax allowances as a tax credit for family dependents. The credit is subtracted from the IRPEF tax calculated on gross income.

For example, for fiscal year 1994 the personal allowances are:

Lire 791,588 for a dependent spouse if not legally and factually separated;

The amounts indicated below with respect to children:

NUMBER OF CHILDREN LIRE

one 91,438
two 182,875
three 274,313
four 365,750
five 457,188
six 548,625
seven 640,063
eight 731,500

for each additional child 91,438

Deductions for personal allowances for a spouse and family dependents are not allowed for non-resident individuals.

11.13 Tax reductions from employment income

If employment income is included in aggregate income, the gross IRPEF tax otherwise payable can be reduced by Lire 727,000. This amount may need to be prorated based on the months worked or months during which a pension was received during the year.

1.1.14 Calculation of the IRPEF tax (for calendar year 1994)

The gross tax shall be calculated by applying to aggregate income the following graduated rates:

income up to 7.2 million lire 10%
income over 7.2 up to 14.4 million lire 22%
income over 14.4 up to 30 million lire 27%
income over 30 up to 60 million lire 34%
income over 60 up to 150 million lire 41%
income over 150 up to 300 million lire 46%
income over 300 million lire 51%

1.2 Local Income Tax (ILOR) - Individuals

Local income tax (ILOR) applies to the Italian source income of individuals. Italian source income of non-residents (such as rents and royalties) is also subject to ILOR, if not excluded under a tax treaty with Italy.

The following income is excluded when computing taxable income for ILOR purposes:

Income from sources outside Italy, if a permanent establishment exists with a separate system of accounting;

Income from lands and buildings;
Income from employment;
Income from independent work;
Income from holdings in all types of partnerships and companies;

Income subject to a final withholding tax;
Other exempt income;
Income exempted under tax treaties with other countries.

All items above, except for the first item, are excluded from taxable income for ILOR purposes whether the income is derived within or without Italy.

1.3 Tax Returns and Payments

Direct taxes are assessed by the tax authorities based on an annual return filed by taxpayers. The return must be filed by June 30 with the local tax office in the area of fiscal domicile, to report income for the previous calendar year.

An advance payment of 98% (divided into two installments of 39.2% and 58.8%, respectively) of the previous year's personal tax or of the estimated tax for the current year (whichever is the lower) must be made during the tax year.

The advance payments must be made as follows:

The first payment (39.2%) within the fifth month of the calendar year (before May 31 of each year);

The second payment (58.8%) before the eleventh month of the calendar year (before November 30 of each year).

The balance must be paid before May 31 of the following year.

1.4 Taxation of Partnership Income

1.4.1 General

A partnership ('Societá di persone') includes general partnerships ('Societá in nome collettivo' - S.n.c.) and limited partnerships ('Societá in accomandita semplice' - S.a.s.). The partnership itself is only subject to local income tax (ILOR).

A partnership is regarded as a conduit for determining the net income of the partners. Net partnership income is automatically attributed to the partners in proportion to their percentage of participation in the profits. Even if the apportioned profits are not actually received by the partners, the income is included with their aggregate income and is subject to individual income tax (IRPEF). When, in a later tax period, the income is actually received by the partners, it does not constitute taxable income. Losses are also apportioned to the partners.

1.4.2 Tax returns

Partnerships must file a tax return (Form 750) before June 30 of the following year.

This return is filed only for the payment of ILOR on the business income earned by the partnership.

Partnerships are also obliged to pay in the course of the year advance payments on ILOR with formalities similar to those for individuals.

1.5 Corporate income tax (IRPEG)

1.5.1 General

All income earned in Italy, whether by a corporation (S.p.A.), a limited partnership by shares (S.a.p.A.), a limited liability company (S.r.l.) or a permanent establishment in Italy of a non-resident company, is subject to the following income taxes:

IRPEG (Corporate Income Tax) 36%

ILOR (Local Income Tax) 16.20%

The aggregate tax burden is 52.2%.

1.5.2 Tax returns

Resident joint-stock companies (S.p.A., S.r.l.) and limited partnerships by shares (S.a.p.A.) must file an income tax return for IRPEG and ILOR purposes (Form 760). The return must be filed within one month of the approval of the annual financial statements by the shareholders' meeting.

Permanent establishments of non-resident entities must file the annual tax return within one month of the approval of the annual financial statement by the Head Office or within six months of the financial statement's closing date.

The tax year of a corporation is the accounting year, which may differ from the calendar year.

An advance payment of 98% (divided into two installments of 39.2% and 58.8%, respectively) of the previous year's corporate tax or of the estimated tax for the current year (whichever is the lower) must be made during the entity's tax year.

The advance payments must be made as follows:

The first payment (39.2%) within 30 days of the shareholders' approval of the prior-year financial statements (usually before May 31 each year);

The second payment (58.8%) before the eleventh month of the tax year (usually before November 30 each year).

The balance is payable with the tax return.

From the tax due the following deductions are made:

Advance payments;
Advance withholding taxes;
Tax credit for taxes paid abroad;
Tax credit on dividends collected.

If the total of the tax credits, withholdings and advance payments exceeds the tax due, the taxpayer may carry forward the tax credit or request a refund. The credit may also be used against the first installment of the advance payment.

1.5.3 Assessments

The tax authorities may issue final assessments by the end of the fifth year following the filing of the tax return. This period is increased to six years when no return has been filed.

1.5.4 Principal components of income

1.5.4.1 Revenues

Revenues from the sale of goods and services rendered are included as income under the following principles:

for goods, at the date of delivery or shipment;

for real property, at the date of the signing of the transfer deed;

for services, at the date of the completion of the service. However, for services to be rendered under lease, loan insurance and other contracts involving periodic payments, at the date such payments become due.

For contracts with a duration exceeding 12 months, revenues are recognized on the basis of the stage of completion. However, the valuation can be made on a cost basis with authorization from the tax office.

1.5.4.2 Capital Gains

Capital gains from the disposal of assets are included in taxable income for corporate income tax purposes.

However, the taxation of capital gains may be deferred for up to five fiscal periods if certain conditions are met.

Gains from the sales of shares are treated as revenue and subject to ordinary taxation.

1.5.4.3 Dividends

Dividends paid by a resident joint-stock company to another resident company are fully taxable in the fiscal year in which they are received (cash principle) for IRPEG purposes only.

Dividends are exempt for ILOR purposes.

For dividends received by a resident company from another resident company, a tax credit system applies.

At present, this tax credit is equal to 9/16 (56.25%) of total dividends received.

In calculating the tax due by the resident company, the amount of the tax credit is added to the total taxable income.

This tax credit, therefore, has a double nature:

Positive component of income, since it is added to the total income of the company receiving the dividends;

Credit towards the Tax Office, which will be used upon filing the tax return by the company receiving the dividends.

The receiving company is taxed on the dividends at the rate of 36% (IRPEG).

A tax of 10% is withheld from dividends paid by resident companies to resident shareholders. This withholding tax constitutes a tax credit a resident company may use when filing its tax return:

EXAMPLE:

Dividend distributed by
resident Company A 100.00
less Withholding at source (10.00)
Net cash received by resident
Company B 90.00
Determination of taxable dividends:
Taxable income for Company B 100.00
(gross dividend received from A)
Tax credit (9/16 = 56.25%) 56.25
Total taxable income for Company B 156.25
IRPEG (corporate income tax) 36% (56.25)
ILOR (local income tax) 16.20% -
Total income, net of taxes 100.00
Position in relation to the Tax Office:
Tax credit on dividends 56.25
Withholding at source on dividends 10.00
IRPEG due (156.25 x 36%) (56.25)

Total credit towards the Tax Office 10.00

The income earned from the dividend is fiscally neutral for the resident company; since the tax credit on dividends forms part of the taxable income, but is then deducted from the tax due.

The tax credits recorded in the financial statements may be:

Claimed as a refund paid by the tax authorities within four or five years, with a current annual interest rate of 6%, or

Carried forward to be used in subsequent periods to offset taxes due.

Dividends from a non-resident company

If a resident company owns more than 20% of the capital of a foreign company (or 10% if the shares are listed on a stock exchange), only 40% of the dividends received from that foreign company are subject to corporate income tax.

Dividends from a company resident in an E.U. Member State

Dividends distributed by companies resident in an E.U. member state, subject to certain conditions, are 95% exempt from corporation tax in the hands of the Italian company. This exemption applies only if the Italian company held at least 25% of the shares of the distributing company for an uninterrupted period of one year.

These provisions reduce the double taxation that may occur on dividends distributed to an Italian resident by a non-resident company, unless a double taxation treaty provides for a more favorable regime.

1.5.5 Deductions

As a general principle, all costs and expenses relating to business activities are deductible (e.g. capital losses, extraordinary losses, labor expenses, royalties), with some limitations for interest paid, income taxes, and charitable contributions.

1.5.5.1 Fringe Benefits

Payments in kind, including goods and services, made to the employee shall be included in the employees income in an amount equal to the cost incurred by the employer. Certain fringe benefits granted to directors and employees are deductible (e.g. housing) if they are taxable income for the employee.

1.5.5.2 Repairs and Maintenance

Expenses for maintenance, repairs, modernization and transformation (not reported on the balance sheet as increases in the cost of assets) are deductible. The maximum deductible amount is limited to 5% of the total cost of all depreciable assets carried in the journal of depreciable assets at the start of the fiscal year. The excess is deductible in equal amounts during the subsequent five fiscal periods.

1.5.5.3 Expenses Relating to More Than One Fiscal Year

Expenses relating to research and development are deducted in the fiscal year in which incurred or in equal installments in the current year and subsequent years but not beyond the fourth subsequent year.

Advertising and publicity expenses are deducted in the fiscal year in which incurred or in equal installments in that year and the two subsequent years.

1.5.5.4 Bad debts

The accounts receivable can be written-down for bad debts to a percentage of the total accounts receivable carried on the balance sheet. The global devaluation may not, however, exceed 5% of the accounts receivable on the balance sheet at the end of the year.

1.5.5.5 Exchange Risks

The provision for the reserve for exchange risk is deductible, with a special method of calculation. It is deductible to the extent of the negative difference between the sum of foreign currency receivables and payables valued at the exchange rate of the last month of the accounting period and the sum of the same items valued at the exchange rate of the day on which they arose.

1.5.5.6 Depreciation

The depreciation rates are fixed by a Ministerial Decree, and vary according to the sector in which the company operates. Depreciation is calculated on a straight-line basis.

The principal rates of depreciation permitted by the tax authorities are (on average):

Buildings and plant 3% - 7%
Machinery and equipment 10% - 16%
Tools 25% - 40%
Office furniture and fixtures 12%
Motor vehicles 25%
Electrical and electronic equipment 20%

In the first year in which the asset comes into use, depreciation is reduced by half. In the case of new assets, the depreciation rates may be increased (doubled) for the first three years as accelerated depreciation.

Intangible assets - Patents, trademarks, know-how, intellectual property and inventions can be depreciated up to a maximum expense of one-third of their cost per year. Goodwill may not be depreciated at more than 20% per year.

1.5.6 Valuation

1.5.6.1 Inventories

The following methods of inventory valuation are allowed:

FIFO (first in, first out)

LIFO (last in, first out)

Average cost

A write-down of the closing inventory is permitted if the value during the last month of the tax period is lower than the valuation determined by one of the above methods.

1.5.6.2 Securities

The same valuation criteria provided for inventories apply to securities. However, the value of securities may be written down as follows:

Quoted shares: a write-down is permitted based on the average price in the last month of the fiscal year;

Non-quoted shares: a write-down is permitted proportionally to the reduction in net worth between the date of the last balance sheet before the date on which the shares were acquired and the most recent balance sheet.

1.5.7 Anti-tax haven legislation

Article 11 of Law n. 413 of December 30, 1991 amended Art. 76 of the Income Tax Code by providing that, except for transfer pricing, the deduction of expenses and other negative items is disallowed when the expenses relate to transactions between resident enterprises and companies domiciled in non E.U.-states and which have a preferred tax regime, if the latter companies directly or indirectly control or are controlled by the Italian enterprise, or are controlled by the same company which controls the Italian enterprise.

A preferred tax regime is defined as one of a foreign State which exempts the income of the aforementioned companies from income taxes or charges them a tax lower than half of the total tax charged on income of a resident company.

The deduction of expenses is allowed when enterprises resident in Italy can prove that the foreign companies principally carry on an effective commercial activity, or that the transactions are carried out for effective economic purposes.

1.6 Local Income tax (ILOR) - Corporations

A local income tax (ILOR) is imposed in addition to corporate income tax (IRPEG). In computing the total income subject to tax, the same rules and exemptions apply as for corporate income tax, with the following exceptions:

Only income from Italian sources is subject to local income tax; however, business income derived from foreign sources is considered to be produced in Italy unless the business income is derived through a permanent establishment abroad that has separate administration and accounts;

Dividends received from resident and non-resident companies are not subject to local income tax.

The rate of the local income tax is 16.2%.

1.7 Withholding taxes

1.7.1 General

Withholding tax is applied to various payments, the most important of which are the following:

Professional fees;
Royalties;
Interest;
Dividends.

1.7.2 Professional Fees

Professional fees and directors' remuneration are subject to a withholding tax of 19% for residents or 20% if paid to a non-resident (unless otherwise provided by a tax treaty).

1.7.3 Royalties

Royalties paid to non-residents by an Italian subsidiary are subject to a withholding tax of 30% calculated on 70% of the gross amount. The total tax burden is 21% unless a lower rate is provided by a tax treaty. This type of withholding ends any further tax liabilities.

Therefore, when there are no tax treaties, the non-resident foreign recipient is subject only to the withholding tax and is not obliged to file a tax return in Italy.

Royalties paid by a resident company to other resident companies are not subject to any withholding tax.

Royalties paid by a resident company to a non-resident are subject to value added tax at the rate of 19%. If the non-resident company does not have a permanent establishment in Italy, VAT is payable by the payer of the royalties by issuing a self-invoice ('autofattura').

1.7.4 Interest

A withholding tax on interest applies to certain interest payments. The rates are:

30% for interest on bonds issued by non-quoted companies;

30% for interest on deposits and current accounts with credit institutions;

12.5% on public bonds;

12.5% on bonds issued by quoted joint-stock companies and banks.

The withholding taxes outlined above are final taxes if paid by non-residents. If paid by taxpayers with business activity in Italy, the tax withheld is a prepayment of the taxpayer's final tax liability.

Certain types of interest paid on public bonds abroad are exempt from tax. In addition, Law 467/1993 provides for a tax exemption on Italian securities interest paid to residents of tax treaty countries.

Other interest payments not outlined above paid to a non-resident are subject to a 15% withholding tax (unless reduced by a tax treaty).

1.7.5 Dividends

Dividends paid by an Italian company to resident shareholders are subject to a withholding tax of 10%. The withholding tax is paid as an advance payment on the recipient's income tax.

Dividends paid to non-resident shareholders are subject to a withholding tax of 32.4%, unless a lower rate is provided by a tax treaty.

A refund, not exceeding two-thirds of the withholding tax paid in Italy, may be claimed by shareholders who can prove that they paid tax on the dividend to their country of residence.

Dividends paid to companies resident in an E.U. Member State

Dividends paid to companies resident in an E.U. Member State are not subject to any withholding tax in Italy, if the following conditions are met:

the foreign company owns more than 25% of the stock capital of the Italian subsidiary;

the foreign company is resident in an E.U. Member State and is subject to tax by that Member State.

1.8 Non-Resident Companies and Entities

For Italian tax law purposes, non-resident companies and entities are those which, for most of the tax period, do not have either their registered office, their administrative headquarters or their principal business in Italy.

1.8.1 Aggregate income

Aggregate income of non-resident companies and entities consists only of income produced within Italy under the criteria discussed above.

Business income includes any gains and losses on goods destined for, or related to, business activities undertaken within Italy, even though not realized through a permanent establishment. It also includes profits distributed by resident companies and entities and capital gains relating to interests held in limited liability companies or general and limited partnerships resident in Italy.

If these companies and entities carry out commercial activities in Italy through a permanent establishment, the taxable income (subject to IRPEG and ILOR) is calculated on the basis of balance sheets and profit and loss accounts for the permanent establishment and for the other activities that produce taxable income in Italy.

The permanent establishment must file a tax return (Form 760) and is subject to the same regulations as illustrated previously. It is subject to corporate tax (IRPEG 36%) and local income tax (ILOR 16.2%) as previously discussed.

Different rules may be provided under double taxation treaties.

1.8.2 Capital gains taxation

Capital gains derived from commercial activities are considered to be income and are subject to taxation.

When capital gains are produced by one of the following:

individuals;
non profit organizations;
non-resident individuals;
non-resident companies with no permanent establishment in Italy;

they are subject to a separate taxation scheme (see below).

The tax is imposed on capital gains realized through sale or assignment of shares of any kind of company or partnership. The transfer of bonds, including government bonds, are exempted.

Capital gains may be taxed under one of two methods, subject to the taxpayer's election:

a.Analytical System

The taxpayer is required to list every capital gain or loss realized during the year on his income tax return.

The tax payable is calculated as 25% of capital gains less all capital losses. When capital losses exceed capital gains, the difference is deductible from capital gains realized in the following five years. The tax is paid when the income tax return is filed.

The analytical system is compulsory if the capital gain is realized through a share sale exceeding 2% of negotiated stock, or 5% of non negotiated stock or 10% of other companies or partnerships.

b.Lump-sum (Forfait)

The tax rate applicable is equal to 1.05% calculated on the sales price (without deducting any cost or loss).

This system can be chosen by the taxpayer if the transfer is made by means of an authorized broker or a notary public and the share or quota transfer does not exceed the above-mentioned percentages. The election to use this method must be made at the time of the first share or quota transfer of the year.

The tax is paid at the time of the transfer.

The lump-sum system does not allow the taxpayer to deduct capital losses.

The taxpayer is required to change to the analytical system if, during the year, the share transfers exceed the above-mentioned limits.

c.Exemptions:

Transfers of shares not exceeding the above limits if owned for more than 15 years;

Transfers of inherited shares;

Transfers of stocks negotiated on the Italian stock exchange after November 24, 1992. This exemption is scheduled to expire on June 30, 1994.

1.9 Other income tax matters

1.9.1 Anti-avoidance

At present there is no general tax anti-avoidance rule in Italy, except for those related to mergers, divisions, concentrations, transformations, spin-offs and reductions of capital.

For these transactions, a specific law was introduced to limit fiscal evasion. As a result, the tax authorities may not recognize, for tax purposes, the tax benefits deriving from transactions performed without valid economic reasons with the sole aim of fraudulently obtaining a tax saving.

Furthermore, the law states that 30% of any additional tax and interest assessed by the tax authorities must be paid before the taxpayer appeals to the first level of the Tax Court.

Additional payments may be due if the case progresses beyond the first level of the Tax Court.

1.9.2 Thin capitalization

There are no relevant provisions regarding thin capitalization in Italian tax law.

1.9.3 Exchange of information with tax authorities of foreign countries

It is expressly provided by Italian law that the E.U. Tax Authorities proceed with the exchange of information necessary to ensure a correct assessment of both income tax and VAT.

The presence in Italy of tax officers from the other member countries for this purpose is authorized.

In accordance with the laws contained in treaties against double taxation, it is also granted that the Tax Office can collect from other States, any information that may be useful for the purpose of tax assessments.

1.9.4 Intercompany transactions (Transfer Prices)

Transfer price regulations (arm's-length basis) apply not only between a controlled Italian company and the foreign parent company (or vice versa). They also apply if the foreign company is a sister company to the Italian company and if the foreign company is controlled by the same company (resident or non resident) that controls the Italian company.

1.9.5 Royalties paid to non-residents

The payment of royalties is deductible for affiliates engaged in manufacturing goods, in accordance with Ministry of Finance Notice n. 9/2267 of 1980.

Rates exceeding 5% of sales are only accepted in exceptional cases, justified by the high technological level of the economic sector in question or by other circumstances.

1.9.6 Management fees paid to non-residents

Expenses incurred for management fees are deductible provided precise and unquestionable advantages result for the Italian subsidiary or branch.

1.9.7 Carryforward of tax losses

The loss in any tax period may be carried forward to reduce income in no more than five subsequent tax periods for IRPEG purposes. No carryback is allowed.

No loss relief exists for ILOR purposes.

The provision for the carryforward is also applicable to permanent establishments.

1.9.8 Tax credit for foreign source income

If income earned abroad is included in the computation of aggregate income, taxes paid abroad upon such income are allowed as credits against net tax in an amount equal to that part of the Italian tax that is proportional to the ratio between foreign source income and aggregate income, without reduction for losses of prior tax periods carried forward.

1.9.9 Tax treaties

Italy has concluded a number of income tax treaties for the avoidance of double taxation. These treaties may alter the rules regarding such items as residence, tax credits and the taxation of non-residents. The treaties generally provide for more favorable taxation of Italian non-residents than the treatment provided under local Italian law. The provisions of each applicable treaty should be consulted for the manner in which tax relief is granted.

Italy has tax treaties with the following countries:

Argentina Indonesia Rumania
Austria Ireland Russia
Australia Israel Singapore
Belgium Ivory Coast Slovak Republic
Brazil Japan Spain
Bulgaria Kenya Sri Lanka
Canada Korea Sweden
China Kuwait Switzerland
Cyprus Luxembourg Tanzania
Czech Republic Malaysia Thailand
Denmark Malta Trinidad
Ecuador Morocco & Tobago
Egypt The Netherlands Tunisia
Finland New Zealand Turkey
France Norway United Kingdom
Germany Pakistan United States
Greece Philippines Venezuela
Hungary Poland Zambia
India Portugal

1.9.10 Net worth tax

Effective in 1992, Italian tax law provides for a net worth tax that must be paid by all business entities. The taxable basis is the company's net worth (subscribed capital, reserves and retained earnings) and the tax rate is 0.75%. This tax is scheduled to expire in 1994.

2. INDIRECT TAXES

2.1 Value-added tax (VAT)

VAT is imposed on virtually all transactions involving goods and services.

The VAT paid by an entrepreneur on goods and services received may normally be credited against the tax payable on his own turnover, so that in effect only the value added is taxed.

The normal rate of the tax is 19%. Reduced rates of 4%, 9% and 13% apply to basic necessities. For example, basic food stuffs are taxed at 4%, restaurant and hotel services are taxed at 9%, and textiles are taxed at 13%.

Companies must calculate their VAT debt or credit on a monthly basis. If there is a balance due, the payment must be made the following month.

If certain conditions are met, the VAT can be calculated and settled on a quarterly basis. The annual VAT return must be completed before March 15th.

2.1.1 VAT refunds to non-resident companies and individuals

The requirements under the VAT laws that apply to transactions in Italy by non-residents without a permanent establishment may be executed by a representative resident in Italy. This procedure allows a request for the refund of VAT paid in Italy. Non-resident companies subject to VAT in their own country may apply directly for the refund of VAT paid in Italy without appointing a fiscal representative, if they have no transactions in Italy (apart from those concerning international transport) and do not have a permanent establishment in Italy.

A VAT refund is also available on the purchase of goods for personal use (exceeding Lire 300,000) by non-resident visitors to Italy. The refund of VAT is possible only if certain procedures are followed. Most stores can provide the necessary information at the time of purchase. To obtain the VAT refund it is mandatory to obtain a validation stamp on the invoice. In order to obtain this stamp, the items purchased plus the documentation must be presented at customs upon departure from Italy (or at the border of final departure from the E.U.).

2.2 Local tax on increase in value of real estate (INVIM)

A local tax on the increase in value of immovable property (Imposta Comunale sull'Incremento di Valore degli Immobili) is imposed on gains realized on the disposal of immovable property.

The tax is imposed at progressive rates (between 5% and 30%) on the difference between the value of the real estate on December 31, 1992 and on the date when it was originally acquired.

Companies are not only subject to this tax on the disposal on their immovable property, but also on the increase in value of immovable property they owned for each period of ten years, unless the property is used directly in the company's own business activities.

The rates, which are applied to the ratio of the 'reference increase' value to original cost, are as follows:

Ratio of increased value to original cost Rate

up to 10% of reference increase 5%
10% - 50% of reference increase 10%
50% - 100% of reference increase 15%
100% - 150% of reference increase 20%
150% - 200% of reference increase 25%
Over 200% of reference increase 30%

The INVIM is scheduled to expire on December 31, 2003.

2.3 Registration Tax

All written deeds and documents having legal effect and executed in Italy must be registered with the Registry Office within 20 days from the date of execution. In addition, certain oral agreements specified in the Registry Tax Law must be registered. Agreements relating to payments that are subject to VAT are required to be registered only in the event of use, and then at nominal fixed rates. For example, royalties payable by an Italian licensee to a foreign licensor are subject to a self-invoicing VAT system kept by the licensee. The license agreement, therefore, must be registered only in special cases of use and at a fixed rate.

Contracts executed abroad must be registered before they are used in judicial, administrative or arbitration proceedings. The registration may be done at any time prior to production of the documents as evidence and upon payment of the normal registration tax, otherwise the official of the court or government office will proceed to register it after the decision.

Where a transaction is subject to VAT, the registration tax is at a normal flat rate amount. For transactions that are not subject to VAT, registration tax is levied at the following rates:

aggregate of 10% on conveyances of property and rights in property;

upon incorporation of a company or contribution to share capital, 1% is payable on the financial statement used for the incorporation or for a contribution in kind.

2.4 Land registration taxes

These taxes are due on sales of real estate at the rate of 2%.

2.5 Stamp tax

Almost all legal documents must be drafted on stamp paper, which may be purchased from public offices or authorized private dealers. The stamped papers generally cost Lire 15,000.

If a legal document required to be on stamped paper is drafted abroad, it may be written on ordinary paper and subsequently stamped in Italy at a public office upon payment of the appropriate stamp tax.

2.6 Stock transfer tax

All stock transfers are subjected to a tax on every Lire 100,000 of declared value as follows:

Lire/000

a.If the contract is direct between the parties:

*** shares, quotas of every kind of company 140**
*** currency including foreign currency 100**
*** bonds and treasury bonds 16**
b.If the contract is between a bank and a private person:
*** shares, quotas of every kind of company 50**
*** currency including foreign currency 90**
*** bonds and treasury bonds 9**

c.If the contract is between stock-holders:
*** shares, quotas of every kind of company 12**
*** currency including foreign currency 40**
*** bonds and treasury bonds 9**

2.7 Inheritance and gift tax

The amount of tax is determined according to a dual rate schedule as shown in the table below. The first rate (column A) is applied to the total value of the taxable estate. Where there are several heirs or beneficiaries, the tax is assessed proportionately between them. The other rates (columns B) represent additional tax payable only by an heir or beneficiaries who are neither a spouse or parent nor a direct descendant of the deceased and apply to each legacy or inheritance.

Rate on amount of inheritance or legacy

(A)Rate on (B)Brothers, (B)Relatives in

total value sisters and 4th degree,

of net direct or 3rd

Taxable value inheritance relatives of degree of (B)

(in millions of Lire) (%) spouse(%) spouse(%) Others(%)

10 - 100 - - 3 6
100 - 250 - 3 5 8
250 - 350 3 6 9 12
350 - 500 7 10 13 18
500 - 800 10 15 19 23
800 - 1,500 15 20 24 28
1,500 - 3,000 22 24 26 31
over 3,000 27 25 27 33

The taxable estate includes, in the case of Italian residents, all assets transferred, wherever situated, and, in the case of non-residents, all assets located in Italy.

Legacies to the Italian state, local governments, recognized non-profit making organizations (entri morali) foundations, and non-profit making public hospitals are exempt from tax and excluded from the total value of the estate on the basis of the tax rate in column A.

Italian death duty is reduced by the amount of foreign death duty paid on assets located in a foreign country to the extent that this amount does not exceed the proportion of total inheritance tax assessable on assets. It is also reduced by the amount of tax on the increase in value of property (INVIM) paid on property up to the amount of inheritance tax payable on such property.

2.8 Municipal tax on productive activities (ICIAP)

Companies conducting commercial activities must pay the ICIAP tax annually. The tax is based on:

The type of activity performed by the company (industrial, commercial, banking, etc.);

The surface area utilized by the company (square meters).

2.9 Municipal tax on buildings (ICI)

Effective January 1, 1993, a municipal tax on real estate property (I.C.I.) was introduced replacing ILOR on real estate. The taxable basis is the cadastral value of the building. In the event that the cadastral value has not been determined by the tax office, the taxpayer must determine by itself the cadastral value of the building on the basis of certain parameters. For industrial buildings without cadastral value, the taxable basis is the historical cost of the real estate property reevaluated by certain fixed parameters depending on the of the cost. The tax rate can range from 0.4% to 0.7% of the taxable basis.

GOVERNMENT ORGANIZATIONS AND ASSOCIATION IN SELECTED COUNTRIES

ALBANIA

Ministry of Industry, Mining and Energy

Tirana
Albania
Tel: 355 42 32746
Fax: 355 42 26717

ALGERIA

Agence pour l'Utilisation Rationnelle de l'Energie

c/o Ministry of Energy, 80 Rue Ben M'Hidi Larbi, Alger
Algeria
Tel: 213 2 739 410
Fax: 213 2 650 997

Centre for Development of Renewable Energies

B.P. 62, Route de l'Observatoire, Bouzareah, Alger
Algeria
Tel: 213 2 784 229
Fax: 213 2 799 862

Ministere de l'Energie et des Mines

80, Avenue Ahmed Ghermoul, Algiers
Algeria
Tel: 213 267 3300
Fax: 213 265 0997

Ministry of Mines and Industry

4 rue Ahmad Bey, Immeuble le Colisee, Algiers
Algeria
Tel: 213 260 1326.

Societé Nationale de Recherches et d'Exploitation Minieres

BP 860, Algiers
Algeria

ANGOLA

Chamber of Commerce and Industry

Largo do Kinaxixi no. 14 1º andar
CP 92
Luanda
Angola
Tel: 244 2 344 506

Ministry of Geology and Mines

PO Box 1260, Luanda
Angola
Tel: 244 2 322 766
Fax: 244 2 321 655

ARGENTINA

Buenos Aires Dirección de Recursos y Geológicas y Mineros

Torre Gubernamental II, Calle 53 esq 12 - piso 15°, 1900 La Plata, Buenos Aires
Argentina
Tel: 54 21 37281
Fax: 54 21 254828

Catamarca Secretaria de Mineria

Esquiu 503, 1°, 4700 San Fernando del Valle de Catamarca
Argentina
Tel: 54 833 25951
Fax: 54 833 24308

Chubut Dirección General de Minas y Geológica

Julio Argentino Roca 582, 9103 Rawson, Chubut
Argentina
Tel: 54 965 81462
Fax: 54 965 82603

Córdoba Secretaria de Mineria

Belgrano 347, 1°, 5000 Cno 347, Córdoba
Argentina
Tel: 54 51 221349
Fax: 54 51 245115

Entre Rios Dirección de Mineria y Recursos Hidricos

Corrientes 480, 3100 Parana, Entre Rios
Argentina
Tel: 54 43 214847

Ingenieria y Asistencia Tecnica Argentina SA (IATASA)

Tacuari 32, 9th, Buenos Aires 1071
Argentina
Tel: 54 1 331 4865
Fax: 54 1 331 9867

Instituto De Economia Energetica (IDEE)

Casilla de Corre, No. 138,, 8400 San Carlos, De Bariloche
Argentina
Tel: 54 9 442 0700
Fax: 54 9 442 2050

Instituto Nacional de Tecnologia Industrial

CC 157 - 1650 San Martan, Buenos Aires
Argentina
Tel: 54 1 755 6161
Fax: 54 1 753 4015

Instituto Nacional de Tecnologia Minera (INTEMIN)

Av Gral Paz entre Avda Constituyentes y Albarellos, Parque Tecnológico Miguelete, 1650 San Martín, Buenos Aires
Argentina
Fax: 54 1 754 4070
Email: luc@inti.edu.ar

Jujuy Dirección Provincial de Mineria

Lamadrid 438, 1° piso, 4600 San Salvador de Jujuy
Argentina
Tel: 54 882 26332
Fax: 54 882 30263

La Pampa Dirección de Minas

Centro Civico, 3° piso, 6300 Santa Rosa, La Pampa
Argentina
Tel: 54 954 33010
Fax: 54 954 31595

La Rioja Secretaria de Industria, Comercio y Mineria

Pelagio Luna 812, 1°, 5300 La Rioja
Argentina
Tel: 54 822 28519
Fax: 54 822 28570

Mendoza Dirección General de Mineria

Boulogne Sur Mer 3051, 5500 Mendoza
Argentina
Tel: 54 61 256442
Fax: 54 61 232934

Misiones Dirección General de Minas y Geologia

San Lorenzo 480, 3300 Posadas, Misiones
Argentina
Tel: 54 752 37436

Neuquén Dirección Provincial de Mineria

Casilla Postal 101, 8340 Zapala, Neuquén
Argentina
Tel: 54 942 21475
Fax: 54 942 21282

PROCOBRE - Argentina

Alsina 1607, 1er Piso, 1088 Buenos Aires
Argentina
Tel: 54 1 40 5063
Fax: 54 1 814 4407

Rio Negro Dirección de Mineria e Hidrogeolgia

Garrone 156, 8500 Viedma, Rio Negro
Argentina
Tel: 54 920 23833
Fax: 54 920 24604

Salta Dirección Provincial de Mineria

Centro Civico, Grand Bourg, 440 Salta
Argentina
Tel: 54 87 222184
Fax: 54 87 222384

San Juan Departamento de Mineria

Paula de Sarmiento 134, Oeste Edifico 9 de Julio, 4° piso 5400 San Juan
Argentina
Tel: 54 64 221984
Fax: 54 64 213732

San Luis Dirección Provincial de Mineria

Pedernera 1065, 5700 San Luis
Argentina
Tel: 54 652 25048
Fax: 54 652 26991

Santa Cruz Dirección General de Mineria

Mariano Moreno 123 y Fagnano, 9400 Rio Gallegos
Argentina
Tel: 54 966 20189
Fax: 54 966 24650

Santa Fe Dirección General de Industria y Mineria

Pellegrini 3100, 3000 Santa Fe
Argentina
Tel: 54 42 40181

Santiago del Estero Dirección General de Mineria y Geologica

25 de Mayo 60, 4200 Santiago de Estero
Argentina
Tel: 54 85 215022
Fax: 54 85 224238

Secretariat of Energy

Av Paseo Colon 171, Piso 8 of 803, 1063
Buenos Aires
Argentina
Tel: 54 1 349 8003
Fax: 54 1 343 6404

Tierra del Fuego Dirección General de Minas y Geologica

San Martin 1401, 9410 Ushuaia, Tierra del Fuego
Argentina
Tel: 54 901 22576
Fax: 54 901 22576

Tucumán Dirección de Minas

24 de Septiembre 848, 4000 San Migual de Tucumán
Argentina
Tel: 54 81 212645
Fax: 54 81 311138

AUSTRALIA

Association of Mining and Exploration Companies

3rd Floor, 33 Ord Street, West Perth,
Western Australia 6872
Australia
Tel: 61 9321 3999
Fax: 61 9321 3260
Email: amec@amec.asn.au

Australasian Institute of Mining and Metallurgy

Level 3/31, Pelham Street, Carlton, Victoria
3053
Australia
Tel: 61 3 9662 3166
Fax: 61 3 9662 3662
Email: editor@ausimm.com.au
URL: www.ausimm.com.au/

Australian Coal Association

39 Brisbane Avenue, Barton
Canberra, ACT
2600
Australia
Tel: 61 02 6273 6044
Fax: 61 02 6273 6060
Email: info@australiancoal.com.au
URL: www.australiancoal.com.au

Australian Geodynamics Cooperative Research Centre

CSIRO Exploration and Mining, 39 Fairway,,
PO Box 437, Nedlands WA 6009
Australia
Tel: 61 9 389 8421
Fax: 61 9 389 1906
Email: g.price@ned.dem.csiro.au
URL: www.agcrc.csiro.au/

Australian Geological Survey Organisation

PO Box 378, Canberra ACT 2601
Australia
Tel: 61 6 249 9111
Fax: 61 6 249 9777
Email: http@agso.gov.au
URL: www.agso.gov.au/

Australian Geoscience Information Association

63 Conyngham Street, Glenside, South Australia 5065
Australia
Tel: 61 8 8379 0444
Fax: 61 8 8379 1088
Email: kbond@amf.com.au
URL: www.agso.gov.au/agia/

Australian Mineral Foundation

63 Conyngham Street, Glenside, South Australia 5065
Australia
Tel: 61 8 8379 0444
Fax: 61 8 8379 4634
Email: amf@amf.com.au

Australian Mining and Petroleum Law Association

4th Floor, 360 Lt Bourke Street, Melbourne, VIC 3000
Australia
Tel: 61 3 967 02544
Fax: 61 3 967 02616

Australian Society of Exploration Geophysicists

P.O. Box 42,
Everton Park,
Queensland 4053.
Australia
Tel: 61 07 3855 8144
Fax: 61 07 3855 8177
Email: secretary@aseg.org.au
URL: www.aseg.org.au

Chamber of Minerals and Energy of Western Australia

7th floor, 12 St George's Tce, Perth WA 6000
Australia
Tel: 61 9 325 2955
Fax: 61 9 221 9848
Email: info@mineralswa.asn.au
URL: www.mineralswa.asn.au/

Commonwealth Scientific and Industrial Research Organization, Division of Energy Technology

PO Box 26, Highett, Victoria 3190
Australia
Tel: 61 3 555 0333

Commonwealth Scientific and Industrial Research Organization, Div of Exploration and Mining

Floreat Park Laboratories, Private Bag, Wembley, Western Australia 6014
Australia
Tel: 61 9 387 0232
Fax: 61 9 387 8642
Email: webmaster@ned.dem.csiro.au
URL: www.dem.csiro.au/

Commonwealth Scientific and, Industrial Research Organization (CSIRO), Division of Minerals

Box 312, Clayton South, Victoria 3169
Australia
Tel: 61 3 9545 8500
Fax: 61 3 9562 8919
URL: www.minerals.csiro.au/

Cooperative Research Centre for Mining Technology and Equipment

PO Box 883, Kenmore, Queensland 4069
Australia
Tel: 61 7 3346 2521
Fax: 61 7 3346 2523
Email: info@cmte.org.au
URL: www.cmte.org.au/

Copper Development Association of Australia

GDN FLR 8-10 Palmer Street, North Paramatta, Sydney 2151
Australia
Tel: 61 2 9289 7854
Fax: 61 2 9289 7222

Department of Primary Industries and Energy

Edmund Barton Building, Kings Avenue
Barton
Australian Capital Territory
Australia
Tel: 61 6 272 3933
Email: webmaster@dpie.gov.au
URL: www.dpie.gov.au/

Energy Research and Development Corporation

GPO Box 629, Canberra, ACT 2601
Australia
Tel: 61 6 274 4800
Fax: 61 6 274 4801

Energy Victoria

5/115 Victoria Parade, Fitzroy, Victoria 3065
Australia
Tel: 61 3 412 5666
Fax: 61 3 412 5677

Engineers Australia

11 National Circuit
Barton
ACT 2600
Australia
Tel: 61 6 270 6555
Fax: 61 6 273 1488
Email: contact_cust_service@ieaust.org.au
URL: www.engineersaustralia.org.au

Geological Society of Australia

1203 Wynyard House, 301 George St, Sydney NSW 2000
Australia
Tel: 61 2 290 2194
Fax: 61 2 290 2198
Email: misha@gsa.org.au
URL: www.agso.gov.au/gsa/

Institute of Metals and Materials Australasia

Suite 205 / 21 Bedford Street, North Melbourne, Victoria 3051
Australia
Tel: 61 3 9326 7266
Fax: 61 3 9326 7272

Julius Kruttschnitt Mineral Research Centre

University Mine, Isles Road, Indooroopilly, Queensland 4068
Australia
Tel: 61 7 3365 5888
Fax: 61 7 3365 5999
Email: jkmrc@mailbox.uq.edu.au
URL: www.jkmrc.uq.edu.au

Metal Mining Agency of Japan

PO Box 253, Civic Square, Canberra, A.C.T. 2608
Australia
Tel: 61 2 6248 0870
Fax: 61 2 6247 5865
Email: mmajau@cyberone.com.au

Mineral Resources Tasmania

PO Box 56, Rosny Park, Tasmania 7018
Australia
Tel: 61 3 6233 8333
Fax: 61 3 6233 8338
Email: info@mrt.tas.gov.au
URL: www.mrt.tas.gov.au/

Minerals Council of Australia

PO Box 363, Dickson ACT 2602
Australia
Tel: 61 6 279 3600
Fax: 61 6 279 3699
Email: minerals@ozemail.com.au
URL: www.minerals.org.au/

National Safety Council of Australia

322 Glenferrie Road,
Malvern,
VIC 3144
Australia
Tel: 61 03 9832 1555
Fax: 61 03 9824 6896
Email: vicsafe@nsca.org.au
URL: www.nsca.org.au

Northern Territory Department of Mines and Energy

GPO Box 2901, Darwin NT 0801
Australia
Tel: 61 8 89995511
Fax: 61 8 89817861
URL: www.minerals.nt.gov.au

Northern Territory Minerals Council

Suites 6-7, Raffles Plaza, Buffalo Court, Darwin, NT 800
Australia
Tel: 61 89 814 486
Fax: 61 89 411 625

Safety in Mines Testing and Research Station (SIMTARS)

PO Box 467, Goodna, Queensland 4300
Australia
Tel: 61 7 3810 6333
Fax: 61 7 3810 6363
Email: enquiries@dme.qld.gov.au

Standards Australia

1 The Crescent, Homebush 2140, PO Box 1055, Strathfield NSW 2135
Australia
Tel: 61 2 746 4600
Fax: 61 2 746 3333
Email: sales@sai-global.com
URL: www.standards.com.au/

Sydney Mineral Exploration Discussion Group

Australia
URL: www.smedg.org.au/

University of New South Wales, School of Mines

Sydney 2052, NSW
Australia

Tel: 61 2 9385 5006
Fax: 61 2 9313 7269
Email: r.benninghaus@unsw.edu.au
URL: www.mines.unsw.edu.au/

University of Queensland, Department of Mining and Metallurgical Engineering

Brisbane, Queensland 4072
Australia
Tel: 61 7 3365 3738
Fax: 61 7 3365 3888
Email: admin@minmet.uq.edu.au

University of South Australia, Mining Engineering Research Group

Mawson Lakes, South Australia
Australia
Tel: 61 8 8302 3248
Fax: 61 8 8302 3379
Email: a.meyers@unisa.edu.au
URL: www.unisa.edu.au/egg/merg/

Uranium Information Centre

GPO Box 1649N
Melbourne 3001
Australia
Tel: 61 3 9629 7744
Fax: 61 3 9629 7207
Email: uic@mpx.com.au
URL: www.uic.com.au/

West Australian Mining Club

PO Box 552, West Perth, WA 6872
Australia
Tel: 61 8 9341 2891
Email: bartjohn@iinet.net.au

Western Australian School of Mines

PMB 22, Kalgoorlie, Western Australia 6430
Australia
Tel: 61 9088 6101
Fax: 61 9088 6103
Email: wasm@wasm.curtin.edu.au
URL: www.wasm.curtin.edu.au

AUSTRIA

Verwertungsagentur (EVA)

Linke Wienzeile 18, A-1060 Wien
Austria
Tel: 43 1 586 1524
Fax: 43 1 586 9488

Geologische Bundesanstalt

Rasumofskygasse 23, POB 127, A-1031, Wien
Austria
Tel: 43 1 712 56 74 0
Fax: 43 1 712 56 74 56
Email: webmaster@cc.geolba.ac.at
URL: www.geolba.ac.at/

International Social Security Association

Allgemeine Unfallversicherungsanstalt,
Adalbert-Stifter-Strasse 65, A-1200 Wien
Austria
Tel: 43 1 33 111 558
Fax: 43 1 33 111 469

Technische Universitat Wien, Institut fur Energiewirtschaft

Gusshausstrasse 27-29/357, A-1040 Wien
Austria
Tel: 43 1 58 801 5201
Fax: 43 1 505 4371

University of Leoben, Department of Mining Engineering and Mineral Economics

Franz-Josef-Strasse 18, A-8700 Leoben
Austria
Tel: 43 3842 402 0
Fax: 43 3842 402 308
URL: www.unileoben.ac.at/

BANGLADESH

Ministry of Energy and Mineral Resources (MEMR)

Dhaka
Bangladesh
Tel: 880 2 832 045
Fax: 880 2 241 4060

BELGIUM

Comité Européen de Normalisation

Rue de Stassart 36, B-1050 Brussels
Belgium
Tel: 32 2 550 0811
Fax: 32 2 550 0819
URL: www.stri.is/CEN/

Copper Development Association Benelux

168/4, Avenue de Tervuren, 1150 Brussels
Belgium
Tel: 32 2 7760090
Fax: 32 2 7760096

European Committee for Standardization

Rue de Stassart 36
B-1050 Brussels
Belgium
Tel: 32 2 550 0811
Fax: 32 2 550 0819

Federal Energy Committee Belgium

Tenbroeklaan 3, B-3090 Overijse
Belgium
Tel: 32 2 511 1830
Fax: 32 2 511 8111

International Iron and Steel Institute

12 Rue Colonel Bourg, B-1140 Brussels
Belgium
Tel: 32 2 702 89 00
Fax: 32 2 702 88 99
Email: steel@iisi.be
URL: www.iisi.be/

International Zinc Association

168 Avenue de Tervueren/Box 4, B-1150 Brussels
Belgium
Tel: 32 2 776 0070
Fax: 32 2 776 0089
Email: email@iza.com
URL: www.iza.com/

BELIZE

Ministry of Natural Resources

Cayo District, 34-36 Unity Blvd, Belmopan
Belize
Tel: 501 822 630

BENIN

Ministry of Energy, Mines and Hydraulica

BP 04-1412, Cotonou
Benin
Fax: 229 31 35 46

BOTSWANA

Botswana Technology Centre

Private Mail Bag 0082
Gaborone
Botswana
Tel: 267 314 161
Fax: 267 374 677

Department of Mines

Private Bag 0049, Gaborone
Botswana
Tel: 267 352 641

Ministry of Commerce and Industry

Private Bag 004
Gaborne
Botswana
Tel: 267 360 1200
Fax: 267 371 539

Ministry of Mineral Resources and Water Affairs

Private Bag 0018, Gaborne
Botswana
Tel: 267 360 4600
Fax: 267 352 738

BRAZIL

Brazilian Aluminium Association

Av República do Líbano, 671, 04501-000, São Paulo
Brazil
Tel: 55 11 885 0222
Fax: 55 11 885 5822

Brazilian Association of Ferroalloys Producers

Av Brigadeiro Faria Lima, 2223/cj.16, 01451-001, São Paulo
Brazil
Tel: 55 11 814 1552
Fax: 55 11 210 1114

Brazilian Cement Association

Av Torres de Oliveira, 76, 05347-902, São Paulo
Brazil
Tel: 55 11 268 5111
Fax: 55 11 268 5984

Brazilian Copper Association

Rua Mariana Correia, 52, 01444-000, São Paulo
Brazil
Tel: 55 11 883 2622
Fax: 55 11 883 2814

Brazilian Foundry Association

Av Eng° Billings, 526, 05321-000, São Paulo
Brazil
Tel: 55 11 819 2515
Fax: 55 11 819 3783

Brazilian Lime Association

Rua Marconi, 131/11° andar, 01047-910, São Paulo
Brazil

Tel: 55 11 258 5366
Fax: 55 11 257 4228

Brazilian Metals Association

Rua Antônio Comparato, 218, 04605-035, São Paulo
Brazil
Tel: 55 11 536 4333
Fax: 55 11 240 4273

Brazilian Mining Institute

SCS - Edif. Camargo Correia 1 Bl. F, 9º andar, CEP 70397-900, Brasília - DF
Brazil
Tel: 55 61 226 9367
Fax: 55 61 226 9560

Brazilian Phosphate Institute

Praça Dom José Gaspar, 30/9º andar, 01047-901, São Paulo
Brazil
Tel: 55 11 255 9277

Brazilian Steel Institute

Av Rio Branco, 181/28º andar, 20040-007, Rio de Janeiro
Brazil
Tel: 55 21 210 3255
Fax: 55 21 262 2234

Companhia Baiana de Pesquisa Mineral (CBPM)

4ª Avenida, 460 Centro Administrativo da Bahia, 41750-300 Salvador, Bahia
Brazil
Tel: 55 71 371 4432
Fax: 55 71 371 7024
URL: www.cbpm.com.br/

Department of Mining

Rua Lefgreen 2225, CEP 04040-033, São Paulo - SP
Brazil
Tel: 55 11 549 5533
Fax: 55 11 549 5826

Energy Application Agency

Av. Paulista, 1776-22 Andar, 01310-921 Sao Paulo
Brazil
Tel: 55 11 284 0704
Fax: 55 11 287 0609

Geological Survey of Brazil

Companhia de Pesquisa de Recursos Minerais, Av. Pasteur, 404, Urca 22292-240, Rio de Janeiro
Brazil
Tel: 55 21 295 5897
Fax: 55 21 295 6347
Email: seus@sgb.cprm.gov.br
URL: www.cprm.gov.br/

Ministry of Mines and Energy

Esplanana dos Ministérios, Bloco U, 7º andar, CEP 70000, Brasília - DF
Brazil
Tel: 55 61 226 5101
Fax: 55 61 223 0109

National Department of Minerals Production

SAN - Q.01 - Bloco B, 70040-200 Brasilia
Brazil
Tel: 55 21 224 2670
Fax: 55 21 225 8274

National Energy Efficiency Institute

Rua Uruguaiana, 55 - Sala 903, 20005-094
Centro Rio de Janeiro, CEP 20043-900
Brazil
Tel: 55 21 242 0456
Fax: 55 21 242 5148

National Gold Association

Rua Líbero Badaró, 471/5° andar, 01009-000, São Paulo
Brazil
Tel: 55 11 605 0366
Fax: 55 11 605 6992

National Syndicate of the Iron Ore and Base Metals Industry

Av Nilo Peçanha, 50/18° andar gr. 1810, 20044-900, Rio de Janeiro
Brazil
Tel: 55 21 262 0583
Fax: 55 21 262 0318

National Syndicate of the Tin Industry

Rua do Carmo, 11/sl. 1302, 20011-020, Rio de Janeiro
Brazil
Tel: 55 21 220 1704
Fax: 55 21 220 3509

Non-ferrous Metals Institute

Av Nove de Julho, 4015, 01407-100, São Paulo
Brazil
Tel: 55 11 887 2033
Fax: 55 11 885 8124

PROCOBRE - Brasil

CJ 601 Sao Paulo
Brazil
Tel: 55 11 816 6383
Fax: 55 11 816 6383
Email: procobre@homeshopping.com.br

World Energy Council

Rua Real Brandeza, 219-69C, 22283-900
Rio de Janeiro
Brazil
Tel: 55 21 246 8593
Fax: 55 21 226 0508

BULGARIA

Association Energetica

8 Triaditza Str., Sofia, BG-1040
Bulgaria
Tel: 359 2 861 91

Committee of Energy

8 Triaditza Str., Sofia, BG-1040
Bulgaria
Tel: 359 2 861 91
Fax: 359 2 87 58 26

Committee of Geology

Boul. Maria Louisa 22, Sofia
Bulgaria

Tel: 359 2 83 39 76
Fax: 359 2 83 35 68

EC Energy Centre

51 James Boucher Bld, 1407 Sofia
Bulgaria
Tel: 359 2 683 542
Fax: 359 2 681 461

Ministry of Industry and Trade

8 Slavenska Str
1000 Sofia
Bulgaria
Tel: 359 2 867 2695
Fax: 359 2 867 2663

University of Mining and Geology

St Ivan Rilski, Studentski grad, 1110 Sofia
Bulgaria
Tel: 359 2 687 224
Fax: 359 2 627 042
Email: webmaster@www.mgu.bg
URL: www.mgu.bg/

BURKINA FASO

Societé de Recherches et d'Exploitation Minieres du Burkina

BP 5562
Burkina Faso
Tel: 226 306 235

BURUNDI

Ministry of Energy and Mines, Directorate for Energy

BP 745, Bujumbura
Burundi
Tel: 257 22 6579
Fax: 257 22 3528

Research Centre for Alternative Energies

PO Box 255, Bujumbura
Burundi
Tel: 257 22 321 05

CAMEROON

Chamber of Commerce, Industry and Mines

PO Box 4011
Douala
Cameroon
Tel: 237 42 28 88
Fax: 237 42 55 96

Institute for Geological and Mining Research, Energy Research Laboratory

PO Box 4110, Yaounde
Cameroon
Tel: 237 23 0008

Ministry of Industrial and Commercial Development

Yaounde
Cameroon
Tel: 237 21 40 40
Fax: 237 22 27 04

Ministry of Mines and Energy

PO Box 955, Yaounde
Cameroon
Tel: 237 22 01 97
Fax: 237 21 19 93

CANADA

Alberta Chamber of Resources

1410 Oxford Tower, 10235 - 101 St.,
Edmonton, Alberta, T5J 3G1
Canada
Tel: 1 403 420 1030
Fax: 1 403 425 4623

Alberta Department of Energy

300 - 801 - 6th Avenue S.W., Calgary,
Alberta T2P 3W2
Canada
Tel: 1 403 297 5500
Fax: 1 403 263 8144
Email: walkerk@enr.gov.ab.ca

Alberta Energy Utilities Board

640 - 5th Avenue SW, Calgary, Alberta T2P 3G4
Canada
Tel: 1 403 297 8311
Fax: 1 403 297 7336
Email: aeubsys@mail.eub.gov.ab.ca
URL: www.eub.gov.ab.ca/

Alberta Research Council

3rd Floor, 6815 - 8 Street N.E.
Calgary
Alberta T2E 7H7
Canada
Tel: 1 403 297 2600
Fax: 1 403 297 2607
Email: techline@arc.ab.ca
URL: www.arc.ab.ca/

American Society of Mechanical Engineers (ASME)

Simon Fraser University, School of Engineering Science
Burnaby
BC V5A 1S6
Canada
Tel: 1 604 291 4290
Fax: 1 604 291 4951
URL: www.asme.org/

Association of Consulting Engineers of Manitoba

4 Donald Street South Winnipeg
Manitoba R3L 2T7
Canada
Tel: 1 204 475 7774
URL: www.mbnet.mb.ca/acem/

Association of Exploration Geochemists

PO Box 48270, Bentall Centre, Vancouver,
British Columbia, V7X 1A1
Canada
Tel: 1 604 685 4767
Fax: 1 604 684 5392
British Columbia Branch
Dr Kay Fletcher, PEng/PGeo
University of British Columbia, Geological Sciences
6339 Stores Rd, Vancouver BC V6T 1WS
Canada
Tel: +1 604 822 2392
Fax: +1 604 822 6088

Association of Professional Engineers and Geoscientists of British Columbia (APEGBC)

200-4010 Regent Street
Burnaby
British Columbia V5C 6N2
Canada
Tel: 1 604 430 8035

Fax: 1 604 430 8085
URL: www.apeg.bc.ca/

Association of Professional Engineers and Geoscientists of Newfoundland (APEGN)

120 Torbay Rd, PO box 21207
St John's
NF A1A5B2
Canada
Tel: 1 709 753 7714
Fax: 1 709 753 6131

Association of Professional Engineers of Manitoba (APEM)

850A Pembia Hwy
Winnipeg
MB R3M 2M7
Canada
Tel: 1 204 474 2736
Fax: 1 204 474 5960
URL: www.apem.mb.ca/

Association of Professional Engineers of New Brunswick (APENB)

535 Beaverbrook Court, Suite 105
Frederiction NB E3B 1X6
Canada
Tel: 1 506 458 8083
Fax: 1 506 451 9629
URL: ctca.unb.ca/apenb/apenb.html

Association of Professional Engineers of Nova Scotia (APENS)

1355 Barrington St, PO Box 129
Halifax NS B3J 2M4
Canada
Tel: 1 902 429 2250
Fax: 1 902 423 9769
URL: www.apens.ns.ca/

Association of Professional Engineers of Prince Edward Island (APEPEI)

549 North River Rd
Charlottetown
PE C1E 1J6
Canada
Tel: 1 902 566 1268
Fax: 1 902 566 5551
URL: www.apepei.com/

Association of Professional Engineers of the Yukon Territory (APEYT)

PO Box 4125, Whitehorse YT YIA 3S9
Canada
Tel: 1 403 667 6727
Fax: 1 667 6727

Association of Professional Engineers, Geologists and Geophysicists

1500 Scotia Pl Tower One, 10060 Jasper Avenue N.W., Edmonton, Alberta T5J 4A2
Canada
Tel: 1 403 426 3990
Fax: 1 403 426 1877
URL: www.apegga.com/

Association of Professional Engineers, Geologists and Geophysicists of Saskatchewan (APEGS)

2255 13th Ave
Regina SK S4P 0V6
Canada
Tel: 1 306 525 9547 or 1 800 500 9547
Fax: 1 306 525 0851
URL: www.apegs.sk.ca/

Association of Professional Geologists and Geophysicists of Quebec

6700 Avenue du Parc, Ste 110, Montreal, Quebec, H2V 4H9
Canada
Tel: 1 514 270 3851
Fax: 1 514 271 4679

British Columbia and Yukon Chamber of Mines

840 West Hastings Street, Vancouver, British Columbia, V6C 1C8
Canada
Tel: 1 604 681 5328
Fax: 1 604 681 2363
Email: chamber@bc-mining-house.com
URL: www.bc-mining-house.com/

British Columbia Geophysical Society

Placer Dome Inc, PO Box 49330 Bentall Postal Station, Vancouver BC V7X 1P1
Canada
Tel: 1 604 661 3773
Fax: 1 604 661 3798

British Columbia Ministry of Energy and Mines, Communications Division

PO Box 9324, 8th Floor 1810 Blanshard St, Victoria, British Columbia V8W 9N3
Canada
Tel: 1 250 952 0606
Fax: 1 250 952 0254
Email: webmaster.mem@gems4.gov.bc.ca
URL: www.gov.bc.ca/em/

Canadian Association of Mining Equipment and Services for Export

Suite 101, 345 Renfrew Drive, Markham, Ontario, L3R 9S9
Canada
Tel: 1 905 513 0046
Fax: 1 905 513 1834
Email: minesupply@camese.org
URL: www.camese.org/

Canadian Copper and Brass Development Association

10 Gateway Boulevard, Suite 375, Don Mills, Ontario M3C 3A1
Canada
Tel: 1 416 421 0788
Fax: 1 416 421 8092

Canadian Council of Professional Engineers (CCPE)

#401-116 Albert St
Ottawa ON K1P 5G3
Canada
Tel: 1 613 232 2474
Fax: 1 613 230 5759
URL: www.ccpe.ca/

Canadian Diamond Drilling Association

306 - 222 McIntyre Street, W North Bay, Ontario, P1B 2Y8
Canada
Tel: 1 705 476 6992
Fax: 1 705 476 9494

Canadian Energy Research Institute

150, 3512-33 Street, N.W., Calgary, Alberta T2L 2A6
Canada
Tel: 1 403 282 1231
Fax: 1 403 284 4181

Email: cdneri@acs.ucalgary.ca
URL: www.ceri.ca/

Canadian Geoscience Council

Department of Earth Sciences, University of Waterloo, Waterloo, Ontario N2L 3G1
Canada
Tel: 1 619 885 1211
Fax: 1 619 746 7484
Email: avmorgan@sciborg.uwaterloo.ca
URL: www.science.uwaterloo.ca/earth/cgc/

Canadian Geotechnical Society

P.O. Box 937, Alliston, Ontario L9R 1W1
Canada
Tel: 1 705 434 0916
Fax: 1 705 434 0917
Email: cgs@cgs.ca

Canadian Institute of Mining, Metallurgy and Petroleum

Xerox Tower, Suite 1210, 3400 de Maisonneuve Boulevard West
Canada
Tel: 1 514 939 2710 ext 304
Fax: 1 514 939 2714

Canadian Institute of Resources Law

MFH 3330, University of Calgary
Calgary
Alberta T2N 1N4
Canada
Tel: 1 403 220 3200
Fax: 1 403 282 6182
Email: cirl@ucalgary.ca
URL: www.cirl.ca

Canadian Mineral Analysts

Box 894, Sigrid Fast, Manitoba, R0B 0W0
Canada
Tel: 1 204 356 2902
Fax: 1 204 356 2902

Canadian Mining Industry Research Organization (CAMIRO)

935 Ramsey Lake Road, Sudbury, Ontario P3E 2C6
Canada
Tel: 1 705 673 6595
Fax: 1 705 675 1024
Email: info@camiro.org
URL: www.camiro.org/

Canadian Portland Cement Association (CPCA)

201-1155 Pender St W, Vancouver BC V6E 2P4
Canada
Tel: 1 604 685 0582
Fax: 1 604 685 1574

Canadian Society of Exploration Geophysicists

905, 510 5th Street SW, Calgary, Alberta T2P 3S8
Canada
Tel: 1 403 262 0015
Fax: 1 403 262 7383
Email: webmaster@geo.ucalgary.ca

Canadian Society of Industrial Engineers (CSIE)

1149 Montroyal Blvd
North Vancouver BC V7R 2H8
Canada

Tel: 1 604 986 8595
Fax: 1 604 986

Centre for Environmental Monitoring (CEM)

Laurentian University, Willet Green Miller Centre
933 Ramsey Lake Road, Sudbury, Ontario, P3E 6B5
Canada
Tel: 1 705 675 1151 x.5087
Fax: 1 705 675 4838
Email: cem@mirarco.org
URL: www.mirarco.org

Centre for Integrated Monitoring Technology (CIMTEC)

Laurentian University, Willet Green Miller Centre
933 Ramsey Lake Road, Sudbury, Ontario, P3E 6B5
Canada
Tel: 1 705 675 1151 x.5098
Fax: 1 705 675 4838
Email: info@cimtec.ca
URL: www.cimtec.ca

Centre for Mining Technology (CMT)

Laurentian University, Willet Green Miller Centre
933 Ramsey Lake Road, Sudbury, Ontario, P3E 6B5
Canada
Tel: 1 705 675 1151 x.5074
Fax: 1 705 675 4838
Email: cmt@mirarco.org
URL: www.mirarco.org

Chamber of Mines of Eastern British Columbia

215 Hall Street, Nelson, British Columbia, V1L 5X4
Canada

Coal Association of Canada

205 9th Avenue SE Ste 502, Calgary, Alberta T2G 0R3
Canada
Tel: 1 403 262 1544
Fax: 1 403 262 1544

Consulting Engineers of British Columbia (CEBC)

#514-409 Granville St
Vancouver BC V6C 1T2
Canada
Tel: 1 604 687 2811
Fax: 1 604 688 7110
URL: www.cebc.org/

Ecole Polytechnique de Montreal Department of Mineral Engineering

PO Box 6079, Station A Montreal, PQ H3C 3A7
Canada
Tel: 1 514 340 4777

Engineering Institute of Canada (EIC)

104 8475 Ontario St
Vancouver BC V5X 3EX
Canada
Tel: 1 604 324 2441
Fax: 1 604 324 1454
URL: www.eic-ici.ca/

Environmental Mining Council of British Columbia

1216 Broad Street, Victoria, British Columbia, V8W 2A5
Canada
Tel: 1 604 384 2686
Fax: 1 604 384 2620
URL: www.miningwatch.org/emcbc/

Geological Association of Canada

Department of Earth Sciences, Memorial University of Newfoundland,
St. John's,
Newfoundland, A1B 3X5
Canada
Tel: 1 709 737 7660
Fax: 1 709 737 2532
Email: gac@esd.mun.ca
URL: www.gac.ca

Geological Survey of Canada

601 rue Booth St., Ottawa, Ontario K1A 0E8
Canada
Tel: 1 613 996 3919
Fax: 1 613 943 0646
Email: webmaster@gsc.nrcan.gc.ca
URL: www.nrcan.gc.ca/gsc/

Geomechanics Research Centre (GRC)

Laurentian University, Willet Green Miller Centre
933 Ramsey Lake Road, Sudbury, Ontario, P3E 6B5
Canada
Tel: 1 705 675 1151 x.5076
Fax: 1 705 675 4838
Email: grc@mirarco.org
URL: www.mirarco.org

Institute of Electrical and Electronics Engineers Inc (IEEE)

Box 4485, Vancouver BC V6B 4X3
Canada
Tel: 1 604 528 8196
Fax: 1 604 528 1828
Email: jmarusen@eprinet.epri.com

International Association of Hydrogeologists, British Columbia Representative

215-260 Esplanade W, North Vancouver, BC V7N 3G7
Canada
Tel: 1 604 986 8551
Fax: 1 604 985 7286

International Council on Metals and the Environment

294 Albert Street, Suite 506, Ottawa, Ontario, K2P 6E6
Canada
Tel: 1 613 235 4263
Fax: 1 613 235 2865
Email: webmaster@icme.com

Manitoba Government, Department of Energy and Mines

PO Box 1359, 227 King Street, Virden, Manitoba R0M 2C0
Canada
Tel: 1 204 746 1557
Fax: 1 204 746 2208

McGill University, Department of Mining and Metallurgy

3450 University Street, Montreal, Quebec H3A 2A7
Canada
Tel: 1 514 398 4373

Fax: 1 514 398 7099
URL: www.minmet.mcgill.ca/

Mineralogical Association of Canada

Cityview 78087, Nepean, Ontario, K2G 5W2
Canada
Tel: 1 613 226 4651
Fax: 1 613 226 4651
URL: www.mineralogicalassociation.ca/

Mines Accident Prevention Association of Ontario

Box 1468, North Bay, Ontario, P1B 8K6
Canada
Tel: 1 705 472 4140
Fax: 1 705 472 5800

Mining Association of British Columbia

Mining House, 840 West Hastings Street, Vancouver, British Columbia, V6C 1C8
Canada
Tel: 1 604 681 4321
Fax: 1 604 681 5305
URL: www.mining.bc.ca/

Mining Association of Canada

350 Sparks Street, Suite 1105, Ottawa, Ontario, K1R 7S8
Canada
Tel: 1 613 233 9391
Fax: 1 613 233 8897
URL: www.mining.ca/

Mining Association of Manitoba

305 Broadway, Ste 700, Winnipeg, Manitoba, R3C 3J7
Canada
Tel: 1 204 942 2789
Fax: 1 204 943 4371

Mining Exploration Group

Homestake Canada, 1000 - 700 Pender St W, Vancouver BC V6C 1G8
Canada
Tel: 1 604 684 2345
Fax: 1 604 685 3953

Mining Industry Land Use Committee

74 Victoria Street, Ste 1002, Toronto, Ontario, M5C 2A5
Canada
Tel: 1 416 362 1969
Fax: 1 416 757 9505

Mining Industry Technology Council of Canada

350 Sparks Street, Ste 1105, Ottawa, Ontario K1R 7S8
Canada
Tel: 1 613 233 9835
Fax: 1 613 233 0579

Mining Innovation, Rehabilitation and Applied Research Corporation (MIRARCO)

Laurentian University, Willet Green Miller Centre
933 Ramsey Lake Road, Sudbury, Ontario, P3E 6B5
Canada
Tel: 1 705 675 1151 x 5075
Fax: 1 705 675 4838
Email: mirarco@mirarco.org
URL: www.mirarco.org

National Energy Board

311 - 6th Avenue S.W., Calgary, Alberta
T2P 3H2
Canada
Tel: 1 403 292 4800
Fax: 1 403 292 5503

National Energy Conservation Association

PO Box 3214, Winnipeg, Manitoba R3C 4E7
Canada
Tel: 1 204 783 1273
Fax: 1 204 774 6702

National Research Council

Montreal Road, Ottawa, Ontario, K1A 0R6
Canada
Tel: 1 613 993 2024
Fax: 1 613 952 7928

Natural Resources Canada (Department of), Minerals and Metals Sector

580 Booth Street, Ottawa, Ontario K1A OE4
Canada
Tel: 1 613 995 0947
Fax: 1 613 952 8169
Email: llaflech@nrcan.gc.ca
URL: www.nrcan.gc.ca/mms/

New Brunswick Government, Department of Natural Resources And Energy

10 Regent Street, Fredericton, New Brunswick E3B 5H1
Canada
Tel: 1 506 453 2206
Fax: 1 506 453 3671

New Brunswick Mining Association

236 St George Street, Ste 312, Moncton, New Brunswick, E1C 1W1
Canada
Tel: 1 506 857 3056
Fax: 1 506 857 3059

New Brunswick Prospectors and Developers Association

PO Box 1195, Bathurst, New Brunswick, E2A 4H9
Canada
Tel: 1 506 857 5056
Fax: 1 506 546 4088

Newfoundland Department of Mines and Energy

PO Box 8700, St John's, Newfoundland, A1B 4J6
Canada
Tel: 1 709 576 2920
Fax: 1 709 576 0059

Nickel Development Institute

214 King Street West, Suite 510, Toronto, M5H 3S6
Canada
Tel: 1 416 591 7999
Fax: 1 416 591 7987
URL: www.nidi.org/

Northwest Territories Association of Professional Engineers, Geologists and Geophysicists

4807 49th St Unit 5, Yellowknife NT X1A 3T5

Canada
Tel: 1 403 920 4055
Fax: 1 403 873 4058
Email: napegg@tamerack.nt.ca
URL: www.napegg.nt.ca/

Northwest Territories Chamber of Mines

PO Box 2818, Yellowknife, Northwest Territories, X1A 2R1
Canada
Tel: 1 403 873 5281
Fax: 1 403 920 2145
Email: nwtmines@ssimicro.com
URL: www.miningnorth.com/

Nova Scotia Department of Natural Resources

PO Box 698, Halifax, Nova Scotia, B3J 2T9
Canada
Tel: 1 902 424 7943

Ontario Mining Association

110 Yonge Street, Ste 1501, Toronto, Ontario, M5C 1T4
Canada
Tel: 1 416 364 9301
Fax: 1 416 364 5986

Ontario Ministry of Natural Resources

6301 - 99 Wellesley St W, Whitney Block,, Queen's Park, Toronto, Ontario, P3E 6A5
Canada
Tel: 1 416 314 2301
Fax: 1 416 314 2216

Ontario Ministry of Northern Development and Mines, Mines and Minerals Division

933 Ramsey Lake Road, Sudbury, Ontario P3E 6B5
Canada
Tel: 1 705 670 5755
Fax: 1 705 670 5818
Email: marc.leroux@ndm.gov.on.ca
URL: www.mndm.gov.on.ca/mndm/mines/Default_e.asp

Ontario Prospectors Association

PO Box 1665, Timmins, Ontario, P4N 7W8
Canada
Tel: 1 705 235 5800
Fax: 1 705 235 5700

Ordre des Ingenieurs du Quebec (OIQ)

2020 rue University, 18e etage, Montreal PQ H3A 2A5
Canada
Tel: 1 514 845 6141 or 1 800 461 6141
Fax: 1 514 845 1833
URL: www.oiq.qc.ca/

Prince Edward Island Department of Energy and Forestry

PO Box 2000, Charlottetown, Prince Edward Island, C1A 7N8
Canada
Tel: 1 902 368 5020
Fax: 1 902 368 5544

Professional Engineers Ontario (PEO)

25 Sheppard Ave W, Suite 1000, North York ON M2N 6S9

Canada
Tel: 1 416 224 1100
Fax: 1 416 224 8168
URL: www.peo.on.ca/

Prospectors and Developers Association of Canada

34 King Street E, 9th Floor, Toronto, Ontario, M4C 2X8
Canada
Tel: 1 416 362 1969
Fax: 1 416 362 0101

Quebec Asbestos Mining Association

1130 Sherbrooke St W, Montreal, Quebec, H3A 2MB
Canada
Tel: 1 514 842 0382
Fax: 1 514 844 1381

Quebec Department of Energy and Resources, Mines Division

5700 4th Avenue W, Bureau A-308, Charlesbourg, Quebec G1H 6R1
Canada
Tel: 1 418 646 5700

Quebec Mining Association

2635 Blvd Hochelaga, Ste 942 Sainte-Foy, Sainte-Foy, Quebec, G1V 4W2
Canada
Tel: 1 418 657 2016
Fax: 1 418 657 2154

Quebec Prospectors Association

640 3rd Avenue, Bureau 108, Val d'Or, Quebec, J9P 1S5
Canada
Tel: 1 819 925 4335
Fax: 1 819 825 2265

Queen's University at Kingston, Department of Mining Engineering

Kingston, Ontario, K7L 3N6
Canada
Tel: 1 613 545 2230
Fax: 1 613 545 6597
Email: office@mine.queensu.ca
URL: info.mine.queensu.ca/

Saskatchewan Government of Energy and Mines

2101 Scarth Street
Regina, SK
S4P 3V7
Canada
Tel: 1 306 787 2526
Fax: 1 306 787 7338
Email: inquiry@sem.gov.sk.ca
URL: www.gov.sk.ca/enermine/

Saskatchewan Potash Producers Association

2103 11th Avenue, Ste 1071, Regina, Saskatchewan S4P 3Z8
Canada
Tel: 1 306 569 1477
Fax: 1 306 369 1479

Small Explorers and Producers Association of Canada (SEPAC)

1060, 717 - 7th Avenue S.W.
Calgary
Alberta T2P 0Z3

Canada
Tel: 1 403 269 3454
Fax: 1 403 269 3636
Email: info@sepac.ca
URL: www.sepac.ca/

Standards Council of Canada

Suite 1200, 45 O'Connor Street, Ottawa, Ontario K1P 6N7
Canada
Tel: 1 613 238 3222
Fax: 1 613 995 4564
Email: info@scc.ca
URL: www.scc.ca/

Technical University of Nova Scotia, Department of Metallurgical and Mining Engineering

PO Box 1000, Halifax, Nova Scotia B3J 2X4
Canada
Tel: 1 902 420 7674
URL: www.dal.ca/~mmweb/index.html

Université Laval, Départment de Mines et Métallurgie

Cité Universitaire, Québec, G1K 7P4
Canada
Tel: 1 418 656 2160
Fax: 1 418 656 5343
Email: gmn@gmn.ulaval.ca
URL: www.gmn.ulaval.ca/

University of Alberta, School of Mining and Petroleum Engineering

Room 606, Chemical Mineral Engineering Building
Edmonton
Alberta T6G 2G6
Canada
URL: www.ualberta.ca/

University of British Columbia, Department of Mining and Mineral Process Engineering

6339 Stores Road, Vancouver, BC V6T 1Z4
Canada
Tel: 1 604 822 2540

Vancouver Geotechnical Society

Klohn-Crippen, 10200 Shelbridge Way
Richmond
BC V6X 2W7
Canada
Tel: 1 604 273 0311
Fax: 1 604 279 4300

World Rock Boring Association

P.O. Box 1051, Copper Cliff, Ontario, P0M 1N0
Canada
Tel: 1 705 522 0387
Fax: 1 705 673 6572
URL: www.wrba.net

CHAD

Directorate of Geological and Mining Research

BP 906, N'djamena
Chad
Tel: 235 512666
Fax: 235 515330

Ministère des Mines, de l'Energie et du Pétrole

BP 816, N'djamena
Chad
Tel: 235 516157
Fax: 235 512565

CHILE

Centro de Estudios del Cobre (CESCO)

Málaga 114, Of. 1002, Las Condes, Santiago
Chile
Tel: 56 2 228 0700
Fax: 56 2 228 0699

Centro de Informacion de Recursos Naturales

Manuel Montt No 1164, Providencia, 14995, Santiago
Chile
Tel: 56 2 223 6641
Fax: 56 2 209 6407

Centro de Investigacion Minera y Metalurgica

Av Parque Antonio Rabat 6500, Las Condes, 170 correo 10, Santiago
Chile
Tel: 56 2 218 4311
Fax: 56 2 218 6015

Centro de Investigacion y Planificacion del Medio Ambiente (CIPMA)

Av Holanda, No 1109 Providencia, 16362, Las Condes, Santiago
Chile
Tel: 56 2 274 6333
Fax: 56 2 223 2028

Comision Chilena del Cobre (COCHILCO)

Agustinas 1161, Piso 4, Santiago
Chile
Tel: 56 2 672 6219
Fax: 56 2 672 3584

Comision Nacional de Energia

Teatinos 120, 7th Floor, Santiago
Chile
Tel: 56 2 698 1757
Fax: 56 2 695 6404

Empresa Nacional de Mineria (ENAMI)

100 D Santiago
Chile
Tel: 56 2 639 6061
Fax: 56 2 633 3505

Instituto de Ingenieros de Minas (IIMCH)

14668 correo 21, Santiago
Chile
Tel: 56 2 697 1076
Fax: 56 2 697 2351

Instituto de Investigaciones Tecnologicas (INTEC)

Av Santa Maria No 6400, Vitacura, Santiago
Chile
Tel: 56 2 242 8100
Fax: 56 2 218 5307

Instituto Latinoamericano del Fierro y del Acero (ILAFA)

16.065 Correo 9, Santiago
Chile
Tel: 56 2 233 0545
Fax: 56 2 233 0768

Ministerio de Mineria

54, Correo 21, Santiago
Chile
Tel: 56 2 698 6593
Fax: 56 2 698 9262

Organizacion Latinoamericana de Mineria

80-D Santiago
Chile
Tel: 56 2 207 1442
Fax: 56 2 207 1442

PROCOBRE - Chile

Santo Domingo 550, 2 Piso, Santiago
Chile
Tel: 56 2 6331 200
Fax: 56 2 6381 200
Email: procobre@reuna.cl

Servicio Nacional de Geologia y Mineria (SERNAGEOMIN)

1046 Santiago
Chile
Tel: 56 2 737 5050
Fax: 56 2 637 2026

Sociedad Nacional de Mineria (SONAMI)

1807 Santiago
Chile
Tel: 56 2 695 5626
Fax: 56 2 697 1778

University of Chile, Department of Mining Engineering

Av Tupper 2069, Santiago
Chile
Tel: 56 2 696 7273
Fax: 56 2 671 8060

University of Concepción, Department of Metallurgical Engineering

Casilla 53-C, Concepción
Chile
Tel: 56 41 204241
Fax: 56 41 243418
URL: www.met.udec.cl/

CHINA

Institution of Mining and Metallurgy

PO Box 92584, Tsim Sha Tsui Post Office, Kowloon, Hong Kong
China
Tel: 86 +852 2761 5147
Fax: 86 +852 2760 4284
Email: wil@asiaonline.net
URL: www.imm.org.uk/

Ministry of Coal Industry

21 Hepingli North Street, Beijing
China
Tel: 86 1 6421 7766

Ministry of Foreign Economic Relations and Trade Commission

2 Changan East Road
Beijing
China
Tel: 86 1 55 66 44

World Gold Council

13th Floor, Printing House, Hong Kong
China
Tel: 86 +852 2521 0241
Fax: 86 +852 2810 6038
Email: webmaster@gold.org
URL: www.gold.org/

COLOMBIA

Ministry of Mines and Energy

CAN, Santafé de Bogotá
Colombia
Tel: 57 1 222 4555
Fax: 57 1 222 3651

National Commission of Energy

Av. 40 A No. 13-09, Edificio UGI, Piso 5, Bogota
Colombia
Tel: 57 1 285 6726
Fax: 57 1 288 7419

University of Los Andes - Joint Energy Program

Carrera 1 era 18-A-70, Bogota 1
Colombia
Tel: 57 1 282 4066
Fax: 57 1 284 1890

CONGO

Department of Energy

BP 95, Brazzaville
Congo
Tel: 242 814181

CONGO, DEMOCRATIC REPUBLIC OF

Societé de Developpement Industriel et Minier de Democratic Republic de Congo

BP 7064, Kinshasa
Congo, Democratic Republic of
Tel: 243 12 325 11

Societé Miniere de Bakwanga

BP 377, Kasaii Oriental
Congo, Democratic Republic of

COSTA RICA

Ministry of Natural Resources, Energy and Mines

Calle 25, Av 8-10 Barrio, Piso 5, Apartado Postal, 126-2120 San Jose
Costa Rica
Tel: 506 331 955
Fax: 506 337 095

CZECH REPUBLIC

Centre for Energy Efficiency

Slezska 7, CS-12056 Prague 2
Czech Republic
Tel: 420 2 2424 7552
Fax: 420 2 2424 7597
Email: seven@ecn.cz
URL: www.svn.cz

Czech Geological Survey

Klárov 3, 118 21 Prague 1
Czech Republic
Tel: 420 2 24002 1111
Fax: 420 2 5732 0438
URL: www.cgu.cz/

EC Energy Centre

c/o Vupek, Stetkova, 18, Prumstav Building,
CS-14068 Prague 4
Czech Republic
Tel: 420 2 430 948
Fax: 420 2 430 948

Ministry of Economy, Department of Energy

Na Frantisku 32, CS-11015 Prague 1
Czech Republic
Tel: 420 1 285 11 11
Fax: 420 1 231 85 44

DENMARK

Collaborating Energy and Environment Offices (SEK)

Dumpen 6, DK-8800 Viborg
Denmark
Tel: 45 86 612 322
Fax: 45 86 614 146

Danish Energy Agency

c/o Ministry of Energy, Landemaerket 11,
DK-1119 Copenhagen K
Denmark
Tel: 45 33 926 700
Fax: 45 33 114 743

Danish Geotechnical Institute

1 Maglebjergvej, DK-2800 Lyngby
Denmark
Tel: 45 42 884 444
Fax: 45 42 881 240

Danish National Agency of Environmental Protection

Miljostyrelsen, Strandgade 29
DK-1401 Copenhagen
Denmark
Tel: 45 31 578 310

Danish Standards Association

Kollegievej 6
DK-2920 Charlottenlund
Denmark
Tel: 45 39 96 61 01
Fax: 45 39 96 61 02
Email: dansk.standard@ds.dk
URL: www.ds.dk/

Danish Technological Institute

Gregersenvej, POB 141
DK-2630 Tastrup
Denmark
Tel: 45 43 504 350
Fax: 45 43 507 250
Email: info@teknologisk.dk
URL: www.teknologisk.dk/

Department of Energy

Slotsholmsgade 1, DK-1216 Copenhagen K
Denmark
Tel: 45 33 927 500

Energy Centre Denmark

Suhmsgade 3, DK-1125 Copenhagen K
Denmark
Tel: 45 33 118 300
Fax: 45 33 118 333

Geological Survey of Denmark and Greenland (GEUS)

Thoravej 8, DK-2400 Copenhagen NV
Denmark
Tel: 45 38 142000
Fax: 45 38 142050
Email: geus@geus.dk
URL: www.geus.dk/geuspage-uk.htm

Mineral Resources Administration for Greenland

Slotsholmsgade 1, DK-1216 Copenhagen K
Denmark
Tel: 45 33 927 500
Fax: 45 33 133 017

Ministry of Environment and Energy

Hoejlero Plade 4, DK-1200 Copenhagen K
Denmark
Tel: 45 33 927 600
Fax: 45 33 322 227

ECUADOR

Ministerio de Energia y Minas

Santa Prisca 223, Quito
Ecuador
Tel: 593 2 529 640
Fax: 593 2 580 724

National Energy Institute

Mariana de Jesus 2307 y, MartÁn de Utreras Casilla 007-c, Quito
Ecuador
Tel: 593 2 433 573
Fax: 593 2 449 739

EGYPT

Egyptian Energy Consultant Group (EECG)

Building 13, Apt. 52, Ossman Buildings, Maadi, Cairo 11431
Egypt
Tel: 20 2 701 225

Egyptian Geological Survey and Mining Authority (EGSMA)

3 Salah Salem Rd, Abbasiya
Cairo, 11517
Egypt
Tel: 20 2 6855660
Fax: 20 2 4820128
Email: egsma@idsc.gov.eg
URL: www.egsma.gov.eg

Energy Conservation and Efficiency Project (ECEP/TIMS)

Tabbin Institute for Metallurgical Studies, Tabbin, Cairo 11913
Egypt
Tel: 20 2 790 254
Fax: 20 2 790 635

Energy Conservation and Environmental Protection Project (ECEP)

c/o Cairo University, Dar El Oloum Bldg.
PO Box 38
Giza
Egypt
Tel: 20 2 790 254
Fax: 20 2 627 205

Energy Field

Building No. 13, Apartment 52, Ossman Buildings, Maadi, Cairo
Egypt
Tel: 20 2 701 225

Ministry of State for Environmental Affairs

30 Misr-Helwan road
Maadi, Cairo
Egypt
Tel: 20 2 5256452
Fax: 20 2 5256490
Email: eeaa@eeaa.gov.eg
URL: www.eeaa.gov.eg

Organization for Energy Conservation and Planning

32 Mahmoud Khairy St, First Zone, Nasr City, Cairo 11717
Egypt
Tel: 20 2 402 9247
Fax: 20 2 403 7623
Email: oecp@idsc.gov.eg
URL: www.ritsec.com.eg/govern/oecp/

EQUATORIAL GUINEA

Department of Mines and Hydrocarbons

PO Box 778, Malabo
Equatorial Guinea
Tel: 240 9 2086
Fax: 240 9 3353

Ministerio de Minas y Energia

C/12 de Octubre S/N, Malabo
Equatorial Guinea
Tel: 240 9 3567
Fax: 240 9 3353

ERITREA

Ministry of Energy, Mining and Water

PO Box 5285, Asmara
Eritrea
Tel: 291 1 116872
Fax: 291 1 117652

ESTONIA

EC Energy Centre Tallinn

B428 Ministry of Economy, 11 Harju Street, EE-0001 Tallinn
Estonia
Tel: 372 2 449 511
Fax: 372 2 247 857

Geological Survey of Estonia

Kadaka tee 80/82, EE0026, Tallinn
Estonia
Tel: 372 6 579 661
Fax: 372 6 579 664
Email: egk@estpak.ee

Institute of Energy Research

Paldiski Road, 1, EE-0001 Tallin
Estonia
Tel: 372 2 450 303
Fax: 372 2 453 435

Tallinn Technical University, Department of Mining

Kopli 82, 10412, Tallinn
Estonia
Tel: 372 620 38 50
Fax: 372 620 36 96

Email: maeinst@cc.ttu.ee
URL: www.ttu.ee/maeinst/

ETHIOPIA

Ethiopian Energy Authority

PO Box 486, Mexico Square, Addis Ababa
Ethiopia
Tel: 251 1 153 689
Fax: 251 1 517 874

Ministry of Mines and Energy

PO Box 486, Mexico Square, Addis Ababa
Ethiopia
Tel: 251 1 153 689
Fax: 251 1 517 874

FIJI

Department of Energy

Private Mail Bag, Suva
Fiji
Tel: 679 386 677
Fax: 679 321 039

Mineral Resources Department, Ministry of Lands, Energy and Mines

Private Mail Bag, Suva
Fiji
Tel: 679 381 611
Fax: 679 386 684

FINLAND

Finnish Standards Association

Maistraatinportti 2
FIN-00240
Helsinki
Finland
Tel: 358 9 149 9331
Fax: 358 9 146 4925
URL: www.sfs.fi/

Geological Survey of Finland

Information Bureau, Betonimiehenkuja 4,
FIN-02150 ESPOO
Finland
Tel: 358 0 46931
Fax: 358 0 462205
Email: info@gsf.fi
URL: www.gsf.fi/

FRANCE

Agence de l'Environnement et de la Maitrise de l'Energie (ADEME)

27 Rue Louis Vicat, F-75015 Paris
France
Tel: 33 1 4765 2000
Fax: 33 1 4765 2229
Email: bernard.devin@utopia.fnet.fr

Association Française de Normalisation

Tour Europe, 92049, Paris La Défense
Cedex
France
Tel: 33 1 42 91 55 55
Fax: 33 1 42 91 56 56
URL: www.afnor.fr/

Association Technique pour l'Environnement et l'Energie (ATEE)

47, Av. Laplace, F-94110 Arcueil
France
Tel: 33 1 4656 9143
Fax: 33 1 4985 0627

Centre d'Énergétique

Ecole des Mines de Paris, 60, Bld Saint-Michel, F-75272 Paris Cedex 06
France
Tel: 33 1 4051 9249
Fax: 33 1 4634 2491
Email: pougin@cenerg.ensmp.fr
URL: www-cenerg.cma.fr/

Centre d'Études et de Recherches Economiques sur l'Energie (CEREN)

89 Rue de Miromesnil, F-75008 Paris
France
Tel: 33 1 4563 1191
Fax: 33 1 4563 6053

Centre d'Information du Cuivre

58 rue de Lisbonne, 75008 Paris
France
Tel: 33 1 4225 2567
Fax: 33 1 4953 0382

Ecole des Mines d'Alès

6 avenue de Clavières, 30319 Alès cedex
France
Tel: 33 66 78 50 00
Fax: 33 66 78 50 34
Email: pweber@ensm-ales.fr
URL: neptune.ensm-ales.fr/

Ecole des Mines de Paris

60-62 Boulevard Saint Michel, F-75272 Paris cedex 06
France
Tel: 33 1 40 51 90 00
Fax: 33 1 43 54 18 98
Email: webmaster@cc.ensmp.fr
URL: www.ensmp.fr/

Ecole des Mines de Saint-Etienne

158 cours Fauriel, 42023 Saint-Etienne Cedex 2
France
Tel: 33 4 77 42 01 23
Fax: 33 4 77 42 00 00
Email: webmaster@emse.fr
URL: www.emse.fr/

European Federation of Geologists

77-79 rue Claude Bernard, F-75005 Paris
France
Tel: 33 1 47 079 195
Fax: 33 1 47 079 193

European Telecommunications Standards Institute

Route des Lucioles, F-06921
Sophia Antipolis Cedex
France
Tel: 33 4 92 94 42 00
Fax: 33 4 93 65 47 16
Email: webmaster@etsi.fr
URL: www.etsi.fr/

European Union of Geosciences

EOPG, 5 Rue Rene Descartes, Strasbourg Cedex 67084
France
Tel: 33 88 41 63 93
Fax: 33 88 61 67 47
Email: eug@eopg.u-strasbg.fr

Geological Survey of France (BRGM Group)

Avenue Claude Guillemin - BP 6009, 45060 Orleans, Cedex 2
France

Tel: 33 2 3864 3434
Fax: 33 2 3864 3518
Email: w.master@brgm.fr
URL: www.brgm.fr/

Institut Francais de l'Energie (IFE)

3 rue Henri-Heine, F-75016 Paris
France
Tel: 33 1 44 304 100
Fax: 33 1 40 500 754

Institut National de l'Environment Industriel at des Risques

Parc Technologique, ALATA-BP2, 60550 Verneuil-en-halatte
France
Tel: 33 344 55 66 77
Fax: 33 344 55 66 99
Email: ineris@ineris.fr

International Energy Agency

9 rue de la Fédération, 75739 Paris Cedex 15
France
Tel: 33 1 40 57 65 54
Fax: 33 1 40 57 65 59
Email: info@iea.org
URL: www.iea.org/

Ministere de l'Industrie, Direction Generale de l'Energie et des Matieres Premieres

101 Rue de Grenelle, F-75353 Paris Cedex 07
France
Tel: 33 1 4319 3141
Fax: 33 1 4556 4886

Strategie Energie Environnement Developpement

11 Boulevard Brune, F-75014 Paris
France
Tel: 33 1 4545 9032
Fax: 33 1 4545 3108

Union Francaise des Geologues

77-79 rue Claude-Bernard, F-75005 Paris
France
Tel: 33 1 47 079 195
Fax: 33 1 47 079 193

GAMBIA

Ministry of Natural Resources and Environment

5 Marina Parade
Banjul
Gambia
Tel: 220 228 702
Fax: 220 228 628

GERMANY

Berliner Energie-Agentur

Rudower Chaussee 5, D-12489, Berlin
Germany
Tel: 49 30 695495 0
Fax: 49 30 695495 99

Bundesministerium der Wirtschaft

53107 Bonn
Germany
Tel: 49 228 6150
Fax: 49 228 615 4436

Deutsche Wissenschaftliche Gesellschaft für Erdöl, Erdgas und Kohle

Kapstadtring 2, D-22297 Hamburg
Germany
Tel: 49 40 63900411
Fax: 49 40 6300736
Email: dgmk@online.de
URL: www.online.de/home/dgmk/

Deutscher Braunkohlen-Industrie-Verein

Max Planck Strasse 37, 50858 Köln
Germany
Tel: 49 221 18640
Fax: 49 221 55365

Deutsches Institut für Normung

Germany
URL: www.din.de/

Deutsches Kupfer-Institut

Postfach 17 02 07, 40483 Düsseldorf
Germany
Tel: 49 211 479 6300
Fax: 49 211 479 6310

Gesamtverband der Deutschen Buntmetallindustrie in der Wirtschaftsvereinigung Metalle

Am Bonneshof 5, 40474 Düsseldorf
Germany
Tel: 49 211 47960
Fax: 49 211 479 6400

Gesamtverband des Deutschen Steinkohlenbergbaus

Rellinghauser Str. 1, D-45128 Essen
Germany
Tel: 49 201 177 08
Fax: 49 201 177 4288
Email: kommunikation@gvst.de

Gesellchaft für Bergbau, Metallurgie, Rohstoff und Umwelttechnik (GDMB)

Paul-Ernst Srasse 10, 38678 Clausthal-Zellerfeld
Germany
Tel: 49 5323 937 90
Fax: 49 5323 937 937
Email: gdmb@tu-clausthal.de
URL: region.tu-clausthal.de/gdmb/

Internationales Centrum fur Energie und Umwelttechnologie Leipzig

Auenstrasse 25, D-04105 Leipzig
Germany
Tel: 49 341 980 4969
Fax: 49 341 980 3486

IREDES Initiative

Goethestrasse 52, D- 49549 Ladbergen
Germany
Tel: 49 5485 8301 41
Fax: 49 5485 8301 58
Email: info@iredes.org
URL: www.iredes.org/

Mineralölwirtschaftsverband eV (MWV)

Steindamm 55, D-20099 Hamburg
Germany
Tel: 49 40 248 490
Fax: 49 40 248 4953

Ministerium für Finanzen und Energie des Landes Schleswig-Holstein

Krinshagener Weg 130A, 24116 Kiel
Germany
Tel: 49 43 11 6950
Fax: 49 43 11 5169

Niedersachsische Energieagentur (NEA)

Ihmeplatz 7 F, D-30449 Hannover
Germany
Tel: 49 511 924 940
Fax: 49 511 924 9418

PolyurethaneWeb

Andresenstraße 1a,
Wolfen
D-06766
Germany
Tel: 49 34 94 63 83 66
Fax: 49 34 94 63 83 68
Email: b.lotze@PolyurethaneWeb.com
URL: www.polyurethaneweb.com

Saarl³ndische Energieagentur (SEA)

Altenkesseler Str. 17, D- 66115 Saarbrªcken
Germany
Tel: 49 681 9762 170
Fax: 49 681 9762 175

Universitat Munchen Forschungsstelle fur Energiewirtschaft

Am Blutenanger 71, D-80995 Munchen
Germany
Tel: 49 681 9762 170
Fax: 49 681 9762 175

Universitat Stuttgart, Institut der Energiewirtschaft und der Rationalen Energieverwendung (IER)

Pfaffenwaldring 31, P.O. Box 801140, D-70550 Stuttgart
Germany
Tel: 49 711 685 7575
Fax: 49 711 685 7567
Email: rr@iersl.energietechnik.uni-stuttgart.de

Verband Bergbau, Geologie und Umwelt

Köpenicker Strasse 80-82, 10179 Berlin
Germany

Verband Bergbaulicher Organisationen und Bergbauverwandter Organisation

Zittelmannstrasse 9, 53113 Bonn
Germany
Tel: 49 228 540 0255
Fax: 49 228 540 0235

Verband Deutscher Maschinen-und Anlagenbau (VDMA)

Postfach 71 08 64, 60498 Frankfurt
Germany
Tel: 49 69 660 30
Fax: 49 69 660 31511
Email: puoe@vdma.org
URL: www.vdma.org/

Vereinigung der Bergbauspezialgesellschaften

Rüttenscheider Strasse 14, 45128 Essen
Germany
Tel: 49 201 770900
Fax: 49 201 780509

Zweckverband Regional Entwicklung und Energie (ZrE)

Geschaeftsstelle, Wieshuberstrasse 3, D-93059 Regensburg
Germany
Tel: 49 941 464 190
Fax: 49 941 464 1910

GHANA

Ghana Minerals Commission

PO Box M248, Accra
Ghana

Ministry of Energy

PO Box 40, Stadium, Accra
Ghana
Tel: 233 21 663 057.

Ministry of Mines and Energy

PO Box M212, Accra
Ghana
Tel: 233 21 66 59 49

Volta Aluminium Company

PO Box 625, Tema
Ghana
Tel: 233 221 228 15
Fax: 233 221 667 605

GREECE

Hellenic Copper Development Institute

Halandriou & Himaras Str, GR-15125
MAROUSSI
Greece
Tel: 30 1 6861236 8
Fax: 30 1 6861232

Hellenic Organization for Standardization

Acharnon 313
GR-11145 Athens
Greece
Tel: 30 1 228 00 01
Fax: 30 1 228 30 34
Email: webmaster@elot.gr
URL: www.elot.gr/

Ministry of Industry, Energy and Technology

80 Michalacopoulou St
GR-10192 Athens
Greece
Tel: 30 1 7482 762
Fax: 30 1 7712 485

GREENLAND

Bureau of Minerals & Petroleum

Government of Greenland, PO Box 930
DK-3900 Nuuk
Greenland
Tel: 299 34 68 00
Fax: 299 32 43 02
Email: bmp@gh.gl
URL: www.bmp.gl

GUATEMALA

Central American Institute of Research and Industrial Technology

Av La Reforma 4-47, Zona 10
Guatemala City 01010
Guatemala
Tel: 502 2 310 631
Fax: 502 2 317 470
Email: icaitigt@uvg.edu.gt

Ministry of Energy and Mines

Diagonal 17 29 78, Zona 11, Apartado
Postal 1421, Guatemala CA
Guatemala
Tel: 502 2 760 679
Fax: 502 2 763 175

GUINEA

Ministry of Energy and Environment

PO Box 295, Conakry
Guinea
Tel: 224 44 1186

GUINEA-BISSAU

Ministry of Mines and Energy

Caixa Postal 387, Bissau
Guinea-Bissau

HAITI

Bureau of Mines and Energy

PO Box 2174, Port-au-Prince
Haiti
Tel: 509 1 611 63
Fax: 509 1 639 46

HONDURAS

Ministry of Natural Resources, Directorate of Mines and Hydrocarbons

Apartado Postal 981, Blvd Centro America,
Tegucigalpa DC
Honduras
Tel: 504 327 848
Fax: 504 327 848

HUNGARY

EC Energy Centre

Konyves Kalman Korut 76, H-1087
Budapest VIII
Hungary
Tel: 36 1 269 9067
Fax: 36 1 269 9065

Hungarian Copper Promotion Centre

PO Box 62, Oktober 6.u. 7, H-1241
Budapest
Hungary
Tel: 36 1 117 2421
Fax: 36 1 266 6794
Email: hcpc.bp@ind.eunet.hu

Hungarian Energy Association

Budafok Vt 4, H-111, Budapest
Hungary
Tel: 36 1 181 3195
Fax: 36 1 181 3195

Hungarian Geological Survey

Stefánia út 14, 1143 Budapest
Hungary
Tel: 36 1 267 1425
Fax: 36 1 267 1425
Email: webmaster@mgsz.hu
URL: www.mgsz.hu/

Ministry of Industry and Trade

Margit Krt 85
H-1024
Budapest
Hungary
Tel: 36 1 156 5566
Fax: 36 1 175 0219

ICELAND

Icelandic Council for Standardization

Keldnaholti, 112 Reykjavík
Iceland
Tel: 354 587 7000
Fax: 354 587 7409
Email: stri@iti.is
URL: www.stri.is/STRI/

INDIA

British Technology Group India

62 Basant Lok, Vasant Vihar
New Delhi
110057
India
Tel: 91 11 676 554
Fax: 91 11 687 7482

Confederation of Indian Industry

23 Institutional Area, Lodi Road
New Delhi 110 003
India
Tel: 91 11 462 9994
Fax: 91 11 463 3168
Email: s.ray@ciionline.org
URL: www.ciionline.org/

Department of Scientific and Industrial Research

Anusandhan Bhavan, 2 Rafi Marg
New Delhi
110 001
India
Tel: 91 11 371 0472
Fax: 91 11 371 0618

Energy Management Centre

Ministry of Power, 118 Ashirwad Complex
D-1, Green Park
New Delhi
110016
India
Tel: 91 11-6864867
Fax: 91 11-6868914

Geological Survey of India (GSI)

Karnatoka Operations, GOA/BRGM,
Jayanagar, Bangalore 560-011
India
Tel: 91 80 663 1231
Fax: 91 80 663 2253

Indian Copper Development Centre

27B Camac Street, PO Box 9100, Calcutta
700016
India
Tel: 91 33 247 5724
Fax: 91 33 247 2763

Ministry of Mines

'A' Wing, Shastri Bhavan, 3rd Floor, New
Delhi 110 001
India
Tel: 91 11 338 5173
Fax: 91 11 338 6402

Ministry of Non-Conventional Energy Sources

Block 14, CGO Complex, Lodi Road, New
Delhi 110 003
India
Fax: 91 11 436 1298

Tata Energy Research Institute

India Habitat Center, Lodi Road, New Delhi
110003
India
Tel: 91 11 462 7651

Fax: 91 11 462 1770
Email: webgroup@teri.res.in
URL: www.teriin.org/

INDONESIA

Asian Federation of Mining Associations

Jl. Prof Dr Supomo SH No.10, Jakarta 12870
Indonesia
Tel: 62 21 830 3632
Fax: 62 21 828 0763

Association of Indonesian Coal Industries

Perum Batu Bara Building, Jl. Supomo 10, Jakarta Selatan
Indonesia
Tel: 62 21 829 5608
Fax: 62 21 830 3632

Department of Mines and Energy (DEPTAMBEM)

Jl. Medan Merdeka Selatan 18, Jakarta Pusat
Indonesia
Tel: 62 21 384 9063
Fax: 62 21 384 1896

Directorate of Mineral Resources

Jalan Diponegoro No. 57, Bundung
Indonesia
Tel: 62 22 73205 ext 154

Energy Conservation Foundation

Jl. Kalibata Utara III/78, Jakarta Selatan
Indonesia
Tel: 62 21 797 2070

Indonesian Association of Geologists

Gedung Geologi and Sumber Daya Mineral R-401
Jl. Prof.Dr. Soepomo SH No.10
Indonesia
Tel: 62 21 83702848
Fax: 62 21 83702848
Email: abachtiar@cbn.net.id

Indonesian Mining Association

Jl. Prof Dr Supomo SH No.10, Jakarta 12870
Indonesia
Tel: 62 21 838 3632
Fax: 62 21 829 7642

Indonesian State Coal Mining Company

Tanjung Enim, South Sumatra 31716
Indonesia
Tel: 62 711 311104
Fax: 62 734 51095

Mineral Technology Development Centre

Directorate Pertambangan Umum, Jl. Jend. Sudirman No.623, Bandung 40211
Indonesia
Tel: 62 22 630 483
Fax: 62 22 614 168

Ministry of Mines and Energy

Jl. HR Rasuna Said, Blok X-2, Kav 07 dan 08 Kuningan, Jakarta 12950

Indonesia
Tel: 62 21 525 6072
Fax: 62 21 525 6084

IRAN

Iran Ministry of Industry and Mines

Address:
Nejattollahi Street
Tehran Iran
Tel:+98 21-887-7588

Fax:+98 21-880-7817
+98 21-880-7031
Email:mimwebmaster@mim.gov.ir
Website:www.mim.gov.ir

Iran Community

Teheran
1000
Iran
Tel: 98 95220174
Fax: 98 588165901
Email: info@iran-community.com
URL: www.iran-community.com

IRAQ

Ministry of Industry and Minerals

Ministry of Industry and Minerals Building

Al Nidal Street

Aviation Square

P.O. Box 5815

Baghdad

Iraq Tel: +964 1-816-2006
Email:minister_mim@yahoo.com

Website:www.industry.gov.iq

Iraq Forum for Reconstruction and Development

Baghdad
Iraq
Tel: 964 1 7628946
Email: baghdad@ifrad.us
URL: www.ifrad.us

ISRAEL

Energy Engineering Centre

Technion City, Haifa 32000
Israel
Tel: 972 4 292 111
Fax: 972 4 221 581

Geophysical Institute of Israel

PO Box 2286, 1 Hamashbir St, Holon 58122
Israel
Tel: 972 3 5576050
Fax: 972 3 5502925
URL: www.gii.co.il/

Ministry of Energy and Infrastructure

PO Box 13106, Jerusalem, 91013
Israel
Tel: 972 2 316 115
Fax: 972 2 381 444

ITALY

Ente Nazionale Italiano di Unificazione

via Battistotti Sassi 11/b, 20133 Milano MI
Italy
Tel: 39 0 2 70024 1
Fax: 39 0 2 70106149
Email: webmaster@uni.unicei.it
URL: www.unicei.it/

Instituto Italiano del Rame

Milanofiori Str 4-Pal A3, 20090 Assago MI
Italy
Tel: 39 0 2 575 01548
Fax: 39 0 2 892 00774
Email: ist-rame@wirenet.it

International Geothermal Association

Via A. Pisano 120, 56122 Pisa
Italy
Tel: 39 50 535891
Fax: 39 50 535893
Email: igasec@enel.it

World Gold Council

Corso Garibaldi 49, 1-20121 Milan
Italy
Tel: 39 0 2 809 841
Fax: 39 0 2 867 710
URL: www.gold.org/

IVORY COAST

Ministry of Mines and Energy

BP V50, Abidjan
Ivory Coast
Tel: 225 21 50 03
Fax: 225 21 53 20

Societé des Mines d'Ity

BP 872, Abidjan
Ivory Coast

Societé Ivoirienne de Ciment et Materiaux

01 BP 887, Abidjan 01
Ivory Coast
Tel: 225 24 17 34
Fax: 225 24 17 21

JAPAN

Coal and New Energy Department, Coal Industry Division

Ministry of International Trade and Industry, (100) 3-1, Kasumigaseki 1 Chome, Chiyoda-ku, Tokyo 100
Japan
Tel: 81 3 3501 1727
Fax: 81 3 3580 8564

Committee for Energy Policy Promotion (CEPP)

Hibiya-Chunichi Bldg, 1-4 2-chome, Uchisaiwai-cho, Chiyoda-ku, Tokyo 100
Japan
Tel: 81 3 3501 6833
Fax: 81 3 3501 8601
Email: gda00450@niftyserve.or.jp

Energy Conservation Center (ECCJ)

3-19-9 Hatchobori, Chuo-ku, Tokyo 104
Japan
Tel: 81 3 5543 3018
Fax: 81 3 5543 3021

Energy Conservation Policy Planning Office

3-1 Kasumigaseki 1-chome, Chiyoda-ku, Tokyo
Japan
Tel: 81 3 3501 9726
Fax: 81 3 3595 8439

Geographical Survey Institute

Japan
Email: intex@gsi.go.jp
URL: www.gsi.go.jp/ENGLISH/

Geological Survey of Japan

Higashi 1-1-3, Tsukuba, Ibaraki 305
Japan
Tel: 81 298 543 513
Fax: 81 298 543 533
Email: igo@gsj.go.jp
URL: www.aist.go.jp/GSJ/

Institute of Energy Economics (IEEJ)

Shuwa Kamiyacho Bldg, 3-13 Toranomon 4-chome, Minato-ku, Tokyo
Japan
Tel: 81 3 3501 7866
Fax: 81 3 3508 8147

Japan Copper Development Association

Konwa Building, 12-22 1-chome, Tsukiji, Chuo-ku, Tokyo 104
Japan
Tel: 81 3 3542 6631
Fax: 81 3 3542 6599

Ministry of International Trade and Industry

3-1 Kasumigaseki 1-chome
Chiyoda-ku
Tokyo
Japan
Tel: 81 3 3501 4031
Fax: 81 3 3580 9097

Ministry of the Environment

No. 5 Godochosha, 1-2-2 Kasumigaseki, Chiyoda-ku
Tokyo 100-8975
Japan
Tel: 81 3-3581-3351
Email: moe@env.go.jp
URL: www.env.go.jp/en/index.html

National Industrial Research Institute of Nagoya

1-1 Hirate-cho
Kita-Ku
Nagoya 462
Japan
Tel: 81 52 911 2111
Fax: 81 52 916 2802
URL: www.aist.go.jp/NIRIN/

New Energy Development Organization (NEDO)

Sunshine 60 Bldg., 28th , 1-1, 3-chome Higashi-Ikebukuro, Toshima-ku, Tokyo 170
Japan
Tel: 81 3 3987 9403
Fax: 81 3 3981 1059

KAZAKHSTAN

Energy Technology Centre

7 Lenin Av, Almaty, 480002
Kazakhstan
Tel: 7 327 233 10 77
Fax: 7 327 233 39 95

Ministry of Power Engineering and Fuel Resources

221 Kaizakov St, Almaty, 4800096
Kazakhstan
Tel: 7 327 243 33 87
Fax: 7 327 243 23 38

KENYA

African Energy Policy Research Network

PO Box 30979, Nairobi
Kenya
Tel: 254 2 566032
Fax: 254 2 561464
Email: stephen_karekezi@elci.gn.apc.org

Kenya Energy and Environment Organisation

PO Box 48197
Nairobi
Kenya
Tel: 254 2 274 9747
Fax: 254 2 274 9382

Ministry of Energy

PO Box 30582, Nairobi
Kenya
Tel: 254 2 333551

National Chamber of Commerce and Industry

PO Box 47024
Nairobi
Kenya
Tel: 254 2 334413

KYRGYZSTAN

Mininstry of Natural Resources

2 Erkindik B1, 720729, Bishkek, Kyrgyz Republic
Phone: 996(312)664901, 996(312) 62-06-32
Fax: 996(312) 66 03 91
URL: http://www.kgs.bishkek.gov.kg,

Institute of Physics and Mechanics of Rocks

98 Mederova Street
Bishkek
720815
Kyrgyzstan
Tel: 996 312 541115
Fax: 996 312 541117
Email: ifmgp@mail.kg
URL: www.ifmgp.elcat.kg

LESOTHO

Ministry of Water, Energy and Mining

PO Box 77776, Maseru
Lesotho
Tel: 266 32 24 91

LIBERIA

Ministry of Lands, Mines and Energy

PO Box 9024, Monrovia
Liberia
Tel: 231 221 488

Ministry of Lands, Mines and Energy, National Energy Committee

PO Box 9024, Monrovia
Liberia
Tel: 231 262 059

LITHUANIA

EC-Energy Centre

14 Zveju Street, PO Box 2515, LT-2051
Vilnius
Lithuania
Tel: 370 2 750774
Fax: 370 2 290224

Geological Survey of Lithuania

Lithuania
Email: webmaster@lgt.lt
URL: www.lgt.lt/

Lithuanian Energy Agency

Zveju 14,, LT-2600, Vilnius
Lithuania
Tel: 370 2 626748
Fax: 370 2 626748

Lithuanian Energy Institute

Bzeslaujos 3, LT-3035, Kaunas
Lithuania
Tel: 370 7 757405
Fax: 370 7 751271
Email: eei@isag.ciza.rt.ee

MADAGASCAR

Ministry of Energy and Mines

BP 896, Antaninarenina, Antananarivo 101
Madagascar
Tel: 261 2 25515
Fax: 261 2 32554

Societé Malgache d'Exploitations Minieres

BP 266, Antananarivo
Madagascar

MALAWI

Ministry of Energy and Mining

Private Bag 309, Lilongwe 3
Malawi
Tel: 265 722 755

National Research Council

PO Box 30745, Capitol City
Lilongwe
Malawi
Tel: 265 734 694

MALAYSIA

Geological Society of Malaysia

c/o Dept of Geology, University of Malaya, 59100, Kuala Lumpur
Malaysia
Tel: 60 3 757 7036
Fax: 60 3 756 3900

Malaysian Energy Research Network

40450 Shah Alam,, Selangor Darul Ehsan
Malaysia
Tel: 60 3 556 4673

Ministry of Energy, Telecommunications and Posts

Wisma Damansara, 3rd Floor
Jalan Semantan
50668 Kuala Lumpur
Malaysia
Tel: 60 3 256 2222
Fax: 60 3 253 3485

SIRIM Berhad, Standards and Industrial Research Institute of Malaysia

1 Persiaran Dato Menteri, Seksyen 2, 40000 Shah Alam, Selangor Darul Ehsan
Malaysia
Tel: 60 3 559 2601
Fax: 60 3 550 8095
Email: web@sirim.my
URL: www.sirim.my/

Universiti Teknologi Malaysia, Centre for Energy Studies

Mail Bag 791
80990 Johor Bahru
Johor
Malaysia
Tel: 60 3 290 4506
Fax: 60 3 294 0293
URL: www.rmc.utm.my/Centres/ces.html

MALI

Societé de Gestion et d'Exploitation des Mines d'Or de Kalana

BP 2541, Bamako
Mali
Tel: 223 22 224 446

MAURITANIA

Department of Mineral and Energy Affairs

PO Box 199, Nouakchott
Mauritania

Ministry of Hydraulics and Energy

BP 1150, Nouakchott
Mauritania
Tel: 222 533 37

Societé Nationale Industrielle et Miniere-Societé d'Economie Mixte

BP 42, Nouadhibou
Mauritania

MEXICO

Asociación de Mineros de Sonora AC (AMSAC)

Mexico
Email: amsac@amsac.com.mx
URL: amsac.com.mx/

Camara Minera de Mexico

Sierra Vertientes No. 369, Col Lomas de Chapultepec, Deleg Miguel Hidalgo, Mexico DF
Mexico
Tel: 52 5 540 6060
Fax: 52 5 540 6788

Comision de Fomento Minero

Puente de Tecamachalco 26, Lomas de Chapultepec, 11000 Mexico DF
Mexico
Tel: 52 5 540 3400
Fax: 52 5 202 0342

Comisión Reguladora de Energía

Horacio 1750, 11510 Col. Polanco, D.F.
Mexico
Tel: 52 5283 1515
Email: info@cre.gob.mx
URL:
orion.oac.uci.edu/~adiazbau/PowerUNAM.html

PROCOBRE - Mexico

Av Sonora 166, 1er Piso, 06100, Mexico
Mexico
Tel: 52 5 211 1201
Fax: 52 5 286 7723
Email: 74052.3111@compuserve.com

Secretaria de Energia

Insurgentees Sur 552, Piso 8, Colonia Roma Sur, 06769 Mexico DF
Mexico
Tel: 52 5 564 4793
Fax: 52 5 564 9751

MONACO

Crans Montana Forum

41 Hector Otto
Monaco
98000
Monaco
Tel: 377 97707000
Fax: 377 97707040
Email: summit@world-summit.org
URL: www.cmf.ch

MOROCCO

Association Marocaine pour la Gestion de l'Energie

49 OLM Souissi II, Rabat
Morocco
Tel: 212 7 755647
Fax: 212 7 759558

Ministere de L'Energie et des Mines

BP 208, Rabat-Instituts
Morocco
Tel: 212 7 774 752

NAMIBIA

Geological Survey of Namibia

PO Box 2168, Windhoek
Namibia
Tel: 264 61 208 5111
Fax: 264 61 249 146
URL: www.gsn.gov.na/

Institution of Mining and Metallurgy

Iscor (Namibia) Exploration, 6 Hugel Street, Windhoek
Namibia
Tel: 264 61 234712
Fax: 264 61 234712
URL: www.imm.org.uk/

Ministry of Mines and Energy

Private Bag 13297, Windhoek
Namibia
Tel: 264 61 226571
Fax: 264 61 238643

NETHERLANDS

Central Dredging Association

Rotterdamseweg 183c, 2629 HD Delft
Netherlands
Tel: 31 (0)15 268 2575
Fax: 31 (0)15 268 2576
Email: ceda@dredging.org
URL: www.dredging.org/

Economic Affairs Ministry

Bezuidenhoutseweg 6, POB 20201
NL-2500
EC Den Haag
Netherlands
Tel: 31 70 379 6320
Fax: 31 70 379 6358

European Association of Geoscientists and Engineers

PO Box 59
NL-3990 DB Houten
Netherlands
Tel: 31 30 635 40 55
Fax: 31 30 634 35 24

Email: eage@eage.nl
URL: www.eage.nl/

Netherlands Agency for Energy and Environment (NOVEM)

Swentiboldstraat 21, PO Box 17, NL-6130 AA, Sittard
Netherlands
Tel: 31 46 595 234
Fax: 31 46 528 260

Netherlands Association of Energy Distributing Companies (EnergieNed)

Utrechtseweg 310, PO Box 9042
6800 GD Arnhem
Netherlands
Tel: 31 85 569 444
Fax: 31 85 460 146
URL: www.energiened.nl/index.htm

Netherlands Energy Research Foundation

Westerduinweg 3, PO Box 1, 1755 ZG Petten
Netherlands
Tel: 31 224 564949
Fax: 31 2246 4480
Email: info@ecn.nl
URL: www.ecn.nl/

Netherlands Standardisation Institute

Kalfjeslaan 2, Postbus 5059
2600 GB Delft
Netherlands
Tel: 31 15 2 690 390
Fax: 31 15 2 690 190
URL: www.nen.nl/

Organization for Applied Scientific Research (TNO), Institute of Applied Geoscience

PO Box 157, 2000 AD, Haarlem
Netherlands
Tel: 31 23 5300300
Fax: 31 23 5351614
Email: nitg@nitg.tno.nl
URL: www.nitg.tno.nl/

Organization for Applied Scientific Research, Institute of Environmental and Energy Technology

Laan van Westenenk 501, PO Box 342,
7300 AH Apeldoorn, The Netherlands
Netherlands
Tel: 31 55 549 34 93
Fax: 31 55 549 32 01
Email: b.a.heide@mep.tno.nl
URL: www.tno.nl/

NEW ZEALAND

Energy Efficiency and Conservation Authority

Natural Gas House, 22 The Terrace
P.O. Box 388, Wellington
New Zealand
Tel: 64 4 470 2200
Fax: 64 4 499 5330
Email: eecainfo@eeca.govt.nz
URL: www.eeca.govt.nz

Energy Management Association of New Zealand

PO Box 12-241, Wellington
New Zealand
Tel: 64 4 473 9444
Fax: 64 4 473 2324
URL: www.ema.org.nz/

International Geothermal Association

Wairakei Research Centre, Private Bag 2000, Taupo
New Zealand
Tel: 64 7 374 8211
Fax: 64 7 374 8199
Email: igasec@gns.cri.nz
URL:
www.demon.co.uk/geosci/igahome.html

Ministry of Commerce, Energy and Resources Division

PO Box 1473, Wellington
New Zealand
Tel: 64 4 474 2876
Fax: 64 4 473 9930

New Zealand Geophysical Society

c/o PO Box 1320, Wellington
New Zealand
Fax: 64 4 471 0977
URL:
www.geo.vuw.ac.nz/science.orgs/nzgs.html

New Zealand Geothermal Association

Wairakei Research Centre
Private Bag 2000
Taupo
New Zealand
Tel: 64 7 374 8211
Fax: 64 7 374 8199
Email: e.mroczek@gns.cri.nz
URL: www.nzgeothermal.org.nz/

New Zealand Minerals Industry Association (NZMIA)

PO Box 5039, 117-125 Lambton QY, 5th Floor, Public Trust Bldg
New Zealand
Tel: 64 4 499 9871
Fax: 64 4 499 9873
Email: nzmia@xtra.co.nz
URL: www.minerals.co.nz/

NICARAGUA

Instituto Nicaragua de Energia

Iglesia Santa Domingo 2c abajo, Box 3104, Managua
Nicaragua
Tel: 505 022 7817

NIGER

Ministry of Mines and Energy

BP 11700, Niamey
Niger
Tel: 227 735 521

Societé des Mines de l'Air

BP 12910, Niamey
Niger
Tel: 227 723 531
Fax: 227 722 933

Societé Miniere de Tassa N'Taghalgue

BP 10376, Niamey
Niger
Tel: 227 733 666

Societé Miniere du Niger

BP 12443, Niamey
Niger
Tel: 227 734 582

Societé Nigerienne du Charbon d'Anou Araren

BP 51, Agadez
Niger
Tel: 227 441 020

NIGERIA

Centre for Energy Research and Development

Obafemi Awolowo University, ILE-IFE
Nigeria
Tel: 234 036 233 638
Fax: 234 036 232 975

Ministry of Solid Minerals New Federal Secretariat

Shehu Shagari Way, PMB 107, Abuja
Nigeria
Tel: 234 9 523 6519

National Agency for Science and Engineering Infrastructure

PMB 12793, Lagos
Nigeria
Tel: 234 612 952
Fax: 234 617 632

Nigeria Mining Corporation

PMB 2154, Jos
Nigeria
Tel: 234 73 55092

**Nigerian Association of Chambers of Commerce,
Industry, Mines and Agriculture (NACCIMA)**

15a Ikorodu Road, Maryland, PMB 12816, Lagos
Nigeria
Tel: 234 1 496 4727
Fax: 234 1 496 4737

Nigerian Coal Corporation

PMB 01053, Enugu
Nigeria
Tel: 234 335314

NORWAY

EC Energy Information Service

c/o Hjellnes COWI, Plogveien 1, Postboks 91, Manglerud 0612 Oslo
Norway
Tel: 47 22 574 800
Fax: 47 22 190 538

Information Centre for Energy Efficiency

PO Box 7634, Rodelokka, N-0503 Oslo
Norway
Tel: 47 63 379 090
Fax: 47 63 370 058

Institute for Energy Technology (IFE)

Postboks 40
N-2007 Kjeller
Norway
Tel: 47 63 806 000
Fax: 47 63 816 356
Email: viktor.wikstrom@ife.no
URL: www.ife.no/

Ministry of Industry

Ploensgt 8
N-0033
Oslo 1
Norway
Tel: 47 73 595 500
Fax: 47 73 595 776

NORSOK Standards

PO Box 7072 Majorstua, N-0306 Oslo
Norway
Tel: 47 22 59 67 00
Fax: 47 22 59 67 29
Email: arj@nts.no
URL: www.nts.no/norsok/

Norwegian Geological Survey

Postboks 3006 Lade, 7002 Trondheim
Norway
Tel: 47 73 90 40 11
Fax: 47 73 92 16 20
Email: ngu@ngu.no
URL: www.ngu.no/

Norwegian Society of Chartered Engineers (NIF)

Dronning Mauds gt. 15, POB 2312 Solli, N-0201 Oslo
Norway
Tel: 47 22 947 500
Fax: 47 22 947 502

Norwegian Society of Engineers

Lakkegt 3, POB 9100 Gronland, N-0133 Oslo
Norway
Tel: 47 22 173 500
Fax: 47 22 172 480

Norwegian Standards Association

PO Box 353, Skøyen
N-0212 Oslo
Norway
Tel: 47 22 04 92 00
Fax: 47 22 04 92 11
Email: firmapost@nsf.telemax.no
URL: www.standard.no/nsf/

Norwegian Technology Standards Institution

Postboks 7072 Majorstua
0306 Oslo
Norway
Tel: 47 22 59 67 00
Fax: 47 22 59 67 33
Email: nts@nts.no
URL: www.nts.no/norsok/

Norwegian Trade Council

Drammensveien 40
N-0243 Oslo
Norway
Tel: 47 22 926 300
Fax: 47 22 926 400
URL: http://www.ntc.no/

World Energy Council Norwegian National Committee (NEK)

Harbitzalleen 2A, PO Box 280, N-0212 Oslo
Norway
Tel: 47 22 526 950
Fax: 47 22 526 961

PAPUA NEW GUINEA

Department of Minerals and Energy

Box 352, Konedobu, Port Moresby
Papua New Guinea

Tel: 675 214011
Fax: 675 21463

Geological Survey of Papua New Guinea

Box 778, Port Moresby
Papua New Guinea
Tel: 675 212422
Fax: 675 211360

National Institute of Standards

Box 3042
Boroko
Papua New Guinea
Tel: 675 272102
Fax: 675 258793

PERU

Centro de Conservacion de Energia (CENERGIA)

Av Arequipa 3510, Lima 27
Peru
Tel: 51 14 412 129
Fax: 51 14 412 129

Geopet Asociados

Chinchon 901, piso 3, Lima 27
Peru
Tel: 51 14 41 9888
Fax: 51 14 42 4762

Ministerio de Energia y Minas

Av Las Artes 260, piso 3, Lima 41
Peru
Tel: 51 14 75 7674
Fax: 51 14 75 7674

PROCOBRE - Peru

Francisco Grana 671, Magdalena
Peru
Tel: 51 461 8092
Email: postmast@rrproc.org.pe

Sociedad Geofisica del Peru

Arnaldo Marquez 2277, Jesus Maria, Lima 11
Peru
Tel: 51 62 3948

Sociedad Nacional de Minería Petróleo y Energía

Calle Francisco Grana 671, Magdalena del Mar, Lima 17
Peru
Tel: 51 1 4601600
Fax: 51 1 4601616
Email: postmast@snmpe.org.pe
URL: www.snmpe.org.pe/

PHILIPPINES

Anglo-Philippines Oil and Mining Corporation

6/F Quad Alpha Centrum, 125 Pioneer St, Mandaluyong, Metro Manila
Philippines
Tel: 63 2 631 5139
Fax: 63 2 631 3113

Department of Energy

PNPC Complex, Merritt Rd, Fort Bonifacio, Makati, Metro Manila
Philippines
Tel: 63 2 812 4016
Fax: 63 2 817 8603

Department of Science and Technology

Science Community Complex, Bicutan Community Complex
Bicutan Taguig
Metro Manila
Philippines
Tel: 63 2 823 8071
Fax: 63 2 821 9167

Energy Development and Utilisation Foundation

Unit G, 19th Floor, Strata 100 Bldg, Emerald Avenue, Pasig, Metro Manila
Philippines
Tel: 63 2 631 2745
Fax: 63 2 631 5782

Energy Management Association of the Philippines

Suite 6H, 6th Floor, Don Tim Bldg, 5468 South Superhighway Cor, General Mascardo St, Makati, Metro Manila
Philippines
Tel: 63 2 857 771
Fax: 63 2 867 497

Office of Energy Affairs

Merritt Rd, Fort Bonifacio, Makati, Metro Manila
Philippines
Tel: 63 2 851 021
Fax: 63 2 817 8603

Oriental Petroleum and Minerals Corporation

7th Floor, Corinthian Plz Cond., paseo de Roxas, Makati, Metro Manila
Philippines
Tel: 63 2 892 6066
Fax: 63 2 816 0557

Renewable Energy Association of the Philippines

c/o Base Corporation, 700 Lerma Street, Mandaluyong, Metro Manila
Philippines
Tel: 63 2 532 6496
Fax: 63 2 532 6667

POLAND

Association of Polish Geomorphologists

Fredry 10, 61-701 Poznañ
Poland
Tel: 48 61 529 327
Fax: 48 61 530 234
Email: sgp@hum.amu.edu.pl

Central Mining Institute

Plac Gwarkow 1
40-166 Katowice
Poland
Tel: 48 32 258 16 31 to 9
Fax: 48 32 259 65 33
Email: gig@gig.katowice.pl
URL: www.gig.katowice.pl

EC Energy Centre

Jasna 22, PL-00950 Warsaw
Poland
Tel: 48 22 268 888
Fax: 48 22 268 585

Energoprojekt

ul. Krucza 6/14, PO Box 184, PL-00950
Warsaw
Poland
Tel: 48 26 283 699
Fax: 48 26 148 92

Energy Conservation Foundation

ul. Dluga 5, PL-00263 Warsaw
Poland
Tel: 48 22 635 6314
Fax: 48 22 635 6386

Energy Management and Conservation Agency

ul. Zurawia 6/12, PL-00503 Warszawa
Poland
Tel: 48 26 253 940
Fax: 48 26 254 960

IABPO Energy Centre

ul. Jasna 22, Pl-00950 Warsaw
Poland
Tel: 48 22 268 391
Fax: 48 22 260 585

Ministry of Environmental Protection, Natural Resources and Forestry

Wawelska 52/54
PL-00922 Warsaw
Poland
Tel: 48 22 250 001
Fax: 48 22 254 141

Ministry of Industry and Trade, Department of Energy

ul. Wspolna 4, PL-00926 Warsaw
Poland
Tel: 48 26 280 801
Fax: 48 26 280 970
Energy Restructuring Group
ul. Mysia 2
PL-00926 Warsaw
Poland
Tel: +48 26 256 280
Fax: +48 26 256 305

National Agency for Energy Efficiency

ul. Wspolna 2, PL-00926 Warsaw
Poland
Tel: 48 26 618 157
Fax: 48 26 618 167

Polish Copper Promotion Centre

pl. 1 Maja 1-2, 50-136 Wroclaw
Poland
Tel: 48 71 401 502

Polish Foundation for Energy Efficiency (FEWE)

ul. Wierzbowa 11
40-169 Katowice
Poland
Tel: 48 32 203 51 14
Fax: 48 32 203 51 20
Email: office@fewe.pl
URL: www.fewe.pl

Stanislaw Staszic University of Mining and Metallurgy in Cracow

al. Mickiewicza 30, 30-059 Krakow
Poland
URL: www.uci.agh.edu.pl/

Strata Mechanics Research Institute of the Polish Academy of Sciences

27 Reymonta St., 30-059, Krakow
Poland
Tel: 48 12 637 62 00
Fax: 48 12 637 28 84
Email: office@aga.img-pan.krakow.pl
URL: www.img-pan.krakow.pl/

PORTUGAL

Agencia Regional de Energia e Ambiente da Regiao Autonoma da Madeira

Av. do Mar e das Comunidades
Madeirenses, 32
P- 000 Funchal
Portugal
Portugal
Tel: 351 91 226 266
Fax: 351 91 225 126
Email: aream@mail.telepac.pt
URL: www.managenergy.net/

Centro para a Conservacao de Energia (CCE)

Estrada de Alfragide, Praceta 1-Alfragide, P-2700 Amadora
Portugal
Tel: 351 1 471 1454
Fax: 351 1 471 1316

Direccao Geral de Energia

Av. 5 de Outubro, 87, P-1000 Lisboa
Portugal
Tel: 351 1 793 9520
Fax: 351 1 793 9540

Instituto da Energia (INTERG)

Av. Rovisco Pais, P-1096 Lisboa Codex
Portugal
Tel: 351 1 808 257
Fax: 351 1 848 4235

Instituto Nacional de Engenharia e Tecnologia Industrial

Azinhaga dos Lameiros, a Estrada do Paco do Lumiar, P-1699 Lisboa Codex
Portugal
Tel: 351 1 716 5141
Fax: 351 1 716 4635

Instituto Português da Qualidade

Rua C à Avenida dos Três Vales, 2825
Monte de Caparica
Portugal
Tel: 351 1 294 81 00
Fax: 351 1 294 81 01
Email: ipqmail@ipqm.ipq.gtw-ms.mailpac.pt
URL: www.ipq.pt/

International Copper Study Group

R. Almirante Barroso 38-6th Floor, 1000
Lisboa
Portugal
Tel: 351 1 350 4039
Fax: 351 1 350 4035

Ministry of Industry and Energy

Rua da Beneficencia, 241
P-1600 Lisbon
Portugal
Tel: 351 1 771 091

REPUBLIC OF IRELAND

Department of Transport, Energy and Communications

Beggars Bush, Haddington Road, Dublin 4, County Dublin
Republic of Ireland
Tel: 353 1 671 5233
Fax: 353 1 660 4462

Institution of Engineers of Ireland

Cumann na nInnealtoírí
22 Clyde Road
Dublin 4
Republic of Ireland
Tel: 353 1 668 4341
Fax: 353 1 668 5508
Email: info@iei.ie
URL: www.iei.ie/

Institution of Mining and Metallurgy

Tara Mines Ltd, Knockumber, Navan, Co. Meath
Republic of Ireland
Tel: 353 46 22798
Fax: 353 46 21927
Email: taramine@indigo.ie
URL: www.imm.org.uk/

Irish Association for Economic Geology

Beggars Bush, Haddington Road, Dublin 4, County Dublin
Republic of Ireland
Tel: 353 1 660 9511
Fax: 353 1 668 1782

Irish Mining and Exploration Group

Confederation House, Kildare Street, Dublin 2, County Dublin
Republic of Ireland
Tel: 353 1 677 9801
Fax: 353 1 677 7823

Irish Mining and Quarrying Society

87-89 Waterloo Road, Dublin 4, County Dublin
Republic of Ireland
Tel: 353 1 685193

NSAI

1, Swift Square
Santry
Dublin 9
Republic of Ireland
Tel: 353 1 807 3800
Fax: 353 1 807 3838
Email: info@nsai.ie
URL: www.nsai.ie

University College Dublin Energy Research Group

Richview, Clonskeagh, Dublin 14, County Dublin
Republic of Ireland
Tel: 353 1 269 2750
Fax: 353 1 283 8908

ROMANIA

Ministry of Industry and Trade

152 Calea Victoriei, 1-st District, Bucharest
Romania
Tel: 40 1 650 50 20
Fax: 40 1 650 91 40

National Agency for Mineral Resources

36-38 Mendeleev Str, 1-st District, 70169-Bucharest
Romania
Tel: 40 1 212 54 45

Fax: 40 1 212 54 49
Email: mianas@namr.ro

RUSSIA

Centre for Energy Efficiency

54, Korpus 4, Novocheremushkinskaya St.,
117418 Moscow
Russia
Tel: 7 095 883-9526
Fax: 7 095 883-9563
Email: cenef@glas.apc.org

EC Energy Centre

c/o ENIN Leninsky Prospekt 19, 117927
Moscow
Russia
Tel: 7 095 952 5527
Fax: 7 095 952 5527

Institute of Mineralogy and Petrography

Universitetskij pr. 3, 630090 Novosibirsk
Russia
Tel: 7 383 235 6552
Fax: 7 383 235 2692
Email: sobolev@uiggm.nsc.ru

Ministry for Fuel and Power Development

Moscow
Russia
Tel: 7 095 220 5500
Fax: 7 095 220 4818

Russian Academy of Sciences Energy Research Institute

Vavilova Street 44, Building 2, 113186
Moscow
Russia
Tel: 7 095 127 4834
Fax: 7 095 310 7065

Russian Federation Ministry of Fuel and Energy

Moscow
Russia
Tel: 7 095 206 8080
Fax: 7 095 206 8107

Russian Mineralogical Society

21st line 2, 199026 St.Petersburg
Russia
Tel: 7 812 218 8247
Fax: 7 812 327 7359
Email: marin@mineral.ras.spb.ru
URL: www.ripn.net/relarn/members/vmo/

St Petersburg Mining Institute, Department of Petrology

21st line 2, 199026 St Petersburg
Russia
Tel: 7 812 218 8247
Fax: 7 812 327 7359 Telex: 121 494 L
Email: mkp@mineral.ras.spb.ru

SENEGAL

Societé Miniere de Sabodala

BP 206, Dakar
Senegal
Tel: 221 223 736

Societé Nouvelle des Salins du Sine Saloum

BP 200, Kaolack
Senegal
Tel: 221 411 013

Societé Senegalaise des Phosphates de Thies

BP 241, Dakar
Senegal
Tel: 221 233 283
Fax: 221 228 384

SINGAPORE

Copper Development Centre - Southeast Asia

87 Beach Road, 04-02 Chye Sing Building, 0718 Singapore
Singapore
Tel: 65 334 3828
Fax: 65 334 6221
Email: cdcsea@singnet.com.sg

Ministry of Science and Technology

Annex Building, 5th Floor
Government Offices
1025
Singapore

Ministry of Trade and Industry

8 Shenton Way 48-01, Treasury Bldg, Singapore 0106
Singapore
Tel: 65 226 9911
Fax: 65 226 9911

World Gold Council

6 Battery Road #24-02A
Singapore
Tel: 65 227 2802
Fax: 65 227 2798
URL: www.gold.org/

SLOVAKIA

Geological Survey of the Slovak Republic

Slovakia
URL: www.gssr.sk/

Ministry of Industry and Trade, Energy Department

Dienva ul. 24, Bratislava
Slovakia
Tel: 421 7 297 11
Fax: 421 2 373 29

SLOVENIA

Standards and Metrology Institute of the Republic of Slovenia

Kotnikova 6, SI-1000 Ljubljana
Slovenia
Tel: 386 61 178 30 00
Fax: 386 61 178 31 96
URL: www.usm.mzt.si/

SOMALIA

Ministry of Mineral Resources and Water

PO Box 774, Mogadishu
Somalia

SOUTH AFRICA

African Exploration Company

PO Box 61661, Marshalltown 2107
South Africa

Tel: 27 11 403 2930
Fax: 27 11 403 2930

Aggregate and Sand Producers Association of South Africa

PO Box 34, 2006 Auckland Park
South Africa
Tel: 27 11 726 5300
Fax: 27 11 726 8421

Anglo American plc

PO Box 61587, Marshalltown 2107
South Africa
Tel: 27 11 638 9111
Fax: 27 11 638 2455
URL: www.angloamerican.co.uk

Associated Manganese Mines of South Africa

PO Box 62379, Marshalltown 2107
South Africa
Tel: 27 11 634 9111
Fax: 27 11 634 0038

Capital Equipment Export Council of South Africa

Export Promotion: Capital Equipment Section, Private Bag X84, Private Bag X84
South Africa
Tel: 27 12 3109 378
Fax: 27 12 3208 157
Email: mminnies@dti.pwv.gov.za

Chamber of Mines of South Africa

PO Box 61809, Marshalltown, 2107
South Africa
Tel: 27 11 498 7100
Fax: 27 11 834 1884
Email: jmccourt@bullion.org.za
URL: www.bullion.org.za/

Copper Development Association

PO Box 14785, Wadeville 1422
South Africa
Tel: 27 11 824 3916
Fax: 27 11 824 3120

**Council for Scientific and Industrial Research,
Division of Mining Technology**

PO Box 91230, Auckland Park, Johannesburg 2006
South Africa
Tel: 27 11 358 0000
Fax: 27 11 726 7308
URL: www.csir.co.za/miningtek/

Department of Mineral and Energy Affairs

Private Bag X59, Pretoria 0001
South Africa
Tel: 27 12 322 8561
Fax: 27 12 322 3416
URL: www.dme.gov.za/

Geological Survey of South Africa, Council for Geoscience

280 Pretoria Road, Silverton, Pretoria, 0184
South Africa
Tel: 27 12 841 1911
Fax: 27 12 841 1221
Email: webmaster@geoscience.org.za
URL: www.geoscience.org.za/

Mineral and Energy Policy Centre

PO Box 395, Wits 2050
South Africa
Tel: 27 11 403 8013
Fax: 27 11 339 8023
Email: info@mepc.org.za

Minerals Bureau

Private Bag X59, Pretoria 0001
South Africa
Tel: 27 12 317 9498
Fax: 27 12 320 4327
URL: www.dme.gov.za/minerals/

National Union of Mineworkers (NUM)

PO Box 2424, Johannesburg 2000
South Africa
Tel: 27 11 833 7012
Fax: 27 11 836 0201
Email: miner@wn.apc.org
URL: www.anc.org.za/num/

Strategic Fuel Fund

Protea Place, Sandton 2146
South Africa
Tel: 27 21 419 8054
Fax: 27 21 419 8058

University of Cape Town, Energy Research Institute

PO Box 207, Plumstead, 7800 Cape Town
South Africa
Tel: 27 21 705 0120
Fax: 27 21 705 6266
Email: mdv@uctvms.uct.ac.za

SOUTH KOREA

Korea Institute of Geology, Mining and Materials (KIGAM)

30 Kajung Dong, Yusong Ku, Taejon 305-350
South Korea
Tel: 82 42 868 3340 2
Fax: 82 42 861 9720
Email: wmaster@www.kigam.re.kr
URL: www.kigam.re.kr/

SPAIN

Centro Español de Información del Cobre

Princesa, 79, 28008 Madrid
Spain
Tel: 34 1 544 8451
Fax: 34 1 544 8884

Club Español de la Energia

E-28043 Madrid
Spain
Tel: 34 1 413 5112
Fax: 34 1 413 5249

Ente Vasco de la Energia (EVE)

Edificio Albia 1, San Vicente, 8-Planta 14
Bilbao
E-48001
Spain
Tel: 34 94 435 5600
Fax: 34 94 424 9733
Email: jreig@eve.es

Institut Catala d'Energia (ICAEN)

Avgda. Diagonal 453 Bis, Atic, E-08036
Barcelona
Spain

Tel: 34 3 439 2800
Fax: 34 3 419 7253

Instituto de la Mediana y PequeÛa Empresa Valenciana (IMPIVA)

Avellanas 14- 3F, E-46003 Valencia
Spain
Tel: 34 6 392 0005
Fax: 34 6 391 4460

Instituto Tecnológico Geominero de España,
Dirección de Recursos Minerales

Rios Rosas, 23. 28003 Madrid
Spain
Tel: 34 91 3495778
Fax: 34 91 4496216
Email: m.regueiro@itge.mma.es
URL: www.itge.mma.es/

Ministerio de Industria y Energia

Pasceo de la Castellana 160, Planta 6, E-28046 Madrid
Spain
Tel: 34 1 349 4545
Fax: 34 1 457 8066

Universidad de Oviedo, Departamento de Explotación y Prospección de Minas

C/ Independencia, 13, 33004 Oviedo
Spain
Tel: 34 98 510 4301
Fax: 34 98 510 4245
URL: www6.uniovi.es/dptos/epm/

SRI LANKA

Ministry for Energy Conservation

50 C.A. Gardiner Mawatha, Colombo 2
Sri Lanka
Tel: 94 1 428 306
Fax: 94 1 449 572

Ministry of Power and Energy

50 C.A. Gardiner Mawatha, Colombo 2
Sri Lanka
Tel: 94 1 422 050
Fax: 94 1 449 572

National Engineering Research and Development Centre

2P/17B, IDB Industrial Estate, Ekala, Ja-ela
Sri Lanka
Tel: 94 1 536 307
Fax: 94 1 536 278

Natural Resources Energy and Science Authority

47/5 Maitland Place, Colombo 07
Sri Lanka
Tel: 94 1 696 771
Fax: 94 1 691 691
Email: webmastr@naresa.ac.lk
URL: www.naresa.ac.lk/

Sri Lanka Energy Managers Association

PO Box 540, Colombo
Sri Lanka
Tel: 94 1 697 328
Fax: 94 1 449 572

SUDAN

Institute of Energy Research

PO Box 2649, Khartoum
Sudan
Tel: 249 11 80 137

Ministry of Energy and Mining

PO Box 2649, Khartoum
Sudan
Tel: 249 733 15

Ministry of Energy, National Energy Administration

PO Box 2087, Khartoum
Sudan
Tel: 249 755 95

SWAZILAND

Ministry of Natural Resources and Energy

PO Box 57, Mbabane
Swaziland
Tel: 268 46 244
Fax: 268 42 436

SWEDEN

British-Swedish Chamber of Commerce

Nybrogatan 75
S-114 40 Stockholm
Sweden
Tel: 46 8 665 3425
Fax: 46 8 665 0935
Email: britcham@mailbox.calypso.net
URL: bscc.swednet.net/

Geological Survey of Sweden

Mineral Resources Information Office
SGU, Malå
Skolgatan 4, S-930 70
Sweden
Tel: 46 953 107 60
Fax: 46 953 216 86
Email: mala@sgu.se
URL: www.sgu.se/

Scandinavian Copper Development Association

c/o Outokumpu Copper, S-721-88 Vasteras
Sweden
Tel: 46 21 198 620
Fax: 46 21 198 041

Standardiseringen i Sverige (SIS)

Box 6455
113 82 Stockholm
Sweden
Tel: 46 8 610 30 00
Fax: 46 8 30 77 57
Email: info@sis.se
URL: www.sis.se/

Swedish Trade Council Marine and Offshore Department

Box 5513 Storgatan 19, S-114 85 Stockholm
Sweden
Tel: 46 8 783 8500
Fax: 46 8 662 9093

SWITZERLAND

Federal Office of Energy (OFEN)

Kapellenstrasse 14, CH-3003 Berne
Switzerland
Tel: 41 31 322 5637
Fax: 41 31 382 4403

International Electrotechnical Commission

3 Rue de Varembe, BP 131,
Geneva 20
1211
Switzerland
Tel: 41 229190211
Fax: 41 223626622
URL: www.iec.ch

International Organization for Standardization (ISO)

1 rue de Varembé, Case postale 56, CH-1211 Genève 20
Switzerland
Tel: 41 22 749 0111
Fax: 41 22 733 3430 Telex: 41 22 05 i
Email: central@isocs.iso.ch
URL: www.iso.ch/

International Telecommunication Union

Place des Nations,
Geneva
CH1211
Switzerland
Tel: 41 227305111
Fax: 41 227337256
Email: itumail@itu.int
URL: www.itu.int

World Gold Council

rue de la Rôtisserie 1, CH-1204 Geneva
Switzerland
Tel: 41 22 311 96 66
Fax: 41 22 310 81 60
URL: www.gold.org/

SYRIA

Ministry of Petroleum and Mineral Resources Building
Adawi Street
Khateeb Area
P.O. Box 31483
Damascus
Syria
Tel:+963 11-441-7835
+963 11-445-5972
Fax:+963 11-446-3942

Email:mopmr-central@mail.sy
Website:www.petroleum.gov.sy
http://www.mopmr-sy.org/

Shora Group

ABO Firass Street Marjeh
DAMASCUS
Syria
Tel: 963 11 2236991
Fax: 963 2247182 44676741
Email: bachar@shoragroup.com
URL: www.shoragroup.com

TANZANIA

Ministry of Planning and Economic Affairs

PO Box 4302, Kivokuni Front, Dar es Salaam
Tanzania
Tel: 255 25 802

Ministry of Water, Energy and Minerals

PO Box 9000, Dar es Salaam
Tanzania
Tel: 255 51 46147
Fax: 255 21 011

Southern and Eastern African Mineral Centre (SEAMIC)

Kunduchi Beach Area, PO Box 9573, Dar es Salaam
Tanzania

Tel: 255 51 650321
Fax: 255 51 650319
Email: seamic@cats-net.com

THAILAND

Chulalongkorn University, Department of Mining and Petroleum Engineering

Faculty of Engineering, Phya-Thai Road, Bangkok 10330
Thailand
Tel: 66 2 218 6586
Fax: 66 2 218 6587
Email: webmaster@www.eng.chula.ac.th
URL: kankrow.eng.chula.ac.th/~mining/

Department of Energy Development and Promotion (DEDP)

Pibultham Villa, Kasatsuk Bridge, Bangkok 10330
Thailand
Tel: 66 2 223 0021
Fax: 66 2 226 1416

Department of Mineral Resources

Rama VI Road, Bangkok 10400
Thailand
Tel: 66 2 246 0034
Fax: 66 2 245 9855

National Energy Policy Office (NEPO)

78 Rachadamnoen-Nok Avenue, Dusit, Bangkok 10300
Thailand
Tel: 66 2 282 9027
Fax: 66 2 280 0292

TOGO

Ministry of Planning and Mines

BP 1667, Lome
Togo
Tel: 228 215 010

TUNISIA

Agence de Maitrise de l'Energie (AME)

15 Rue 8000 Montplaisir, 1002 Tunis Belv-dÉre
Tunisia
Tel: 216 1 787 700
Fax: 216 1 784 624

Institut National de la Recherche Scientifique et Technique

BP 95, 2050 Hammam LIF
Tunisia
Tel: 216 1 430 044
Fax: 216 1 430 917

Ministry of National Economy

17 Av. Khrddine Pacha 1002 Tunis BelvdÉre
Tunisia
Tel: 216 1 782 668
Fax: 216 1 787 804

Office National des Mines

24 rue 8601, Zone Industrielle Charguia, 2035 Tunis Carthage
Tunisia
Tel: 216 1 788 842
Fax: 216 1 794 016

TURKEY

Association of Anatolian Miners

Gazi Mustafa Kemal Bulv No.12/35, Onur Ishani K3, Kizilay, Ankara
Turkey

Tel: 90 312 425 8655
Fax: 90 312 417 0765

Association of Miners of Turkey

Istiklal Cad, Arda Apt No.471/1, Tünel, Istanbul
Turkey
Tel: 90 212 245 1503
Fax: 90 212 244 8335

Association of Young Mining Businessmen

Gazi Mustafa Kemal Bulv No.12/35, Onur Ishani K3, Kizilay, Ankara
Turkey
Tel: 90 312 425 8655
Fax: 90 312 417 0765

Chamber of Mining Engineers of Turkey

Selanik Cad. No:19/3, 06650 Kizilay Ankara
Turkey
Tel: 90 312 418 36 57
Fax: 90 312 417 52 90
Email: maden@mining-eng.org.tr
URL: www.mining-eng.org.tr/

Ferrous and Non-Ferrous Metals Exporters Association

Inönü Cad, Nevres Han No.96 K4-5, 80090 Gümüssuyu, Taksim
Turkey
Tel: 90 212 293 4010
Fax: 90 212 293 3329

Foundation for Development of Domestic Mining

Istiklal Cad, Arda Apt No.471/1, Tünel, Istanbul
Turkey
Tel: 90 212 245 1503
Fax: 90 212 244 8335

General Directorate of Mineral Research and Exploration of Turkey

MTA Genel Müdürlüðü, 06520 Sogutozu, Ankara
Turkey
Tel: 90 312 287 34 30
URL: www.mta.gov.tr/

Istanbul Mineral and Metals Exporters Association

Inönü Cad. Dever Han No.96 Kat 4-5, 80090 Gümüssuyu, Taksim, Istanbul
Turkey
Tel: 90 212 293 4010
Fax: 90 212 293 3329
Email: mmib-d@servis.net.tr

Ministry of Energy and Natural Resources

Konya Yolu Uzeri, 06100 Bestepe, Ankara
Turkey
Tel: 90 312 212 6420
Fax: 90 312 223 6984

Scientific and Technical Research Council of Turkey

Ataturk Bulvari No. 221, 06100 Kavaklidere, Ankara
Turkey
Tel: 90 312 468 2196
Fax: 90 312 468 2196
Email: aynur.agnel.tusitak@vines.cc.metu.edu.tr

UGANDA

Ministry of Energy, Minerals and Environmental Protection

PO Box 7270, Kampala
Uganda
Tel: 256 41 234 733

Ministry of Natural Resources

PO Box 7270, Kampala
Uganda
Tel: 256 41 230 220
Fax: 256 41 233 331

UKRAINE

Agency for Rational Energy Use and Ecology

PO Box 48, 1 Laboratory St, Kiev 252133
Ukraine
Tel: 380 44 268 8088
Fax: 380 44 268 8451
Email: arena@arena.kiev.ua

EC Energy Centre Kiev

Apt 19, 39 Pushkinskaya Street, Kiev 4
Ukraine
Tel: 380 44 221 2241
Fax: 380 44 229 7522

Ministry of Coal Industry

4 B Bmelnitskogo St., Kiev 252001
Ukraine
Tel: 380 44 229 9946
Fax: 380 44 226 2165

State Committee for Coal Utilisation

Kiev 12
Ukraine
Tel: 380 44 226 2768

UNITED ARAB EMIRATES

Ministry of Energy
The Minister: Mohammed bin Dha'en Al Hamili
Abu Dhabi POB: 59; Tel: 02 6671999; Fax: 02 6664573
Email: mopmr@uae.gov.ae

Dubai World Trade Center, Dubai
United Arab Emirates
Tel: 971 4 314 500
Fax: 971 4 315 514
URL: www.gold.org/

UNITED KINGDOM

Association of British Mining Equipment Companies (ABMEC)

Webster Buidings, Wortley Rd, Rotherham, South Yorkshire S61 1LZ
United Kingdom
Tel: 44 1709 555 402
Fax: 44 1709 555 758

Association of Mining Analysts

c/o Bain Securities, 115 Houndsditch, London, EC3A 7BD
United Kingdom
Tel: 44 207 283 9133

British Combustion Equipment Manufacturers Association

The Fernery, Market Place, Midhurst, West Sussex, GU29 9DP
United Kingdom

Tel: 44 1730 812782
Fax: 44 1730 813366

British Geological Survey

Kingsley Dunham Centre, Keyworth,
Nottingham NG12 5GG
United Kingdom
Tel: 44 1159 363100
Fax: 44 1159 363200
Email: www-bgs@ua.nkw.ac.uk
URL: www.bgs.ac.uk/

British Hardmetal Association

3 Melbourne Avenue, Sheffield, South
Yorkshire S10 2QJ
United Kingdom
Tel: 44 114 2663084
Fax: 44 114 2670910

British Non-Ferrous Metals Federation

10 Greenfield Crescent, Birmingham, B15
3AU
United Kingdom
Tel: 44 121 456 3322
Fax: 44 121 456 1394

British Pump Manufacturers Association

The McLaren Building, 35 Dale End
Birmingham
B4 7LN
United Kingdom
Tel: 44 1212001299
Fax: 44 1212001306
Email: enquiry@bpma.org.uk
URL: www.bpma.org.uk

British Safety Council

70 Chancellor's Road
London
W6 9RS
United Kingdom
Tel: 44 208 741 1231
Fax: 44 208 741 4555
Email: bsc1@mail.britishsafetycouncil.co.uk
URL: www.britishsafetycouncil.co.uk/

British Safety Industry Federation

St Asaph Business Park, St Asaph
Denbighshire
LL17 7LJ
United Kingdom
Tel: 44 1745 585600
Fax: 44 1745 585800
Email: info@bsif.co.uk
URL: www.bsif.co.uk/

British Standards Institute (BSI)

389 Chiswick High Road
Chiswick
London W4 4AL
United Kingdom
Tel: 44 208 996 9000
Fax: 44 208 996 7400
Email: info@bsi-global.com
URL: www.bsi-global.com/

British Timber Merchants Association

Stocking Lane, Hughenden Valley, High
Wycome, Bucks, HP14 4JZ
United Kingdom
Tel: 44 1494 563602
Fax: 44 1494 565487

British Valve and Actuator Manufacturers' Association

The McLaren Building, 35 Dale End,
Birmingham, B4 7LN
United Kingdom
Tel: 44 121 200 1297
Fax: 44 121 200 1308
Email: enquiry@bvama.org.uk
URL: www.bvama.org.uk/

Camborne School of Mines

University of Exeter, Redruth, Cornwall,
TR15 3SE
United Kingdom
Tel: 44 1209 714866
Fax: 44 1209 716977
Email: d.m.summers@csm.ex.ac.uk
URL: www.ex.ac.uk/CSM/

Centre for Energy, Petroleum and Mineral Law and Policy

University of Dundee
Dundee DD1 4HN
United Kingdom
Tel: 44 1382 344300
Fax: 44 1382 322578
Email: cpmlp@dundee.ac.uk
URL: www.dundee.ac.uk/cepmlp/main/

Chamber of Coal Traders

Victoria House, Southampton Row, London,
WC1B 4DH
United Kingdom
Tel: 44 207 405 0034
Fax: 44 207 831 5181

Coal Merchants Federation

Victoria House, Southampton Row, London,
WC1B 4DH
United Kingdom
Tel: 44 207 405 8218
Fax: 44 207 831 5181

Confederation of British Industry (CBI)

103 New Oxford Street
London WC1A 1DU
United Kingdom
Tel: 44 207 379 7400
Fax: 44 207 240 1578
Email: www.ofcom.org.uk/
URL: www.cbi.org.uk

Copper Development Association

Verulam Industrial Estate, 224 London
Road, St Albans, Hertfordshire AL1 1AQ
United Kingdom
Tel: 44 1727 731200
Fax: 44 1727 731216
Email: copperdev@compuserve.com
URL: www.cda.org.uk/

Cornish Chamber of Mines

Gilberts Coombe, New Portreath Road,
Redruth, Cornwall, TR16 4HG
United Kingdom
Tel: 44 1209 313511
Fax: 44 1209 313512

Cornish Mining Development Association

Roundway, Sennen, Penzance, Cornwall,
TR19 7AW
United Kingdom
Tel: 44 1736 871320

Corporacion Venezolana de Guayana

8th Floor, Artillery House, 11-19 Artillery Row, London, SW1P 1RT
United Kingdom
Tel: 44 207 222 0566
Fax: 44 207 222 0698

Department of Trade and Industry, Infrastructure and Energy Projects Directorate

Tay House, 300 Bath Street, Glasgow, G2 4DX
United Kingdom
Tel: 44 141 228 3646
Fax: 44 141 228 3612
URL: www.dti.gov.uk/ots/iep/

Energy Industries Council

Newcombe House, 45 Notting Hill Gate, London W11 3LQ
United Kingdom
Tel: 44 207 221 2043
Fax: 44 207 221 8813

Energy Institute

61 New Cavendish Street
London
W1G 7AR
United Kingdom
Tel: 44 20 7467 7100
Fax: 44 +44 (0)20 7255 1472
Email: info@energyinst.org.uk
URL: www.energyinst.org.uk

Engineering Council

10 Maltravers Street
London
, WC2R 3ER
United Kingdom
Tel: 44 207 240 7891
Fax: 44 207 240 7517
Email: staff@engc.org.uk
URL: www.engc.org.uk/

Engineering Equipment and Materials Users Association

Artillery House, Artillery Row, London SW1P 1RT
United Kingdom
Tel: 44 207 222 3822
Fax: 44 207 222 3922

Federation of Small Mines of Great Britain

29 King Street, Newcastle-under-Lyme, Staffs, ST5 1ER
United Kingdom
Tel: 44 1782 614618
Fax: 44 1782 717287

Geological Society

Burlington House,
Piccadilly,
London W1J 0BG
United Kingdom
Tel: 44 207 434 9944
Fax: 44 207 439 8975
Email: enquiries@geolsoc.org.uk
URL: www.geolsoc.org.uk/

Geologists' Association

Piccadilly, London W1V 9AG
United Kingdom
Tel: 44 207 434 9298
Fax: 44 207 287 0280
Email: geol.assoc@btinternet.com
URL: www.geologist.demon.co.uk/index.htm

Hydrographic Society

University of East London, Longbridge Rd,
Dagenham, Essex RM8 2AS
United Kingdom
Tel: 44 208 597 1946
Fax: 44 208 590 9730
Email: webmaster@hydrosoc.demon.co.uk
URL: www.hydrosoc.demon.co.uk/

IEA Coal Research - The Clean Coal Centre

Gemini House, 10-18 Putney Hill, London
SW15 6AA
United Kingdom
Tel: 44 208 780 2111
Fax: 44 208 780 1746
Email: mail@iea-coal.org.uk
URL: www.iea-coal.org.uk/

Institute of Explosives Engineers

Centenary Business Centre, Hammond
Close, Attleborough Fields, Nuneaton CV11
6RY
United Kingdom
Tel: 44 2476 350846
Fax: 44 2476 350831

Institute of Materials, Minerals and Mining

1 Carlton House Terrace
London
SW1Y 5DB
United Kingdom
Tel: 44 207 451 7300
Fax: 44 207 839 1702
Email: admin@iom3.org
URL: www.iom3.org

Institute of Occupational Medicine

Roxburgh Place, Edinburgh, EH8 9SU
United Kingdom
Tel: 44 131 667 5131
Fax: 44 131 667 0136

Institution of Civil Engineers

1 Great George Street, London, SW1P 3AA
United Kingdom
Tel: 44 207 222 7722
Fax: 44 207 222 7500
Email: international@ice.org.uk
URL: www.ice.org.uk/

Institution of Electrical Engineers

Savoy Place, London, WC2R 0BL
United Kingdom
Tel: 44 207 240 1871
Fax: 44 207 240 7735
Email: postmaster@iee.org.uk
URL: www.iee.org.uk/

Institution of Fire Engineers

148 New Walk, Leicester, Leicestershire,
LE1 7QB
United Kingdom
Tel: 44 116 255 3654
Fax: 44 116 247 1231
Email: info@ife.org.uk
URL: www.ife.org.uk/

Institution of Lighting Engineers

Regent House
Regent Place, Rugby
CV21 2PN
United Kingdom
Tel: 44 01788 576492
Fax: 44 01788 540145
Email: info@ile.org.uk
URL: www.ile.org.uk

Institution of Mechanical Engineers

1 Birdcage Walk
London
SW1H 9JJ
United Kingdom
Tel: 44 207 222 7899
Fax: 44 207 222 4557
Email: corporate_comm@imeche.org.uk
URL: www.imeche.org.uk/

Institution of Mining and Metallurgy

Danum House, South Parade, Doncaster, DN1 2DY
United Kingdom
Tel: 44 1302 320486
Fax: 44 1302 380900
Email: hq@imm.org.uk
URL: www.imm.org.uk/

Institution of Structural Engineers

11 Upper Belgrave Street, London SW1X 8BH
United Kingdom
Tel: 44 207 235 4535
Fax: 44 207 235 4294
Email: istructe.lon@mail.bogo.co.uk

International Institute of Risk and Safety Management

National Safety Centre, Chancellor's Road
70 Chancellors Road, London W6
United Kingdom
Tel: 44 20 8600 5538
Fax: 44 20 8741 1349
Email: info@iirsm.org
URL: www.iirsm.org

International Liaison Group on Gold Mineralisation

Southampton Oceanography Centre,
Empress Dock, European Way,
Southampton, SO14 3ZH
United Kingdom
Tel: 44 2380 595000
Fax: 44 2380 593052
URL: www.emine.freeserve.co.uk/ILGGM/

International Union of Crystallography

2 Abbey Square, Chester, CH1 2HU
United Kingdom
Tel: 44 1244 345431
Fax: 44 1244 344843
Email: execsec@iucr.ac.uk
URL: www.iucr.ac.uk/

Lifting Equipment Engineers Association

Waggoners Court, The Street, Manuden,
Bishop's Stortford, Herts CM23 1DW
United Kingdom
Tel: 44 1279 816504
Fax: 44 1279 816524

Materials Handling Engineers Association (MHEA)

United Kingdom
Tel: 44 1642 570045
Fax: 44 1642 570045
Email: hw@mhea.co.uk
URL: www.mhea.co.uk

Mineral Industry Research Organisation

Expert House, Sandford Street, Lichfield,
Staffordshire, WS13 6QA
United Kingdom
Tel: 44 1543 262957

Fax: 44 1543 262183
Email: miro@mirolich.demon.co.uk
URL: www.miro.co.uk/

Mineralogical Society

41 Queens Gate, London SW7 5HR
United Kingdom
Tel: 44 207 584 7516
Fax: 44 207 823 8021
Email: k-murphy@minersoc.demon.co.uk

Minerals Engineering Society

2 Ryton Close, Blyth, Worksop, S81 8DN
United Kingdom
Tel: 44 1909 591787

Miners Lamp Manufacturers Association

c/o Oldham, Crompton, Mining Division,
Denton, Manchester, M34 3AT
United Kingdom

Mining Association of the United Kingdom

Expert House, Sandford Street, Lichfield,
Staffordshire WS13 6QA
United Kingdom
Tel: 44 1543 262957
Fax: 44 1543 262183
Email: mauk@mauk.org.uk

National Association of Colliery Managers

137 Station Road, Lingfield, Surrey, RH7
6DZ
United Kingdom
Tel: 44 1342 833716

National Association of Colliery Overmen, Deputies and Shotfirers

48 Netherhall Road, Doncaster, DN1 2PZ
United Kingdom

National Association of Licensed Opencast Operators

3 The Bigg Market, Newcastle upon Tyne,
NE1 1UN
United Kingdom
Tel: 44 191 221 0274

National Association of Solid Fuel Wholesalers

Victoria House, Southampton Row, London,
WC1B 4DH
United Kingdom
Tel: 44 207 405 0034
Fax: 44 207 831 5181

National Environmental Technology Centre

AEA Technology Plc, F6 Culham, Abingdon,
Oxon OX14 3DB
United Kingdom
Tel: 44 1235 463060
Fax: 44 1235 463070
Email: ncec@aeat.co.uk

National Union of Mineworkers (NUM)

Holly Street, Sheffield, S1 2GT
United Kingdom
Tel: 44 1742 766900

NetRegs

Environment Agency, Government Buildings, Burghil Road, Westbury-on-Trym
Bristol
BS10 6BF
United Kingdom
Tel: 44 117 915 6284
Fax: 44 117 915 2770
Email: abigail.beavan@environment-agency.gov.uk
URL: www.environment-agency.gov.uk/netregs

North of England Institute of Mining and Mechanical Engineers

Neville Hall, Westgate Road, Newcastle upon Tyne, NE1 1SE
United Kingdom
Tel: 44 191 232 2201

Northern Ireland Coal Importers Association

c/o 28 Arthur Street, Belfast, BT1 4YX
United Kingdom

Pertamina

Representative Office for London, 29 Queen Anne's Gate, London, SW1H 9BU
United Kingdom
Tel: 44 207 222 2371
Fax: 44 207 222 1247

Scottish Enterprise Energy Group

10 Queens Road, Aberdeen AB15 4ZT
United Kingdom
Tel: 44 1224 626310
Fax: 44 1224 627006
Email: energy.info@scotent.co.uk
URL: www.se-energy.co.uk/

Scottish Office Industry Department, Energy Division

New St Andrew's House, St James Centre, Edinburgh EH1 3TG
United Kingdom
Tel: 44 131 244 4661
Fax: 44 131 244 4668

Solid Fuel Association

Victoria House, Southampton Row, London, WC1B 4DH
United Kingdom
Tel: 44 207 405 0034
Fax: 44 207 831 5181

Solids Handling and Processing Association (SHAPA)

United Kingdom
Tel: 44 116 271 3704
URL: www.shapa.co.uk

Trevithick Society

5 Fairfield Close, Lelant, St Ives, Cornwall, TR26 3JY
United Kingdom
Tel: 44 1736 754358

Union of Democratic Mineworkers (UDM)

The Sycamores, Moor Road, Bestwood, Nottingham, NG6 8UE
United Kingdom
Tel: 44 1159 763468
Fax: 44 1159 763474

University of Dundee, Centre for Petroleum and Mineral Law and Policy

Park Place, Dundee DD1 4HN
United Kingdom
Tel: 44 1382 344300
Fax: 44 1382 322578
Email: cpmlp@dundee.ac.uk
URL:
www.dundee.ac.uk/cepmlp/main/html/home.htm

University of Leeds, Department of Mining and Mineral Engineering

Leeds, West Yorkshire, LS2 9JT
United Kingdom
Tel: 44 113 233 2787
Fax: 44 113 246 7310
Email: minwww@gps.leeds.ac.uk
URL: www.leeds.ac.uk/mining/

Uranium Institute

12th floor, Bowater House, 68
Knightsbridge, London SW1X 7LT
United Kingdom
Tel: 44 207 225 0303
Fax: 44 207 225 0308
Email: ui@uilondon.org
URL: www.uilondon.org/

World Bureau of Metal Statistics

27A High Street
Ware, Hertfordshire
SG12 9BA
United Kingdom
Tel: 44 1920 461274
Fax: 44 1920 464258
Email: wbms@dircon.co.uk
URL: world-bureau.com

World Coal Institute

Oxford House, 182 Upper Richmond Rd,
Putney, London SW15 2SH
United Kingdom
Tel: 44 208 246 6611
Fax: 44 208 246 6622
Email: info@wci-coal.com
URL: www.wci-coal.com/

URUGUAY

Ministry of Industry, Energy and Mines

Rincon 747, Montevideo
Uruguay
Tel: 598 2 98 59 29
Fax: 598 2 92 12 45

National Institute for Environmental Preservation

Luis Cartia 3046
Montevideo
Uruguay
Tel: 598 2 793 109

USA

Abrasive Engineering Society

144 Moore Road
Butler
16001
USA
Tel: 1 724 282 6210
Email: aes@abrasiveengineering.com
URL: www.abrasiveengineering.com

Alabama Coal Association

Vestavia Commerce Center, 2090
Columbiana Road,, Suite 2500, Birmingham,
AL 35216

USA
Tel: 1 205 822 0384
Fax: 1 205 822 2016

Alabama Crushed Stone Association

660 Adams Avenue, 254 Montgomery, AL 36104
USA
Tel: 1 205 263 3407
Fax: 1 205 263 3426

Alaska Coal Association

100 Cushman Street, #210,
Fairbanks, AK 99701
USA
Tel: 1 907 452 2625
Fax: 1 907 451 6543

Alaska Department of Natural Resources

400 Willoughby Avenue, 5th Floor
Juneau
AK 99801
USA
Tel: 1 907 465 2400
Fax: 1 907 465 3886
Email: www-pic@dnr.state.ak.us
URL: www.dnr.state.ak.us/

Alaska Geological Society

PO Box 101288, Anchorage, AK 99510
USA
Tel: 1 907 271 3593
Fax: 1 907 263 4986

Alaska Miners Association, Fairbanks Branch

PO Box 73069, Fairbanks, AK 99707
USA
Tel: 1 907 451 0663
Fax: 1 907 451 0668
Email: raha@ptialaska.net

Alaska Mining Association

501 West Northern Lights Blvd, Suite 203, Anchorage, AK 99503
USA
Tel: 1 907 276 0347
Fax: 1 907 278 7997

Alliance of Independent Miners

PO Box 7042, Boise, ID 83707
USA

American Association of Engineering Societies

1111 19th Street, NW, Suite 608
Washington
DC 20036
USA
Tel: 1 202 296 2237
Fax: 1 202 296 1151
Email: aaes@access.digex.net
URL: www.asee.org/

American Association of Professional Landmen

4100 Fossil Creek Blvd, Fort Worth TX 76137-2791
USA
Tel: 1 817 847 7700
Fax: 1 817 847 7704
URL: www.landman.org/

American Bar Association (SONREEL), Section of Natural Resources, Energy and Environmental Law

75 North Lake Shore Drive, Chicago, IL
60611
USA
Tel: 1 312 988 5724
Fax: 1 312 988 5572
Email: meachamc@attmail.com

American Buff International

PO Box 581, Court Street Paris
Illinois
61944-0581
USA
Tel: 1 217.465.1411
Fax: 1 217.465.1210
Email: info@americanbuff.com
URL: www.americanbuff.com/

American Bureau of Metal Statistics

400 Plaza Drive, Secaucus, NJ 07094-0405
USA
Tel: 1 201 863 6900
Fax: 1 201 863 6050

American Coal Ash Association

2760 Eisenhower Avenue, Suite 304,
Alexandria, VA 22314-4569
USA
Tel: 1 703 317 2400
Fax: 1 703 317 2409
Email: acaa-usa@acaa-usa.org
URL: www.acaa-usa.org/

American Coal Foundation

1130 17th Street, NW Suite 220,
Washington, DC 20036-4604
USA
Tel: 1 202 466 8630
Fax: 1 202 466 8632

American Consulting Engineers Council

1015 Fifteenth Street
NW 802
Washington 20005
USA
Tel: 1 2023477474
Fax: 1 2028980068
Email: acec@acac.org
URL: www.acec.org

American Copper Council

Suite 4-C End Ave, Ste 4-C, New York, NY
10280
USA
Tel: 1 212 945 4990
Fax: 1 212 945 4992

American Crystallographic Association

PO Box 96, Ellicott Station,
Buffalo,
NY 14205-0096
USA
Tel: 1 716 898 8694
Fax: 1 716 898 8695
Email: aca@hwi.buffalo.edu
URL: www.hwi.buffalo.edu/aca/

American Galvanizers Association

12200 East Iliff Avenue, Suite 204, Aurora,
Colorado 80014
USA
Tel: 1 800 468 7732
Fax: 1 303 750 2909
Email: aga@netway.net
URL: www.galvanizeit.org/

American Geological Institute

4220 King Street, Alexandria, Virginia
22302-1502
USA
Tel: 1 703 379 2480
Fax: 1 703 379 7563
Email: webmaster@agi.umd.edu
URL: www.agiweb.org/

American Geophysical Union

2000 Florida Avenue N.W., Washington, DC
20009-1277
USA
Tel: 1 202 462 6900
Email: service@kosmos.agu.org
URL: www.agu.org/

American Institute of Minerals Appraisers

5757 Central Avenue, Suite D, Boulder, CO
80301
USA
Tel: 1 303 443 2209
Fax: 1 303 443 3156

American Institute of Mining, Metallurgical and Petroleum Engineers (AIME)

PO Box 270728, 8307 South Shaffer
Parkway
Littleton
CO, 80127
USA
Tel: 1 303 948 4256
Fax: 1 303 948 4260
Email: aime@aimehq.org
URL: www.aimehq.org

American Institute of Professional Geologists

7828 Vance Drive, 103 Arvada, CO 80003
USA
Tel: 1 303 431 0831
Fax: 1 303 431 1332

American Iron and Steel Institute

1101 17th Street NW, Suite 1300,
Washington, DC 20036
USA
Email: webmaster@steel.org
URL: www.steel.org/

American Iron Ore Association

915 Rockerfella Building, 614 Superior
Avenue, Cleveland, OH 44113-1383
USA
Tel: 1 216 241 8261
Fax: 1 216 241 8262

American Land Rights Association

30218 NE 82nd Avenue, Battle Ground, WA
98604
USA
Tel: 1 360 687 3087
Fax: 1 360 687 2973

American Mining Congress

1920 N Street NW, 300 Washington, DC
20036
USA
Tel: 1 202 861 2800
Fax: 1 202 861 7535

American National Standards Institute

11 West 42nd Street
New York
NY 10036
USA
Tel: 1 212 642 4900
Fax: 1 212 398 0023
Email: info@ansi.org
URL: www.ansi.org/

American Society for Surface Mining and Reclamation

21 Grandview Drive, Princeton, WV 24740
USA
Tel: 1 304 425 8332

American Society for Testing and Materials

100 Barr Harbor Drive, West Conshohocken, PA 19428-2959
USA
Tel: 1 610 832 9585
Fax: 1 610 832 9555
Email: webmastr@astm.org
URL: www.astm.org/

American Society of Appraisers

PO Box 17265, Washington, DC 20041
USA
Tel: 1 800 272 8258
Fax: 1 703 742 8471
URL: www.appraisers.org/

American Society of Civil Engineers

USA
URL: www.asce.org

American Society of Mechanical Engineers

22 Law Dr, PO Box 2900, Fairfield, NJ 07007-2900
USA
Tel: 1 201 882 1167
Fax: 1 201 882 5155
Email: infocentral@asme.org
URL: www.asme.org/

American Zinc Association

1112 16th Street NW, Suite 240
Washington
20036
USA
Tel: 1 2028350164
Fax: 1 2028350155
Email: zincinfo@zinc.org
URL: www.zinc.org

Appalachian Geological Society

PO Box 2605, Charleston, West Virginia 25329 - 2605
USA
Email: slcollins@geocities.com
URL: www.geocities.com/CapeCanaveral/6948/

Arizona Geological Society

PO Box 40952, Tucson, Arizona 85717
USA
Tel: 1 602 795 8169
Fax: 1 602 670 5571

Arizona Mining Association

2702 North 3rd Street, Suite 2015, Phoenix, AZ 85004
USA

Tel: 1 602 266 4416
Fax: 1 602 266 4418
URL: www.azcu.org/

Arizona Prospectors and Small Mine Operators Association

PO Box 5345, Tucson, Arizona 85703
USA
Tel: 1 602 887 6812

Arizona Prospectors Association

4138 W Ruth Avenue, Phoenix, Arizona 85051
USA
Tel: 1 602 930 9454

Arizona Rock Product Association

2020 N Central 1080, Phoenix, Arizona 85004
USA
Tel: 1 602 271 0346
Fax: 1 602 255 0363

Arizona State Mine Inspector

1700 West Washington, Suite 400, Phoenix, Arizona 85007
USA
Tel: 1 602 542 5971
Email: admin@mi.state.az.us
URL: www.asmi.state.az.us

Asbestos Information Association of North America

1745 Jefferson Davis Highway, 509
Arlington, AZ 85004
USA
Tel: 1 703 979 1150
Fax: 1 703 979 1152

Association of Energy Engineers

4025 Pleasantdale Rd., Suite 420
Atlanta
GA 30340
USA
Tel: 1 770 447 5083
Fax: 1 770 446 3969
Email: info@aeecenter.org
URL: www.aeecenter.org

Association of Energy Services Professionals

7040 W. Palmetto Park Rd, Suite 2315, Boca Raton, FL 33433
USA
Tel: 1 407 361 0023
Fax: 1 407 361 0027
Email: phxx49b@prodigy.com
URL: www.aesp.org/

Association of Exploration Geochemists

US Geological Survey, Federal Center, MS-973 Denver, CO 80225
USA
Tel: 1 303 236 5521
Fax: 1 303 236 3200

Association of Iron and Steel Engineers

3 Gateway Center, Suite 1900, Pittsburgh, PA 15222-1004
USA
Tel: 1 412 281 6323
Fax: 1 412 471 4858
Email: webmaster@aise.org
URL: www.aise.org/

Association of Mining Financial Professionals

4300 Republic Plaza, Denver, CO 80202
USA
Tel: 1 303 628 4315
Fax: 1 303 628 4550

Association of Women in the Metal Industries

515 King Street, Suite 420, Alexandria, VA 22314-3137
USA
Tel: 1 703 739 8335
Fax: 1 703 684 6048
URL: www.awmi.com/

Australian Institute of Geoscientists (AIG)

PO Box 606, West Perth WA 6872
USA
Tel: 1 8 9226 3996
Fax: 1 8 9226 3997
Email: aig@aig.asn.au
URL: www.aig.asn.au/

Black Hills Mining Association

PO Box 295, Deadwood, SD 57732
USA
Tel: 1 605 578 1363

Bohemia Mine Owners Association

25199 Perkins Road, Veneta, OR 97487
USA
Tel: 1 503 935 1806
Fax: 1 503 935 1806

Cadmium Council

Suite 110, 12110 Sunset Hills Road, Reston, VA 22090
USA
Tel: 1 703 709 1400
Fax: 1 703 709 1402

California and Nevada Miners and Prospectors Association

PO Box 283, Mina, NV 89422
USA
Tel: 1 702 573 2250

California Energy Commission

1516 Ninth Street, Sacramento, CA 95814-2950
USA
Tel: 1 916 654 4989
Fax: 1 916 654 4420
Email: energia@energy.ca.gov
URL: www.energy.ca.gov/

California Mineral Education Foundation

9647 Folsom Boulevard, Suite 148, Sacramento, CA 95827
USA

California Mining Association

1 Capital Mall, Suite 220, Sacramento, CA 95814-3229
USA
Tel: 1 916 447 1977
Fax: 1 916 447 0348

California Society of Professional Engineers

910 Florin Road, Suite 112
Sacramento
CA 95831-3569
USA
Tel: 1 916 422 7788
Fax: 1 916 422 7785
Email: s.vorhees@cspe.com
URL: www.cspe.com/

Carolina Geological Society

PO Box 90234, Durham, NC 27708-0234
USA
Tel: 1 919 684 5321
Fax: 1 919 684 5833
Email: heron@geo.duke.edu
URL: www.geo.duke.edu/cgsinfo.htm

Casper College, Department of Mining Technology

125 College Drive, Casper, Wyoming 82601
USA
Tel: 1 307 268 2110

Center for Energy and Economic Development

1800 Diagonal Road, Suite 370, Alexandria, VA 22314
USA
Tel: 1 703 684 6292
Fax: 1 703 684 6297
Email: webmaster@ceednet.org
URL: www.ceednet.org/

Central Valley Rock, Sand and Gravel Association

PO Box 1464, Los Banos, CA 93635
USA
Tel: 1 209 826 5955
Fax: 1 209 826 6564

Coal and Slurry Association

1156 15th Street NW, Suite 525, Washington, DC 20005
USA

Coal Outlook

13111 NW Freeway, Suite 230, Houston, TX 77040
USA
Tel: 1 713 460 9200
Fax: 1 713 460 9150

Colorado Department of Natural Resources, Division of Minerals and Geology

1313 Sherman Street, Room 215, Denver, CO 80203
USA
Tel: 1 303 866 3567
Fax: 1 303 832 8106
URL: www.dnr.state.co.us/geology/

Colorado Geological Survey

1313 Sherman St., Rm. 715
Denver, CO 80203
USA
Tel: 1 303 866 2611
Fax: 1 303 866 2461
Email: cgspubs@state.co.us
URL: geosurvey.state.co.us

Colorado Mining Association

1600 Broadway, Suite 1770, 600 Broadway,
Denver, Colorado 80202
USA
Tel: 1 303 894 0536
Fax: 1 303 894 8416
Email: comine@aol.com

Colorado Safety Association

4730 Oakland Street, Suite 500, Denver,
Colorado 80239
USA
Tel: 1 303 373 1937
Fax: 1 303 373 1955

Colorado School of Mines

1500 Illinois Street, Golden, Colorado
80401-1887
USA
Tel: 1 303 273 3000
Fax: 1 303 273 3278
Email: webmaster@mines.edu
URL: www.mines.edu/

Columbia University, Henry Krumb School of Mines

500 W 120th Street, New York, NY 10027
USA
Tel: 1 212 854 2905

Computer Oriented Geological Society

PO Box 370246
Denver Colorado
80237-0246
USA
Fax: 1 303 279 0909
Email: tbrez@csn.org
URL: www.cogsnet.org/

Connecticut Crushed Stone Association

46 Avery Road, Newington, CT 06111
USA
Tel: 1 303 273 3493
Fax: 1 303 273 3314

Copper Development Association

260 Madison Avenue, New York, NY 10016
USA
Tel: 1 212 251 7200
Fax: 1 212 251 7234
Email: the-copper-page@cda.copper.org
URL: www.copper.org/

Department of Energy (DOE)

Forrestal Building, 1000 Independence Ave
SW
Washington
D.C. 20585
USA
Tel: 1 202 586 5575
Fax: 1 202 586 3045
URL: www.energy.gov

Department of Labor, Mine Safety and Health Administration

Arlington, Virginia
USA
Tel: 1 703 235 1452
Fax: 1 703 235 4323
Email: webmaster@msha.gov
URL: www.msha.gov/

Department of the Interior, Minerals Management Service

1849 C Street, NW, Washington, DC 20240
USA
Tel: 1 202 208 3985

Fax: 1 202 208 3968
Email: webmaster@smtp.mms.gov
URL: www.mms.gov/

Eastern Mineral Law Foundation

Kentucky Mineral Law Center, Room 21, Law Building, Lexington, KY 40506-0048
USA
Tel: 1 606 257 1161
Fax: 1 606 323 1061

Eastern Oregon Mining Association

PO Box 932, Baker City, OR 97814
USA
URL: www.oregontrail.net/~eoma/

Empire State Concrete and Aggregate Producers Association

421 New Karner Road, 10 Albany, NY 12205
USA
Tel: 1 518 456 0036
Fax: 1 518 456 0644

Engineering Foundation

345 East 47th Street, Suite 303
New York
NY 10017
USA
Tel: 1 212 705 7836
Fax: 1 212 705 7441
Email: engfnd@aol.com
URL: www.engfnd.org/

Environmental and Engineering Geophysical Society (EEGS)

PO Box 4475, Englewood, Colorado 80155
USA
Tel: 1 303 771 6101
Fax: 1 303 843 6232
Email: eegs@www.esd.ornl.gov
URL: www.esd.ornl.gov/societies/EEGS/

Fabricators and Manufacturers Association

833 Featherstone Road, Rockford, IL 61107
USA
Tel: 1 815 399 8775
Fax: 1 815 399 7279
URL: www.fmametalfab.org/

Florida Limerock and Aggregate Institute

1007 Desota Park Drive, 202 Tallahassee, Florida 32301
USA
Tel: 1 904 942 0781
Fax: 1 904 942 5632

Geological Society of America

3300 Penrose Place, Boulder, Colorado 80301
USA
Tel: 1 303 447 2020
Fax: 1 303 447 1133
Email: web@geosociety.org
URL: www.geosociety.org/

Geological Society of Nevada

PO Box 12021, Reno, NV 89510
USA
Tel: 1 702 323 3500
Fax: 1 702 323 3599

Georgia Mining Association

900 Circle, 75 Parkway, Suite 1740, Atlanta, GA 30339
USA
Tel: 1 770 952 7975
Fax: 1 770 952 7986

Geothermal Education Office

USA
Fax: 1 415 435 7737
Email: geo@marin.org
URL: geothermal.marin.org/

Geothermal Energy Association

1025 Thomas Jefferson St, NW, Suite 109, Washington, DC 20007
USA
Tel: 1 202 944 8561
Fax: 1 202 944 8568
Email: gea@geotherm.org
URL: www.geotherm.org/

Geothermal Resources Council

PO Box 1350, Davis, CA 95617
USA
Tel: 1 916 758 2360
Fax: 1 916 758 2389

Gold Institute

1112 16th Street NW, Suite 240, Washington DC 20036
USA
Tel: 1 202 835 0185
Fax: 1 202 835 0155
URL: www.goldinstitute.com/

Gold Prospectors Association

PO Box 507, Bonsall, CA 92003
USA
Tel: 1 619 728 6620
Fax: 1 619 728 4815

Greening Earth Society

4301 Wilson Blvd, Ste 805, Arlington, VA 22203
USA
Tel: 1 703 907 6168
Fax: 1 703 907 6161
Email: info@greeningearthsociety.org
URL: www.greeningearthsociety.org/

Houston Geological Society

7171 Harwin, Suite 314, Houston, TX 77036-2190
USA
Tel: 1 713 785 6402
Fax: 1 713 785 0553
URL: www.hgs.org/

Idaho Mining Association

PO Box 1660, Hoff Building, Boise, ID 83701
USA
Tel: 1 208 342 0031
Fax: 1 208 345 4210
Email: info@idahomining.org
URL: www.idahomining.org

Illinois Association of Aggregate Producers

522 West Burlington Avenue, La Grange, IL 60525
USA
Tel: 1 708 354 8838

Illinois Coal Council

212 South 2nd Street, Springfield, IL 60525
USA
Tel: 1 217 528 2092
Fax: 1 217 523 5191

Illinois Mining Institute

PO Box 20, Pesotum, IL 61863
USA
Tel: 1 217 867 2791
Fax: 1 217 867 2791
Email: p-godwin@ux1.cso.uiuc.edu

Indiana Coal Council

143 West Market Street, Suite 701,
Indianapolis, IN 46204
USA
Tel: 1 317 638 6997
Fax: 1 317 638 7031

Indiana Mineral Aggregates Association

9595 N Whitley Drive, 205 Indianapolis, IN
46240
USA
Tel: 1 317 580 9100
Fax: 1 317 580 9183

Industrial Diamond Association of America

355 Lexington Avenue, New York, NY
10017
USA
Tel: 1 212 661 4261
Fax: 1 212 370 9047

Industrial Safety Equipment Association

1901 N Moore Street, Suite 808, Arlington,
VA 22209
USA
Tel: 1 703 525 1695
Fax: 1 703 528 2148
Email: safetyhq@aol.com
URL: www.safetycentral.org/isea/

Institute of Electrical and Electronics Engineers (IEEE)

445 Hoes Lane, PO Box 1331, Piscataway,
New Jersey 08855-1331
USA
Tel: 1 908 562 3800
Fax: 1 908 562 1571
URL: www.ieee.org/

Institute of Shaft Drilling Technology

1352 Southwest 175th Street, Seattle, WA
98166
USA
Tel: 1 206 243 2558
Fax: 1 206 244 7994

International Association of Geophysical Contractors

PO Box 460209, Houston, TX 77056-8209
USA
Tel: 1 713 850 7981
Fax: 1 713 850 7984

International Copper Association

16th Floor, 260 Madison Avenue New York,
NY 10016
USA
Tel: 1 212 251 7240
Fax: 1 212 251 7245

International Lead Zinc Research Organization

2525 Meridian Parkway, PO Box 12036, Research Triangle Park, NC
USA
Tel: 1 919 361 4647
Fax: 1 919 361 1957
Email: rputnam@ilzro.org
URL: www.ilzro.org/

International Precious Metals Institute

4905 Tilghman Street, 160 Allentown, PA 18104
USA
Tel: 1 215 395 9700
Fax: 1 215 395 5855

International Security Industry Organization (ISIO)

Florida
USA
Email: isiojk@intsi.org
URL: www.intsi.org

International Society of Explosives Engineers

30325 Bainbridge Road
Cleveland
44139
USA
Tel: 1 440 349 4400
Fax: 1 440 349 3788
Email: isee@isee.org
URL: www.isee.org

Iowa Limestone Producers Association

615 E 14th Street, Des Moines, IA 50316
USA
Tel: 1 515 262 8668
Fax: 1 515 262 0299

Kentucky Coal Association

340 South Broadway, Suite 100, Lexington, KY 40508
USA
Tel: 1 606 233 4743
Fax: 1 606 233 4745
Email: kca@mis.net
URL:
www.miningusa.com/associat/kca/kca.htm

Kentucky Coal Marketing and Export Council

PO Box 11578, Lexington, KY 40576-1578
USA
Tel: 1 606 246 2500
Fax: 1 606 246 2497
URL:
www.coaleducation.org/kcmec/default.htm

Kentucky Crushed Stone Association

Depot Plc, Box 326-119, W Broadway, Frankfort, KY 40602
USA
Tel: 1 502 223 2379
Fax: 1 502 223 2370

Kentucky Mining Institute

340 South Broadway, Suite 100, Lexington, KY 40508
USA
Tel: 1 606 233 4743
Fax: 1 606 233 4745
URL: www.miningusa.com/kmi/default.htm

Lead Industries Association

295 Madison Avenue, New York, NY 10017
USA
Tel: 1 212 578 4750

Lignite Energy Council

PO Box 2277, Bismarck, ND 58502
USA
Tel: 1 701 258 7117
Fax: 1 701 258 2755

Louisiana Crushed Stone Association

2900 West Fork Drive, 200 Baton Rouge, LA 70827
USA
Tel: 1 504 292 5272
Fax: 1 504 293 2901

Louisiana State University, Center for Energy Studies

1 East Fraternity Circle, Baton Rouge, Louisiana 70803-0301
USA
Tel: 1 225 578 4400
Fax: 1 225 578 4541
Email: ces@enrg.lsu.edu
URL: www.enrg.lsu.edu/

Maryland Aggregates Association

33 West Street, 110 Annopolis, MD 21401
USA
Tel: 1 410 269 7531
Fax: 1 410 269 7528

Maryland Coal Association

1688 Belhaven Woods Court Pasadena, MD 21122
USA

Michigan Mineral Resources Association

PO Box 80677, Lansing, MI 48908
USA
Tel: 1 517 321 0515
Fax: 1 517 321 3240

Michigan Technological University, Department of Mining Engineering

1400 Townsend Drive, Houghton, MI 49931-1295
USA
Tel: 1 906 487 2610
Fax: 1 906 487 2495
Email: mining@mtu.edu
URL: www.mg.mtu.edu/

Michigan Technological University, Institute of Materials Processing

1400 Townsend Drive, Houghton, MI 49931
USA
Tel: 1 906 487 2600
Fax: 1 906 487 2921
Email: jhwang@mtu.edu
URL: www.imp.mtu.edu/

Mineral Economics and Management Society

PO Box 721, Houghton, MI 49931
USA
Tel: 1 906 487 2771
Fax: 1 906 487 2994

Mineral Information Institute

1125 17th Street, 1800 Denver, CO 80202
USA
Tel: 1 303 297 3226
Fax: 1 303 297 3526
Email: mii@mii.org
URL: www.mii.org/

Mineral Insulation Manufacturers Association

44 Canal Center Plaza, 310 Alexandria, VA 22314
USA
Tel: 1 703 684 0084
Fax: 1 703 684 0427

Mineralogical Society of America

1015 Eighteenth St NW, Suite 601, Washington, DC 20036
USA
Tel: 1 202 775 4344
Fax: 1 202 775 0018

Mineralogical Society of Southern California

PO Box 41027, Pasadena, CA 91114-8027
USA
Fax: 1 818 338 4617
Email: 74131.524@compuserve.com
URL: www.mineralsocal.org/

Minerals Exploration Coalition

1019 8th Street, Suite 305, Golden, Colorado 80401
USA
Tel: 1 303 277 1155
Fax: 1 303 277 1212
Email: mec@henge.com

Miners Advocacy Council

PO Box 73824, Fairbanks, AK 99707
USA
Tel: 1 907 488 6453

Mining and Metallurgical Society of America

9 Escalle Lane, Larkspur, CA 94939
USA
Tel: 1 415 924 7441
Fax: 1 415 924 7463

Mining Association of South Carolina

PO Box 1368, Irmo, SC 29063
USA
Tel: 1 803 772 5354
Fax: 1 803 798 0670

Mining Association of Wyoming

PO Box 866, Cheyenne, WY 82003
USA
Tel: 1 307 635 0331
Fax: 1 307 778 6240

Mining Industry Council of Missouri

PO Box 725, Jefferson City, MO 65102
USA
Tel: 1 314 635 730
Fax: 1 314 635 6030
Email: info@momic.com
URL: www.momic.com/

Minnesota Exploration Association

Suite 622, 12 South 16th Street,
Minneapolis, MN 55402-0521
USA
Tel: 1 612 338 5584
Fax: 1 612 338 5457

Mississippi Valley Coal Trade and Transport Council

2 Canal, Suite 1013, New Orleans, LA 70130
USA

Missouri Limestone Producers Association

PO Box 1725, Jefferson City, MO 65102
USA
Tel: 1 314 635 0208
Fax: 1 314 635 8006

Modern Gold Miners Association

PO Box 47, Happy Camp, CA 96039
USA
Tel: 1 916 493 2062
Fax: 1 916 493 2095

Montana Coal Council

2301 Colonial Drive, Helena, MT 59601
USA
Tel: 1 406 442 6223

Montana College of Mineral Science and Technology, Department of Mining Engineering

W Park Street, Butte, MT 59701
USA
Tel: 1 406 496 4261

Montana Mining Association

2301 Colonial Drive, Helena, MT 59601
USA
Tel: 1 406 443 7297
Fax: 1 406 443 7299

National Aggregates Association

900 Spring Street, Silver Spring, MD 20910
USA
Tel: 1 301 587 1400
Fax: 1 301-587-9419
Email: webmaster@nationalaggregates.org
URL: www.nationalaggregates.org/

National Coal Association

1130 17th Street NW, Washington, DC 20036
USA
Tel: 1 202 463 2653
Fax: 1 202 833 1965

National Coal Council

PO Box 17370, Arlington, VA 22216-7370
USA
Tel: 1 703 527 1191
Fax: 1 703 527 1195

National Fire Protection Association

1 Butterymarch Park, Quincy, Massachusetts 02269-9101
USA
Tel: 1 617 770 3000
Fax: 1 617 770 0700
Email: library@nfpa.org
URL: www.nfpa.org/

National Geophysical Data Center

325 Broadway E/GC4, Boulder, CO 80303-3328
USA
Tel: 1 303 497 6826
Fax: 1 303 497 6513
Email: info@ngdc.noaa.gov
URL: www.ngdc.noaa.gov/

National Institute of Standards and Technology

Administration Bldg A903, Gaithersburg, MD 20899-0001
USA
Tel: 1 301 975 3058
Email: inquiries@enh.nist.gov
URL: www.nist.gov/*NIST Boulder, Colorada Laboratories*
325 Broadway
Boulder, CO 80303
United States of America
Tel: +1 303 497 3017
Fax: +1 303 497 3371
E-mail: webmaster@boulder.nist.gov
URL: http://www.boulder.nist.gov/

National Lime Association

3601 N. Fairfax Drive, Arlington, VA 22201
USA
Tel: 1 703 243 5463
Fax: 1 703 243 5489

National Mining Association

1130 17th Street, NW, Washington, DC 20036
USA
Tel: 1 202 463 2662
Fax: 1 202 833 9636
Email: nma@planetcom.com
URL: www.nma.org/

National Safety Council

1121 Spring Lake Drive
Illinois
60143320
USA
Tel: 1 6302851121
Fax: 1 6302851315
Email: customerservice@nsc.org
URL: www.nsc.org

National Society of Professional Engineers

1420 King Street, Alexandria
Virginia
223142794
USA
Tel: 1 7036842800
Fax: 1 7038364875
Email: webmaster@nspe.org
URL: www.nspe.org

National Stone Association

1415 Elliott Place, Washington, DC 20007
USA
Tel: 1 202 342 1100
Fax: 1 202 342 0702
URL: www.aggregates.org/

Natural Resources Law Center

University of Colorado School of Law,
Campus Box 401, Boulder, CO 80309-0401
USA
Tel: 1 303 492 1286
Fax: 1 303 492 1297
Email: katherine.taylor@colorado.edu

Nebraska Conservation and Survey Division (NebraskaGeological Survey)

University of Nebraska-Lincoln, 113 Nebraska Hall, Lincoln, Nebraska 68588-0517
USA
Tel: 1 402-472-3471
Fax: 1 402-472-4608
Email: csdsales@unl.edu
URL: csd.unl.edu/

Nevada Bureau of Mines and Geology

Mail Stop 178, University of Nevada, Reno, Nevada 89557
USA
Tel: 1 702 784 6691
Fax: 1 702 784 1709
Email: info@nbmg.unr.edu
URL: www.nbmg.unr.edu/

Nevada Division of Minerals

400 W King St, Ste 106, Carson City, Nevada 89703
USA
Tel: 1 702 687 5050
Fax: 1 702 687 3957
Email: ndom@govmail.state.nv.us
URL: www.state.nv.us/b&i/minerals/

Nevada Energy Office

41050 E. Williams St, Suite 435
Carson City
Nevada 89710
USA
Tel: 1 702-6874910
Fax: 1 702-6874914
URL: energy.state.nv.us

Nevada Geological Association

PO Box 283, Mina, NV 89422
USA
Tel: 1 702 323-7775

Nevada Landmen's Association

PO Box 21351, Reno, NV 89515-1351
USA
Tel: 1 702 358 9500

Nevada Mining Association

5250 South Virginia Street, Suite 220, Reno, Nevada 89502
USA
Tel: 1 702 829 2121
Fax: 1 702 829 2148
URL: www.nevadamining.org/

New Jersey Concrete and Aggregate Association

770 River Road, West Trenton, NJ 08628
USA
Tel: 1 609 771 0099
Fax: 1 609 771 2095

New Mexico Bureau of Mines and Mineral Resources

Campus Station, Socorro, NM 87801
USA
Tel: 1 505 835 5420

New Mexico Energy, Minerals and Natural Resources Department

2040 S Pacheco Street, Santa Fe, NM 87505
USA
Tel: 1 505 827 5950

New Mexico Geological Society

Campus Station, Socorro, NM 87801
USA
Tel: 1 505 835 5410

New Mexico Mining Association

1470 St Francis Drive, Sante Fe, NM 87505-4038
USA
Tel: 1 505 820 6662
Fax: 1 505 986 0091

Nickel Producers Environmental Research Association

2605 Meridian Parkway, Suite 200, Durham, NC 27713
USA
Tel: 1 919 544 7722
Fax: 1 919 544 7724
Email: nipera@asciences.com
URL: www.nipera.org/

North Carolina Aggregates Association

PO Box 30603, Raleigh, NC 27622
USA
Tel: 1 919 782 7055

Northwest Mining Association

10 North Post Street, Suite 414, Spokane, WA 99201-0772
USA
Tel: 1 509 624 1158
Fax: 1 509 623 1241
Email: nwma@on-ramp.ior.com

Ohio Aggregates Association

20 South Front Street, 200 Colombus, OH 43215
USA
Tel: 1 614 224 2717

Ohio Mining and Reclamation Association

50 South Young Street, Suite 204
Columbus, OH 43215
USA
Tel: 1 614 228 6336
Fax: 1 614 228 6349

Ohio State University, Department of Mining Engineering

177 Watts Hall, 2041 College Rd, Columbus, OH 43210
USA
Tel: 1 614 292 2079

Oklahoma City Geological Society

USA
Email: ocgs@oklahoma.net
URL: www.ocgs.org

Oklahoma Energy Resources Board

PO Box 18738, Oklahoma City, Oklahoma 73154 - 0738
USA
Email: general@oerb.com
URL: www.oerb.com/

Oregon Metals Industry Council

101 SW Main, 245, One World Trade Center, Portland, OR 97204
USA
Tel: 1 503 223 0719

Oregon Mining Council

1201 SW 12th Avenue, 200 Portland, OR 97205
USA
Tel: 1 503 227 5591

Pacific Mining Association

7906 La Palma Avenue, Buena Park, CA 90620
USA

Pennsylvania Coal Association

212 North Third Street, Suite 102, Harrisburg, PA 17101
USA
Tel: 1 717 233 7909
Fax: 1 717 231 7610

Pennsylvania Department of Environmental Protection, Bureau of Deep Mine Safety

USA
URL: www.dep.state.pa.us/dep/deputate/minres/dms/dms.htm

Pittsburgh Research Laboratory, National Institute for Occupational Safety and Health

USA
Tel: 1 412 892 6601
Fax: 1 412 892 6614
URL: www.cdc.gov/niosh/mining/

Portland Cement Association

5420 Old Orchard Road
Skokie
Illinois 60077
USA
Tel: 1 847 966 6200
Fax: 1 847 966 8389
Email: info@cement.org
URL: www.portcement.org

Potash and Phosphate Institute

2801 Burord Highway NE, 401 Atlanta, GA 30329
USA
Tel: 1 404 634 4274
Fax: 1 404 536 8733

Prospector and Miners Coordinating Council

PO Box 508, Sanger, CA 93657
USA
Tel: 1 209 299 1265

Rocky Mountain Association of Environmental Professionals

PO Box 46171, Denver, CO 80201
USA
Tel: 1 303 771 0900

Rocky Mountain Association of Geologists

820 16th Street, Suite 505, Denver, CO 80202

USA
Tel: 1 303 573 8621
Fax: 1 303 628 0546
Email: rmag@henge.com
URL: www.rmag.org/

Rocky Mountain Association of Mineral Landmen

PO Box 2000, Broomfield, CO 80020
USA
Tel: 1 303 469 8844

Rocky Mountain Coal Mining Institute

8057 S. Yukon Way
Littleton, Colorado 80128-5510
USA
Tel: 1 303 948 3300
Email: mail@rmcmi.org
URL: www.rmcmi.org

Rocky Mountain Mineral Law Foundation

7039 East 18th Ave., Denver, CO 80220
USA
Tel: 1 303 321 8100
Fax: 1 303 321 7657
Email: info@rmmlf.org
URL: www.rmmlf.org/

Safety Equipment Institute

Suite 3A, 1307 Dolley Madison Boulevard,
McLean, Virginia 22101
USA
Tel: 1 703 442 5732
Fax: 1 703 442 5756
Email: sei_headquarters@msn.com
URL: www.seinet.org/

Society for Mining, Metallurgy and Exploration

PO Box 277002,
Littleton, CO 80127-7002
USA
Tel: 1 303-973-9550
Fax: 1 303 973 3845
Email: sme@smenet.org
URL: www.smenet.org/

Society of Economic Geologists Foundation

PO Box 926, De Kalb, IL 60115
USA
Tel: 1 815 753 0495

Society of Exploration Geochemists

PO Box 571, Golden, CO 80402
USA
Tel: 1 303 236 5538

Society of Exploration Geophysicists (SEG)

8801 South Yale, Tulsa, Oklahoma 74137
USA
Tel: 1 918 497 5500
Fax: 1 918 497 5557
Email: web@seg.org
URL: www.seg.org/

Society of Manufacturing Engineers

One SME Drive, PO Box 930, Dearborn, MI 48121-0930
USA
Tel: 1 313 271 1500
Email: webmaster@sme.org
URL: www.sme.org/

Society of Mineral Analysis

PO Box 26, Elko, NV 89801
USA
Tel: 1 702 738 8043

South Carolina Mining Association

PO Box 1184, Inno, SC 29063
USA
Tel: 1 803 772 5354
Fax: 1 803 798 0670

South Dakota Council for Natural Resources Development

PO Box 8250, Rapid City, SD 57709
USA
Tel: 1 605 342 2592

South Dakota Mining Association

3801 South Kiwanis Avenue, 5, Sioux Falls, SD 57105
USA
Tel: 1 605 332 3803
Fax: 1 605 334 1938

South Dakota School of Mines and Technology

501 East Saint, Joseph Street, Rapid City, SD 57701
USA
Tel: 1 800 544 8162
Fax: 1 605 394 2400
Email: jsmoragi@msmailgw.sdsmt.edu
URL: www.hpcnet.org/cgi-bin/global/a_bus_card.cgi?SiteID=21

Southern California Rock Products Association

1811 Fair Oaks Avenue, Box 40, South Pasadena, CA 91030
USA
Tel: 1 626 441 3107
Fax: 1 626 441 0649

Southern Illinois University, Department of Mining Engineering

Carbondale, IL 62901
USA
Tel: 1 618 536 6637

Southwestern Mineral Exploration Association

PO Box 40938, Tucson, AZ 85725
USA
Tel: 1 602 622 6257

Spokane Research Laboratory, National Institute for Occupational Safety and Health

315 E Montgomery, Spokane, WA 99207
USA
Tel: 1 509 354 8000
Fax: 1 509 354 8099
Email: efc8@cdc.gov
URL: www.cdc.gov/niosh/mining

Texas Mining and Reclamation Association

300 Highland Mall Boulevard, Suite 100, Austin, TX 78752
USA
Tel: 1 512 467 1300
Fax: 1 512 451 9556

TMS (Minerals, Metals and Materials Society)

184 Thorn Hill Rd
Warrendale, PA 15086
USA
Tel: 1 724 776 9000
Fax: 1 724 776 3770
Email: tmsgeneral@tms.org
URL: www.tms.org

TMS (The Minerals, Metals, & Materials Society)

184 Thorn Hill Rd
Warrendale, PA 15086
USA
Tel: 1 724 776 9000
Fax: 1 724 776 3770
URL: www.tms.org

United States Geological Survey

MS804 National Center, Reston VA 20192
USA
Tel: 1 703 648 4000
Fax: 1 703 648 4888
Email: webmaster@www.usgs.gov
URL: www.usgs.gov/

United States Mine Rescue Association

PO Box 1010, Uniontown, PA 15401
USA
Email: usmra@usaor.net
URL: www.usmra.com/

University of Alabama, Department of Metallurgical and Materials Engineering

Dean's Office, Box 870200, Tuscaloosa, AL 35487
USA
Tel: 1 205 348 6578
URL: www.eng.ua.edu/~mtedept/

University of Alaska, School of Mineral Engineering

Fairbanks, AK 99701
USA
Tel: 1 907 474 7565
URL: sme.uaf.edu

University of Arizona, College of Mines

Building 12, Room 229, Tucson, AZ 85721
USA
Tel: 1 602 621 2147

University of Kentucky, College of Mining Engineering

230 Mining and Mineral Resources Bldg, Lexington, KY 40506-0107
USA
Tel: 1 606 257 8026
URL:
www.engr.uky.edu/MINING/mintmb.html

University of Missouri-Rolla, Department of Mining Engineering

129 McNutt Hall, Rolla, MO 65401
USA
Tel: 1 573/341-4753
Fax: 1 573/341-6934
Email: mining@umr.edu
URL: www.umr.edu/~mining/

University of Nevada, Mackay School of Mines

MS 168, Reno, NV 89557
USA
Tel: 1 702 784 6961

University of North Dakota, School of Engineering and Mines

PO Box 8086, University Station, Grand Forks, ND 58202
USA
Tel: 1 701 777 2811
URL: www.und.edu/dept/sem/

University of Utah, Department of Mining Engineering

1320 East 500 South 506, Salt Lake City, UT 84112-1183
USA
Tel: 1 801 581 7162

University of Wisconsin, Department of Metallurgical and Mining Engineering

1509 University Avenue, Madison, WI 53706
USA
Tel: 1 608 262 1821

Utah Department of Natural Resources

1594 West North Temple
Salt Lake City
Utah 84114
USA
Tel: 1 801 538 7200
Email:
nrdomain.nrmain.help@email.state.ut.us
URL: www.nr.state.ut.us/

Utah Mining Association

136 South Main #709, Salt Lake City, Utah 84101
USA
Tel: 1 801 364 1874
Fax: 1 801 364 2640
Email: mining@xmission.com
URL: www.utahmining.org/

Utah Office of Energy and Resource Planning

1594 West North Temple, Suite 3610
Salt Lake City
Utah 84114-6480
USA
Tel: 1 801-5385428
Fax: 1 801-5210657
Email: nradm.jcurry@state.ut.us
URL: www.nr.utah.gov/energy/home.htm

Virginia Aggregates Association

6243 River Road, Suite 6
Virginia
23229
USA
Tel: 1 8042829401
Fax: 1 8042828134
Email: va_aggregates@vaagg.org
URL: www.vaagg.org

Virginia Coal Association

Old City Hall, Suite 425, 1001 East Broad Street, Richmond VA 23219
USA
Tel: 1 804 643 6697
Fax: 1 804 643 6699

Virginia Coal Council

PO Box 858
Richlands
VA 24642
USA

Virginia Tech, Department of Mining and Minerals Engineering

213 Holden Hall, Blacksburg, VA 24061
USA
Tel: 1 703 231 6671
URL:
www.eng.vt.edu/eng/mining/minehome.html

Washington Energy Policy Group

PO Box 43172, Olympia, Washington
98504-3172
USA
Tel: 1 360 956 2096
Fax: 1 360 956 2180
Email: wepg@wseo.wa.gov
URL: www.energy.cted.wa.gov

West Texas Geological Society

PO Box 1595, Midland, TX 79702
USA
Tel: 1 915 683 1573
Email: wtgs@basinlink.com
URL: www.wtgs.org/

West Virginia Coal Association

1301 Laidley Tower, Charleston, WV 25301
USA
Tel: 1 304 342 4153
Fax: 1 304 342 7651
Email: braney@wvcoal.com
URL: www.wvcoal.com/

West Virginia Mining and Reclamation Association

1624 Kanawha Boulevard, East Charleston,
WV 25311
USA
Tel: 1 304 346 5318
Fax: 1 304 346 5310
Email: wvmra@newwave.net
URL: www.wvmra.com/

West Virginia University, Department of Mining Engineering

PO Box 6070, Morgantown, WV 26505-6070
USA
Tel: 1 304 293 7680
Fax: 1 304 293 5708
Email: speng@wvucomer1.comer.wvu.edu
URL: www.wvu.edu/~minengin/

Western Fuels Association

Magruder Building, 1625 M Street NW,
Washington, DC 20036
USA
Tel: 1 202 463 6580
Fax: 1 202 223 8790

Western Interstate Energy Board

1515 Cleveland Place, Suite 200
Denver, CO 80202
USA
Tel: 1 303 573 8910
Fax: 1 303 534 7309
Email: dlarson@westgov.org
URL: www.westgov.org/wieb/

Wisconsin Mining Association

PO Box 352, 501 E Washington Avenue,
Madison, WI 53701-0352

USA
Tel: 1 608 258 3400
Fax: 1 608 258 3413

World Energy Efficiency Association

1400 16th Street NW, Suite 340,
Washington, DC 20036
USA
Tel: 1 202 797 6570
Fax: 1 202 797 6573
Email: info@weea.org
URL: www.weea.org/

World Gold Council

900 Third Avenue, New York, NY 10022
USA
Tel: 1 212 688 0005
Fax: 1 212 688 0411
URL: www.gold.org/

Wyoming Geological Association

PO Box 545, Casper, WY 82602-0545
USA
Tel: 1 307 237 0027

Wyoming Mining Association

Hitching Post Inn, PO Box 866, 1700 West
Lincoln Way, Cheyenne, WY 82003
USA
Tel: 1 307 635 0331
Fax: 1 307 778 6240
URL: www.wma-minelife.com/

VENEZUELA

Bitumenes del Orinoco (BITOR)

Edif Bitumenes del Orinoco SA, Calle Cali,
Las Mercedes, Caracas
Venezuela
Tel: 58 2 907 5111
Fax: 58 2 908 3982

Corporacion Venezolana de Guayana (CVG)

Av La Estancia, Torre General, Piso 2,
Chuao, Caracas Venezuela
Venezuela
Tel: 58 2 993 0363
Fax: 58 2 993 8549

Industry Development Corporation (CORPOINDUSTRIA)

Av Las Delicias, Edif Corpoindustria, Piso 6,
Maracay, Edo Aragua Venezuela
Venezuela
Tel: 58 43 339309
Fax: 58 43 331264

Mining Chamber

Av Leonardo da Vinci, Edif centro Comercial
Bello Monte, Piso 7, Ofic D Colinas de Bello
Monte, Caracas
Venezuela
Tel: 58 2 752 0304
Fax: 58 2 752 3657

Ministry for Energy and Mines

Centro Simon Bolivar, Torre Oeste, Piso 12,
El Silencio, Caracas
Venezuela
Tel: 58 2 575 4686
Fax: 58 2 574 4101

Ministry for Trade and Industry

Avenida Libertador, Centro Comercial Los Cedros
PH
Caracas
Venezuela
Tel: 58 2 762 3810
Fax: 58 2 731 3027

National Council of Industries (CONINDUSTRIA)

Esquina Puente Anauco, Edif Camara de Industriales
Piso 1
La Candelaria, Caracas
Venezuela
Tel: 58 2 573 0222
Fax: 58 2 576 0972
URL: www.conindustria.org/

Venezuelan Association of Metal and Mining Industries

Esquina Puente Anauco, Edif Camara de Industriales, Piso 1, La Candelaria, Caracas
Venezuela
Tel: 58 2 471 3549
Fax: 58 2 575 0186

Venezuelan Iron and Steel Institute

Esquina Puente Anauco, Edif Camara de Industriales, Piso 1, La Candelaria, Caracas
Venezuela
Tel: 58 2 572 9468
Fax: 58 2 575 2935

Venezuelan Society of Mining and Metallurgical Engineers

Apartado Postal 64903, CCC Tamanaco, Caracas 1064-A
Venezuela
Tel: 58 2 2642481
Fax: 58 2 9458062
Email: inespro@ccs.internet.ve

VIETNAM

Chamber of Commerce and Industry

33 Ba Trieu Street
Hanoi
Vietnam
Tel: 84 48 252961
Fax: 84 48 256446

Ministry of Industry

54 Hai Ba Trung Street
Hanoi
Vietnam
Tel: 84 48 267870
Fax: 84 48 269003

YEMEN

Ministry of Energy and Minerals

PO Box 5780, Maala'a, Aden
Yemen
Tel: 967 42 141

YUGOSLAVIA

Ministry of Mining and Energy
Kralja Milana 36
11000 Belgrade
Serbia
phone: +381113346755
fax: +381-11-36-16-603

University of Belgrade, Faculty of Mining and Geology

Djusina 7, 11000 Belgrade
Yugoslavia
Tel: 381 11 3238 832
Fax: 381 11 3235 539

ZAMBIA

Department of Energy

Ministry of Energy and Water Development,
PO Box 36079, Lusaka 10101
Zambia
Email: doe@zamnet.zm

Ministry of Mines and Mineral Development

PO Box 31939, Lusaka
Zambia
Tel: 260 211 220

National Energy Council

PO Box 37631, Great East Road, Bobil Oil Building, Lusaka 10101
Zambia
Tel: 260 292 165

ZIMBABWE

Industry, governmental and related organisations in Zimbabwe

Chamber of Mines of Zimbabwe

PO Box 712, Harare
Zimbabwe
Tel: 263 4 702841
Fax: 263 4 707983

Confederation of Zimbabwe Industries

PO Box 3794
Harare
Zimbabwe
Tel: 263 4 739830
Fax: 263 4 750953
Email: czi@primenet.co.zw

Ministry of Mines

Private Bag 7709, Causeway, Harare
Zimbabwe
Tel: 263 4 703781
Fax: 263 4 793065

National Chamber of Commerce

PO Box 1934
Harare
Zimbabwe
Tel: 263 4 708611
Email: info@zncc.co.zw
URL: www.zncc.co.zw

Zimbabwe Mining Development Corporation

PO Box 4101, Harare
Zimbabwe
Tel: 263 4 487014
Fax: 263 4 487022

BUSINESS TRAVEL TO ITALY

BUSINESS CUSTOMS

By and large, what is considered good business practice in the United States also applies when doing business in Italy. Businesspeople in Italy also appreciate prompt replies to their inquires, and they expect all correspondence to be acknowledged. Before embarking on a business venture to tap the market in Italy, the review of travel guides would be especially helpful. These guides contain useful hints on cultural differences and business protocol.

TRAVEL ADVISORY AND VISAS

Every U.S. traveler must have a valid passport. No visa is required of U.S. citizens visiting Italy for less than 3 months, but one is required for longer stays. An American citizen entering for permanent residence must register within 8 days of entering the country. Application for a Residence Permit (Permesso di Soggiorno) is made at the local police station:

U.S. citizens planning to work in the country must first obtain a work visa. Work permit approval must first be obtained by the Italian employer and is usually granted only for specialized work or skills. Management and skilled workers have no difficulty in obtaining work permits. The Italian employer files an application at a Provincial Labor Office. If clearance is granted, the prospective employer is further required to obtain a work permit with the approval of the regional and central authorities. The permit is then sent to the worker so that he or she may apply for the entry visa. There are Italian consular offices in all of the largest American cities. The application process should be initiated three to four months before it will be needed.

For further information concerning entry requirements for Italy, travelers can contact the Embassy of Italy at 1601 Fuller Street, NW, Washington, DC 20039, telephone: (202) 328-5558, or the nearest Italian Consulate General in Boston, Chicago, Houston, Los Angeles, New Orleans, New York, Philadelphia, or San Francisco.

A person seeking to work in Italy in an independent or self-employed capacity, files an application directly with the Italian Consulate along with needed credentials demonstrating experience in the field of work.

Italy has a very low rate of violent crime, little of which is directed toward tourists. Petty crime (pickpocketing, theft from parked cars, purse snatching) is a significant problem, especially in large cities. Most reported thefts occur at crowded tourist sites, on public buses, or at the major railway stations, including Rome's Termini, Milan's Centrale, Florence's Santa Maria Novella, and the Centrale in Naples.

U.S. Citizens are reminded that certain Alitalia flights between Italy and various middle eastern points (usually Damascus or Amman) make en route stops in Beirut. The State Department warns U.S. Citizens to avoid all travel to or through Lebanon.

Embassy and Consulate locations
The U.S. Embassy in Rome is located at Via Veneto 119/A, telephone: 39-06-46741, fax: 39-06-488-2672 or 4674-2356.

There are U.S. Consulates at the following locations: Florence, at Lungarno Amerigo Vespucci 38, telephone: 39-055-239-8276/7/8, or 217-605;

fax: 39-055-284088; Milan, at Via Principe Amedeo 2/10, telephone: 39-02-290351; fax: 39-02-2900-1165; Naples, at Piazza della Repubblica, telephone: 39-081-583-8111; fax: 39-081-761-1869; Palermo (consular Agent), at Via Vaccarini 1, telephone: 39-091-305857 or 39-337-793421 (cellular); fax: 39-091-6256026. Trieste (consular agent), at Via Roma 15, telephone: 39-040-660177, fax: 39-040-631240; Genoa (consular agent), Via Dante 2, telephone/fax: 39-010-584492.

BUSINESS INFRASTRUCTURE

Italian is the official language and is spoken in all parts of Italy, although some minority groups in the Alto Adige and Aosta regions speak German and French, respectively. Correspondence with Italian firms, especially if the letter is the first sent, should be in Italian. If a reply comes in English then the subsequent correspondence with the Italian firm can be in English. The use of Italian is not only regarded as a courtesy, but assures prompt attention, and prevents inaccuracies which might arise in translation. Most large commercial firms, however, are able to correspond in various languages in addition to English and Italian, but a business overture or proposal is given more serious attention if written in Italian.

The importance of having trade literature, catalogs, and instructions for the use of servicing of products printed in Italian cannot be overemphasized. The agent representative in Italy who has such material is in a far better competitive position than the one who can only show prospective customers and consumers literature in English.

The usual Italian business hours are from 8 or 9 A.M. to Noon or 1 P.M. and from 3 to 6 or 7 P.M. Working hours for the various ministries of the government are normally from 8 A.M. to 2 P.M. without intermission. Bank hours are from 8:30 A.M. to 1:30 P.M. and 3:00-4:00 P.M.; they are closed on Saturdays.

With the ease of telephone communications, international calls are frequently the best method of arranging appointments and maintaining solid commercial relations. Fax machines have increased the speed and ease of international communications and should be used to maintain strong business ties. The Italians are usually adept at handling business calls in English; however, be prepared to expect some language differences and be able to make simple requests in Italian. The time zone for Italy is 6 hours ahead of the U.S. eastern standard time.

As in many Western European countries, Italy's telephone dialing procedures are in the process of being changed. With regards to dialing procedures within Italy, by November 1998, the present city code will become part of each telephone number. An example of a local call within Rome would be: 06-46741 (06 is the city code).

Incoming long distance calls to Italy already require that the "0" in the city code now be included when dialing. An example of an incoming long distance call from the U.S. to Rome is as follows: 011-39-06-46741 (39 being the country code, 06 the city code for Rome). Milan's city code 02.

Many Italian companies are now beginning to use E-mail communications; requests for E-mail addresses are becoming more frequent from Italian businesspersons.

Medical services are excellent and hospitals compare with those in the United States. Common medical needs are readily obtained, and special supplies are normally available on short notice. An international certificate of vaccination is not required for travelers from the United States. Drinking water is acceptable
and most pharmaceuticals are available, and sanitation is at American standards.

Rental automobiles are available at numerous locations. An international or state driving license is acceptable. Tipping is as appropriate in Italy as it is in the United States. Generally, tip waiters 10 percent if "servizio" has not been added to the check.

Conservative business attire is recommended at all times. Business appointments are also required, and visitors are expected to be punctual.

There is solid sales potential for U.S. goods and services in the Italian market. It is a highly competitive market and the U.S. exporter must keep certain factors in mind to achieve maximum success. The "golden keys" of customary business courtesy, especially replying promptly to requests for price quotations and to orders, are a prerequisite for exporting success. In general, European business executives are more formal than their American counterparts; therefore, it is best to refrain from using first names until a solid relationship has been formed.

During the first stages of conducting business, it is best to let the prospective buyer take the lead since the American approach of "getting down to business" may be considered abrupt. Avoid commenting on political events or negative comments about the country. Some positive and sincere observations about the Italian culture, style, art, history, cuisine, or music are always appropriate. Italian business executives tend to use titles indicating their position in the firm. Friendship and mutual trust are highly valued, and once an American has established this relationship a productive business association can usually be counted upon.

Italian buyers appreciate style, quality, and service, but are also interested in delivered price. Care must be taken to assure that stated delivery dates will be maintained and that after-sales service will be promptly honored. Italians, and Europeans in general, are concerned that after placing an order with a supplier that the delivery date be honored. While there are numerous factors that may interfere with prompt shipment, the U.S. exporter must allow for additional shipping time and keep in close contact with the buyer.

Meeting delivery schedules is of prime importance. It is much better to quote a later delivery date that can be guaranteed than promise an earlier delivery that is not completely certain.

CURRENCY

The basic monetary unit is the lira (plural: lire) and is usually indicated as L or Lit. The value of the lira changes with respect to the U.S. dollar. Check the financial section of the daily newspaper for the current exchange rate.

Major U.S. credit cards are usually accepted with proper identification, such as a passport but visitors should always ask if a particular card is accepted prior to ordering meals or making hotel reservations. Travelers checks are accepted, but visitors should first inquire on the policy of the bank, hotel, or store before attempting to use them.

SUPPLEMENTS

ITALIAN EMBASSIES

AMBASSY	E-MAIL	HOME PAGE
ALBANIA	ambittia@icc.al.eu.org	
ALGERIA	ambitalgeri@ist.cerist.dz	
ANGOLA	embitaly@ebonet.net	
ARABIA SAUDITA	info@italia-embassy-riyadh.org	http://www.italia-embassy-riyadh.org
ARGENTINA	stampa@ambitalia-bsas.org.ar	http://www.ambitalia-bsas.org.ar
AUSTRALIA	embassy@ambitalia.org.au	http://www.ambitalia.org.au
AUSTRIA	ambitalviepress@via.at	
AZERBAIJAN	ambbaku@azeuro.net	
BANGLADESH	ambdhaka@citechco.net	http://www.citechco.net/italydhaka
BELGIO	ambit.bxl@ibm.net	http://soi.cnr.it/ambitbe
BIELORUSSIA	ambitminsk@belsonet.net	
BOLIVIA	ambitlap@ceibo.entelnet.bo	
BOSNIA ERZEGOVINA	ambsara@bih.net.ba	
BRASILE	embitalia@zaz.com.br embitalia@embitalia.org.br	http://www.embitalia.org.br
BULGARIA	italdiplsofia@online.bg	
CAMERUN	ambyaounde@gcnet.cm	
CANADA	ambital@italyincanada.com	http://www.italyincanada.com
CILE	italcom@entelchile.net	
CINA	ambpech@italianembassy.org.cn	http://www.italianembassy.org.cn
CIPRO	italian.embassy@cytanet.com.cy	
CITTA' DEL VATICANO	amb.scv@esteri.it	
COLOMBIA	ambitbog@inter.net.co	
COREA	ambseoul@ktnet.co.kr	
COSTA D'AVORIO	ambitali@aviso.ci	
COSTA RICA	ambitcr@sol.racsa.co.cr	http://www.ambitcr.com
CROAZIA	veleposlanstvo-italije@zg.tel.hr	
CUBA	ambitcub@ceniai.inf.cu	http://www.ceniai.inf.cu/italia/index.htm

DANIMARCA	italambcph@get2net.dk	
ECUADOR	ambital@ambitalquito.org	
EGITTO	ambcairo@brainy1.ie-eg.com	http://www.italembassy.org.eg
EL SALVADOR	italemb@sal.gbm.net	
EMIRATI ARABI UNITI	AMBITAL@emirates.net.ae	
ERITREA	iea@eol.com.er	
ESTONIA	italemb@online.ee	http://www.online.ee/~italemb
ETIOPIA	italembadd@telecom.net.et	
FILIPPINE	Ambitaly@iname.com	
FINLANDIA	ambhel@clinet.fi	http://www.clinet.fi/~ambhel/
FRANCIA	stampa@dial.oleane.com	
GABON	ambasciata-italia@internetgabon.com	
GERMANIA	ambitalia.segr@t-online.de	http://www.ambasciata-italia.de/ http://www.botschaft-italien.de/ http://www.italian-embassy.de/
GHANA	ambital@ghana.com	
GIAPPONE	itembtky@gol.com	http://SunSite.sut.ac.jp/embitaly/
GIORDANIA	Italemb1@go.com.jo	http://www.italembamman.org
GRAN BRETAGNA	emblondon@embitaly.org.uk	http://www.embitaly.org.uk
GRECIA	ambaten@hol.gr	
GUATEMALA	ambaguat7@infovia.com.gt	
HONDURAS	ambitalia@sigmanet.hn	
INDIA	italemb@nde.vsnl.net.in	http://www.italembdelhi.com
INDONESIA	italemba@rad.net.id	http://www.italambjkt.or.id
IRAN	itaembtehe@kanoon.net	
IRLANDA	italianembassy@eircom.net	http://homepage.eircom.net/~italianembassy/
ISRAELE	italemb@netvision.net.il	http://www.italian-embassy-israel.org
JUGOSLAVIA	italbelg@EUnet.yu	
KAZAKHSTAN	ambalma@nursat.kz	
KENYA	ambnair@swiftkenya.com	
KUWAIT	ambkuwa@ncc.moc.kw	
LETTONIA	ambitalia.riga@apollo.lv	

LIBANO	amb@italyemb-beirut.org	
LITUANIA	ambitvilnius@post.omnitel.net	
LUSSEMBURGO	italamb@tcp.ip.lu	
MACEDONIA (Ex Repubblica Jugoslava di)	pr.segr@unet.com.mk	
MADAGASCAR	ambanta@simicro.mg	
MALAYSIA	embassyit@italy-embassy.org.my	http://www.italy-embassy.org.my
MALTA	ambitalia@vol.net.mt	
MAROCCO	Ambraba@onpt.net.ma	
MESSICO	embitaly@data.net.mx	http://www.pentanet.com.mx/Embitaly
MOZAMBICO	ambital.moz@virconn.net	
NAMIBIA	ambitwin@iafrica.com.na	
NICARAGUA	italdipl@tmx.com.ni	
NIGERIA	ambitnig@alpha.linkserve.com	
NORVEGIA	ambitalia.oslo@online.no	
NUOVA ZELANDA	ambwell@xtra.co.nz	
OMAN	ambmasc@omantel.net.om	
PAESI BASSI	italemb@worldonline.nl	http://www.italy.nl
PAKISTAN	ambisl@isb.comsats.net.pk	http://www.italia.com.pk
PANAMA	panitamb@cwp.net.pa	
PARAGUAY	ambasu@uninet.com.py	
PERU'	italemb@chavin.rcp.net.pe	
POLONIA	ambvars@medianet.com.pl	
PORTOGALLO	embital@individual.EUnet.pt	http://www.embital.pt/
QATAR	itembqat@qatar.net.qa	http://www.qatar.net.qa/itembqat
REPUBBLICA CECA	Italemba@mbox.vol.cz	http://www.italianembassy.cz
REP. DEMOCRATICA DEL CONGO	ambitalykin@raga.net	
REPUBBLICA DOMINICANA	ambital@codetel.net.do	
REPUBBLICA SLOVACCA	amb@ambitaba.sk	
ROMANIA	primosegretario@ambitalia.ro	

RUSSIA	Itembmsk@astelit.ru	http://www.astelit.ru/embitaly
SAN MARINO	AMBSMAR@OMNIWAY.SM	
SENEGAL	ambitsen@telecomplus.sn	
SINGAPORE	ambitaly@italyemb.org.sg	http://www.italyemb.org.sg
SIRIA	italamb@net.sy	http://www.ambitsir.org
SLOVENIA	amblubiana@siol.net	
SPAGNA	ambitalsp@cempresarial.com	
SRI LANKA	itembgen@sri.lanka.net	http://www.italianembassy.lk
STATI UNITI D'AMERICA	stampa@itwash.org	http://www.italyemb.org/
SUD AFRICA	ambital@iafrica.com	http://www.ambital.org.za
SUDAN	italsd@usa.net	
SVEZIA	itemb@itemb.se	http://itembassy-sweden.bo.cnr.it/
SVIZZERA	ambital.berna@spectraweb.ch	http://www3.itu.int/EMBASSY/Italy
TANZANIA	italdipl@raha.com	http://www.italdipl-dar.org
THAILANDIA	ambitbkk@loxinfo.co.th	
TUNISIA	AMBITALIA.TUN@Email.ati.tn	
TURCHIA	itaamb@superonline.com	http://itaamb.org.tr
UCRAINA	ambital.kiev@utel.net.ua	
UGANDA	ambkamp@imul.com	http://www.imul.com/embitaly
UNGHERIA	ambital@pronet.hu	
URUGUAY	amburuit@netgate.com.uy	http://ww.ambitalia.com.uy
UZBEKISTAN	ambita@silk.org	
VENEZUELA	ambcara@italamb.org.ve	http://www.italamb.org.ve
VIETNAM	embitaly@netnam.org.vn	
YEMEN	ITALIANEMBASSY@y.net.ye	
ZAMBIA	italyzam@zamnet.zm	
ZIMBABWE	amitalia@samara.co.zw	

CONSUALTE GENERAL

COUNTRY	CONSULATE	EMAIL	HOMEPAGE

ARABIA SAUDITA			
Gedda	Cons. Gen.	ITCONGED@TRI.NET.SA	
ARGENTINA			
Bahia Blanca	Cons. Gen.	consitbbl@infovia.com.ar	http://www.advance.com.ar/usuarios/consitbbl
Buenos Aires	Cons. Gen.	consitba@sminter.com.ar	http://www.consitalia-bsas.org.ar
Cordoba	Cons. Gen.	italcons@cpsarg.com.ar	
La Plata	Cons. Gen.	italcons@sminter.com.ar	http://www.sminter.com.ar/consla plata
Rosario	Cons. Gen.	titolare@consit-rosario.org.ar	http://www.consit-rosario.org.ar
Mendoza	Consolato	consitalia@impsat1.com.ar	http://www.consitalia-mendoza.com.ar
Mar del Plata	Consolato	itconmdp@statics.com.ar	http://www.cons-italia.com.ar
Corrientes	V. Consolato On.	brianti@compunort.com.ar	
Paranà	V. Consolato On.	bellum@infovia.com.ar	
Lomas de Zamora	Ag. Cons.	aclomas@sminter.com.ar	
Moron	Ag. Cons.	itamoron@sinectis.com.ar	
San Jorge	Ag. Cons. On.	est.durando@sme.com.ar	
AUSTRALIA			
Melbourne	Cons. Gen.	itconmel@netlink.com.au	
Sydney	Cons. Gen.	itconsyd@itconsyd.org	
Adelaide	Consolato	consadel@chariot.net.au	
Brisbane	Consolato	italcons.brisbane@bigpond.com	
Perth	Consolato	itconper@wantree.com.au	
Cairns	V. Consolato On.	flanza@c130.aone.net.au	
Darwin	V. Consolato On.	randproperties@octa4.net.au	
Lismore	Ag. Cons. On.	sumtrav1@lis.net.au	
Mount Isa	Ag. Cons. On.	nortaski@tpgi.com.au	

AUSTRIA			
Innsbruck	Cons. Gen.	coninns@tirol.com	
Klagenfurt	Cons. Gen.	CONKLU@happynet.at	
Vienna	Consolato	italconsul-vienna@vienna.at	
BARBADOS			
Bridgetown	V. Consolato On.	pbaldi@sunbeach.net	
BELGIO			
Anversa	Cons. Gen.	conanve@euronet.be	
Charleroy	Cons. Gen.	consolato.italia.charleroi@euronet.be	
Liegi	Cons. Gen.	consolato.italia.liegi@skynet.be	
Bruxelles	Consolato	consitbxl@infoboard.be	http://www.euronet.be/consitbxl/
Mons	Vice Cons.	italconsmons@skynet.be	
Genk	Ag. Cons.	ac.italy.genk@skynet.be	
BIELORUSSIA			
Minsk	Canc. Cons.	ambitminsk@belsonet.net	
BRASILE			
San Paolo	Cons. Gen.	segreteria@italconsul.org.br	http://www.italconsul.org.br
Curitiba	Cons. Gen.	concuri@ifnet.com.br	http://bbs2.sul.com.br/italia
Porto Alegre	Cons. Gen.	italconpal@myway.com.br	
Rio De Janeiro	Cons. Gen.		www.conrio.org.br
Belo Horizonte	Consolato	consitaliabh@metalink.com.br	
Recife	Consolato	conrecife@marte.torricelli.com.br	
CAMERUN			

Douala	V. Cons. On	giorgetti@camnet.cm	
CANADA			
Toronto	Cons. Gen.	consolato.it@toronto.italconsulate.org	http://www.toronto.italconsulate.org/
Montreal	Cons. Gen.	cgi@italconsul.montreal.qc.ca	
Vancouver	Cons. Gen.	italcons@axion.net	
Quebec	Cons. On.	rrossini@videotron.ca	
Edmonton	V. Cons.	consitedm@compusmart.ab.ca	
Hamilton	V. Cons.	vicham@primus.ca	
CAPO VERDE			
Praia	Ag. Cons. On.	annariga@mail.cvtelecom.cv	
CINA			
Canton	Cons. Gen.	itconsgz@gtic.com.cn	
Hong Kong	Cons. Gen.	itconshk@netvigator.com	http://www.ust.hk/~italy/
Shanghai	Cons. Gen.	conitsha@public4.sta.net.cn	
CIPRO			
Larnaca	Cons. On.	plotin@spidernet.com.cy	
Limassol	Cons. On.	mantocy@zenon.logos.cy.net	
CROAZIA			
Fiume	Cons. Gen.	confium@ri.tel.hr	http://www.tel.hr/confium/
Spalato	Vice Cons.	consitalsplit@st.tel.hr	
DANIMARCA			
Copenhagen	Sez. Cons.	italconscph@get2net.dk	
Aarhus	Cons. On.	holmenmo@post2.tele.dk	

EGITTO			
Alessandria d'Egitto	Cons. Gen.	conales@internetalex.com	
EMIR. ARABI UNITI			
Dubai	Ag. Cons.	consulit@emirates.net.ae	
FINLANDIA			
Turku	Cons. On.	benito.casagrande@pp.atlasnet.fi	
FRANCIA			
Parigi	Cons. Gen. I C.	italconsulparigi@mailcity.com	
Lione	Cons. Gen.	Cogen.Lyon@wanadoo.fr	
Marsiglia	Cons. Gen	consolato.italia.marseille@wanadoo.fr	
Metz	Cons. Gen	Iticonmetz@wanadoo.fr	www.cgi-metz.com
Nizza	Cons. Gen	consulit@nicematin.fr	
Grenoble	Cons. I C.	dirdidattica.grenoble@wanadoo.fr	
Lilla	Cons. I C.	italconslilla@wanadoo.fr	
Tolosa	Cons. I C.	Cons.Tolosa@magic.fr	http://perso.magic.fr/cons.tolosa
Bastia	Consolato	consbastia@aol.com consitbastia@free.fr	
Chambery	Consolato	italconsul.chambery@icor.fr	
Mulhouse	Consolato	italcons-mulh@aiing.com	
GERMANIA			
Francoforte sul Meno	Cons. Gen. I C.	italia.consolato.francoforte@t-online.de	
Monaco di Baviera	Cons. Gen. I C.	italcons.monaco@t-online.de	http://www.consolati.italiani.de/monaco/
Amburgo	Cons. Gen.	segreteria@italconsul-hamburg.de	http://www.consolati.italiani.de/amburgo/
Colonia	Cons. Gen.	italcons.colonia@t-online.de	

Hannover	Cons. Gen.	italia.consolato.hannover@t-online.de	
Lipsia	Cons. Gen.	ITALIA.CONSOLATO.LIPSIA@t-online.de	
Stoccarda	Cons. Gen.	Italia.Consolato.Stoccarda@t-online.de	http://www.consolati.italiani.de/stoccarda/
Saarbrucken	Cons. I C.	ITALIA.CONSOLATO.SAARBRUCKEN@T-ONLINE.DE	
Dortmund	Consolato	ITALIA.CONSOLATO.DORTMUND@T-ONLINE.DE	
Friburgo	Consolato	italia.consolato.friburgo@t-online.de	http://www.consolati.italiani.de/friburgo/
Norimberga	Consolato	ital.konsulat.nbg@t-online.de	
Mannheim	Ag. Cons.	italconsul.mannheim@t-online.de	
Wolfsburg	Ag. Cons.	agenzia-consolare-italia-wob@t-online.de	
GERUSALEMME			
Gerusalemme	Cons. Gen.	Congeru@netvision.net.il	
GIAPPONE			
Osaka	Cons. Gen.	conosak@osk.3web.ne.jp	
GRAN BRETAGNA			
Edimburgo	Cons. Gen	consedimb@consedimb.demon.co.uk	
Manchester	Consolato	passaporti@italconsulman.demon.co.uk	
Bedford	Vice Cons.	consulat@netcomuk.co.uk	
GRECIA			
Salonicco	Cons. Gen.	italcons@the.forthnet.gr	http://users.forthnet.gr/the/italcons/
Atene	Consolato	itconath@hol.gr	

GUATEMALA			
Quetzaltenango	Ag. Cons. On.	hicea@c.net.gt	
GUINEA			
Conakry	Cons. On	soguicom@mirinet.net.gn	
INDIA			
Calcutta	Cons. Gen.	italy@cal2.vsnl.net.in	
Chennay	Vice Cons. On.	rjs@alc.rpgms.vsnl.net.in	
Mumbay	Cons. Gen.	consmumb@bom5.vsnl.net.in	
Panjim	Vice Cons. On.	gualaclosures@vsnl.com	
INDONESIA			
Denpasar	Vice Cons. On.	italconsbali@italconsbali.com	http://www.italconsbali.com
JUGOSLAVIA			
Bar	Cons. Gen.	consit@cg.yu	
LUSSEMBURGO			
Esch-Sur-Alzette	Cons. I C.	consitesch@tcp.ip.lu	
MADAGASCAR			
Nosy Be	Vice Cons. On.	murri@dts.mg	
MALDIVE			
Male	Ag. Cons. On.	cyprea@dhivehinet.net.mv	
MALI			
Bamako	Cons. On.	loriana@malinet.ml	
MAROCCO			
Casablanca	Cons. Gen.	italconsul.casa@casanet.net.ma	

Tangeri	Vice Cons.	conitang@cybermania.net.ma	
MAURITANIA			
Nouakchott-Tevragh-Zeina	Cons. On.	TRANSAC@toptechnology.mr	
MONACO (Principato di)			
Monaco	Cons. Gen. I C.	italconsul@monte-carlo.mc	
NORVEGIA			
Bergen	V.Cons.On	erikno@enor.no	
Tromsö	V.Cons.On	barlindhaug@barlindhaug.no	www.barlindhaug.no
Stavanger	V.Cons.On	firmapost@norskagip.no	
Trondheim	V.Cons.On	federico.venzi@sds.no	
NIGER			
Niamey	V.Cons.On	profor@intnet.ne	
NUOVA ZELANDA			
Dunedin	Ag. Cons. On.	ssalis@clear.net.nz	
PAESI BASSI			
Amsterdam	Cons. Gen.	consital@euronet.nl	
Maastricht	V.Cons. On.	p.agostini@worldonline.nl	
PAKISTAN			
Karachi	Cons. Gen.	consecr@italcons.org.pk	
ROMANIA			
Bucarest	Canc. Cons.	info@ambitalia.ro	
RUSSIA			

San Pietroburgo	Cons. Gen.	itconspb@astelit.ru	
SLOVENIA			
Capodistria	Cons. Gen.	cg.capodistria@siol.net	http://www.consolatocapodistria.si
SPAGNA			
Barcellona	Cons. Gen.	cgbarcconsolare@infonegocio.com	
Madrid	Cons. Gen.	italconsul.madrid@futurnet.es	http://www.area.fi.cnr.it/spagna/servizi.htm
STATI UNITI			
New York	Cons. Gen. I C.	ItalConsNY@aol.com	http://www.italconsulnyc.org
Boston	Cons. Gen.	postmaster@italconsboston.org	http://www.italconsboston.org
Chicago	Cons. Gen.	consul@italconschicago.org	http://www.italconschicago.org
Houston	Cons. Gen.	italyconsulate@pdq.net	
Los Angeles	Cons. Gen.	cglos@conlang.com	http://www.conlang.com
Miami	Cons. Gen.	italcons@netrox.net	http://www.italconsmiami.com
Philadelfia	Cons. Gen.	conphila@op.net	
San Francisco	Cons. Gen.		http://www.italconsfrisco.org
Detroit	Cons. I C.	conitdet@crl.com	http://www.crl.com./~conitdet
Saint Paul	Cons. On.	sarahr360@aol.com	
Newark	Vice Cons.	ITALVCNK@ix.netcom.com	http://www.reference.it/vcnewark
SUD AFRICA			
Johannesburg	Cons. Gen.	conjoha@global.co.za	
Cape Town	Consolato	itacons@mweb.co.za	
Durban	Consolato	italdurb@mweb.co.za	
SVIZZERA			
Lugano	Cons. Gen. I C.	consluga@bluewin.ch	
Zurigo	Cons. Gen. I	consolato.it.zh@bluewin.ch	http://www.consolato-italia-zh.ch

	C.		
Losanna	Cons. Gen.	italconsul.losanna@vtx.ch	http://www3.itu.int/Consulate/Italy/Losanna
Locarno	Vice Cons.	conloca@bluewin.ch	http://www3.itu.int/Consulate/Italy/Locarno/
TANZANIA			
Zanzibar	V. Cons. On.	mario@zanzinet.com	
TRINIDAD E TOBAGO			
Port of Spain	Cons. On.	dabb@trinidad.net	
TURCHIA			
Istanbul	Cons. Gen.	italcons@ttnet.net.tr	http://web.turnet.net.tr/~italcons
Smirne	Consolato	izmir@italcons-izmir.com	http://www.italcons-izmir.com
URUGUAY			
Colonia	V. Cons. On.	ITALIA@COLONIA.COM.UY	
Montevideo	Consolato	consit@netgate.com.uy	
VENEZUELA			
Caracas	Cons. Gen.	consitvzla@cantv.net	http://www.italamb.org.ve/consolato.html
Maracaibo	Consolato	consul@conmara.com	http://www.conmara.com/
Maracaj	V. Cons. On.	giovanpetr@cantv.net	
Punto Fijo	Ag. Cons. On.	SVALLES@TELCEL.NET.VE	

LARGEST LAW FIRMS

- Adonnino - Ascoli, 7, Via Principessa Clotilde, Rome, Italy, Tel:(39)6-3220585-6-7, Fax:(39)6-3219128, Contact: Dr. Roberto Ascoli
- Alegi & Associates, Via Venti Settembre 1, Rome, 00187, Italy, Tel:(39)6--482-0147, Fax:(39)6-4871149, Contact: Christine Marciasini
- Amenta Biolato Corrao LongoRidola, Via del Babuino 51, Rome, 00187, Italy, Tel:(39)6-3233001, Fax:(39)96-3234238, Contact: Antonio Corrao

- Becchis, Roverati, Pasquetto & Masetti, Via XX Settembre, 1, Rome, 00187, Italy, Tel:(39)6 4743830, Fax:(39)6 482531, Contact: Dr. Proc. Raimondo Becchis
- Borgognoni vimercati & Romano, 20, Viale di Villa Grazioli, Rome, 00198, Italy, Tel:(39)6/8558846, Fax:(39)6/853424, Contact: Gianbenso Borgognoni Vimercati
- Brosio,Casati e Associati, Via Manzoni 41, Milan, 20121, Italy, Tel:(39)2-29010200, Fax:(39)2-29010278, Contact: Guido Brosio
- Capello & Associati, 47, Piazza Barberini, Rome, 00187, Italy, Tel:(39)6 4824781, Fax:(39)6 4881327, Contact: Riccardo Cappello
- Capua Varrenti e Associati, Via di Porta Pinciana, 6, Rome, 00187, Italy, Tel:(39)6 4881907, Fax:(39)6 4882611, Contact: Allessandro Varrenti
- Cesaris e Nunziante, Piazza di Pietra, 26, Rome, 00186, Italy, Tel:(39)6-69.518.1, Fax:(39)6-69.518.333, Contact: Filippo Cesaris
- Chiomenti Studio Legale, Via Bertoloni 44/46, Rome, 00197, Italy, Tel: (39) 6-809701, Fax: (39) 6-809706, Contact: Filippo D. Vassalli
    - Chiomenti e Associati is among the three largest firms in the country, with over 40 attorneys. It was founded in 1946 by Avv. Pasquale Chiomenti and was one of the first firms in Italy to introduce the concept of partnership. The firm is in general practice. Chiomenti e Associati is the Italy member of Lex Mundi, a global association of 152 independent law firms.
- Collodel, Leone, Ligi, Queirolo, Via Emanuele Gianturco, 11, Rome, 00196, Italy, Tel:(39)6 3224262, Fax:(39)6 3224282, Contact: Roberto Collodel
- Dobson & Sinisi, Via Santa Radegonda 16, Milan, 20121, Italy, Tel:(39)2-809816, Fax:(39)2-86464648, Contact: David Dodson
- Gianni Origoni & Partners, Piazza Belgioioso, 2, Milan, 20121, Italy, Tel:(39)2-76009756, Fax:(2-76009628, Contact: Gian B. Origoni della Croce
- Grippo, Associati e Simmons & Simmons, Corso Vittorio Emanuele, 1, Milan, 20122, Italy, Tel:(39)2-76003012, Fax:(39)2-782770, Contact: Eugenio Grippo
- Macchi di Cellere e Gangemi, Via G Serbelloni 4, Milan, 20122, Italy, Tel:(39)2-76009756, Fax:(39)2-76001618, Contact: Luigi Maccgi di Cellere
- Magrone & Associati, Via del Banco Di S. Spirito 42, Rome, 000186, Italy, Tel:(39)6-6879962, Fax:(39)6-6751240, Contact: Gian Domenico Magrone
- Pavia Ansaldo e Verusio, -Via dell' Annunciata 7, Milan, 20123, Italy, Tel:(39)2-63381, Fax:(39)2-28100308, Contact: Giuseppe Ansaldo
- Piergrossi Villa Manca Graziadei, Studio Legale, Via Festa del Perdono 10, Milan, 20122, Italy, Tel:(39)2-58303657, Fax:(39)2-58303818, Contact: Franco P. Villa
- Puopolo Sistilli Geffers & Luise, Via Lisbona 11, Rome, 00198, Italy, Tel: (39)6-8841535, Fax: (39)6-884-2094, Contact: Gianfranco Puopolo
    - Puopolo Sistilli Geffers & Luise is an international law firm based in Rome, Italy serving the legal and business needs of corporations and individuals in Italy and abroad. Staffed with European and American attorneys it offers services in more than five languages.
- Studio Avv. Emauele Turco, Viale G. Rossini 9, Rome, 00198, Italy, Tel:(39)6-8088244/6/7, Fax:(39)6-8088980, Contact: Emanuelo Turco

- Studio Avv. Ercole Graziadei, Via Vittorio Veneto 96, Rome, Italy, Tel:(39)6-479801, Fax:(39)6-4873402, Contact: Enrico Zaffarani
- Studio Avvocato Pacchiani, Via Dante, 4, Milan, 20121, Italy, Tel:(39)2-86461172, Fax:(39)2-864358, Contact: Avv. Giancarlo Pacchiani
- Studio Carnelutti, Via Parigi 11, Rome, Italy, Tel:(39)6-473901, Fax:(39)6-4819833, Contact: Avv. Marino Bastianini
- Studio Legale Albert-Gomboli, Salita Santa Caterina 6/1, Genova, 16123, Italia, Tel:(39)10-540614, Fax:(39)10-543397, Contact: Alessandro Albert
- Studio Legale Albisinni & Associati, Via Ciro Menotti N.4, Rome, 00195, Italy, Tel:(39)6-3216171, Fax:(39)-63217034, Contact: Avv. Ferdinando Albisinni
- Studio Legale Associato & Frere Cholmeley Bischoff, Viale Bruno Buozzi 47, Rome, 00197, Italy, Tel:(39)6 8080133, Fax:(39)6 8080134, Contact: Andrea Russo
- Studio Legale Associato con Carnelutti London, Largo della Fontanella di Borghese, 19, Rome, 00186, Italy, Tel:(39)6-6889911, Fax:(39)6-6878644, Contact: Marino Bastianini
- Studio Legale Associazione Professionale Scassellati-Sforzolini, Piazza Picinino N.13, Perugia, 06122, Italy, Tel:(39)75-5725244, Fax:(39)75-5728398, Contact: Annalissa Segoloni
- Studio Legale Beltramo, 20/C, Via Lazio, Rome, 00187, Italy, Tel:(39)6-4817747, Fax:(39)6-4820281, Contact: Lucio Francario
- Studio Legale Biamonti, Lungotevere Michelangelo, 9, Rome, 00192, Italy, Tel:(39)6-3236940, Fax:(39)6-3211959, Contact: Avv. Filippo Biamonti
- Studio Legale Bisconti, Via Bissolati, 76, Rome, 00187, Italy, Tel:(39)6 479881, Fax:(39)6 487-2070, Contact: Carlo Garbarino
- Studio Legale Camilotti-Ceccon-Polettini, Galleria Borromeo 3, Padua, 35137, Italy, Tel:(39)498763200, Fax:(39)49666086, Contact: Francesco Camilotti
- Studio Legale Cavasola, Scamoni e Associati, Via Agostino Depretis, 86, Rome, 00184, Italy, Tel:(39)6-478151, Fax:(39)6-483755, Contact: Pietro Cavasola
- Studio Legale Cieri, Crocenzi, Saldutti e Visconti, Via Cesare Beccaria 18, Rome, 00196, Italy, Tel:(39)6-36003892, Fax:(39)6-36003328, Contact: Francesco Paolo Crocenzi
- Studio Legale Emanuele Turco, Viale G. Rossini 9, Rome, 00197, Italy, Tel:(39)6-809701, Fax:(39)6-809706, Contact: Filippo D. Vassalli
- Studio Legale Giordano Associazione Professionale, Piazza Salvemini, 2, Padua, 35131, Italy, Tel:(39)49-8753575, Fax:(39)49-8752304, Contact: Claudio Giordano
- Studio Legale Lauro, 19 Via Depretis, Naples, 80133, Italy, Tel:(39)81-5800199, Fax:(39)81-5800195, Contact: Francesco Lauro
- Studio Legale Sutti, Via Monteapoleone 8, Milan, 20121, Italy, Tel:(39)276-2041, Fax:(39)276-204805/806, Contact: Dr. Davide Braghini
- Studio Legale Tesauro, Via Pergolesi 1, Naples, 80122, Italy, Tel:(39)81-761.50.60, Fax:(39)81-761.15.20, Contact: Bruno De Maria
- Studio Legale Trucillo-De Zigno, Via Monte diPieta, 1/A, Milan, 20121, Italy, Tel:(39)287.82.88, Fax:(39)27.02.00.20, Contact: Avv. Pierluigi Trucillo

- Studio Legale Ugi e Nunziante, Via Venti Settembre 1, Rome, 00187, Italy, Tel:(39)6-476841, Fax:(39)6-4870397, Contact: Gianni Nunziante
- Studio Legale Vuoli Lanza e Associati, Viale Majno, 17/A, Milan, 20122, Italy, Tel:(39)2-76.01.37.91, Fax:(39)22-76.00.87.67, Contact: Federica Vuoli
- Studio Legale Zambelli-Luzzati-Meregalli, Via Carducci, 15, Milan, 20123, Italy, Tel:(39)2-86451933, Fax:(39)2-86451997, Contact: Paolo M. Zambelli
- Toffoletto, Studio Legale, Via Eugenio Chiesa, 4, Milan, 20122, Italy, Tel:(39)2-54164.1, Fax:(39)2-54164.500, Contact: Avv. Franco Toffoletto
- Tosi & Bontempo, Via Paolo Da Cannobio 10, Milan, 20122, Italy, Tel:(39)2-8052890, Fax:(39)2-72021655, Contact: Stefano Bontempo
- Traverso & Associati, Studio Legale, Via Sant'Andrea 19, Milan, 20121, Italy, Tel:(39)2-76020566, Fax:(39)2-76020430, Contact: Maurizio Traverso
- Trevisan & Cuonzo, Avvocati, Via Brera 6, Milan, 20121, Italy, Tel:(39)2/86463313, Fax:(39)2/86463892, Contact: Luca Trevisan
- Villa, Broglio, Mameli & Kucerova, Via Conservatorio 17, Milan, 20122, Italy, Tel:(39)276028597, Fax:(39)276028598, Contact: Adriano Villa

REGIONAL GOVERNMENT

Regione Abruzzo

Consiglio Regionale
-v. Michele Iacobucci 4,
Palazzo Emiciclo
67100 L'Aquila
Tel. +39 (0)862 - 64.41

Giunta Regionale
-p. S.Giusta, Palazzo Centi
67100 L'Aquila
Tel. +39 (0)862 - 42.00.46/
65.59.4/ 65.02.4
Fax +39 (0)862 - 41.93.83/
64.75.34

-v. Bovio 425
65125 Pescara
Tel. +39 (0)85 - 47.13.03.1/
75.96.2/ 75.96.4
Fax +39 (0)85 - 47.11.78.9

Regione Basilicata

Consiglio Regionale
-v. Manhes 33
85100 Potenza
Tel. +39 (0)971 - 33.21

Giunta Regionale
-v. Pretoria 277
85100 Potenza
Tel. +39 (0)971 - 33.21

Regione Calabria

Consiglio Regionale
-p. Italia, Palazzo S.Giorgio
89122 Reggio Calabria
Tel. +39 (0)965 - 85.51

Giunta Regionale
-vle. de Filippis
88100 Catanzaro
Tel. +39 (0)961 - 85.11/
77.15.05/ 77.20.95

Regione Campania

Consiglio Regionale
-v. Palepoli 20
80132 Napoli
Tel. +39 (0)81 - 79.74.11.1

Giunta Regionale
-v. S.Lucia 81
80132 Napoli
Tel. +39 (0)81 - 79.61.11.1

Regione Emiglia Romagna

Consiglio Regionale
-vle. Aldo Moro 50
40127 Bologna
Tel. +39 (0)51 - 63.95.11.1

Giunta Regionale
-vle. Aldo Moro 52
40127 Bologna
Tel. +39 (0)51 - 63.95.11.1/
28.31.11/ 28.41.11

Regione Lazio

Consiglio Regionale
-v. della Pisana 1301
00163 Roma
Tel. +39 (0)6 - 65.93.1
Fax +39 (0)6 - 65.00.06.71

Giunta Regionale
-v. Cristoforo Colombo 212
00147 Roma
Tel. +39 (0)6 - 51.68.1

Regione Liguria

Consiglio Regionale
-v. Fieschi 15

16121 Genova
Tel. +39 (0)10 - 54.85.1
Fax +39 (0)10 - 54.05.79

Giunta Regionale
-v. Fieschi 15
16121 Genova
Tel. +39 (0)10 - 54.85.1
Fax +39 (0)10 - 59.02.18

Regione Lombardia

Consiglio Regionale
-v. Ugo Bassi 2
20159 Milano
Tel. +39 (0)2 - 69.75.1

Giunta Regionale
-v. Fabio Filzi 22
20124 Milano
Tel. +39 (0)2 - 67.65.1

Regione Friuli Venezia Giulia

Consiglio Regionale
-p. Oberdan 6
34133 Trieste
Tel. +39 (0)40 - 37.71.11.1
Fax +39 (0)40 - 37.73.19.0

Giunta Regionale
-p. Unita' d'Italia 1
34121 Trieste
Tel. +39 (0)40 - 37.71.11.1
Fax +39 (0)40 - 37.73.72.3

Regione Marche

Consiglio Regionale
-v. Oberdan 1
60122 Ancona
Tel. +39 (0)71 - 22.98.1
Fax +39 (0)71 - 20.47.82

Giunta Regionale
-v. Gentile da Fabriano 9
60125 Ancona
Tel. +39 (0)71 - 80.61

Regione Molise

Consiglio Regionale
-v.4 Novembre 87
86100 Campobasso
Tel. +39 (0)874 - 42.91/ 42.96.65
Fax +39 (0)874 - 48.11.81.6/ 48.20.89

Giunta Regionale
-v. XXIV Maggio 130
86100 Campobasso
Tel. +39 (0)874 - 42.91/ 42.97.25
Fax +39 (0)874 - 42.96.14/ 42.96.90

Regione Piemonte

Consiglio Regionale
-v. Alfieri 15
10121 Torino
Tel. +39 (0)11 - 57.57.1/ 57.57.21.3
Fax +39 (0)11 - 51.82.72/ 57.57.27.7

Giunta Regionale
-p. Castello 165
10122 Torino
Tel. +39 (0)11 - 43.21.1/ 43.23.25.6/ 43.23.31.7

Regione Puglia

Consiglio Regionale
-v. Calpruzzi 204
70124 Bari
Tel. +39 (0)80 - 54.01.11.1
Fax +39 (0)80 - 22.48.27

Giunta Regionale
-v. Capruzzi 212
70124 Bari
Tel. +39 (0)80 - 54.01.11.1
Fax +39 (0)80 - 54.02.00.8
Internet:
http://www.pandora.it/medimage

Regione Autonoma Sardegna

Consiglio Regionale
-v. Roma 25
09125 Cagliari
Tel. +39 (0)70 - 60.14.1
Fax +39 (0)70 - 65.55.25

Giunta Regionale
-vle. Trento 69
09123 Cagliari
Tel. +39 (0)70 - 60.61

Regione Siciliana

Assemblea Regionale
-p. Parlamento 1, Palazzo dei Normanni
90133 Palermo
Tel. +39 (0)91 - 65.61.11.1

Giunta di Governo
-p. Indipendenza, Palazzo d'Orleans
90129 Palermo
Tel. +39 (0)91 - 69.61.11.1

Regione Toscana

Consiglio Regionale
-v. Cavour 2, Palazzo Panciatichi
50129 Firenze
Tel. +39 (0)55 - 23.87.1
Fax +39 (0)55 - 21.09.47

Giunta Regionale
-v. De' Servi 51, Palazzo Budini Gattai
50122 Firenze
Tel. +39 (0)55 - 43.82.11.1
Fax +39 (0)55 - 21.28.20

Regione Autonoma Trentino Alto Adige / Trentino Suedtirol

Consiglio Regionale
-v. Piazza Dante 16
38100 Trento
Tel. +39 (0)461 - 20.11.11

-v. Crispi 9
39100 Bolzano

Tel. +39 (0)471 - 97.32.85/ 97.32.86

Giunta Regionale
-v. Gazzoletti 2
38100 Trento
Tel. +39 (0)461 - 20.11.11
Internet: (Provincia di Bolzano/ Bozen)
http://www.provincia.bz.it/index-i.htm

Regione dell'Umbria

Consiglio Regionale
-p. Italia 2, Palazzo Cesaroni
06100 Perugia
Tel. +39 (0)75 - 57.61
Fax +39 (0)75 - 57.20.25.3

Giunta Regionale
-c. Vannucci 96, Palazzo Donini
06121 Perugia Tel. +39 (0)75 - 50.41
Fax +39 (0)75 - 50.42.50.9

Regione Autonoma Valle d'Aosta/Vallée d'Aoste

Consiglio Regionale
-p. Albert Deffeyes 1
11100 Aosta
Tel. +39 (0)165 - 30.31
Fax +39 (0)165 - 30.34.02

Giunta Regionale
-p. Albert Deffeyes 1
11100 Aosta
Tel. +39 (0)165 - 30.31
Fax +39 (0)165 - 30.34.02
Internet:
http://www.aostavalley.com

Regione del Veneto

Consiglio Regionale
-sestiere di San Marco 2322, Palazzo Ferro Fini
30124 Venezia
Tel. +39 (0)41 - 27.01.11.1
Fax +39 (0)41 - 27.01.23.9

Giunta Regionale
-sestiere Dorsoduro 3901, Palazzo Balbi
30123 Venezia
Tel. +39 (0)41 - 79.21.11
Fax +39 (0)41 - 79.28.6

MAJOR NEWSPAPERS

AVVENIRE Piazza Garbonari, 3 20159 Milano tel. 39-02-67801 fax. 39-02-678-0208

CORRIERE DELLA SERA Via Solferino, 28 20121 Milano tel. 39-02-6339/628-27246 fax. 39-02-2900-9668/2900-9705

LA DISCUSSIONE Piazza del Gesu', 46 00186 Roma tel. 39-06-6920-9318 fax. 39-06-6920-9333

IL FOGLIO Via Victor Hugo, 1 20123 Milano tel. 39-02-863-9181 fax. 39-02-878-596

LA GAZZETTA DEL MEZZOGIORNO Viale Scipione l'Africano, 264 70124 Bari tel. 39-080-547-0400 fax. 39-080-547-0488

GAZZETTA DEL SUD Via Ubeto Bonino, 15/C 98124 Messina tel. 39-090-2261 fax. 39-090-2936-359/2932-063

GIORNALE DI SICILIA Via Lincoln, 21 90133 Palermo tel. 39-091-662-7111 fax. 39-091-662-7280/617-7517

IL GIORNALE Via Gaetano Negri, 4 20123 Milano tel. 39-02-85661 fax. 39-02-7202-3859/80

IL GIORNO Piazza Cavour, 2 20123 Milano tel. 39-02-77681 fax. 39-02-7600-6656

IL MANIFESTO Via Tomacelli, 146 00186 Roma tel. 39-06-687-191 fax. 39-06-689-2600/6871-9573

IL MATTINO Via Chiatamone, 65 80121 Napoli tel. 39-081-794-7111 fax. 39-081-794-7288

IL MESSAGGERO Via del Tritone, 152 00187 Roma tel. 39-06-47201 fax. 39-06-472-072

LA NAZIONE Via Ferdinando Paolieri, 2 50121 Firenze tel. 39-055-87951 fax. 39-055-234-3646

L'OPINIONE Piazza S. Lorenzo in Lucina, 40 00186 Roma tel. 39-06-690071 fax. 39-06-6849-4336

L'OSSERVATORE ROMANO Via del Pellegrino 00120 Citta' del Vaticano tel. 39-06-6988-3461/3385 fax. 39-06-6988-3675

IL PICCOLO Via Guido Reni, 1 34123 Trieste tel. 39-040-373-3111 fax. 39-040-373-3312 IL POPOLO Via del Gesu', 62 00186 Roma tel. 39-06-695071 fax. 39-06-6994-2377

LA REPUBBLICA Piazza Indipendenza, 11/b 00185 Roma tel. 39-06-49821 fax. 39-06-4982-2923

IL RESTO DEL CARLINO Via Mattei, 106 40138 Bologna tel. 39-051-536-111/530-202 fax. 39-051-532-990

IL SECOLO XIX Via Varese, 2 16122 Genova tel. 39-010-53881 fax. 39-010-538-8560

LA SICILIA Viale Odorico da Pordenone, 50 95126 Catania tel. 39-095-330-544 fax. 39-095-338-073/336-466

IL SOLE-24 ORE Via Paolo Lomazzo 52 20154 Milano tel. 39-02-31031 fax. 39-02-312-055/317-519

LA STAMPA Via Marenco, 32 10126 Torino tel. 39-011-65681 fax. 39-011-655-306/310-0759

IL TEMPO Piazza Colonna, 366 00187 Roma tel. 39-06-675-881 fax. 39-06-675-8869/315

L'UNITA' Via dei Due Macelli, 23/13 00187 Roma tel. 39-06-699-961 fax. 39-06-678-3555/ foreign desk: 679-1988 Major Italian Business Journals L'ESPRESSO Via Po, 12 00198 Roma tel. 39-06-84781 fax. 39-06-884-5167

ITALIA OGGI Via Marco Burigozzo, 5 20122 Milano tel. 39-02-582-191 fax: 39-02-5831-7559 MILANO FINANZA Via Puligozzo, 5 20122 Milano tel. 39-02-582-191 fax: 39-02-5831-7509

PANORAMA Viale Mondadori 1 20090 Segrate (MI) tel. 39-02-75421 fax. 39-02-7542-2769 Via Sicilia 136 00187 Roma tel. 39-06-474-971 fax. 39-06-4749-7345

IL MONDO Via Angelo Rizzoli, 2 20132 Milano tel. 39-02-25841 fax. 39-02-2720-1158

BANKS WITH CORRESPONDENT U.S. BANKING ARRANGEMENTS

A large number of Italian banks have correspondence relationships with U.S. banks.

Below is a listing of Italian banks with branch offices in the U.S. Istituto Bancario San Paolo di Torino S.p.A. Piazza San Carlo, 156 10121 Turin Tel: 39-11-5551 Fax: 39-11-555-6650 245 Park Avenue, Suite 3500 New York, NY 10022 Tel: (212) 692-3000 Fax: (212) 599-5303/599-5304

Banca di Roma Via Marco Minghetti, 17 00187 Rome Tel: 39-6-670-71 Fax: 39-6-678-1929 34 East 51st Street New York, NY 10022 Tel: (212) 407-1600/407-1707/407-1726 Fax: (212) 407-1704 225 West Washington Street, Suite 1200 Chicago, IL 60606 Tel: (312) 368-8855 Fax: (312) 726-3058 Market Stewart Tower San Francisco, CA 94105 Tel: (415) 357-0800 Fax: (415) 357-9869 CARIPLO - Cassa di Risparmio delle Provincie Lombarde S.p.A. Via Monte di Pieta', 8 20121 Milan Tel: 39-2-886-61 Fax: 39-2-8866-2302 190 South La Salle Street, Suite 2890 Chicago, IL 60603 Tel: (312) 444-1-500 Fax: (312) 444-1-501 One Embarcadero Center, Suite 2820 San Francisco, CA 94117-3717 Tel: (415) 439-6780 Fax: (415) 439-6785

Banca Nazionale del Lavoro BNL S.p.A. Via V. Veneto, 119 00187 Rome Tel: 39-6-470-21 Fax: 39-6-470-7298 25 W. 51st Street New York, NY 10019 Tel: (212) 314-0707 Fax: (212) 489-9088 Xerox Center 55 West Monroe Street, Suite 1690 Chicago, IL 60603 Tel: (312) 444-9410, 444-9251, 444-9252, 444-9253, 444-9254

Banca Commerciale Italiana S.p.A. Piazza della Scala, 6 20121 Milan Tel: 39-2-88501 Fax: 39-2-8850-3026 1 William Street New York, NY 10004 Tel: (212) 607-3500 Fax: (212) 809-2124 150 North Michigan Ave., Suite 1500 Chicago, IL 60601 Tel: (312) 346-1112 Fax: (312) 346-5758 555 S. Flowers Street, Suite 4300 Los Angeles. CA 90071 Tel: (213) 624-0440 Fax: (213) 624-0457

Banco di Napoli S.p.A. Via Toledo, 177/178 80132 Naples Tel: 39-81-791-1111 Fax: 39-81-580-1343 277 Park Avenue New York, NY 10172 Tel: (212) 872-2400 Fax: (212) 644-8246 Banco di Sicilia S.p.A. Via Generale Vincenzo Magliocco, 1 90141 Palermo Tel: 39-91-608-1111 Fax: 39-91-608-5964/3227 250 Park Avenue New York, NY 10017 Tel: (212) 692-4300 Fax: (212) 370-5790

Credito Italiano Direzione Centrale Via S. Protaso 1/3 20121 Milan Tel: 39-02-88621 Fax: 39-02-8646-5399 375 Park Avenue New York, NY 10152 Tel: (212) 546-9600 Fax: (212) 546-9675 Two Prudential Plaza 180 North Stetson Suite 1310 Chicago, IL 60601-6713 Tel: (312) 946-1-111 Fax: (312) 946-1-112

Monte dei Paschi di Siena Piazza Salimbeni, 3 53100 Siena Tel: 39-0577-294-111 Fax: 39-0577-294-653 26th Floor 245 Park Avenue New York, NY 10167 Tel: (212) 557-8111 Fax: (212) 557-8039

BASIC TITLES ON ITALY

IMPORTANT!

All publications are updated annually!

Please contact IBP, Inc. at ibpusa3@gmail.com for the latest ISBNs and additional information

Title
Italy A "Spy" Guide - Strategic Information and Developments
Italy A Spy" Guide"
Italy Air Force Handbook
Italy Air Force Handbook
Italy Army Weapon Systems Handbook
Italy Army Weapon Systems Handbook

Title
Italy Army Weapon Systems Handbook
Italy Aviation and Aerospace Industry Handbook
Italy Aviation and Aerospace Industry Handbook
Italy Banking & Financial Market Handbook
Italy Business and Investment Opportunities Yearbook
Italy Business and Investment Opportunities Yearbook
Italy Business and Investment Opportunities Yearbook Volume 1 Strategic Information and Opportunities
Italy Business Intelligence Report - Practical Information, Opportunities, Contacts
Italy Business Intelligence Report - Practical Information, Opportunities, Contacts
Italy Business Law Handbook - Strategic Information and Basic Laws
Italy Business Law Handbook - Strategic Information and Basic Laws
Italy Business Law Handbook - Strategic Information and Basic Laws
Italy Business Law Handbook - Strategic Information and Basic Laws
Italy Clothing & Textile Industry Handbook
Italy Clothing & Textile Industry Handbook
Italy Company Laws and Regulations Handbook
Italy Constitution and Citizenship Laws Handbook - Strategic Information and Basic Laws
Italy Country Study Guide - Strategic Information and Developments
Italy Country Study Guide - Strategic Information and Developments
Italy Country Study Guide - Strategic Information and Developments Volume 1 Strategic Information and Developments
Italy Customs, Trade Regulations and Procedures Handbook
Italy Customs, Trade Regulations and Procedures Handbook
Italy Diplomatic Handbook - Strategic Information and Developments
Italy Diplomatic Handbook - Strategic Information and Developments
Italy Ecology & Nature Protection Handbook
Italy Ecology & Nature Protection Handbook
Italy Ecology & Nature Protection Laws and Regulation Handbook
Italy Economic & Development Strategy Handbook
Italy Economic & Development Strategy Handbook
Italy Education System and Policy Handbook
Italy Energy Policy, Laws and Regulation Handbook
Italy Export-Import Trade and Business Directory
Italy Export-Import Trade and Business Directory
Italy Foreign Policy and Government Guide
Italy Foreign Policy and Government Guide
Italy Government and Business Contacts Handbook
Italy Government and Business Contacts Handbook
Italy Immigration Laws and Regulations Handbook - Strategic Information and Basic Laws
Italy Industrial and Business Directory
Italy Industrial and Business Directory
Italy Intelligence & Security Activities & Operations Handbook
Italy Intelligence & Security Activities & Operations Handbook
Italy Intelligence, Security Activities & Operations Handbook
Italy Intelligence, Security Activities & Operations Handbook
Italy Internet and E-Commerce Investment and Business Guide - Strategic and Practical Information: Regulations and Opportunities
Italy Internet and E-Commerce Investment and Business Guide - Strategic and Practical Information:

Title
Regulations and Opportunities
Italy Investment and Business Guide - Strategic and Practical Information
Italy Investment and Business Guide - Strategic and Practical Information
Italy Investment and Business Guide - Strategic and Practical Information
Italy Investment and Business Guide - Strategic and Practical Information
Italy Investment and Trade Laws and Regulations Handbook
Italy Justice System and National Police Handbook
Italy Justice System and National Police Handbook
Italy Labor Laws and Regulations Handbook - Strategic Information and Basic Laws
Italy Land Ownership and Agriculture Laws Handbook
Italy Medical & Pharmaceutical Industry Handbook
Italy Medical & Pharmaceutical Industry Handbook
Italy Mineral & Mining Sector Investment and Business Guide - Strategic and Practical Information
Italy Mineral & Mining Sector Investment and Business Guide - Strategic and Practical Information
Italy Mining Laws and Regulations Handbook
Italy Parliament Guide
Italy Parliament Guide
Italy Recent Economic and Political Developments Yearbook
Italy Recent Economic and Political Developments Yearbook
Italy Recent Economic and Political Developments Yearbook
Italy Research & Development Policy Handbook
Italy Research & Development Policy Handbook
Italy Research & Development Policy Handbook
Italy Space Agency and Programs Handbook
Italy Space Agency and Programs Handbook
Italy Space Programs and Exploration Handbook
Italy Space Programs and Exploration Handbook
Italy Starting Business (Incorporating) in....Guide
Italy Tax Guide
Italy Tax Guide
Italy Taxation Laws and Regulations Handbook
Italy Telecom Laws and Regulations Handbook
Italy Telecommunication Industry Business Opportunities Handbook
Italy Telecommunication Industry Business Opportunities Handbook
Italy Transportation Policy and Regulations Handbook
Italy Wine Industry Investment and Business Opportunities Yearbook
Italy: Economic Development of Italian Regions Yearbook

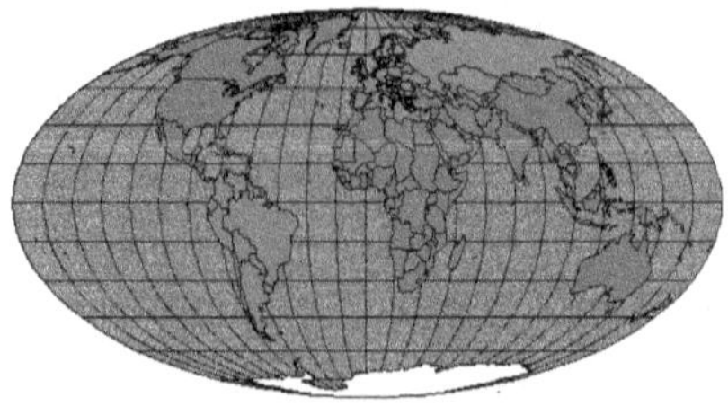

WORLD MINING LAWS AND REGULATIONS HANDBOOK LIBRARY

Price: $149.95 Each

Title
1. Afghanistan Mining Laws and Regulations Handbook
2. Albania Mining Laws and Regulations Handbook
3. Algeria Mining Laws and Regulations Handbook
4. Angola Mining Laws and Regulations Handbook
5. Argentina Mining Laws and Regulations Handbook
6. Armenia Mining Laws and Regulations Handbook
7. Australia Mining Laws and Regulations Handbook
8. Austria Mining Laws and Regulations Handbook
9. Azerbaijan Mining Laws and Regulations Handbook
10. Bahrain Mining Laws and Regulations Handbook
11. Bangladesh Mining Laws and Regulations Handbook
12. Belarus Mining Laws and Regulations Handbook
13. Belgium Mining Laws and Regulations Handbook
14. Benin Mining Laws and Regulations Handbook
15. Bolivia Mining Laws and Regulations Handbook
16. Bosnia and Herzegovina Mining Laws and Regulations Handbook
17. Botswana Mining Laws and Regulations Handbook
18. Brazil Mining Laws and Regulations Handbook
19. Brunei Mining Laws and Regulations Handbook
20. Bulgaria Mining Laws and Regulations Handbook
21. Burkina Faso Mining Laws and Regulations Handbook
22. Burundi Mining Laws and Regulations Handbook
23. Cambodia Mining Laws and Regulations Handbook
24. Cameroon Mining Laws and Regulations Handbook

Title
25. Canada Mining Laws and Regulations Handbook
26. Cape Verde Mining Laws and Regulations Handbook
27. Cayman Islands Mining Laws and Regulations Handbook
28. Central African Republic Mining Laws and Regulations Handbook
29. Chad Mining Laws and Regulations Handbook
30. Chile Mining Laws and Regulations Handbook
31. China Mining Laws and Regulations Handbook
32. Colombia Mining Laws and Regulations Handbook
33. Comoros Mining Laws and Regulations Handbook
34. Congo Mining Laws and Regulations Handbook
35. Congo, Dem. Republic Mining Laws and Regulations Handbook
36. Cook Islands Mining Laws and Regulations Handbook
37. Costa Rica Mining Laws and Regulations Handbook
38. Cote d'Ivoire Mining Laws and Regulations Handbook
39. Croatia Mining Laws and Regulations Handbook
40. Cuba Mining Laws and Regulations Handbook
41. Czech Republic Mining Laws and Regulations Handbook
42. Denmark Mining Laws and Regulations Handbook
43. Djibouti Mining Laws and Regulations Handbook
44. Dominican Republic Mining Laws and Regulations Handbook
45. Dubai Mining Laws and Regulations Handbook
46. Ecuador Mining Laws and Regulations Handbook
47. Egypt Mining Laws and Regulations Handbook

For additional analytical, business and investment opportunities information, please contact Global Investment & Business Center, USA at (202) 546-2103. Fax: (202) 546-3275. E-mail: rusric@erols.com

Title
48. El Salvador Mining Laws and Regulations Handbook
49. Equatorial Guinea Mining Laws and Regulations Handbook
50. Eritrea Mining Laws and Regulations Handbook
51. Estonia Mining Laws and Regulations Handbook
52. Ethiopia Mining Laws and Regulations Handbook
53. Fiji Mining Laws and Regulations Handbook
54. Finland Mining Laws and Regulations Handbook
55. France Mining Laws and Regulations Handbook
56. Gabon Mining Laws and Regulations Handbook
57. Gambia Mining Laws and Regulations Handbook
58. Georgia Mining Laws and Regulations Handbook
59. Germany Mining Laws and Regulations Handbook
60. Ghana Mining Laws and Regulations Handbook
61. Greece Mining Laws and Regulations Handbook
62. Guatemala Mining Laws and Regulations Handbook
63. Guinea Mining Laws and Regulations Handbook
64. Guinea-Bissau Mining Laws and Regulations Handbook
65. Guyana Mining Laws and Regulations Handbook
66. Haiti Mining Laws and Regulations Handbook
67. Honduras Mining Laws and Regulations Handbook
68. Hungary Mining Laws and Regulations Handbook
69. Iceland Mining Laws and Regulations Handbook
70. India Mining Laws and Regulations Handbook
71. Indonesia Mining Laws and Regulations Handbook
72. Iran Mining Laws and Regulations Handbook
73. Iraq Mining Laws and Regulations Handbook
74. Ireland Mining Laws and Regulations Handbook
75. Israel Mining Laws and Regulations Handbook
76. Italy Mining Laws and Regulations Handbook
77. Jamaica Mining Laws and Regulations Handbook
78. Japan Mining Laws and Regulations Handbook
79. Jordan Mining Laws and Regulations Handbook
80. Kazakhstan Mining Laws and Regulations Handbook
81. Kenya Mining Laws and Regulations Handbook
82. Korea, North Mining Laws and Regulations Handbook
83. Korea, South Mining Laws and Regulations

Title
Handbook
84. Kuwait Mining Laws and Regulations Handbook
85. Kyrgyzstan Mining Laws and Regulations Handbook
86. Laos Mining Laws and Regulations Handbook
87. Latvia Mining Laws and Regulations Handbook
88. Lesotho Mining Laws and Regulations Handbook
89. Liberia Mining Laws and Regulations Handbook
90. Libya Mining Laws and Regulations Handbook
91. Lithuania Mining Laws and Regulations Handbook
92. Macedonia Republic Mining Laws and Regulations Handbook
93. Madagascar Mining Laws and Regulations Handbook
94. Malawi Mining Laws and Regulations Handbook
95. Malaysia Mining Laws and Regulations Handbook
96. Mali Mining Laws and Regulations Handbook
97. Mauritania Mining Laws and Regulations Handbook
98. Mauritius Mining Laws and Regulations Handbook
99. Mayotte Mining Laws and Regulations Handbook
100. Mexico Mining Laws and Regulations Handbook
101. Micronesia Mining Laws and Regulations Handbook
102. Moldova Mining Laws and Regulations Handbook
103. Mongolia Mining Laws and Regulations Handbook
104. Morocco Mining Laws and Regulations Handbook
105. Mozambique Mining Laws and Regulations Handbook
106. Myanmar Mining Laws and Regulations Handbook
107. Namibia Mining Laws and Regulations Handbook
108. Nepal Mining Laws and Regulations Handbook
109. Netherlands Mining Laws and Regulations Handbook
110. New Zealand Mining Laws and Regulations Handbook
111. Nicaragua Mining Laws and Regulations Handbook
112. Niger Mining Laws and Regulations Handbook
113. Nigeria Mining Laws and Regulations Handbook
114. Norway Mining Laws and Regulations Handbook
115. Oman Mining Laws and Regulations Handbook

For additional analytical, business and investment opportunities information, please contact Global Investment & Business Center, USA at (202) 546-2103. Fax: (202) 546-3275. E-mail: rusric@erols.com

Title
116. Pakistan Mining Laws and Regulations Handbook
117. Papua New Guinea Mining Laws and Regulations Handbook
118. Paraguay Mining Laws and Regulations Handbook
119. Peru Mining Laws and Regulations Handbook
120. Philippines Mining Laws and Regulations Handbook
121. Poland Mining Laws and Regulations Handbook
122. Portugal Mining Laws and Regulations Handbook
123. Qatar Mining Laws and Regulations Handbook
124. Romania Mining Laws and Regulations Handbook
125. Russia Mining Laws and Regulations Handbook
126. Rwanda Mining Laws and Regulations Handbook
127. Sao Tome and Principe Mining Laws and Regulations Handbook
128. Saudi Arabia Mining Laws and Regulations Handbook
129. Scotland Mining Laws and Regulations Handbook
130. Senegal Mining Laws and Regulations Handbook
131. Serbia Mining Laws and Regulations Handbook
132. Sierra Leone Mining Laws and Regulations Handbook
133. Slovakia Mining Laws and Regulations Handbook
134. Slovenia Mining Laws and Regulations Handbook
135. Somalia Mining Laws and Regulations Handbook
136. South Africa Mining Laws and Regulations Handbook
137. Spain Mining Laws and Regulations Handbook
138. Sri Lanka Mining Laws and Regulations Handbook
139. Sudan Mining Laws and Regulations Handbook
140. Suriname Mining Laws and Regulations Handbook
141. Swaziland Mining Laws and Regulations

Title
Handbook
142. Sweden Mining Laws and Regulations Handbook
143. Syria Mining Laws and Regulations Handbook
144. Taiwan Mining Laws and Regulations Handbook
145. Tajikistan Mining Laws and Regulations Handbook
146. Tanzania Mining Laws and Regulations Handbook
147. Thailand Mining Laws and Regulations Handbook
148. Togo Mining Laws and Regulations Handbook
149. Trinidad and Tobago Mining Laws and Regulations Handbook
150. Tunisia Mining Laws and Regulations Handbook
151. Turkey Mining Laws and Regulations Handbook
152. Turkmenistan Mining Laws and Regulations Handbook
153. Uganda Mining Laws and Regulations Handbook
154. Ukraine Mining Laws and Regulations Handbook
155. United Arab Emirates Mining Laws and Regulations Handbook
156. United Kingdom Mining Laws and Regulations Handbook
157. United States Mining Laws and Regulations Handbook
158. Uruguay Mining Laws and Regulations Handbook
159. Uzbekistan Mining Laws and Regulations Handbook
160. Venezuela Mining Laws and Regulations Handbook
161. Vietnam Mining Laws and Regulations Handbook
162. Yemen Mining Laws and Regulations Handbook
163. Zambia Mining Laws and Regulations Handbook
164. Zimbabwe Mining Laws and Regulations Handbook

www.ingramcontent.com/pod-product-compliance
Lightning Source LLC
LaVergne TN
LVHW080029210926
848481LV00011B/3141